Critical Issues in User Interface Systems Engineering

Springer
London
Berlin
Heidelberg
New York
Barcelona
Budapest
Hong Kong
Milan
Paris
Santa Clara
Singapore
Tokyo

David Benyon and Philippe Palanque (Eds)

Critical Issues in User Interface Systems Engineering

With 50 figures

Springer

David Benyon
Computing Department, The Open University
Walton Hall, Milton Keynes MK7 6AA, UK

Philippe Palanque
LIS-IHM, University of Toulouse I, Place Anatole France
31042 Toulouse cedex, France

ISBN-13:978-3-540-19964-9 e-ISBN-13:978-1-4471-1001-9
DOI: 10.1007/978-1-4471-1001-9

Springer-Verlag Berlin Heidelberg New York
British Library Cataloguing in Publication Data
Critical Issues in User Interface Systems Engineering
I. Benyon, David II. Palanque, Philippe
004.019
ISBN-13:978-3-540-19964-9

Library of Congress Cataloging-in-Publication Data
A Catalog record for this book is available from the Library of Congress

Typesetting: Camera ready by editors

34/3830-543210 Printed on acid-free paper

Foreword

This book developed from an IFIP workshop which brought together methods and architecture researchers in Human Computer Interaction and Software Engineering. To an extent this introduction is a little unfair to the authors, as we have distilled the results of the workshop to give the reader a perspective of the problems within integrated approaches to usability engineering. The papers could not hope to address all of the issues; however, we hope that a framework will help the reader gain further insights into current research and future practice.

The initial motivation was to bring together researchers and practitioners to exchange their experiences on Graphical User Interface (GUI) design problems. The two groups represented methodological and architecture/tools interests, so the workshop focused on intersection of how methods can support user interface development and vice versa, how tools, architectures and reusable components can empower the design process. There is, we believe, a constructive tension between these two communities. Methodologists tend to approach the design problem with task/domain/organisational analysis while the tool builders suggest design empowerment/envisioning as a means of improving the way users work rather than relying on analysis of current systems. This debate revolves around the questions of whether users' current work is optimal, or whether designers have the insight to empower users by creating effective solutions to their problems. Tool builders typically want to build something, then get the users to try it, while the methodologists want to specify something, validate it and then build it. In spite of these divergent views the workshop was more successful than may have been expected and this book arose as a consequence of seeing how design methods and architectures can fit together.

To anchor discussion a case study, the IFIP WG 8.1 Conference planning problem, was circulated beforehand. This gave a brief description of requirements for an information system to manage collection of conference paper submissions, handling refereeing, communicating with authors, planning a conference programme etc. Discussions within the workshop raised a series of interesting questions for future research and technology transfer, which are reflected in the papers within this book.

One key issue is the fit between human factors (e.g. work context, task/user analysis, dialogue design, etc.) and software engineering (e.g. requirements specification, domain/functional modelling, dialogue design, software architecture, etc.) in the development process. A recurrent theme is the transition from natural language and informal visualisation in early stages of development to more formal specification. Three critical leaps are necessary to bridge gaps in the design process, each one representing currently unsolved problems:

Leap 1: from understanding the user's task and work context to producing the design. Bridging this gap requires methods and notations to identify critical paths and generic tasks, solving the dilemma of making task descriptions more formal but still usable, and developing tools to transform task descriptions into dialogue designs.

Leap 2: from visualisation of an external design to technical specification, particularly for novel designs. This gap required tools to make explicit the constraints coming from the implementation environment, to specify system behaviour in a form which is usable by interaction designers, and to support design of new objects and widgets.

Leap 3: between formal specification of system requirements and implementation. Issues here are deriving and verifying properties from the task description within a formal design process which also allows violations of properties to be identified and relaxed if necessary.

Different views of requirements are possible, ranging from user needs statements relevant to a work context to software-oriented approaches that come close to being complete design descriptions. Four different starting points are possible:
(a) the roles people fulfil; the tasks performed by people and the information needed to fulfil the task for that role; (b) the tasks that needed to be performed to 'solve' the problem; (c) the information that will be needed in a task, and the information that is available to be presented;
(d) designer's (or user's) vision of new products which change and improve current work practice.

Current notations and evaluation techniques are inadequate for expressing complex requirements with different mixes of stakeholders, roles and tasks on one hand, and design realisation on the other for the more concrete aspects of user interface design, i.e. appearance and presentation, especially for richer media (e.g. links between audio and video). Object oriented techniques may help by allowing iterative modification, while specific methods such as MUSE and Discounted Rich Pictures offer a more comprehensive framework for the integrated HCI/SE development process. The MUSE methodology developed at the UCL Ergonomics Unit in London, supports parallel development of human factors and software engineering. Although it may suggest possible objects to a software architect, it stops short of detailed design. Other design representations e.g. ETAG, provide different views, as well as more detail, to help designers. New uses can be found for old notations, such as exploring task allocation via data flow diagrams; however, some notations have serious restrictions (e.g. inherent sequentially of most task description languages). There is an argument for using multiple notations in order to stimulate creativity while prototypes are a key alternative for communicating designs to users.

Requirements, specification and design become inevitably intertwined. Design options become 'pointers' back to the context and requirements analysis, exposing issues that had not been addressed in the initial top-down analysis. Designers may become misled by analysis of existing systems; boundaries between task and domain (object) analysis are unclear; and there is poor integration of task analysis with social analyses. Furthermore, identification of objects for high level interaction design depends critically on earlier human-computer task allocations and these decisions can place constraints on the designer's options. These problems are only beginning to be recognised by methodologists. The interaction during the design process of context information influencing design and design suggestions affecting the work context is an interesting perspective. Empowering users with new technical capabilities versus supporting current work practices is an established HCI debate, however, maybe development should be seen as a co-routine of design empowerment and work/task analysis.

Some engineering approaches prefer to transform context information into requirements and/or designs. However, it is not clear whether all the contextual information can, or should be, transformed, or used in other ways, for example, as constraints during design formation, or as scenarios and criteria for formative evaluation. Issues of how context information can be used in the design process, as non functional requirements, are also being debated in the software engineering and requirements engineering communities. However it is not clear how much context information to gather and then how to integrate it into design. When rapid design sketching is employed, prototype design may precede context analysis and thus wholly drive requirements elicitation, while designed artefacts can suggest further requirements. Carroll's task-artefact cycle captures this relationship in contrast to the more traditional top-down structured design. Research is needed into the pros and cons of each approach, and their implications for development choices.

In methodologies like MUSE, software and human factors engineering proceed in parallel, but it is not clear how to synchronise these processes. What happens if the right inputs aren't available at the right time, and what needs to be done to re-integrate late analyses? Late commitment in requirements is a constant problem but this needs to account for technical decisions (e.g. inter-operability with existing environments). More research is necessary to integrate technological factors and the effects of early and delayed commitments on design decisions. Human Factors methodologies do not currently address such problems, neither do they tackle cost-benefit trade-offs and project management. How should effort be divided between task analyses, domain analysis, organisational analysis, stakeholder analyses and technical designs ? We are still a long way from understanding different trade-offs; for instance, systems with different time scales might need different development tools, i.e. a small system with a short life time should not require the rigorous analysis and design that a larger system with an expected long lifetime might assume.

The architectures approach looks at system properties and how these match HF requirements. This leads to problems of functional partitioning and locating these properties in parts of the design by, for instance, task mapping on to hierarchies of agents and developing enhanced UIMS (User Interface Management systems) models which go beyond the traditional 'Seeheim' perspective. Architectures need to be refined so clear mappings are possible between functionality of the application, dialogue management, presentation and different aspect of usability onto discrete components. As new design conceptions, e.g. design for and with reusable components becomes more widespread the role of UI architecture will become a vital concern. Software engineering criteria (e.g. portability, maintainability) often influence choices between user interface design and software architecture. More research is needed to establish relationships between human issues and software architecture. Anecdotal evidence of such relationships is widespread, e.g. change A took less than a minute, change B took 6 months and required extensive software restructuring.

Few tools or methods, if any, are self-contained; i.e. they start with informal requirements and generate complete solutions, indeed there are few clear boundaries between current development approaches. For example a specification language may produce output to be consumed by a system builder tool, but do executable specifications become 'the system' ? How do metaphor designers and interface builders interact and where does Programming by Demonstration fit in; is it a system building tool, or part of a user interface builders toolkit ? The dividing line between methods, specification language and tools is not as neat as we may think. This highlights the different choices between methods and tools according to the context and generality of the desired system. For instance, requirements, tasks and designed components differ radically according to whether a bespoke application is being built for a specific task, or a generic product is being developed, or a reusable library of components for a class of applications is being constructed.

In conclusion, the implications of alternative approaches to design, the rationalisation of software engineering and HCI design objectives are key concerns, as are shared and usable notations, the need for more powerful UI architectures and different conceptions of design ranging from specific products to reuse libraries. The papers in this book go some way towards resolving some of the issues, explore others, and point towards many future research and practice directions for integrating usability and system engineering.

Alistair Sutcliffe and Len Bass

Preface

In September 1994 the International Federation of Information Processing (IFIP) sponsored a workshop between technical committee TC13 - Human-Computer Interaction and TC2 - Software Theory and Practice. The workshop was organised by two working groups: WG13.2 - Methodologies for Human-Computer Interaction and WG2.7 - Software for User Interface Design. The object of this meeting was to exchange ideas from people with different backgrounds - software engineers and user interface developers - so that the issues could be better understood.

The result of that meeting is presented in this book under the title Critical issues in User Interface Systems Engineering (CRUISE). We chose this title in order to reflect the interests of the researchers and practitioners involved; the software engineers who have to develop and implement systems, the system modellers who are charged with developing representations for systems, tool-builders who seek to empower developers with enhanced software tools. The emerging discipline of User Interface Systems Engineering (UISE) combines this variety of interests and perspectives on user interface development - seeking to bridge the gap between the user interface and the underlying software system.

Following the workshop, we invited the participants to submit chapters for this volume. Authors were asked to reflect upon the presentations given at the workshop and the discussions which took place and to position their work clearly within the field. The result is a coherent, integrated and comprehensive book covering the field of UISE. Moreover, we believe that this is the first book to bring together all sides of the user interface systems engineering community and represents the first step along the road of better integration and enhanced understanding between these groups of previously distant practitioners.

In bringing together the material on UISE, we resisted the temptation to divide the volume into design and implementation. Our aim, in contrast, is to *integrate* these two aspects of user interface development. We believe that the concerns of designers and implementors of user interfaces have remained separate for too long and that it is important to bridge this gap of communication. We also believe that the process of systems development cannot be separated into 'design' first and then 'build'. There must be an iterative and integrated approach to developing user interfaces. So, instead of design and development we have divided the book into five parts each of which reflects a different perspective on the products, processes, behaviour and construction of user interface software.

Part I is concerned with issues of domain modelling - capturing a user-centred and yet software relevant representation of the application domain. Part II is concerned with approaches to UISE which are based on an underlying domain model. Whereas a typical user interface management system (UIMS) requires the designer to focus on the syntactic and lexical levels of design (such as command names, screen and icon design, menu organisation, sequencing rules, and interaction techniques), in a model-based approach, the designer creates an interface for an application by describing the application at the semantic or conceptual level. The designer then chooses the various interface components (such as radio buttons, text boxes and so on) which best fit the application. A further advantage of model-based development is that the formality of certain models can be used to prove aspects of the design. The third part shifts attention to the idea of methodology for UISE. Whereas model-based design is concerned with supporting system developers by providing notations and tools, the papers in this part are more concerned with the approach. Underlying all these tools, methods and approaches is a need for novel and flexible software architectures. The two chapters in part IV deal with architectural issues. The final part is concerned with future developments and aspects which are currently missing from the world of UISE.

Critical issues in User Interface Systems Engineering is appropriate for a wide range of general and specialist courses on user interface development. Most importantly - since it marries the software engineering and the user interface developers views - it is appropriate for software engineering courses on user interface design and for courses on human-computer interaction which emphasise the need to implement and not simply to discuss interfaces. Students on such courses at final year undergraduate level and masters level will find the book an invaluable source of review and new material.

For other students and practitioners of HCI, the book provides a rich source of up-to-date new and review material which encapsulates many of the current areas of HCI. For example, chapter 9 presents a comprehensive review of models and notations for conceptual design, chapter 11 summarises the work on software architectures, chapter 13 covers the material on contextual enquiry and chapter 14 brings together much of the research on metaphor design. Each of these is an important area of study in HCI. Other chapters deal with generic applications such as information display (chapter 3), computer supported cooperative work (chapter 8), complex systems (chapter 10) and consumer goods (chapter 9). CRUISE will satisfy those looking for a critical approach to HCI, but will disappoint those seeking a simple recipe for user interface development.

The Human-Computer Interaction community has argued that user interfaces are often the most important part of the software system. This position, based on the assumption that it is not worth building a system if the result is not usable, has led to a wealth of research concerning the cognitive, social, organisational and ergonomic aspects of people using computers. The emphasis of HCI is on the usability of interactive systems. The Software Engineering community has argued that it is not worth building a system if it does not do what it is meant to do, efficiently and reliably. Why build an attractive and ergonomic system if it breaks down every thirty seconds? Clearly the software engineering considerations affect the usability of a system. Equally the user interface affects the efficiency and reliability of a system. User interface systems engineering brings these aspects of software systems development together and seeks to provide robust methods, tools and notations for developing user interfaces.

David Benyon and Philippe Palanque
Milton Keynes - Toulouse
September 1995

Contents

Contributors

Chapter 1: Domains Models for User Interface Design

David Benyon
Computing Department, Open University, Milton Keynes, MK7 6AA, UK.
Tel. +44 (0) 908 652679. Email. D.R.Benyon@open.ac.uk

Chapter 2: Domain Specific Design of User Interfaces – Case Handling and Data Entry Problems.

Jan Gulliksen & Bengt Sandblad
Uppsala University, Center for Human-Computer Studies, Lägerhyddv. 18, S-752 37 Uppsala, Sweden.
Uppsala University, Systems and Control Group, Dept. of Technology, Lägerhyddv. 2, house 8, PO Box 27, S-752 37 Uppsala, Sweden.
Email: jg@syscon.uu.se, bengt.sandblad@cmd.uu.se

Chapter 3: A Method for Task-Related Information Analysis

Alistair Sutcliffe
Centre for HCI Design, School of Informatics, City University,
Northampton Square, London EC1V 0HB, UK
Tel: +44-171-477-8411. Email: sf328@uk.ac.city

Chapter 4: Task Models - System Models: a Formal Bridge over the Gap

Philippe Palanque & Rémi Bastide
LIS-IHM, Université Toulouse I
Place Anatole France, 31042 Toulouse cedex, FRANCE
Tel: +33 61 63 35 88. Email: {bastide, palanque}@cict.fr

Chapter 5: ETAG-based Design: User Interface Design as User Mental Model Design

Geert de Haan
Department of Computer Science, Vrije Universiteit, de Boelelaan 1081a, 1081 HV Amsterdam The Netherlands
Email: dehaan@cs.vu.nl

Chapter 6: A Methodology for a Task-driven Modelling of Interactive Systems Architectures

Fabio Paterno'
CNUCE - C.N.R., Via S.Maria 36, 56100 Pisa, Italy
Email: paterno@vm.cnuce.cnr.it

Chapter 7: Key Activities for a Development Methodology of Interactive Applications

François Bodart[1], Anne-Marie Hennebert[1], Jean-Marie Leheureux[1], Isabelle Provot[1], Jean Vanderdonckt[1] & Giovanni Zucchinetti[2]
[1] Facultés Universitaires Notre-Dame de la Paix, Institut d'Informatique, rue Grandgagnage, 21, B-5000 NAMUR (Belgium)
Tel. +32 (0)81-72.49.75. Email: {fbodart, amhennebert, jmleheureux, jvanderdonckt}@ info.fundp.ac.be
[2] Université de Lausanne, Ecole des Hautes Etudes Commerciales, CH-1015 LAUSANNE (Switzerland)
Tel. +41 21-692.34.17. Email: gzucchin@hec.unil.ch

Chapter 8: Design of Workplace-Integrating User Interfaces based on Work Scenario Graphs

Hans-W. Gellersen[1] & Max Mühlhäuser[2]
[1] Telecooperation Office (TecO), University of Karlsruhe, Vincenz-Prießnitz-Str. 1, D-76131 Karlsruhe, GERMANY.
Tel. +49-721-6902.49. Email: hwg@teco.uni-karlsruhe.de
[2]University of Linz, A-4040 Linz, AUSTRIA.
Tel. +43-732-2468.9238. Email: max@tk.uni-linz.ac.at,

Chapter 9: Methods & Tools for Supporting the User Interface Design Process

David Bell[1], Ashok Gupta[1], Raghu Kolli[2] & Martina Manhartsberger[3]
[1] Philips Research Laboratories, Crossoak Lane, Redhill, UK. RH1 5HA
Email: {bell,gupta}@prl.philips.co.uk
[2] Delft University of Technology, Faculty of Industrial Design Engineering Jaffalaan 9, 2628 BX Delft, The Netherlands
Email: r.kolli@io.tudelft.nl
[3] Vienna User Interface Group University of Vienna, Lenaug. 2/8, 1080 Vienna, Austria
Email: mm@ani.univie.ac.at

Chapter 10: User Centred Complex System Design: Combining Strategy, Methods and Front End Technology

Bryan Murray, Linda Candy & Ernest Edmonds
LUTCHI Research Centre , Loughborough University of Technology
Loughborough, U.K. LE11 3TU
Email: l.cnady@lut.ac.uk

Chapter 11: Agent-Based Architecture Modelling for Interactive Systems

Jöelle Coutaz., Laurence Nigay & Daniel Salber
CLIPS - IMAG, BP 53, 38041 Grenoble Cedex 9, France
Tel. +33 76 51 48 54.
Email: {Joelle.Coutaz, Laurence.Nigay, Daniel.Salber}@imag.fr

Chapter 12: Towards A Flexible Software Architecture of Interactive Systems
Michael Goedicke & Betina Sucrow
University of Essen, Maths & Computer Science
Specification of Software Systems
D-45117 Essen, Germany
Tel. +49 201 183 3481. Email: {goedicke,sucrow}@informatik.uni-essen.de

Chapter 13: Literate Development: Weaving Human Context into Design Specifications
Gilbert Cockton, Steven Clarke, Phil Gray & Chris Johnson
GIST Group, Department of Computing Science, University of Glasgow, Glasgow G12 8QQ
Tel. +44 141 339 8855. Email: {gilbert, clarkesj, pdg, johnson}@dcs.gla.ac.uk.

Chapter 14: Metaphors in User Interface Development: Methods and Requirements for Effective Support
Manfred Tscheligi [1] & Kaisa Väänänen-Vainio-Mattila[2]
[1] Vienna User Interface Group, Universität Wien, Lenaugasse 2/8, A-1080 Wien
[2] Computer Graphics Center (ZGDV), Wilhelminenstr. 7, D-64283 Darmstadt

Part I: Domain Modelling

Human-Computer Interaction (HCI) is concerned with developing computer-based systems which help people undertake their work or other activities and which demonstrate a high degree of usability. Both the process of development and the various products which are produced during development are critical to the success of the final human-computer system. Within HCI there is an increasing awareness of the importance of developing abstract representations - or models - of the area of activity which is to be the subject of the system. Such a representation is known as a domain model.

This section deals with a number of important aspects of domain models. Chapter 1 discusses the philosophical and practical aspects of developing domain models in HCI. Three generic approaches to domain modelling are identified; task-based, object-oriented and data-centred. Task-based approaches view HCI primarily in terms of the activities which people want to do. Object-oriented approaches describe the domain from the perspective of 'real world', user-centred objects and how these objects interact with one another. Data-centred approaches focus on the information structure and the ways in which information flows through the overall human-computer system.

Domain models can exist at many different levels of abstraction. The domains described in chapter 2 are whole work systems. For example, instead of seeing banking as a different domain from health care or tax returns as a different domain from insurance, the focus is on case work in general. Different work environments have different requirements for user interfaces. Most user interfaces at present are so generic that they can actually hinder people pursuing their work needs. Users often experience problems caused by the demands of window management; resizing windows, moving windows, scrolling, etc. This imposes a large and unnecessary load on the user. Instead, interfaces should aim to optimise work activities in a particular domain by providing an interface which is obvious and which uses an appropriate language.

Style guides should be based on domain-specific interface elements which are meaningful for the users with their work environment. This raises a number of issues concerning the correct level of abstraction which can be answered by considering how the information is used. Thus we can see the three generic perspectives identified in chapter 1 being applied sensitively to a large domain. User tasks are important for structuring the information displays, but equally important is the information which is required to support the users tasks. This information may be best structured in terms of objects which the users understand - again in terms of their work.

The importance of adopting various representations of the domain is also a theme in chapter 3. Although the domain here is narrower than that in chapter 2, it is still a broad domain. The chapter discusses a method for HCI design - particularly aimed at developing appropriate displays of information - illustrated using the domain of shipboard information systems. The domain is not *a* shipboard information system; it is shipboard information systems in general. Indeed the chapter abstracts from the needs of these systems to information presentation systems in general. One of the problems with task -based design is that the information requirements are not specified in enough detail. Hence there is a need for task and information (i.e. data-centred) analysis.

Throughout this section, then, the emphasis is on understanding the domain at various levels of abstraction. The discussion covers whole work areas, to particular types of information system. It looks at the need for information to support tasks, at the language needed to support work, at the methods of presentation needed to support the information requirements, at the interface style needed to structure the information and at the concrete interface objects which are appropriate for the users and their work.

Chapter 1: Domains Models for User Interface Design

David Benyon

1. Introduction

Human-Computer Interaction (HCI) is concerned with developing computer-based systems which help people undertake their work or other activities and which demonstrate a high degree of usability. Both the process of development and the various products which are produced during development are critical to the success of the final human-computer system (Hix and Hartson, 1993; Preece, et al., 1994). Within HCI there is an increasing awareness of the importance of developing abstract representations - or models - of the area of activity which is to be the subject of the system. Such a representation is known as a domain model, or an application model.

Any domain model must be built upon some conceptualisation of the domain which it is representing. Indeed the primitive constructs, or concepts, from which a model is built will reflect that conceptualisation. In HCI, however, there is no universally agreed conceptualisation on which we can base a model; there is no agreed theory of HCI. For example, there is the question of whether we interact *with* the computer or we interact *through* the computer; a debate which has been well-rehearsed in the pages of *Interacting with Computers* (Bench-Capon and McEnery, 1989a; Barlow, Rada and Diaper, 1989; Bench-Capon and McEnery, 1989b; Keeler and Denning, 1991). In (Bench-Capon and McEnery 1989b) the authors point out that both perspectives are important, but that the interacting through view should not be overlooked.

Another aspect of this debate concerns the importance of the concept of a 'task' in HCI. This concept has dominated the ontology of HCI in recent times as the wealth of literature on task analysis techniques will demonstrate (e.g. Diaper, 1989; Wilson, et al. 1988). Tasks are central to Carroll's (1990) conceptualisation of the task-artefact cycle. Long's (Long, 1989) conceptualisation of HCI includes the concept along with humans, computers and effectiveness. More recently however, the concept of 'task' has come in for criticism (Suchman, 1987; Benyon, 1992a; Benyon 1992b; Draper 1993).

Others (e.g. Fischer, 1989; Storrs 1989) challenge the dominance of tasks, arguing for a communication model of HCI. This model recognises the existence of shared knowledge in a particular problem domain. Humans and computers possess different but complementary knowledge and skills and should cooperate in the problem-solving activity. HCI should be viewed as the result of 'an interplay between [human] mental processes and external computational and memory aids'. (Fischer, 1989, p. 45).

It is likely that different conceptualisations of HCI have different strengths in different circumstances. In this paper, the philosophical and practical aspects of developing domain models of HCI are discussed. In section 2 a very general conceptualisation of HCI is provided. The following three sections examine three fundamental and contrasting modelling paradigms; task-based approaches, object-oriented approaches and data-centred approaches. The discussion section 7 provides a comparison of these.

2. HCI as a System

When we sit in front of a VDU it is natural and easy to focus attention on the human-computer interaction and the tasks which we undertake. For example, to download a file from a remote computer I might have the tasks; log on to remote computer, enter a password, locate the directory and type 'get <filename>'. Yet when we take a picture with a modern, automatic camera or we navigate the globe using the internet it is equally easy to overlook the role of information technology (and increasingly intelligent information technology) in these activities. Using the world-wide web to get a file I click on an icon. A software system locates the remote computer, another logs on, another locates the directory and yet another sends me the file.

Software systems are now embedded in a multitude of devices. Consequently we need to consider HCI not so much as a human using a computer, but more as a network of interacting systems; some interacting with each other and some interacting with the end-users. Ultimately users are interacting with other people through the computer - with the person who put the file in the directory, or wrote the software - but there are so many software systems operating at different levels of the interaction that such a description of the interaction on its own is not very enlightening.

Instead of teasing HCI apart into humans, tasks, interfaces, computers and so on, it may be more fruitful to begin with a more basic concept; a system. A system is a more or less complex object which is recognised, from a particular perspective, to have a relatively stable, coherent structure (Checkland, 1981). For example, I might wish to consider a human interacting with a computer as a system. Another person might wish to consider the computer as a system in its own right. Another person might wish to consider the users of networked computers distributed across the globe as system.

The concept of a system is a useful place to start because it can be applied at many different levels of abstraction and from many perspectives. However, it is not so general a concept that it has no foundation. Checkland's (1981) theory of systems is perhaps the clearest exposition. He stresses the need to declare explicitly as part of the system definition, the perspective (or *weltanschauung*) from which the phenomenon is being considered as a system and the aspects of the system which are considered to be stable and coherent. Systems theory also recognises that all systems are composed of other systems and exist within wider systems.

Another important aspect of systems theory is the recognition that systems interact with other systems. Systems interact with their sub-systems, with their super-systems and with systems at the same level of abstraction. The interaction of a systems' component subsystems results in the system having properties which *emerge* from the relationships existing between its sub-systems. In other words,

systems possess properties which are not possessed by any of its subsystems. For example, if I consider water to be a system composed of the subsystems hydrogen and oxygen, then water clearly possesses properties not possessed by either hydrogen or oxygen. The properties of water emerge from the relationship between its subsystems. If I consider the Internet to be a system (defined as all the people, software, computers and communication mechanisms who are able to access the 'net), then its properties (e.g. being able to read today's *Daily Telegraph* from South America or participating in the virtual communities of computer conferences) are not possessed by any of the component systems. The properties emerge from the relationships between those component systems.
In order to illustrate the system concept, consider the systems illustrated in Figure 1. The environment under consideration in this figure is the banking system. The banks themselves exist within this environment (and indeed in other environments which are not under consideration). There will be other institutions which are part of the banking system which are not banks. My various accounts exist within the banks and stray outside (e.g. into Building Societies.) Automatic Teller Machines (ATMs) exist within the banks. Some are related to my accounts but others are not. The interfaces to ATMs exist within the ATM system. In Figure 1 we see a variety of systems, defined at a variety of levels of abstraction and from a variety of perspectives. The systems engage in a variety of interactions.

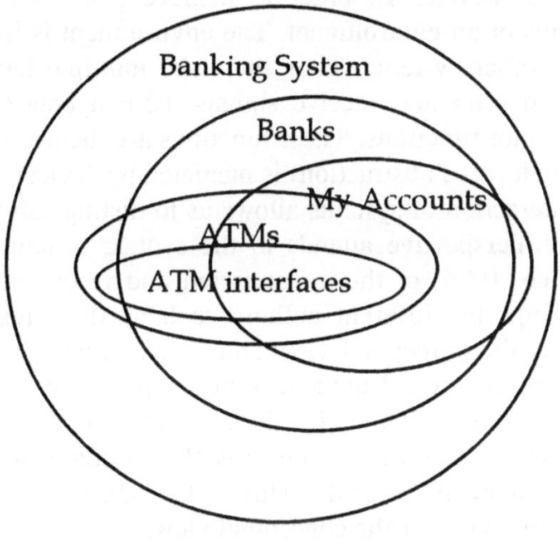

Figure 1 Some interacting systems in a Banking environment

Viewing HCI as a system focuses attention on the existence of multiple levels of networks of interacting systems. Observers, designers or participants in such a network can choose to identify and describe systems and their interactions at a level of abstraction appropriate for their purpose at hand. This purpose and the level of description needs to be openly declared as it is part of the modelling process.

Interacting Systems

In HCI we are primarily concerned with interaction, but how do systems interact? Theorists from many disciplines such as communication theory (e.g. Cherry, 1966), semiotics (e.g. Eco, 1976), systems theory (e.g. Laszlo, 1969), linguistics (Lyons, 1977) and information theory (Shannon and Weaver, 1949) recognise that systems interact through the exchange of signals which travel through a communication channel. Signals are the elementary particle of interaction (Benyon, 1993). Signals are binary in that they either exist or do not exist (Eco, 1976). However, they rarely travel alone and we refer to a structured collection of signals as a message. Like systems, however, signals and messages need to declared and viewed at a given level of abstraction. From my perspective pressing a button labelled 'withdraw cash' is the way I send signals to the ATM. From the perspective of the computer, the signals might be described as a series of bits.

In this conceptualisation of HCI as a network of interacting systems, it is useful to recognise two main classes of participants; agents and devices. Agents are intentional, autonomous systems in that they have beliefs and desires and can formulate their own goals (Laurel, 1990). People are agents and we are beginning to create artificial agents (e.g. Maes and Kozeriok, 1993; Maes, 1994). Devices are not autonomous. They may demonstrate sophisticated behaviour, but they do so without the sense of volition attached to agents.

Agents and devices are systems. They interact through the exchange of signals. Agents make use of devices in order to achieve goals within the actual and perceived constraints of an environment. The environment is itself a system which is interacting with other systems. Thus there are multiple levels of agent-device systems. In order to send and receive signals, both agents and devices require transmitter and receptor functions. These functions are themselves devices. Thus all interaction (at some level of abstraction) is mediated by devices.

Focusing on the interaction of systems allows us to distinguish two perspectives on those systems. One perspective attends to the syntax, semantics and pragmatics (Stamper, 1977; Eco, 1976) of the transmission and reception of signals. This is called different things by different authors such as the 'presentation' view, the 'view', the interface, the perceptual view and so on. Coutaz, *et al.*, (this volume) provide a comparison of several nomenclatures. Some authors (e.g. Goedicke and Sucrow, this volume) like to distinguish the internal presentation from the external presentation. The other perspective concerns the mechanisms by which systems structure and manipulate the signals. This is the 'abstract' view, also called the 'model', the abstraction view or the conceptual view.

There may be several presentation views on a system according to the other systems with which it interacts. For example, the ATM has one presentation view in order to interact with the human user of the ATM, another to interact with the bank card and another in order to communicate with the central computer. Similarly we may view the user of an ATM from the presentation view of pressing keys on the keypad, from inserting the card into the machine and so on. Clearly there are many other presentation views of humans; when they interact with other humans or with other devices.

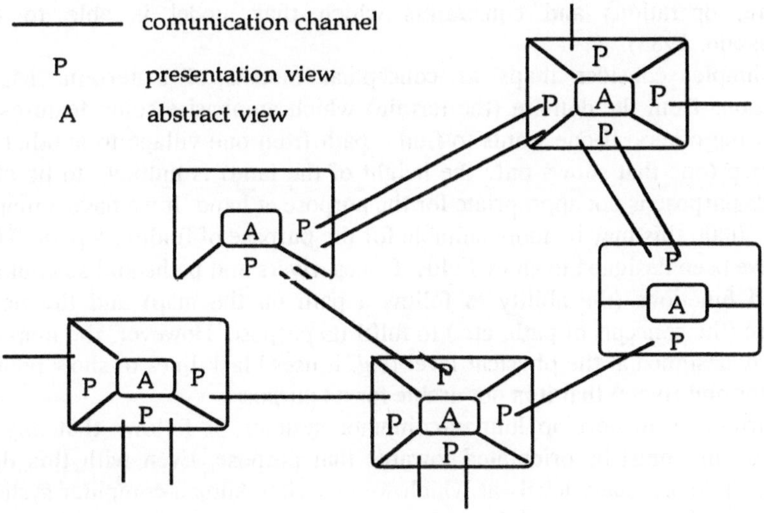

Figure 2 Systems have a variety of presentation views and a variety of interactions

This systems perspective of HCI shifts attention from the characteristics of humans and computers. Instead it focuses on interactions and the exchange of messages between the components of a human-computer system. Different views of those systems and their interaction will reveal different aspects of the interaction. This is illustrated schematically in Figure 2.

3. Modelling the Domain

The domain of HCI is a network of interacting systems some of which are agents and some of which are devices. If we wish to think about HCI, and to design human-computer systems, we need to conceptualise the domain using appropriate representations - or conceptual models. Conceptual models are devices for understanding, communicating, testing or predicting some aspects of some system. They are 'professional' languages which both constrain and focus a discourse by limiting the range of concepts which can be expressed in the language (Kangassollo, 1983, Lyttinen, 1983). Conceptual models provide a certain perspective of the domain by employing abstraction mechanisms which are reflected in the content and the structure of the concepts employed by the model.
A conceptual model will be more or less effective depending on the characteristics of the model. First we need to consider the purpose and use of the model. Second we need to consider whether the model possesses the necessary structure and processing capability to fulfil its purpose and third we need to consider the physical characteristics of the model - its notation and its usability. The analytic, explanatory and communicative power of a conceptual model arises from the

structure, operations and constraints which that model is able to capture (Kangassalo, 1983).
For example, consider maps as conceptual models of a terrain. Maps are abstractions from the domain (the terrain) which emphasise some features whilst suppressing others. If one wants to find a path from one village to another then a relief map (one that shows only the height of the land) is unlikely to be of much help. It's purpose is not appropriate for the purpose at hand. If we have a map of the scale 1:50000 this may be more suitable for the purpose of finding a path. The map may have been designed to show fields, fences, rivers and paths and so contains the required functions (the ability to follow a path on the map) and the necessary structure (the concepts of path, etc.) to fulfil its purpose. However, the map may be so poorly designed at the physical level (e.g. it uses black lines to show boundaries and paths and rivers) that it is not usable for its purpose.
Our purpose is to develop human-computer systems. It follows that any model which we use must be orientated towards that purpose. Even with this declared purpose there are many levels at which we can view human-computer systems. At the organisation level we might wish to consider the design of working practices and the impact of new technologies on organisations. At the environmental level, we might wish to look at health and safety issues or office layout. At another environmental level we may wish to look at legal and ethical issues concerning human-computer systems. At a physical level we could examine the use of colour or font style on the usability of systems. At a more detailed physical level we may consider hardware and software issues concerned with rendering accurate representations of real world objects. At each of these levels there are a variety of devices and models which can help the designer.
The focus of attention here - and the models considered in the following sections - are at the logical, or conceptual level of the design of a suitable human-computer system which can deliver the required functionality and usability. We are concerned with an abstract view which can support the various presentations (or interactions) required by the component agents and devices in the system. We are concerned with who or what will perform which functions and provide which pieces of knowledge and at the structure of the human-computer dialogue.
The models which are considered in the next three sections have been chosen because they represent important paradigms within systems design and which are all candidates for the domain model which should underlie the development of human-computer systems. The three approaches differ in the type and level of abstraction which they use, the underlying concepts and notation which they employ and the constraints and operations which they support. Task-based approaches focus on what the user has to do. Object-oriented approaches exploit a representation based on the exchange of messages between objects. Data-centred approaches focus on the data which exists and which flows through the system. As is discussed in section 7, many methods in HCI utilise more than one of these generic modelling approaches.
One important aspect of modelling which is frequently misunderstood is that the concepts employed by a model constitute the material from which that model is

constructed; they are not the object of the model. Thus an algebraic model of a circle, $x^2 + y^2 = z^2$, is not a model *of* algebra. It is a model *of* a circle *made from* algebra. This could be contrasted with a model *made from* programming constructs expressed in a language such as Logo (which may be represented as To Circle, Forward 1, Right 1, Circle). Thus task-based models are models of a human-computer system made from tasks, object-oriented models are models of a system made from objects and data-centred models are models of a system made of data.

4. Task Models

Task models seek to represent the domain in terms of tasks. The emphasis of task-based approaches is primarily on human tasks and the need to understand what people (rather than computers) have to do. Task-models were developed because of the emphasis in HCI on people interacting with computers. The essence of the task-based paradigm is summed up by Carroll in his plea for an 'ontologically minimised' HCI (Carroll 1990). He argues that 'A task implicitly sets requirements for the development of artefacts, and the use of an artefact often redefines the task for which the artefact was originally developed' (p. 323). This task-artefact cycle would certainly appear to characterise one of the main problems which HCI faces. Carroll justifies the importance of task by saying 'conceiving of HCI activity in this way clearly implies that to design more useful artefacts we must better understand the tasks people undertake and better apply our understanding of tasks in the design process'. Although there is a sense in which this view appears self-contradictory (surely if the artefact is going to change the task, understanding the task during design is going to be of little help in the longer term), Carroll's view of the centrality of tasks is one that is pervasive in HCI circles.

Task-based approaches have as their basic concept the idea of a user 'task'. Although there are many variations in the definition of the term - and different authors define task in different ways - the concept of a task may be defined as 'a goal together with some procedure or ordered set of actions that will achieve that goal' (Amodeus, 1994). (But see Benyon, 1992a, Draper, 1993 or Diaper, 1989 for more discussion). Other basic concepts such as 'goal', (a state of the environment or agent which is desired by the agent) 'operation' 'simple task', 'unit task' or 'action' (a task which involves no problem solving or control component), 'plan' or 'procedure' (a sequence of tasks, sub-tasks and/or actions), 'job' and 'role' ('the collection of tasks that a person occupying that role performs'; Johnson, 1992 p. 162) are defined in terms of this basic concept. Task-based approaches date back to the earliest exposition of HCI theory (Card, Moran and Newell, 1980; Moran, 1981) and continue to be popular today (e.g. Browne, 1994). The wide variety of task-based models and the different uses to which they are put adds to the confusion.

The notation used in task-based methods is either based on a grammar type of representation or it is based on the structure chart notation. Structure charts represent a sequence of tasks, sub-tasks and actions as a hierarchy and include notational conventions to show whether an action can be repeated a number of times (iteration) and the execution of alternative actions (selection).

The most recent and complete description of a task-based approach is provided by Lim and Long (1994). Their method - MUSE - follows the structured approach advocated in information systems development circles and hence models the systems development process as well as the domain. The method is a well-researched and detailed scheme for integrating human factors into information systems development approaches based on a structure chart notation.

The process advocated by Lim and Long (1994) is to construct task models of existing or extant systems, develop a Generic Task Model and from this produce a Composite Task Model for the new system. This Composite Task Model describes both user and system activities and is used to derive a System and User Task Model which divides the tasks and actions required between the user and the computer. User interface specification may then be undertaken.

In MUSE, Lim and Long are careful to emphasise the role of abstraction and 'generification' in modelling. Thus the move from extant task models to Generic Task Model is vital. They recommend the following steps;

1. Take as input task information described in the statement of requirements. Temporal and conditional aspects of task execution should also be noted.
2. Summarise the task (and sub-tasks) in device-independent terms to reveal the logic underlying the design of the task.
3. Re-express the task description using structured diagrams to derive a target Generalised Task Model, and record any additional notes.

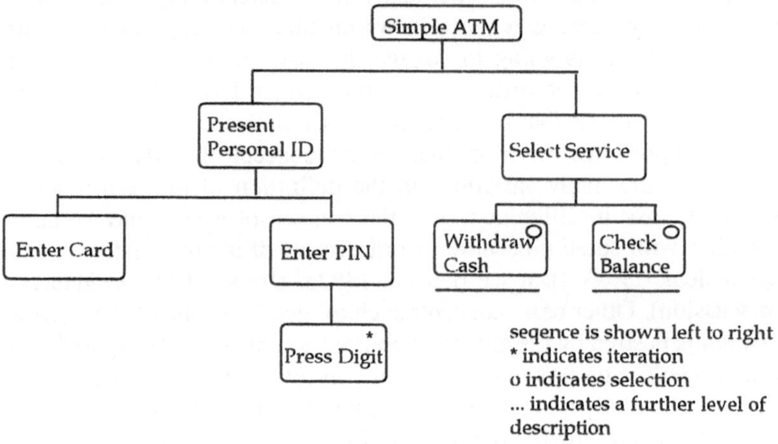

Figure 3 Generic Task Model for a portion of an ATM

Lim and Long (1994) illustrate their approach using two main case studies; an ATM and a network security system. A portion of their ATM example is shown in Figures 4 and 5. Following an analysis of current (or extant) systems, a Generalised Task Model for an ATM has been produced.

Although Lim and Long (1994) do not provide their version of the Generalised Task Model for the ATM, we may assume that it is similar to Figure 3. This shows that the 'Simple ATM' consists of two sub-tasks which are completed in sequence;

Present Personal ID and Select Service. Present Personal ID consists of two sub-tasks Enter Card and Enter PIN and in its turn Enter PIN consists of a number of iterations of the Press Digit action. Select Service consists of either Withdraw Cash or Check Balance. Each of these is further redescribed (indicated by the dotted line, but not shown in this example).
Taking on board a statement of user needs, the Composite Task Model for the new system has been developed. A portion of this is shown in Figure 4. This model must now be decomposed into the user and system tasks (Figure 5).

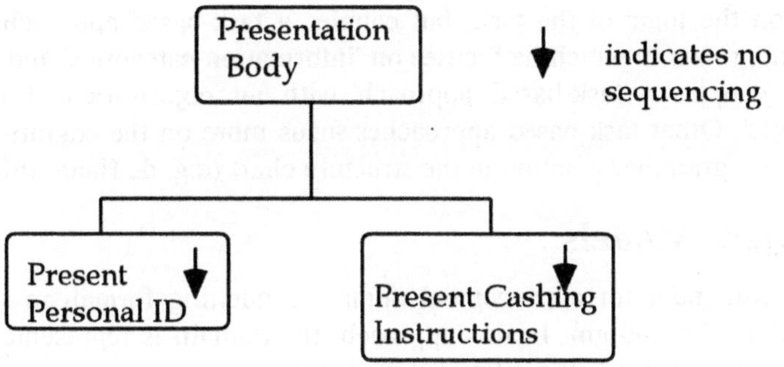

Figure 4 Portion of a Composite Task Model for an ATM (from Lim and Long, 1994).

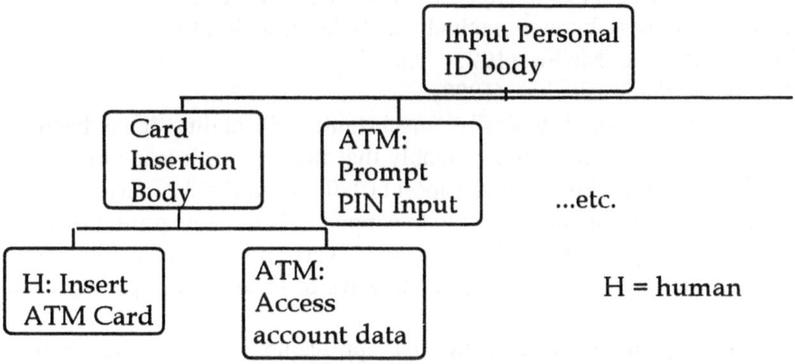

Figure 5 Portion of a User and System Task Model (from Lim and Long, 1994)

This small snippet of the task-based approaches to developing conceptual models of the domain illustrates several important features of the approach. First, two important aspects of modelling are emphasised - abstracting from current systems and aiming for device independence (so, for example the composite task model in Figure 4 allows for the processes Present Personal ID and Present Cashing Instructions to be undertaken in any sequence). Second the approach uses a notation which can be used to model the whole human-computer system and to subsequently identify human and computer activities (as illustrated by the human and ATM activities in Figure 4). This aspect has also been emphasised by (Sutcliffe and McDermott, 1991).

The purpose of the task-based approach is to facilitate the design of systems through analysing and abstracting current practice. The concepts employed by the model are tasks and sub-tasks. The physical notation and representation of the model is the structure chart notation. Task-based models are able to show the sequencing, iteration and selection of sub-tasks and actions and to show the allocation of tasks to human or to computer.

MUSE focuses primarily on the logic of the task. Sutcliffe (this volume) also focuses on the logic of the task, but couples a task-based approach with a data-centred approach in which he focuses on 'information categories' and Paterno' (this volume) couples a task-based approach with an object-oriented model of the 'interactors'. Other task-based approaches focus more on the cognition of the task and prefer a grammar notation to the structure chart (e.g. de Haan, this volume).

5. Object Models

Another contender for a conceptual domain modelling formalism in HCI is the object-oriented paradigm. In this approach, the domain is represented in terms of the objects which exist, the relationships between objects and the messages which are passed between objects. The proliferation in object modelling methods has resulted in a large amount of confusion over exactly what is being represented, how it should be represented and how to approach application modelling using the OO approach. McBride (1994) suggests that there are over sixty OO methods in existence. The best known methods include; Booch (1991), Rumbaugh, et al. (1991), Shlaer and Mellor (1992), Jacobson, et al. (1993), Coad and Yourdon (1992) and Wirfs-Brock et al. (1990).

Many extravagant (and typically unsubstantiated) claims have been made for object-oriented techniques; most notably that the approach leads to a more natural design. For example, Rosson and Alpert (1990) claim that ' A particularly attractive aspect of OO design is that it seems to support a better integration of problem and solution' (p. 361)....whilst admitting that 'very little empirical evidence exists concerning the naturalness of objects as ways of representing problem entities' (p. 363).

Objects are the basic concept in OO approaches. Objects are defined as 'an encapsulation of attributes and exclusive services [behaviours]; an abstraction of the something in the problem space,...' (Coad and Yourdon, 1992). Davis (1993), like many OO theorists stresses that objects correspond to real world entities.

In OO design analysts/designers are encouraged to identify objects in the domain and use these as the basis for the conceptual model. Various advice is offered on how to spot objects. For example 'identifying classes and objects involves finding key abstractions in the problem space and important mechanisms that offer the dynamic behaviour over several such objects.' (Booch. 1992).

The analysts should 'develop an object model which describes the static structure of the system with classes and relationships. The dynamic model captures the temporal aspects, the functional model describes the computation '(Rumbaugh, et al. 1991).

'The designer looks for classes of objects trying out a variety of schemes in order to discover the most natural and reasonable way to abstract the system. ...In this phase the major tasks are to discover the classes required to model the application and to determine what behaviour the system is responsible for and assign these specific responsibilities to classes'. (CACM, 1990).

OO modelling focuses first of all on structure - it is the objects which are paramount. The system's processing is defined in terms of the objects - different classes of object allow for different types of processing. The notation for object diagrams varies considerably from Entity-relationship diagrams to 'roundtangles' to represent objects to cloud type diagrams. Sully (1994) provides a comparison.

One of the problems of describing and analysing the OO approaches is that they often employ a nomenclature which is unfamiliar and which uses a variety of concepts. Thus apart from objects and classes, OO approaches use concepts of scenarios, 'use cases', methods, messages, roles and so on. There is also a problem in distinguishing object-oriented programming and object-oriented analysis and design.

The claims for the benefits of OO techniques include abstraction and encapsulation (otherwise known as 'information hiding'). Objects are viewed from the outside and users need not be concerned about how they are implemented. Objects can send and receive messages; they encapsulate the structure and processing which enables them to deal with those messages. Other features of the OO paradigm such as polymorphism (that different object classes will treat the same message in different ways), inheritance, late binding and tight cohesion relate more to the programming benefits than to any conceptual benefits of the approach.

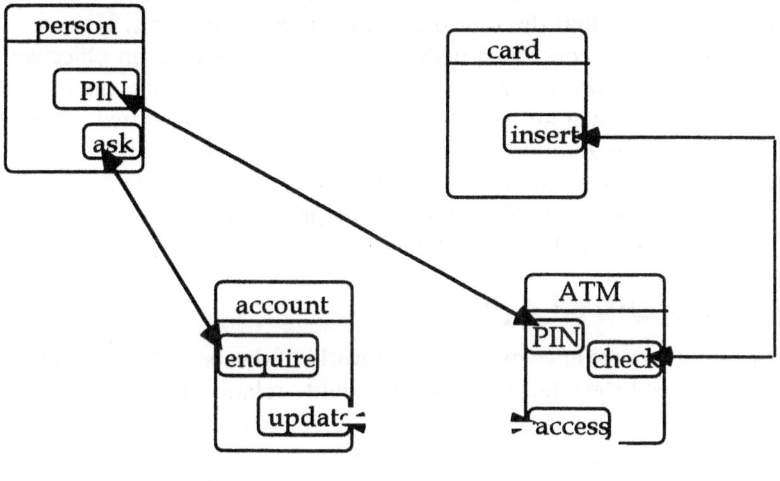

Figure 6 Object model of the ATM

The most significant difference between the OO paradigm and the data-centred paradigm is that OO approaches avoid the separation of data from procedures typified by the data-centred approaches. Instead of the functional decomposition into processes on a dataflow diagram, OO decomposes a system into messages flowing between objects. However, a number of authors (e.g. Sully, 1994) describe two approaches to OO design; moving from a data-centred approach to an object model and going directly from a domain or application to an object model.
In the ATM example, a OO analysis would result in diagrammatic representation as shown in Figure 6. The objects of interest in the application; person, card, account and ATM are shown as objects with the major messages which they can send and receive shown. The internal description of the objects (the structure of the objects in terms of the attributes which they have and the processing which the objects can perform) would be shown in separate object description tables.
The object-oriented paradigm again emphasises abstraction and generification through the notion of object classes. This is similar to the idea of generic tasks, where, for example, the task of entering a PIN is similar in all circumstances. Generification recognises, for example, that all bank cards will have common attributes and will send and receive similar messages. OO also recognise sub-types which inherit behaviours and/or attributes from the super-class. For example if there are various types of bank card which provide different types of facilities, these different types would inherit the basic characteristics of all bank cards. The focus of the approach is on structure rather than processing (unlike the task-based approaches). Objects also stress encapsulation - the 'black box' view approach of hiding information which is not relevant to a particular view of the object. The emphasis is on the existence of the object and on its presentation in terms of the messages which it can send or receive rather than on the abstract, internal view of the structure.
The attraction of the OO approaches is that the system can be described in terms which the users should be able to understand. The objects which the analyst discovers are those that the user deals with in concrete terms. However, there are philosophical issues concerned with whether or not there is an objective reality to be modelled and even given an agreed reality to model, the analyst can find it difficult to know when an object has been successfully identified. Objects are also very popular in programming; in implementing a system. If they are clearly defined then the programmer can re-use objects which have been previously defined. The ability of objects to inherit the structure and processing of other objects means that the writing of code can be more efficient.

6. Data-Centred Approaches

Data-centred models have existed in the world of database design since 1976 when Peter Chen published his paper on the entity-relationship model (Chen, 1976). Shortly afterwards, in 1979 the dataflow diagram was established (e.g. DeMarco, 1979) and in the early 1980s the entity-life history evolved (Rosenquist, 1982). Typically details of the entities, dataflows and processes are recorded in a data dictionary. All of these models use as their basic concept the notion of a data item or data element. The structure of the domain is abstracted as a network of entities and the functions of the domain by a network of dataflows and processes. Other representations associated with the data-centred approach include state transition diagrams (which come in a variety of guises). These focus on the data which is necessary to move the system from one state to another.

The basic concept of a data model is a data element (or data item). A data item consists of one or more symbols, a name (and usually a more comprehensive description of the meaning of the data item) and a context. The name, description and context ascribe the semantics to the data item. Data items are generalisations of the actual and potential values which that data item can take. These values are known as the domain of the data item (Benyon, 1990).

For example, in the context of the ATM we may have some data, say '2341', associated with a name, PIN. This would allow us to represent that a particular PIN is 2341. This can be generalised in terms of the domain of PIN which may be any 4-digit number. The concept of a domain is very similar to that of an object in the OO approaches as the domain defines the operations which are allowable. For example in the ATM application we might define the data items PIN and Card where PIN has the domain of 4-digit numbers and Card has a domain of BankCard (and hence supports certain operations such as 'insert', 'swipe', etc.).

Another level of abstraction in data-centred approaches is provided by something which is usually known as an *entity*. Although some authors argue that entities are things which exist in the 'real world', others prefer to focus on an entity as a purer data-centred concept. An entity is an aggregation of data items, expressing the semantics that certain data items belong together. Once these groupings have been established, the analyst can refer to the collection of data items - the entity - by name, thus suppressing detail which would otherwise clutter the model. Relationships between entities - expressed in terms of the number of instances of one entity which are associated with the instances of another entity - can then be considered.

Figure 7 shows an entity-relationship diagram of the ATM example. It may be interpreted as follows. An Account (identified by Accountnumber) must have just one owner (identified by Name and Address), though an owner may have many accounts (but must have one). An (account) owner may be a (ATM) user. A user (defined as a Card + PIN) makes use of ATMs (identified by an ATMnumber). A use is defined as a user using an ATM. An ATM accesses accounts.

One of the interesting things which arises once one starts looking at the data is that further insight is gathered; for example, that the entity User may be different from the entity Owner. Indeed that we define a User as a person who is in possession of (a valid combination of) PIN and Card and this may be different from the owner of the account.

Representing the domain in terms of data items, how they are grouped together into entities and the relationships which pertain between entities describes the structure of the domain. Another way to model the domain is to look at how data flows between processes. A process, or functional, model made of data concentrates on the data which is strictly necessary for processing to occur.

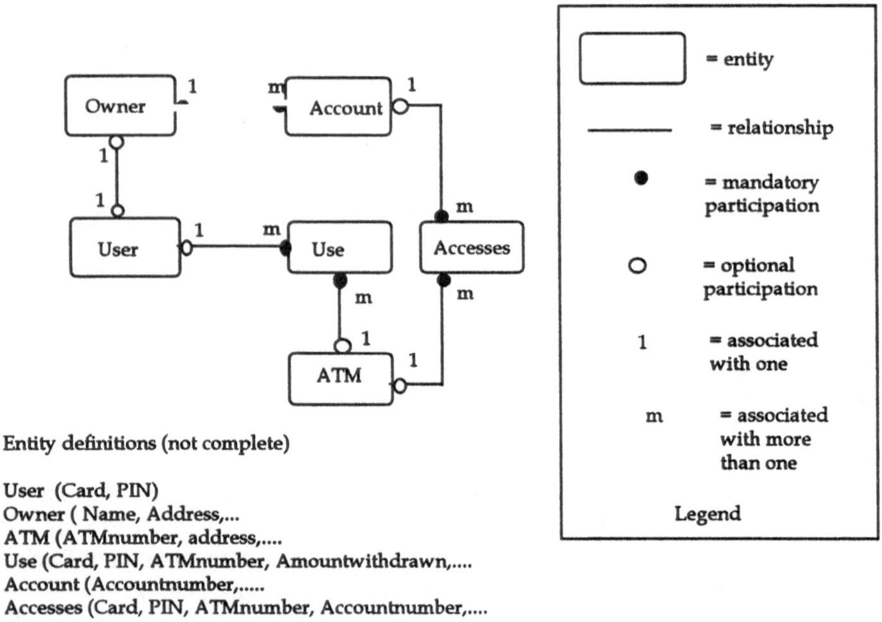

Figure 7 Entity-relationship model for portion of an ATM.

Functional data models are abstractions of systems which do not show flow of control i.e. they strive to be as independent of the device as possible. This may be contrasted with a model of the physical system (such as a flowchart) which models the movement of physical objects such as documents and the control flow (i.e. the sequencing of actions) of particular implementations. Functional data models concentrate on the data processing which is strictly necessary for some process to function in a given domain. For example, in order to get cash from an ATM, a user *has* to be validated and to have enough money in the account (Figure 8) and these things have to take place in sequence. The cash retrieval process, logically, needs both of these data items in order to function. In contrast, Present Personal ID and Present cashing instructions are not dependent on each other. Importantly dataflow models *do* show the data which is necessary for certain processes to happen (compare this representation with Figure 4 which does not show the data which needs to flow between processes.)

Several well-developed techniques are available to assist the designer develop a conceptual data model. Normalisation enables the analyst to explore the semantics of the data by examining the relationships between data items (Date, 1986). The entity-relationship (ER) model represents aggregations of data items and the relationships which exist between them (Benyon, 1990). Dataflow diagrams (DFDs) concentrate on consistent and complete descriptions of data flow, showing the minimum amount of sequencing required for processing to occur and the data dictionary describes the semantics of data items, stores and processes (DeMarco,

1979). Entity Life Histories (ELH) use a structure chart notation to show the behaviour of entities over time.

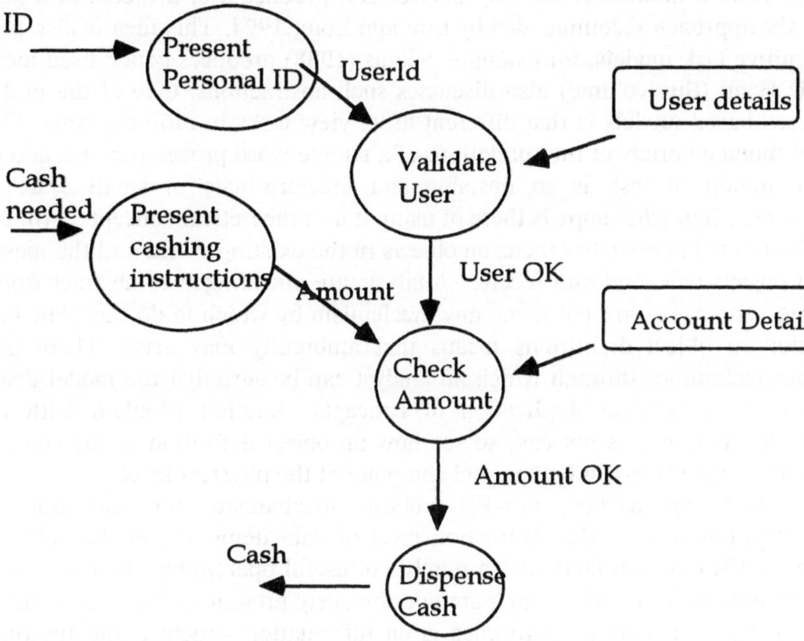

Figure 8 Portion of Dataflow diagram for ATM

7. Discussion

Developing an appropriate domain model is critical for the success of interface design. For model-based approaches to HCI a domain model is strictly necessary. Even where a model-based approach is not employed, the analyst needs to be able to abstract the domain and represent it in a way which facilitates analysis of the problem situation and design of an effective solution.

The purpose of developing a conceptual model of the application domain is to support both the analysis of the extant system (understanding the requirements of the whole human-computer system) and the design of a replacement system. The two important requirements of a modelling method are

(i) that it must be at an appropriate level of abstraction for these purposes

and

(ii) that it should support a useful and relevant conceptualisation of HCI.

The task-based approaches focus on the sequences of actions which are necessary to accomplish a goal. They do not represent the data or information which flows between these actions. Nor do they represent the knowledge required to undertake an action successfully. The notation of task-based models includes control flow (i.e. the sequencing, selection and iteration of actions). Task-based models - because they show control flow - are device dependent; the sequencing of actions is dependent on the device being used to achieve the goal. Of course the analyst can abstract from a number of existing devices and produce a task model of a generic task - the approach recommended by Lim and Long 1994. This idea is also present in cognitive task models; for example, Kieras (1988) produces generalised methods and de Haan (this volume) also discusses such abstractions. One of the problems with task-based models is that different users view tasks in different ways. Draper (1993) found a variety of interpretations of a simple word processing task and notes 'If the notion of task is so unstable and indeterminate in small scale word processing...then what hope is there of using it as a theoretical concept...? (p. 207).

Object-oriented approaches focus on objects in the existing world and the messages which objects can send and receive. Analysts are encouraged to abstract from the existing system, but are not given any mechanism by which to do this. The lack of precision in object definitions means that ambiguity may arise. There are no rigorous techniques through which an analyst can be sure that the model does not contain any redundant duplication of concepts. Another problem with object approaches is that it is not easy to see how an object definition at the conceptual level can be split between human and computer at the physical level.

Data-centred approaches provide robust mechanism for detecting poor representations both at the abstraction level of data items and at the entity level where the ER diagram facilitates a number of useful operations which can be used to determine useful entities which are *not* obviously present in the 'real world'. The focus of the data-centred approaches is on information structure and information flow. The main problems with data-centred approaches is that the entities in a structural model of the domain or the dataflows in a procedural model may not correspond to user concepts or user tasks.

Besides the material from which the model is constructed - tasks, objects or data - the approach to HCI development needs to be considered. The approaches may be classified as structured, iterative or 'toolkit' (Benyon and Skidmore, 1987). A structured method offers a prescribed step by step approach. An iterative approach emphasises the cyclical nature of development. A tool-kit approach encourages the selection of models which are appropriate for the purpose at hand.

One of the difficulties with examining the different paradigms and methods is that they are frequently confused. First, there is a confusion between structured methods and data-centred approach. A structured method can be based on any modelling formalism. Thus MUSE is a structured method based on tasks. The data-centred approach does not have to be structured; one can undertake data-centred analysis and design without following a method (e.g. a tool-kit approach).

Second the same notations are used to support multiple methods. For example ER models are used in a number of object-oriented approaches and structure charts are used in both data-centred and task-based approaches. Third, there are many hybrid techniques. For example, in the task-based technique KAT, Johnson (1992) explicitly states that the knowledge required by users to undertake a task must be represented and uses object models for this. Many of the methods described in this volume combine aspects of the different paradigms. For example, the object approach of Palanque and Bastide shows the data which flows between objects. Sutcliffe's task-based approach also shows data whereas Paterno's task-based approach uses objects. Fourth, different authors usurp the advantages of other methods, claiming them for their own. For example, the claim that the object paradigm takes a modelling point of view is equally true for both the data-centred and task-based approaches. Certainly task-based approaches are more procedural, but they clearly take a modelling perspective.

In order to develop effective human-computer systems we need to develop techniques which capture a conceptual model of the whole domain. These conceptual models must be expressed using a medium which is applicable to both agents and devices. The conceptualisation of HCI presented in section 2 emphasised that communication in agent-device systems takes place through the exchange of signals and that both the signals and the systems need to be described at various levels of abstraction.

Data modelling makes the semantics of, and relationships between data items explicit. At the level of abstraction appropriate for human-computer systems, data are the signals which are exchanged between systems. Thus data-centred approaches are suitable for describing the abstract view of both agents (whether human or not) and devices. For the presentation view concerned with the interaction with users, data must be organised into user-centred objects and processing must be organised into user-centred tasks. For the internal presentation views both data-centred and object-oriented models have their place.

The tasks which we design when we develop computer-based systems must be openly declared and evaluated with users. The objects which users think about and interact with when using the system must correspond to objects which they understand and use. However, shifting attention from existing tasks and existing objects to the tasks and objects of the new system requires an abstract view to be taken. Developing appropriate conceptual models of domains demands that the material from which the model is constructed is suitable for that purpose. A well-constructed, abstract model means that the allocation of tasks, knowledge, functions and control to human, to artificial agent or to a device becomes a more considered, rational and open activity.

Chapter 2: Domain Specific Design of User Interfaces – Case Handling and Data Entry Problems

Jan Gulliksen & Bengt Sandblad

1. Introduction

The use of graphical user interfaces in a computerised work environment is often considered to substantially improve the work situation. The outcome however, can be the opposite. Inappropriate use of windowing techniques, scrolling and colours can result in confusing and tedious interaction with the computer. The problem solving process of professional work is constantly interrupted by the need for "re-design" of the interface, e.g. open, resize and move windows, start different applications etc. This results in low efficiency, a high level of anxiety and stress, bad acceptance and even health problems. Studies on different types of work situations show that properties of the work environment can limit efficient use of skills by persons performing the work. We call these limitations 'cognitive work environment problems' and they are often associated with the human-computer interface. To minimise the cognitive load caused by the interface, design of the interface must be based on an analysis of it's load on the user. In our research we have seen examples of computer systems where up to 80% of the working time is spent managing the interface. In a work situation, where computerised information systems are used, e.g. health care, the purpose of the work performed by the work domain professionals is never to operate the computer. The computer is only a tool that will be used and appreciated only as long as it efficiently supports the purpose of the work, e.g. to provide good health care for a patient. This means that the user interface must be designed on the basis of optimisation of the work activities as such, instead of just optimising computer use. Design of user interfaces for skilled workers in professional work settings should be based on style guides that certify efficiency.

Unnecessary cognitive work-load, related to the interface, rather than to the work process as such, is often a severe obstacle for skilled professionals using computer artifacts. Studies of skilled workers in a variety of contexts imply that an extremely important part of the design of a system for such workers is the mapping of certain types of relevant information onto graphical properties that can be automatically perceived. The interface can be made "obvious" to the user (Nygren, Johnson, Lind & Sandblad 1992). Other problems encountered in the design and implementation phases are the difficulties for end-users to participate efficiently in prototyping and experimental development. This can be facilitated by performing the dialogue in a terminology familiar to the involved professionals, i.e. in domain specific terms.

The practical problems can be illustrated by the following example. In a large Swedish governmental authority most of the case handling is performed using intensive computer support. The total number of case handlers are approximately

14.000, and the computer support consists of some 200 different applications. To develop, run, support and maintain this complex system is of course associated with many different problems and high costs. If the structure of different applications, the involvement of users in the specification and development processes and the methods and techniques for systems development and implementation could be improved the potential gain, in terms of time, money, work efficiency and improved work environment, would be substantial. One way of achieving parts of this is to base the development on a domain specific approach.

2. Experimental System Development

Our research at CMD has, among other things, been dealing with methods for design and construction of human-computer interfaces in professional work settings. Research activities have covered areas such as task and information analysis, design methodology; e. g. domain specific design, specification of new interface elements, construction tools etc. When the different steps, and the methods and tools supplied for them, now are to be integrated, this leads to new requirements concerning their coordination (Gulliksen, Lind, Lif & Sandblad 1995). This paper gives a framework for the entire domain specific design process. Of special importance is the specification of the bridges between the different steps and the definition of languages for documentation of the results from each step. In such a language it must be possible to specify the result from one step in a form interpretable to the next step.

A decision on investments to improve usability in a company requires results immediately measurable with respect to efficiency and increased acceptance by the users. It also requires proof of shorter development times at a minimum of costs. The laborious and time consuming development of user interfaces directly based on an existing style guide, like e. g. Motif, has to be reviewed and remodelled to meet the coming demands on usability of the information systems and on the design and development process. With a domain specific design methodology, user interface development can be improved with respect to efficiency of use, development time and cost. We have currently been using this methodology in the Helios project within the CEC/ AIM-programme – where a style guide specific for the medical health care ward domain has been developed (Borälv, Göransson, Olsson & Sandblad 1994). Based on large domain specific user interface development projects, the reuse of interface components and theories for skilled professional users in routine work situations become important. The possibilities to reuse components at different levels are enhanced through object oriented techniques.

Following is a summary of some important parts of our model for system development:

- System development, including interface design and construction, according to an experimental model means that requirements specifications, system design and construction are performed in a user centred dialogue involving both domain experts (e. g. end-users) and system and user interface designers.
- A task analysis is always performed, treating work activities and organisational aspects simultaneously, resulting in a development plan. After this, two things

follow in parallel: information analysis and data modelling for the specification of the database and analysis of information utilisation for the specification of interaction requirements.
- Design of the user interface based on analysis of information utilisation combined with more general design knowledge. An efficient interface must minimise cognitive load caused by the computer artifact.
- Domain specific design, incorporating domain knowledge in the design process, to improve design and construction and make the resulting interface more efficient.
- New tools for construction of interfaces, which are more efficient than today's tools, and that are consistent with the rest of the development process.

An important concept relating to interface design and construction is the interface *style guide* (OSF/Motif Style Guide), that however has an ambiguous definition. With an interface style guide we mean a document specifying a set of basic interface elements, normally called widgets, and a set of rules for how these elements can and should be used to be compliant with the style guide. It has been debated whether the definition of the basic element, the widgets, is a part of the style guide or not. We consider the widget set to be a part of the style guide even if it normally is specified separately, although, it should not be confused with the implementation of it. Today's standards and style guides define basic design principles but are insufficient for design of interfaces to end-user applications, because they give no higher level guidance concerning design of an interface for a certain application. They also over-emphasise general aspects, or aspects relevant to novices. To increase efficiency both of the design process and of the resulting interface, more domain knowledge should be included. In order to develop style guides that aid the design of interfaces on a much higher level, we have defined the concept of a domain specific style guide (Gulliksen, Johnson, Lind, Nygren & Sandblad 1993).

3. Domain Specific Style Guides

With a domain specific style-guide we mean a specification of a class of appropriate interface elements together with guide-lines for interface design using these elements for a given domain of applications. If a domain is defined too narrow, its usage will be very limited, if too broad, the advantages of using such a style-guide will be reduced. Including domain knowledge earlier in the development process is advantageous since it enables development of more efficient user interfaces as well as simplifies the development of applications by basing it on a domain specific style guide. End-user participation in the experimental development process can be facilitated if the dialogue is performed in a terminology familiar to the involved professionals, i.e. in domain specific terms. Minimal cognitive work load for the end-users is ensured since the design can be based on a very detailed analysis of information utilisation in the domain. The design is formulated in a special design language interpretable by an interface emulating tool. Domain specific design of user interfaces for skilled professionals in working life can heavily reduce development times, efforts and costs, since it is based on high level elements and detailed domain relevant guidelines (Gulliksen & Sandblad 95). One might argue that the development of a domain specific interface style-guide will be expensive compared to the direct application specific analysis and development of applications directly on an existing style guide e. g. Motif. This might be true for the first application, but the possibilities of saving time and resources, by reusing the domain specific interface style-guide when developing new applications in this domain, is dramatically increased. Domain specific style guides can serve as a tool to accomplish a uniform and well-functioning design, but requires a high consistency between design concepts and interface elements to enable efficient implementation.

4. A Framework for a Domain Specific Interface Design Process

Schematically the domain specific development process can be described as follows (c. f. Figure 1). A general information utilisation analysis over a representative sample of possible work situations in a domain is performed with the purpose of establishing both the datamodel, describing relevant objects as instances of information, and how this information is being used. Based on this, the developer, the designer and user representatives can specify a domain specific style guide on a relevant level for coming application development. In the second phase a designer, together with the user, can perform the final specifications of the user interface, since design is performed in a language relevant to the end-user. Only a simplified analysis of information utilisation is needed, resulting in an information system with an object oriented separation of included artifacts, to ensure modularity and reuse of interface components.

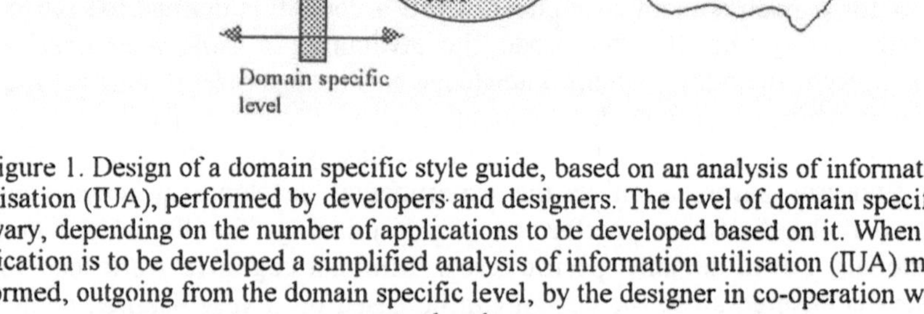

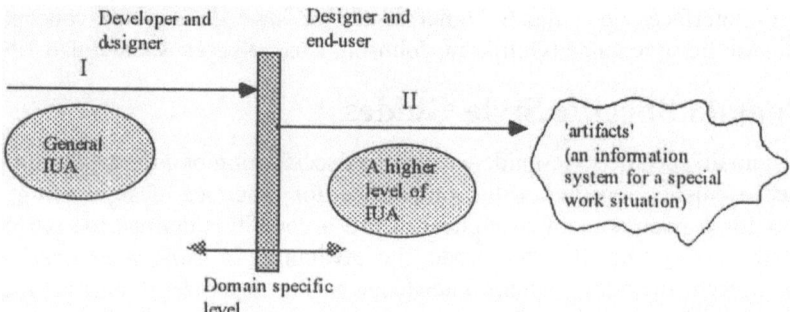

Figure 1. Design of a domain specific style guide, based on an analysis of information utilisation (IUA), performed by developers and designers. The level of domain specificity can vary, depending on the number of applications to be developed based on it. When a new application is to be developed a simplified analysis of information utilisation (IUA) must be performed, outgoing from the domain specific level, by the designer in co-operation with the actual end-users.

The level of domain specificity is determined by the number of applications to be developed based on it. The higher the number of applications, the higher the level of domain specificity can promote better cost efficiency. A domain specific style

guide can be specified to a level where design of a user interface could be performed e. g. by drag-&-drop techniques. The designer, with extensive knowledge in human-computer interaction, cognitive psychology, software engineering, organisational theory and some basic artistic experiences, should never be eliminated from the domain specific design process.
Analysis of information utilisation aims at identifying instances of information and their use in the work process. Relevant information is also automatically obtained for establishing and validating the datamodel. Instances of information relate to the information concept of the user, and are formulated in terms of information sets normally used in a work situation. An object modelling process identifies objects in the datamodel (Rumbaugh, Blaha, Premerlani, Eddy & Lorensen 1991). Interface elements are presentation objects shown by the interface. The concepts are, however, related; an interface element can refer to information sets in a work situation, an information set can be presented in one or several ways by an interface element. Every information set has a clear position in the datamodel, the basis for database design, and vice versa just as every object in the datamodel has mappings on interface elements. Representation of interface elements has been discussed in earlier publications (Olsson, Göransson, Borälv & Sandblad 1993). It is important to separate the semantic and syntactic specifications of elements from the presentation. When semantic meaning is added to an interface element it has domain specific behaviour.
Traditional application development based on a general style guide is today performed using a UIMS (User Interface Management System) or an IDT (Interactive Design Tool). A UIMS is a 'tool' in which elements are created without the use of a programming language and the dialogue is written in a special high-level language. The design is specified in high level forms that automatically generate executable code. The database search, the network communication and the communication with the main application, normally are to be coded. A IDT is a direct manipulated tool box with which the interface is specified in forms by 'drag-&-drop' that generate executable code. The dialogue is specified using some kind of high level language. Designing user interfaces using a tool box at this level is tedious and time consuming and requires programming skills. Development with a UIMS is abstract for a potential end-user without computer knowledge. General critique on UIMSs is that they generate to much overhead, that they do not support the main application or the communication with the main application, and that they do not support direct manipulated interfaces directly, being based on logical models of the user interface.

5. Structure of the Domain Specific Development Process

The domain specific development process has evolved based on experiences from application development with an experimental model. It is a dialogue between domain experts and computer experts using analysis of information utilisation to specify interaction requirements, and prototyping methods to evaluate design decisions. By incorporating prototyping in the development tool, one turn in the spiral model is defined as follows (c. f. Figure 2), assuming an already existing datamodel.

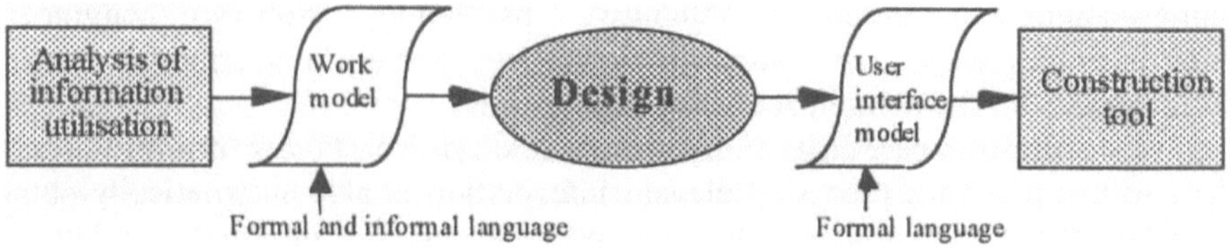

Figure 2. The user interface development process based on a general style guide like e. g. Motif.

A major part of the work performed in the domains we are interested in can be described as making judgements and decisions. Decision making is a demanding cognitive process and human cognitive capacity is limited. Thus computer systems should support such decision making. Decision making and control of the user interface can be regarded as two concurrent tasks competing for the users' cognitive resources. The main objective when constructing interfaces intended for use in decision making situations is to make sure that the interface requires as little action as possible from the user during the decision. The need for paging or scrolling should be avoided as well as calling up additional windows, replying to modal dialogue boxes, resizing and rearranging windows etc. Decision relevant properties of data should be coded demanding less cognitive resources for interpretation. This is done by letting the content of a variable control the appearance in a systematic and relevant way i.e. by controlling font, size, colour etc.

As a prerequisite to the design the designer of the interface has to identify:

- **Major decision making situations** of the intended users in an hierarchical fashion with one level of high granularity suitable for construction of interface elements and another level of a lower granularity suitable for the construction of complete interfaces based on these elements.
- **Data needed for these decisions.** This is a very demanding task. Users tend to describe general properties of their work, leaving out exceptions.
- **Properties of these data** – if variables are continuous, ordinal or nominal (a set of possible values should be described) and the frequency of use in relation to each decision making situation. Important aspects of the data might not be captured in the datamodel. An example is the property of having status of a value i.e. if estimated but not validated, estimated and validated, objectively measured etc. This must be added to the datamodel if missing.

Based on the analysis of information utilisation it is possible to design a user interface that lets the user use cognitive resources for decision making instead of manipulating the interface. It is focused on the entire line of work, specifying interaction requirements, which can be translated into a formal design specification, and an informal part in natural language that is impossible to formulate in a specific way. Informal parts of the analysis of information utilisation are treated and

coded in the design process. Due to limitations in natural language the person performing the analysis of information utilisation should be the same person performing the design. Design is a question of assembling work decisions with the information needed for each decision adding necessary special features. Design is partly an issue of art and taste and should never be performed automatically.
The output of the design phase must be entirely in formal language, compatible with the database. It must describe the design fully in terms of the datamodel and interface elements, and be enough to generate the user interface. The design is specified in a formal language that is understood by a construction tool, either user or construction dependent. A interface construction tool is currently being developed in our group which interprets a user interface description file and an existing object-oriented database and produces an interface with total functionality. The tool acts upon an object model and a set of dialogue elements and defines a view of the data stored.

6. Development of the Domain Specific Style Guide

To be able to develop the domain specific style guide one first has to categorise information sets, referring to classes of elements separable in the data model (c. f. Figure 3). We assume an already existing data model, but with the possibility of refining and changing it due to changes implied by the analysis of information utilisation. A domain specific approach uses a high degree of granularity in identifying decision making components, highly related to the domain and therefore common to many different work situations within the domain. To each of these components a domain-specific interface component is designed and constructed, with the previously stated goal of minimising the cognitive effort needed for its use.

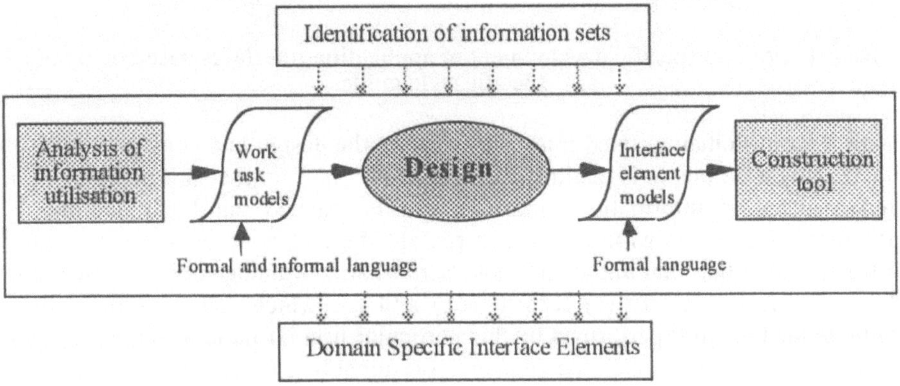

Figure 3. Development of a dynamic domain specific style guide, is a question of adopting the old model in a revised form to instances in the datamodel, established through analysis of information utilisation.

The work is similar to a complete analysis of information utilisation, without attempting to describe decision making, using a low degree of granularity and without constructing complete interfaces. The analysis of information utilisation is performed on 'general' end-users in a specific application area in a domain with the quality to derive information relevant for the construction or revision of the datamodel. Every information set, referring to a class of objects in the datamodel, undergoes an information utilisation analysis etc. The datamodel may not exist in its final form in this phase. The language for the interaction requirements only describes the information in data modelling terms, the presentation of the objects is irrelevant at this level. When the style guide design process is finished we have a set of interface elements at different levels of domain specificity e. g. a patient record, a patient card or a laboratory report. This process is performed for every interface element until our domain specific style guide is complete for the time being. Development is performed in a bottom-up manner.

7. Application Development Based on Domain Specific Style Guides

Developing applications based on a domain specific style guide is a top-down process. A simplified information utilisation analysis is performed in co-operation with the end-user for whom we are developing an artifact. The possibility for efficient user participation in the design process is facilitated, using a domain relevant language (c. f. figure 4).

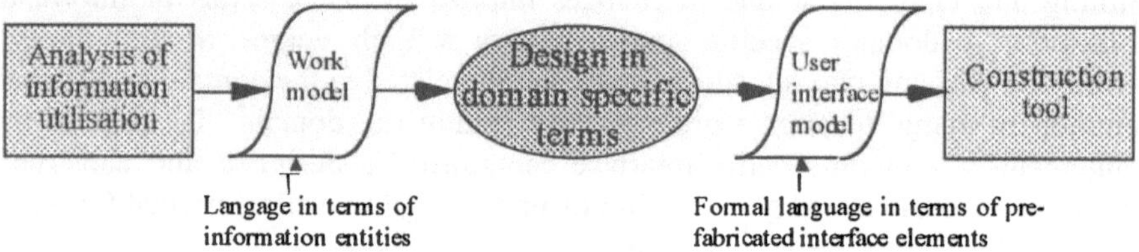

Figure 4. Domain specific development of application interfaces based on a domain specific style guide.

With a set of domain related interface elements the design and construction of user interfaces for a domain is facilitated. A combination of on-the-spot interface design and analysis of information utilisation can be carried out fairly rapidly. The designer, in dialogue with a user, can present the collection of interface elements (please remember that these are not "scroll-bars", "dialogue-boxes" etc., but a "customer form", a "patient record" etc.) and see which subset of these that is suitable for the work performed by this particular user. If parts of the work are not supported by existing interface elements, presumably a fairly rare occurrence, this must be analysed and a new interface element constructed. Since all interface elements are objects, this is mostly a easy task from the programmers viewpoint. With an appropriate set of interface elements, an analysis in terms of decision making must be performed on a low level of granularity. No analysis of the data used is needed, merely a list of interface elements used per decision making situation. This analysis is the basis for design of a complete user interface in terms of available and simultaneously visible interface elements, their logical inter-relationships etc. such as the mutual response to alterations and which elements

should react to which global commands. The outcome of the analysis of information utilisation, forming the interaction requirements, is formulated in a totally different language, easily understood by the end-user, in terms of information sets rather then presentation related. Information sets in the design should be related to interface elements and correspond to objects in the data model. The design process is mainly concentrated on customising and layout, depending on the degree of domain specificity in the domain specific style guide.
We will now exemplify this domain specific approach to development of information systems by regarding aspects relevant from the case handling domain.

8. The Domain of Case Handling

A domain covering a wide range of work in the public sector is the domain of case handling, which can be defined as a domain containing work situations with similar aspects on administrative office work routines. Examples are; tax work, personal administration work, banking or insurance business, credit card administration, and in some aspects even health care. Working with case handling is an interaction mainly between a case administrator and a client, striving to achieve the clients wish, which puts demands on the computer support. Computer support is here both essential and necessary. Increasing amounts of information concerning the individual client and rules and regulations needed to make decisions and judgements in specific cases is needed. Anyone having a bank relation has come across situations where a case can not be performed due to ‘something wrong with the computer'. The reason is not always a system error but often usability problems in the communication between the end-user and the computer system.
People working with case handling are normally not trained in handling computers. They have large skills in their work domain; nurses are best suited to provide good health care, bank clerks are better suited for aiding clients with withdrawals or loans etc. rather than being computer operators. A main goal in the design of a computer system for these workers is a design dedicated to their work, minimising the cognitive work environment problems, with an 'obvious' functionality for the end-user. Case handling means interaction with a client. The main goal must be to facilitate operations and collection of relevant information. To be able to 'put the client in the centre' the case administrators computer system has to be designed so that he can keep total focus on the client, handling the computer support on an automatic level. The relation to customers can vary according to media (a telephone call, a meeting, a letter or a form) but there is no contradiction in having a computer system optimal for the physical meeting with a client, with good functionality for interaction on other modes as well.
Case handling, with an immediate contact with the client, can cause stress for the case administrator. Errors that have occurred due to lack of communication can cause frustration and anger with the client, putting mental pressure on the case administrator. All available information about a person can be relevant, which is why the possibility, to get an overview by globally searching on the clients personal identification number, is important. Interacting with customers needs as efficient computer support and case handling as possible. Long and tedious case handling is

annoying for all parts involved, creating anger and frustration with the client and causing stress with the case administrator.
We see a need for dividing cases into two different categories; simple cases or complex cases (contracts). A case is here defined as any work performed under workflow, handling a clearly defined activity, limited in time and concern, collecting and specifying information and, based on certain rules, making a decision or judgement that in its turn has to be kept in a record and communicated to the concerned part. A case involves mainly two parties; the client and the case administrator (one or many). Every case has to be limited in time with a start and end. The basic case is initialised through an application from a client to a case administrator. A case does not exist for the case administrator until initialised and entered into a record. We can categorise a few phases (c. f. figure 5):

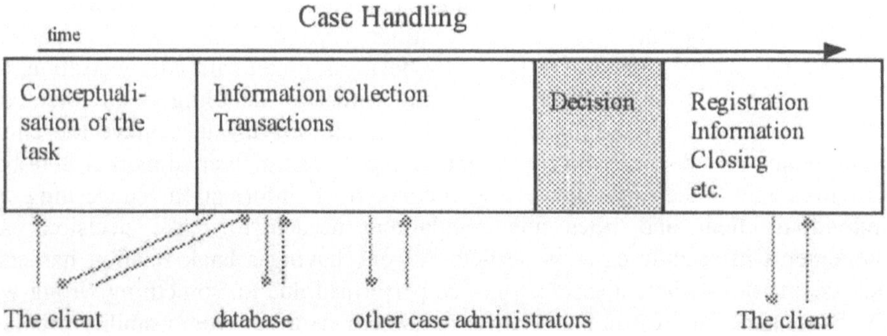

Figure 5. Phases in case handling seen from the case administrators perspective, and the physical interaction needed between the case administrator, the client, other case administrators and the computer.

- **Initialisation** – a case is initialised through an application; verbal meeting, telephone call, formal questionnaire, form or informal letter. It needs to be registered. An application is not a case until established so that it fulfils above mentioned definitions.
- **Information collection** – the interaction with the computer, the rule book, the client and other case administrators, to find essential information for making a decision according to the initial application.
- **Decision** – the judgement the case administrator has to make based on a set of rules and the accessible information about the client. This important process that demands responsibility and concentration from the case administrator is cognitively demanding and claims absolute attention from the case administrator.
- **Record keeping** – all processes following a decision; execution, informing the client, possibilities to appeal, continuation etc.

Field studies show that this model is a suitable description of case handling. Differences occur in the scope of time, from cases that are handled so quickly that they can not be interrupted without needing to be restarted, to cases that need up to a year or more. Otherwise all cases follow the above mentioned structure.

Complex cases do not entirely follow the above mentioned model. A case that travels through many case administrators does not exist until it is introduced to one special case administrator, and ceases to exist when terminated for that case administrator. A case can also start without the client being the initialising part. We need to define the complex case, which can be exemplified by the first initialising contact with a bank (c. f. figure 6).

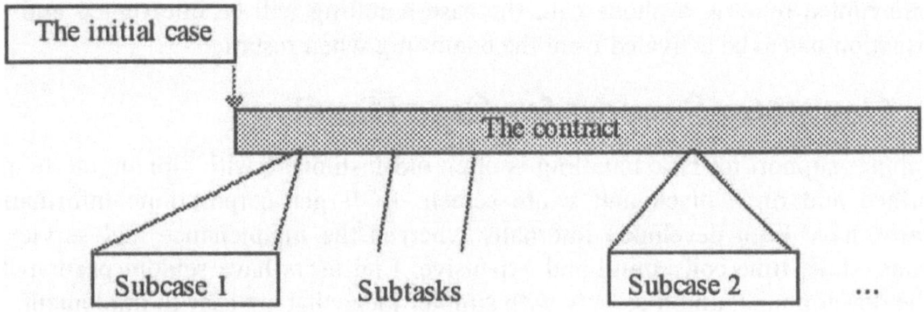

Figure 6. The complex case; an initial case with a positive outcome starts a contract, identifying interaction, and that in its turn can initialise subcases or subtasks.

An initialising case is needed to establish a connection and to get entered into the computer system. A positive decision on this initial case starts a *contract*, valid for as long as interaction is necessary. The contract can initialise *subcases* or *tasks* without a decision. To transfer a case to a new case administrator, a task is transferred if an inquiry needs answering (function in computer terminology) and if the entire case administration is to be transferred a subcase is transferred (procedure according to computer terminology).

9. The Case Administrator

The demands on a case administrator education can vary greatly. Work is often complex depending on large amounts of rules and the complexity in utilising the computer support. An informal application has to be translated to a formal application and relevant information has to be organised in a perspicuous and proper way. The need for simultane capacity with the case administrator is big. A case administrator usually handles many different concurrent cases in pseudo parallel, by sharing his time between different tasks. He can momentarily only handle one case at a time why the necessity to signal the status of a case becomes increasingly important. The important cognitively stressing decision process in case handling should never be interrupted. The majority of the cases are small cases that are handled from start to stop without interruption.

Important features of a case is the case status e. g. in progress, sent, informed to a client, remitted to another case administrator, guarded, awaiting further inquiry as well as which case administrator currently responsible. If administrated by many case administrators every single case administrator's case handling can be seen as the handling of a simple case. The transfer of the case between administrator is to be seen as the first case administrator distributing a subtask, which from the second case administrator perspective is to be regarded as a new case to be treated as a simple case, with the exception that the client information phase is an information back to the inquiring party. The transfer of information and case status between case administrators is a source of problems. The majority of cases are of a limited size, and can be treated without interruption. Field studies show that if a small cases is interrupted by e. g. a phone call, the case handling will be interrupted and the transaction has to be activated from the beginning when restarted.

10. Computer Support for Case Handling

Computer support for case handling is often old-fashioned, with alphanumeric user interface and on a black and white screen. In larger corporations information systems have been developed internally whereas the maintenance and service is tedious, slow, time consuming and expensive. End-users have seldom participated in the development, and if so only with simpler ideas that are easy to implement.

Work flow is the modelling of how cases, and relevant information about cases travels through a computer network, how it can be transferred between different case administrators, how case status is visualised and how work with a case can be postponed to be resumed later, i. e. a flow chart of activities involved in a case. Case handling has often erroneously been equalised with work flow. Work flow management systems are, however, good general tools for capturing important, recurrent aspects of the work process. Possibilities of changing the status of a case while processed are limited and above all complicated. In most situations the case administrator can not tell the category of the case until all information about the case has been captured and he is ready to make his decision. Work flow management system has an automatic way of categorising a case, and therefore restrict the processing possibilities, the path. These systems do seldom support the informal ways of capturing unusual features when handling a case, since merely the specification of the work flow can cover these aspects. The future of work flow capabilities will emerge from the traditional imaging vendors with enhanced network based work flow management, visualising the work flow definition and design areas, making them system independent, enhancing the paper document intense business process and interlocking different work flow designs rather than a single work flow repository (Howard 1993). The work management market will undergo a rapid change and expansion, with a risk of systems with redundant and isolated functions rather then a powerful tool. Ultimately message based applications, closer to the operating system with agents and objects will interconnect various work management models. A work flow process chart modelling of case handling is only meaningful if cases are complex, of great length and involves many case administrators. Also a limited amount of different case events must be the fact.

The domain of case handling is large and often it has primitively developed tools for the work situation requiring efforts in the design and development of computer support. Field studies show similarities in case administrators way of addressing their work tasks. With a methodology and a style guide specific for the case handling both the development process domain and the work situation could be facilitated and effectiviced. The interaction with clients imply extensive use of personal identification numbers, names, addresses, telephone numbers and monetary amounts to be entered into the system. The main part of the data entered is data for controlling the user interface. The case handling domain can also make use of a large amount of standardised forms for the application phase. Finally, there are many aspects to diary notes, archive processes and information retrieval that could be efficiently designed by incorporating domain knowledge. Following, we will study an example from the case handling domain of how to design input fields that can be automatically perceived, which is very useful when there is limited screen space available.

11. Domain Specific Interaction Elements

So far many domains, e. g. the health care domain, have been studied, mainly addressing information retrieval by pattern recognition and by perceiving characteristics of the information media (Nygren & Henriksson, 1992; Nygren, Johnson, & Henriksson, 1992). In the case handling domain we have extended these studies also to cover data entry procedures. Data for categorisation of problems and client privileged information have to be entered in search controlling fields. Field studies and experiments show that one of the most common search sensitive data, the personal and organisational identification numbers, have a misinterpretable structure.
A smaller preliminary survey on the perception of un-entered input fields was performed (c. f. Figure 7). Based on the knowledge that people tend to divide numbers into its components of digits and then chunk them into larger units, we hypothesised that subjects would recognise what types of numbers would be entered into the un-entered input fields. A sequence of fields of the size of one digit each was shown to subjects and the frequency of recognition was noted and compared with the recognition of filled fields with well known number types.

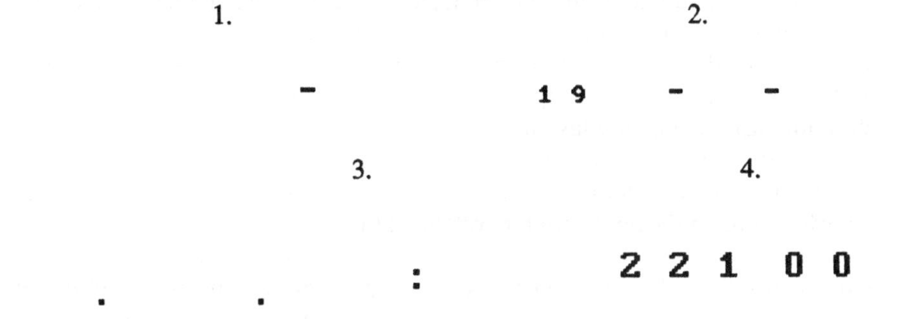

Figure 7. Domain specific input field for input and output of (1) personal identification numbers, bank accounts or organisational numbers, (2) dates, (3) monetary amounts and (4) post codes, usually appearing in context with the city.

Personal identification numbers – As well as organisational numbers are important and extensively used. They are easy to characterise, due to the fixed structure. Automatic pattern recognition is possible without stressing higher cognitive levels.
Dates – Are easily recognised, especially if enhanced by an editable default century figure. In this case it becomes obvious that international standard for entering dates are not adapted to computerisation.
Monetary amounts – Are easily recognised if displayed as in the example. Problems can occur whether right-shift or left-shift entering is preferred.
Postal code (Zip code) – The Swedish postal code always appears together with the city and the address why the context enables automatic perception.

The survey show that the structure of the personal identification number, dates, monetary amounts and postal codes in context is fully recognisable without information entered. Therefore separated digits in data entry fields, would relieve the user in its categorisation of what data to enter, and prevent activation of higher cognitive levels.

12. Discussion

Domain specific design of user interfaces for skilled professionals in working life can heavily reduce development costs and time. The possibilities for efficient user participation in the development process is enhanced. The domain specific user interface applications are more efficient and require less cognitive load compared with interfaces developed directly from an existing style guide. This methodology has successfully been tested in several different domains. However, some problems remain:

- Which level of domain specificity is the best for a specific project? A number of different possible levels of development both between and within domain specific style guides are possible but the cost efficiency varies. What arguments are crucial for the specification of the level of domain specificity?
- The level and syntax of the design language determines whether it can be a description file automatically interpretable by the interface modelling tool or if a translation and compilation from the design language is needed. Is the goal to eliminate the developer in application development based on the domain specific style guide in a way that design can be performed directly using e. g. drag-and-drop for customising and layout?
- What parts of the analysis of information utilisation must be performed in the development of the domain specific style guide, and how can knowledge be transferred on to the application development phase?

A domain specific style guide must be developed down to a specific level of detail through a controlled and well structured process, following a pre-engineering model. Based on this, or starting at higher levels of domain specificity, further development of end-user applications occurs. A domain specific structured dynamic tool box can be the basis for further development of applications (c. f. Figure 8). It is a dynamic document that is updated with the latest developed elements to create a basis for further development. This tool box is extended while performing the first part of the development process according to bottom-up design methodology, but might be extended with newly needed elements if top-down development according to phase II is adopted.

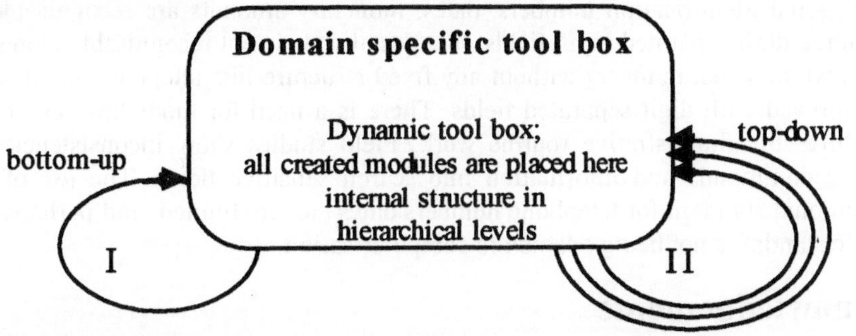

Figure 8. The development process as the structured dynamic, domain specific tool box.

In future research the integration of different steps of the design and construction process into a more complete methodology will continue. This includes the identification of areas where specifications are not complete, further specifications of the languages needed for bridging different steps of the design process and further development of tools to interpret both the results of the analysis of information utilisation and design. It is our belief that this framework for domain specific design could be the basis for a model of the entire design process. Future development should emphasise properties typical for larger domains and include domain knowledge into both the design of the style guide as well as the design of the application based on this style guide.

The case handling domain has especially been studied with respect to the interaction requirements of the operations. We distinguish two main types of cases, the simple case containing the application phase, information retrieval, the decision process and documentation and communication, and the complex case that defines a contract between a client and an institution, in itself generating new cases and subtasks. Central in the case handling domain is the similarities in the interactions with clients. The end-users of a computer system, the case administrators, are not educated computer experts, but rather experts in their main line of work, that is, to make decisions related to the cases they are employed to handle. Computer support for case handling are either self developed oldfashioned systems designed especially for the work situation, with increasing difficulties handling the demands on system expansion and flexibility, or an adaptation of work flow software systems, that does not specifically focus on case handling. For the important interaction with clients and the encountering of information about the clients in a computerised information system the use of personal identification numbers and other domain specific fields in forms is extensive. In the future domain specific design methodologies will be used to specify, define, design and apply domain specific style guide and guidelines

for case handling on various projects within the Swedish income tax authority (RSV – Riksskatteverket).
Suggestions on domain specific data entry fields for different numbers occurring in administrative routine domains, digit separated fields to enhance recognition of un-entered information, have been designed and evaluated. A smaller survey implied that personal identification numbers, dates, monetary amounts are recognisable as un-entered digit separated input fields, that postal code is not recognisable alone but in context, and that numbers without any fixed structure like telephone numbers is not improved with digit separated fields. There is a need for modelling data entry procedures in administrative routine work. Field studies show inconsistencies in entering commands and information into search sensitive fields. The use of the international standard for telephone numbers dates etc. are limited, and perhaps due to these standards not being adapted to computerisation.

Acknowledgements

The combined competence of the user interface group at the Center for Human Computer Studies at Uppsala University are greatly appreciated. This work has been performed with financial support from the Swedish Work Environment Fund and the Swedish Working Life Fund in a co-operation project with the Swedish Tax Handling Authorities (Riksskatteverket). The cooperation with the participants from the Helios project (A1004) within the CEC/AIM-programme is greatly appreciated.

Chapter 3: A Method for Task-related Information Analysis

Alistair Sutcliffe

1. Introduction

A fundamental yet neglected part of human computer interaction is design of the presentation interface. Although guidelines offer advice about the display ergonomics, and standards are being prepared for interface presentation (ISO1994), there is little help for designers in HCI methods when it comes to analysing and specifying information displays. Task analysis methods, (Johnson1985, Johnson et al. 1988) do not explicitly define users' information requirements; however, task models produced by such methods do describe objects which may become the subject matter of the presentation interface. Structured system development methods, such as SSADM, (Downs et al. 1991) give data models such as entity relationship diagrams but only general heuristics for screen design. Clearly there is a need for methodical guidance to define users' information requirements in the context of task analysis, synthesise this with data modelling, and then produce specifications for the presentation interface.

This paper aims to address this need by proposing a Task-based Information analysis Method (TIM). The initial motivation stems from the needs of the Esprit project p6593, INTUITIVE, which is developing information retrieval tools for multimedia databases. Information retrieval may be either general, i.e. searches for information linked to goals of learning or entertainment, however, frequently it is embedded in a task context. This implies that information requirements should be specified in a task sensitive manner.

Several different means of delivering information have been proposed ranging from standard displays, to hypertext/hypermedia and information retrieval languages. Hypertext and information retrieval tools are usually considered as separate technologies which bear little relationship to applications or the tasks contained therein. A further motivation for this paper is to address information provision in a unified manner which integrates the disparate technologies of hypertext, Information Retrieval (IR) tools and custom-designed displays. In many applications a combination of all three may be necessary.

Linking data modelling, task analysis and HCI design has been proposed (Benyon 1991), and there have been some suggestions about using entity relationship analysis as a basis for design of graphical user interface displays (Sutcliffe & McDermot 1991). Lim and Long (Lim & Long 1992) described a framework for integration of HCI and software engineering methodology which shows where presentation design should fit into the design process, although they offer only general advice about how this may be achieved. Other proposals for integrating information requirements in the specification of human computer dialogues do not address the problem of specifying those requirements in the first place (Sutcliffe &

Wang 1991). This paper takes these proposals forward by developing a method for defining information requirements and specification of the presentation interface. The paper is organised by describing the method in four main sections; task and information analysis, information resources, and presentation design. Application of the method is illustrated in each section by a case study carried out in Esprit project 6593, INTUITIVE. Finally the implications for further method development are reviewed.

2. A Method for Task-based Information Analysis

Information analysis presupposes a task analysis method. As it is not the intention of this paper to devise yet another task analysis method, the recommendations can be applied to specific methods such as HTA (Annett et al. 1971) or TKS (Johnson & Johnson 1988, Johnson 1989). Furthermore, as interface specification should be a normal part of structured systems analysis, information analysis should be easy to incorporate in structured methods such as SSA (De Marco 1978) or SSADM (Downs et al.1991).

2.1 Task Analysis

The basic assumption is that task analysis proceeds by top down functional decomposition. First the top level goals are identified, then sub-goals and so on, to produce a task goal tree (see Figure 1).

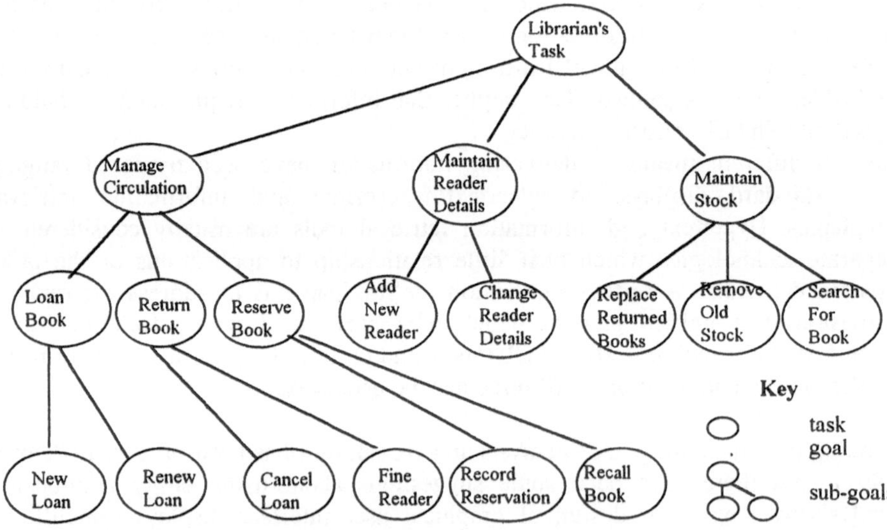

Figure 1. TKS goal tree of Librarian's task

Most task analysis methods create a hierarchy of goals, composed of sub-goals which in turn contain procedures, actions and objects. The semantic primitives of task models are therefore taken to be :

- Goals- purposeful activities composed of procedures.
- Procedures- sequences of actions, structured by the control constructs, sequence, selection and iteration.
- Actions- non decomposable primitives of the task model, units of mental or physical activity.
- Objects- conceptual or physical things which are used or changed by actions.

There are variants on this approach, such as addition of pre and post conditions for procedures (Johnson 1989, Johnson 1992) and more object oriented views, such as Methode Analytique de Description (Pierret-Golbreich et al. 1989). More grammatical approaches to task knowledge e.g. TAG (Payne 1989), may not adopt the same model; however, the guide-lines and techniques for information analysis should be mappable to grammars in a wide variety of task analysis methods. As the functional decomposition is also practised in Structured Systems Analysis (De Marco 1978) and similar methods familiar to many software developers, information analysis should be easy to integrate within mainstream software engineering. The question to be resolved is how units of information are to be specified and then related to the task structure.

2.2 Taxonomy of Information types

Before proceeding further, a classification of information types is proposed for describing information requirements. The information types are 'tools for thought' to help refine descriptions of the necessary information content. The motivation is to provide informal categories which help assessment of what type of information is required to support user and system tasks.

A pragmatic approach is taken to classifying information starting with entity relationship type data, facts in text based documents, and progressing to more complex information such as task related knowledge, i.e. how to do something and abstract facts referred to as concepts. Information can broadly be divided into static data about objects and dynamic data describing actions, events and changes in the environment. Information types are based on the schema of Task Knowledge Structures (Johnson & Johnson 1988, Johnson 1992) such as actions and procedures. The following information types extend TKS definitions, and are listed in approximate ascending order of complexity:

Dynamic Information types

Events- messages recording some change of state in the world. These may be regarded as triggers for action or as a transient datum which does not belong to an object, and therefore more closely related to static information.

Rules- have a condition consequence-action structure and express activity declaratively rather than in procedures, e.g. If Book loan date is more than 30 days ago then recall Book from loan.

Heuristics- rules of thumb which have a less deterministic consequence, i.e. the action is advisory and may or may not have the desired effect, e.g. If tasks can not be described in 10-12 lines of procedure then try further decomposition.

Plans- higher level goals which are organised in an order, e.g. plans for organising workload allocation in an office.

Static information types use standard ERA definitions e.g. entities, relationships, attributes and value domains, with the following additions:
Domain properties- facts or states pertaining to the universe of discourse which are not associated with any particular entity, e.g. information about physical structures and spatial distributions e.g. air corridors on a map of the airspace for air traffic control.
Propositions- assertions about some truth or state of the universe of discourse, for instance, a cup may have attributes of volume, colour and material, but assertions about its use e.g. 'holds liquid', 'is used for drinking' are propositions.
Concepts- these are based on high level objects and their relationships. Concepts are higher order aggregates of objects, relationships and dynamic information which explain some part of the world. For instance, knowledge about how an object works or a rationale for what causes its behaviour (e.g. explanation of how the rainbow spectrum is created).
The categories are informal definitions to preserve ease of use which more formal definitions may impair. The taxonomy helps to identify the necessary source of information. This helps planning the match between information requirements and available data resources, as covered in section 2.5. For instance, rules and heuristics may have to be constructed specifically for the application, propositions and concepts are more likely to be text based explanations derived from bibliographic sources, whereas entity relationship information is more readily accessed from standard databases. Event information has to be captured from external sources, while plans and procedures come from task analysis.

2.3 Information Analysis

The first part of the method specifies task related information needs. Figure 2 gives an overview of the TIM method stages. In practice task and information analysis proceed concurrently. This stage may be integrated with either data analysis or task analysis using interviews, observations and investigation of source documents where appropriate. The main objective of information analysis is to specify what type of information is required during a task.

The first part of the method concentrates on eliciting information to classify information requirements in their task context. The information/knowledge types are used in 'walkthroughs' in which the analyst progresses through the task model asking questions about information needs. At each step the level of the required information/knowledge is assessed, although the quantity and quality of information may need to be modified in light of the user's knowledge. For instance, trained users will require little task knowledge whereas novices will require considerable knowledge as prompts, and instructions. The walkthrough uses lower level goals in the task hierarchy (i.e. sub-goals which are not decomposed further), as follows:

(i) Progress through the task description for each sub-goal to determine answers to the following questions:

- What are the information inputs to this task-goal ?
- What are the information outputs from the goal ?
- What other information is required to achieve this goal ?

If structured analysis is being used, datastores and dataflows in DFD diagrams are good indicators of information required by a task process. Requirements are identified from the input and output dataflows, combined with descriptions of the datastores. Information from files (or datastores in SA/SD terminology) implies a data retrieval from a database or file. The analysis is then refined at the procedure-action level where necessary. Information may be a necessary input for, or created by task action, i.e. output. Other information may be required throughout the task; for instance, continuous monitoring data, or knowledge about how to carry out the task.

(ii) For each goal check each action within the procedures to ascertain:

- What input information is required for this action ?
- What output information is produced by this action ?
- Is any other information required to help the user complete this action ?

  at each Selection or Iteration step :

- Is any information required to help the user take a decision ?

  and for the whole procedure:

- Is any information required throughout the procedure ?

Input for actions will usually be simple data, although for more complex actions several information types may be required. Similarly, decisions may require a single fact or attributes from several entities to be tested for a complex decision. Hence for the task goal of 'Return Books' in a library system, the user will need attributive information about the reader and the book, including the loan date. The quantity of information will depend on the granularity of the task analysis as well as the complexity of the domain.

One of the purposes of task analysis is to design computerised support for the user's job of work. In fully automated tasks, information requirements simply become input data for a software process; while for human operation, information may be input for the task in hand or descriptions of the task itself as operational procedures. In partially automated tasks information output from a software process may be required to support users' activity . Definition of information requirements is therefore bound up with the process of task and dialogue design. For instance, in user operated tasks, novices will require considerable task knowledge to help them operate a system with more information for training purposes. Allocation of information types is therefore liable to be iterative as the interface design progresses. An important distinction to bear in mind is whether information is required as part of the task or if information is needed to help the user to perform the task. To illustrate the point:

Operational information: is required as input for processing, hence in a library loans, for the task action 'loan book' the necessary information is reader details, book identity, date, etc.

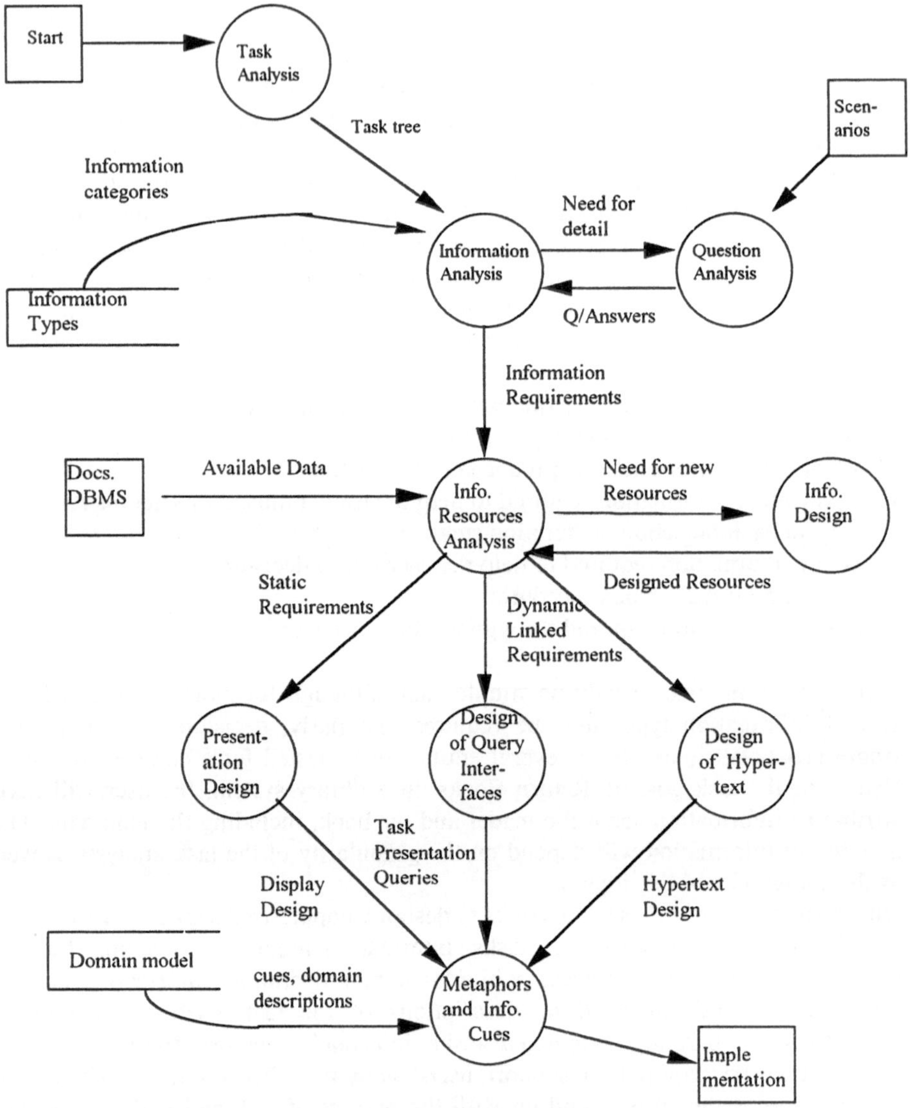

Figure 2. Method Overview, shown in Dataflow Diagram format

Task support information: procedures may be required to help a user carry out the task, although it may not be necessary for all users, so for the action 'fine reader' when book returns are overdue, a set of heuristics could be provided to give the librarian a policy for mitigating circumstances when fines should be waived.

Novice librarians may need the information; however, experienced librarians should already possess such information as part of their task knowledge.

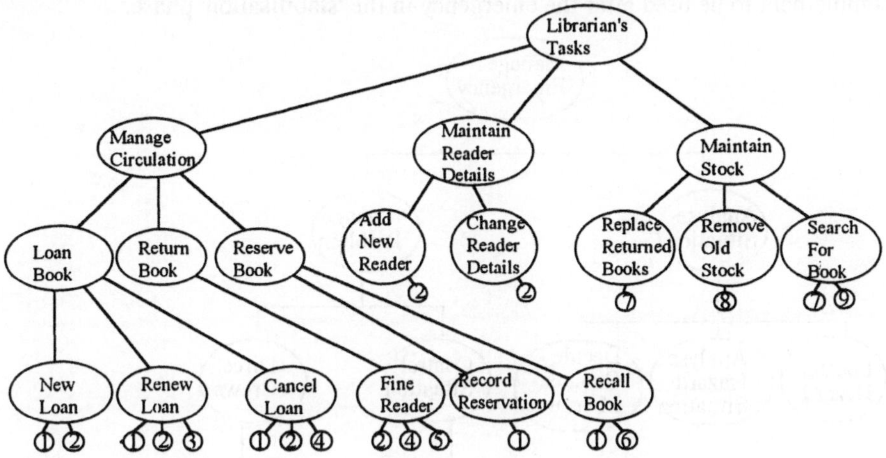

Figure 3. TKS goal tree of Librarian's task after information analysis

The following questions can help elucidate needs for operational and support information in manual and semi-automated actions:

- What information does the user need to carry out the action manually ?
- What information should the user supply the computer as input ?
- What supporting information should the computer supply to help the user complete a task-action ?

The answers to these questions are linked to specification of the presentation interface, so the needs will unfold gradually as the nature of the task support is clarified. Another important need is to discover which data items are vital for task operation. This will feed through into presentation design for highlighting key information for the users' attention. Important items for the users' attention (e.g. warning or safety critical information) are specified by annotation on the task model. The results of information analysis are illustrated in Figure 3. If more detailed analysis is necessary, the next step is to elicit users' requests for information in a task scenario and investigate the answers they expect to get.

2.3.1 Shipboard Information System Case Study

The case study of an information system for shipboard emergency management is used to illustrate each method stage. Initial fact capture was carried out with 8 practising ship's captains using scenario elicitation techniques (Hobday et al. 1994). In this application the ship's captain has to control an emergency and give orders to the crew to deal with a fire hazard. Once the immediate hazard is over the captain has to assess the damage and check on any cargo damage, and possible injuries to passengers and crew. The requirements for decision support information during the emergency control task have to be analysed and specified. Secondary requirements are for a more general information system covering cargo and ships complement to be used after the emergency in the 'stabilisation' phase.

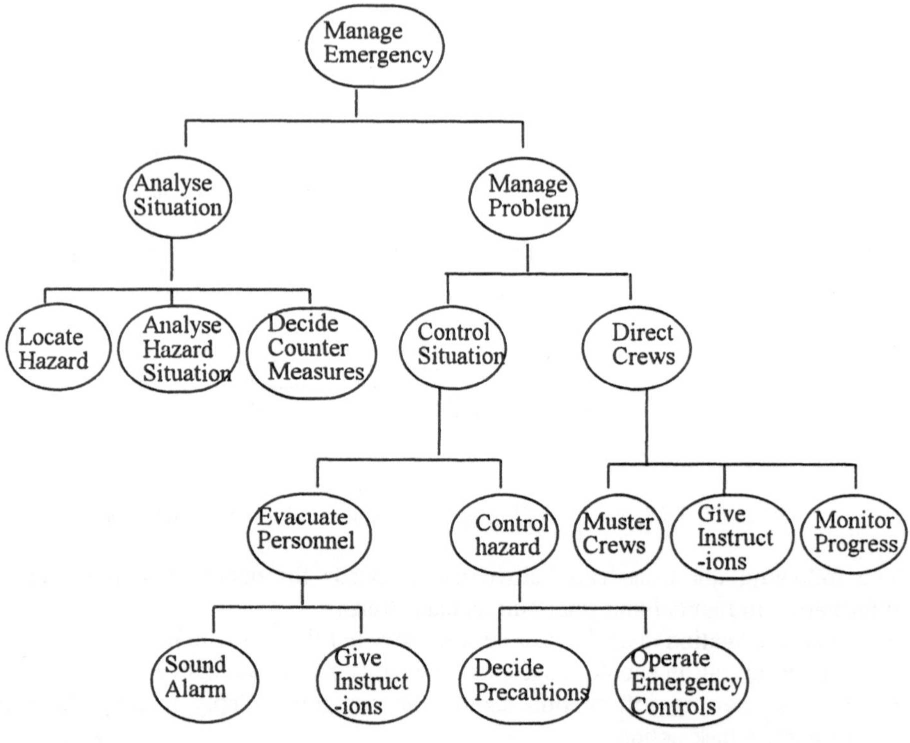

Figure 4. Task model as a Goal hierarchy for the Manage Emergency Task

The task model at this stage is recorded as a task goal hierarchy (see Figure 4). The overall task deals with a shipboard emergency. This decomposes into sub-goals for Locating the Problem, Evacuating Personnel, Mustering Emergency Crews, and Managing Hazard. Each sub-goal is decomposed further, hence Locating the Problem has lower level goals for Deciding Hazardtype, Locating Hazard, and Evaluating Problem. The low level goals are described in further detail as procedures which have been omitted for brevity.

2.3.2 *Information Analysis*

An entity relationship diagram of the ship's data is shown in Figure 5. Some of the data will be fixed (e.g. the ship's diagrams); however, most of the data will be updated, hence information requirements can not be completely ascertained at design time.

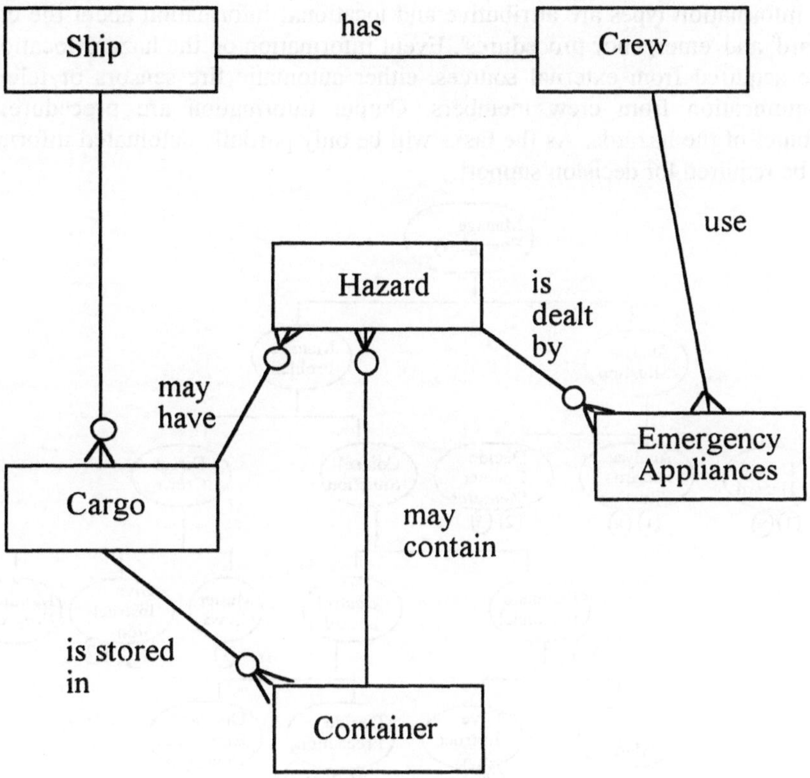

Figure 5. Entity Relationship Diagram: Ship Emergency Control Domain

The next step is to allocate responsibility for the task. Most of the sub-tasks require human judgement so little direct automation is appropriate. The computer system needs to provide decision support to help the captain check that the appropriate actions have been carried out. Task support is also required for status monitoring, and more general information retrieval once the immediate emergency is over. The analysis from the information needs using the task walkthrough techniques yielded the task model shown in Figure 6.

Goal: Analyse Hazard type

Information input::

Notified Hazard< emergency type, status, location, compartment>

Hazard description <emergency type, hazard properties, danger warnings>

Information output::

Analysed problem< hazard type, properties, location, status>

Emergency msg< danger signal>

Evac plans< instructions, location>

The information types are attributive and locational information about the entities 'hazard' and 'emergency procedures'. Event information on the hazard location has to be acquired from external sources, either automatic fire sensors or telephone communication from crew members. Output information are procedures and attributes of the hazards. As the tasks will be only partially automated information will be required for decision support.

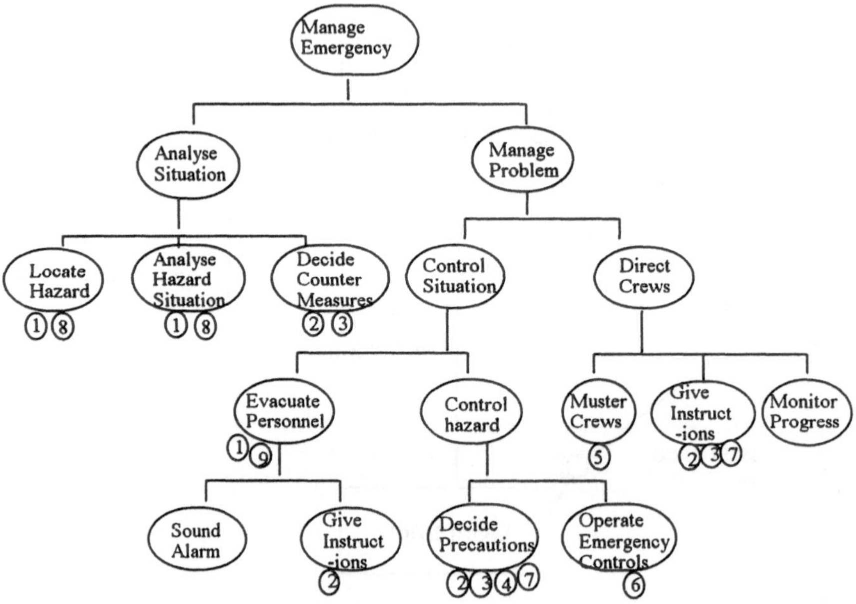

Figure 6. Task Model with information categories for the Manage Emergency Task

Goal: Decide counter measures
Information input

Analysed problem< hazard type, properties, location, status>
Emergency procedures< hazard type, action list, warnings>

Information output

Appropriate measures< instructions, action list, warnings>
Crew moves< instructions, locations>

In this task information is needed on how to deal with an identified hazard type. Procedural, object-attribute and spatial information is required (see fig 6), implying access to text databases for hazard management procedures, relational type data on cargo and possibly image data on the ship's layout.

2.4 Question Analysis

This step focuses on information seeking questions that a real user (or designer acting as a hypothetical user) may ask during a dialogue. Question analysis can be conducted by trial user sessions using scenarios, task scripts, story boards or

Wizard of Oz techniques. The procedure is to elicit a restricted verbal protocol including questions about the information necessary to complete a task, take a decision, carry out an action, etc. This technique therefore complements task information analysis in identifying requirements and, moreover, may yield further data about how information should be presented. Questions elicited in scenarios are critiqued by a playback walkthrough which asks the user to validate the recorded questions.
A functional taxonomy of question and answer types is used based on Rhetorical Structure Theory (Mann & Thompson 1988) which has been extensively used in intelligent question answering systems (Sarantinos & Johnson 1991, Maybury 1993). Heuristics guide the identification of the question by linking linguistic markers and the main subject in the utterance and an expected answer type, e.g.

Question form	Implied answer type
Where + physical object	location
When + event	time
Who + animate agent	identity
What is in + physical object	content
Which + object + possessive verb	identity
How <can, should> + action-verb	procedure.

These heuristics suffice for simple questions which are answerable without knowledge based processing. Unfortunately the variation in syntactic expression of questions means that analysis still requires considerable human interpretation. If electronic transcripts of the users' questions are available then this analysis can be semi-automated by simple string searches using a standard word processor.
Some questions may expect more than one answer. In this case linked answers are specified, for instance, as in the following library example:
Which books do I need for the 'introduction to statistics' course ?
The answer here may just list the books marked as essential; however, a more co-operative reply would also make the user aware that there are supplementary readings as well.
This introduces co-operative answering into question analysis. Unfortunately there is no short cut to the analysis effort in specifying co-operative answers. Each question has to be inspected and a judgement made about what information the user might want in order to answer the question directly and help completion of the immediate and future task steps. A complete description of the analysis procedure and mapping rules for classifying questions and answers is beyond the scope of this paper; however, the approach follows the work of Sarantinos and Johnson (1991) in mapping question types to answer predicates taking topic focus into account. Many of the question types are too complex for basic presentation needs as they require intelligent processing by deductive databases and knowledge based systems. These questions, requiring answers for justification (e.g. from a question 'why should I do this ?), motivation, evaluation and causal information, are useful for

defining the needs of explanation systems, but this complexity defeats ordinary databases, unless text entities are indexed for causality, motivation, etc.. The question/answer types usually processable by standard data retrieval languages (e.g. SQL) are:

Attributive- questions about the properties of objects, e.g. what make is the car ?
Identity- requests for information about an instance of an entity or its status, e.g. what is the car registration number ?
Content- requests for information on entities contained within a larger entity, e.g. what cargo is in the ship ?
Location- questions about the location of an entity, e.g. where is the safety switch ?

The ability to answer other questions, e.g. ownership, procedure, justification, etc. depends on the indexing and content of database relations, so questions analysis has implications for database design.

Case Study- Question Analysis

Questions were captured from user interviews and observation of tasks scenarios. A corpus of dialogues was collected from 8 ships captains however, a full sub-language analysis is expensive in terms of resources, hence and abbreviated question analysis was carried out.
The questions concerned the attributes of the entities Compartment, Cargo, Emergency Appliance, Crews, Control-device and text based documents, Hazard description, Hazard procedure and Emergency procedure. The information requests to the ship's plans database were of the canonical pattern: "Find compartment ID where location = co-ordinates (x,y)". Requests directed to the hazard description had the form: "Find the hazard properties associated with this particular type of emergency", or "Find all procedures for dealing with hazard type (x)".
Most tasks had several questions so sub-dialogues were designed for the user to choose the appropriate questions (e.g. for the 'give instructions' and 'decide counter measures' goals). Questions with anaphoric or elliptical ambiguity (e.g. How far has it spread ?) were expanded by inserting the object reference. Duplicate questions were eliminated and, after consultation with the users, questions were revised and placed in order of importance or expected frequency of use. This was used to order questions in menus, design dialogue boxes using the task model to link questions with task action, and finally to decide which questions are cued from hotspots on the interface metaphor.

2.5 Information Resources Analysis

So far the method has captured the user's information requirements; the next stage is to describe the available resources to satisfy those needs. It is necessary to decide whether the required data can be accessed by database queries or found in a paper form (e.g. report or instruction manual). Electronic data resources may be in relational or text databases, or in other physical media such as digitised images. However, the resources may not exist for some requirements and these will have to be created by the designer. This step involves mapping the identified information needs to the target data resources. The method then proceeds to design the presentation interface in light of the requirements and resources by selecting displays, hypertext, data retrieval languages or a mix of these methods.

Task characteristics can influence the modality of resource used; for instance, rules and heuristics information are appropriate for reasoning and decision making tasks. These information needs imply linguistic information as text based resources or speech. In contrast, visual information is suitable for spatial tasks involving moving, positioning and orienting objects, so image resources will be appropriate. Selection rules are proposed for the information type required for the task sub-goal type. Selection rules guide choice of resources according to the match of information types and resources as follows:

Selection Rule (SR)1: if the task sub-goal requires spatial information then prefer visual media resources

SR2: if the task sub-goal requires information for physical procedures then select visual media resources. Use animation media resource with complex action sequences; still image media resource with simple actions .

SR3: if task sub-goal requires abstract procedural information then, prefer linguistic media with:

(a) speech for simple, short operations,
(b) text for complex, longer procedure.

SR4: if the task sub-goal requires attributes with descriptive information for :

(a) situation, physical objects then prefer visual media, still images ,
(b) abstract object properties, or values, then prefer linguistic media.

SR5: if the task sub-goal requires rules or heuristics for decision making then use linguistic media as text. Speech may be used but beware it is not a persistent medium.

SR6: if conceptual information is required then prefer linguistic media as text but also use image media for illustrations if available.

SR7: for event information use audio media for sound warning but present the context of event messages using text for descriptive/status information and image for physical/spatial detail

SR8: for propositional information use linguistic media as text with image illustrations if available.

SR9: entity and property information with values implies relational tabular information, descriptive property information implies text resources.

SR10: relationship information should use diagrams to show associations with text captions to describe the relationships.

Using these rules the task information model is consulted and the relevant media resources are matched to each sub-goal.

Important considerations are addressability and unit size of resources. This effects the potential for designing media and information units. Unit size dictates how much hypertext nodes or data base records will contain whereas indexing determines how they may be accessed. For example if information is required about objects within an image this data will usually have to be semantically encoded onto the image. If text is accessible in paragraphs several different combinations are possible whereas if the resource is only accessible as a whole document then the design alternatives are limited.
Occasionally the necessary information or knowledge may not exist. Furthermore, complex information may not be readily available in documents or existing databases. Task related knowledge can be acquired from the task analysis; however, conceptual and propositional knowledge may have to be specially designed. Requirements for complex knowledge ultimately leads into consideration of an explanation sub-system and when information analysis is used in conjunction with a knowledge analysis method e.g. KADS (Wilenga et al. 1993) .Treatment of this problem is beyond the scope of this paper.

Case Study- Information Resources

The available resources were:
(i) A text database on emergency procedures, describing the actions to deal with particular types of hazards.
(ii) Relational data on ships cargo, with details of cargo owners, cargo descriptions, notes on hazards, container location; personnel data, ships crew including name, rank, responsibility and training records
(iii) Image data in the form of diagrams of the ship's architecture, showing compartments, labelled with their approximate contents, entrances, and location of important equipment. This implies the image resource will have to be semantically encoded with identities of equipment, entrances and contents.

A further need is for access to a text database containing descriptions of dangerous chemicals and other hazardous cargo indexed according to International Maritime Organisation hazard types. Access is by keyword search using the emergency descriptions. As the ship's diagrams existed, these were used for developing screen metaphors showing the locations of objects and pathways between compartments. The diagrams had to be designed as an information resource by creating an image encoded to identify compartments, location of appliances, hatches and pathways between compartments.
Applying the selection rules to the 'Fight Fire' procedure, procedural information is required, and this is assigned to text media as the overall instructions for fire fighting are complex. The 'Find Fire' task sub-goal calls upon spatial and descriptive information, so selection rules (SR1 & 3) favour a still image; while the 'Find Team' sub-goal is similar, favouring a still image. The 'Muster Team' sub-goal requires spatial, descriptive and physical procedure information to find the

team's location and then guide them to the appropriate compartment. The selection rules (SR2,3) favour images and animation for complex operational procedures.

3. Selecting the Information Presentation Style

Information may be presented as hypertext, screen displays or retrieved by query languages. For many applications a mixture of techniques will be required depending partly on the users' requirements, but also on the nature of the data resources and task context. This part of the method starts the design phase by selecting the presentation styles which may be required. Selecting presentation styles involves comparing the resources' properties with the requirements.

Information resources may be static and not change, or dynamic with change at the instance level or schema level. The changeability of resources impacts on presentation design. Dynamic data can only be accessed by a query interface because updating at the instance and probably schema level makes design of display screens difficult. The type of information may be identifiable but the instances are impossible to predict because of continuous database updating. In this situation the problem changes to specification of an information access interface. Table 1 gives a comparison matrix for selecting the appropriate mix of presentations from the following design alternatives:

(i) Information displays: these are hard coded into a dialogue so the information display will be the same each time.

(ii) Pre-formed-queries: the contents of these displays are determined by a performed query which is known at design time but executed at run time.

(iii) Query templates: these are a variation of pre-formed queries which allow some user configuration, so the entity and attributes may be specified but the user has to complete the constraint clause with attribute values, .e.g. Find Cargo in Compartment < ...>.

(iv) Linked-queries: the display contents are determined by pre-formed queries but links to related information are added, so the interface functions as a hybrid between hypertext and a query language.

(v) Hypertext, following the standard definitions as a non-linear, linked set of data resources.

(vi) Query languages: any open ended query language which allows full syntactic and semantic expression of data retrieval needs. For most databases this will be SQL.

If query patterns cannot be determined beforehand, then an information retrieval language (e.g. SQL) will have to be used; however, assuming that questions can be predetermined, it should be possible to associate them to specific steps within the task in menus or automatically triggered questions.

The first decision (see table 1) is to enquire whether the information needs are known at the instance level or not. If the answer is yes, then the designer proceeds to create an information display to support that task step. If the answer is no, then only the type of information can be ascertained at design time. While the presentation can be planned in outline, e.g. the approximate order and location of presentation windows, detailed design of formats is only possible if pre-formed templates can be used.

Information Resources Requirements	Static	Dynamic Instance	Dynamic Schema
Single Item**	Displays	Pre-formed Queries	Query Templates Query Language
Information Group**	Displays	Pre-formed Queries	Query Language
Linked Items*	Hotspots Linked Displays	Linked Queries	
Pathway*	Hypertext	Linked Queries	
Unpredictable	Query Language	Query Language	Query Language

** sequential / * non-sequential

Table 1. Decision matrix: information resources analysis and presentation planning

If questions are known in advance and their submission is under user control, the design options are to place questions in explicit lists (menus, radio buttons, etc.) or to embed the question triggers as hot spots in the GUI. Formatting instructions can be attached to preformed queries to determine the layout of the retrieved data. If associated information needs have been identified then either a linked-query or a hypertext interface will be necessary, depending on how stable the data resources are. When questions and follow-up information needs are known but the access path may vary, the design options are to use linked question lists or a hypertext interface. When requirements are difficult to determine or the data resources are very volatile then the only resort is to a query language.

The decision table is used to plan the presentation interface, which will probably require a mixture of different solutions within one application.

Case study- Information Presentation style

Databases were available for text procedures for dealing with hazards, relational data on the ship's cargo and crew with image resources for diagrams of the ship's architecture. The cargo and crew databases changed at the instance level, as did the procedures, although less frequently. Static presentations were therefore not possible. The users' needs were:

(i) for information seeking access with general non-task related questions on shipboard management of cargo and crew. This indicated a query language interface.

(ii) task related queries which were for grouped information and some limited query paths. This suggested a mix of preformed queries and links.

The presentation, therefore, required a task related metaphor which supported preformed query access, with a separate interface for more general information seeking. As a decision support system was required queries were placed under user control in menus attached to task goals and an export facility may be desirable to supply information from databases into models, spreadsheets and formulae for 'what if' type analysis. Queries about hazard location, cargo and crew were specified as templates to be completed by the user. Constraints on location could be added to customise the query. For more well determined needs, such as location of emergency appliance and escape routes, complete queries were constructed. Queries are held in a library with pointers to link them to specific stages in the task model, so the task model step 'decide hazard type' has queries about different fire types. However queries may not occur in isolation. Information seeking may start with one question and then progress through linked queries depending on the user's possible information need. This prompted design of follow-up query button which linked crew queries to information related to their training, equipment and location. Likewise query links between hazard types and procedures to deal with them were specified.

The task related part of the interface was implemented as preformed queries organised in a series of menus. Much of the presentation interface was devoted to information seeking and decision support. The system's role was to support the captains decision making and provide an aide memoir of procedures rather than automate any part of emergency management. The task model was explicitly represented on the user interface as checklist of actions. Sub menus of preformed queries were associated with each action to supply the necessary information. This gave six sub menus for the task-goals: Hazard-description, Analyse Hazard type, Emergency procedures, Decide counter measure, Hazard procedures and Instruct Crews.

4. Specification of the Presentation Interface

The presentation interface is specified in tandem with task design, and specification of the user-system dialogue. Specification of displays progresses from the task information model to information grouping and ordering taking users' needs into account, e.g. according to the user view of priority, importance, security, etc. The main objectives of presentation specification are:

- description of the logical structure of the information and any task related requirements for its organisation including drawing attention to specific items.
- specification of when information should be displayed during a task.

The task model has already been annotated with the users' information requirements, (as depicted in Figure 6). For manual tasks the information requirements feed into design of procedure manuals, operating instructions and forms. Checklists, notepads, aide-memoir lists and forms design will provide information support for user operated tasks. The end point is to describe a number of documents which will help users complete the task. For partially automated systems a more detailed level of specification is necessary. First the information requirements have to be related to the dialogue design. As the dialogue should be based on the task description, the sequence and content of data displays will follow the information requirements annotated on the task model. The next problem is to group data into presentation units which can be mapped to UI components and devices, e.g. screens, windows, messages boxes and speech generators.

To help timing simple bar chart diagrams (see Figure 7) can be used to specify when information groups should be displayed during a dialogue. This technique cross references presentation units to dialogue actions using bar charts or Jackson structure diagrams (Sutcliffe & Wang 1988). Bar charts show the timing of presentation units to be display during dialogue actions, the latter being derived from task actions.

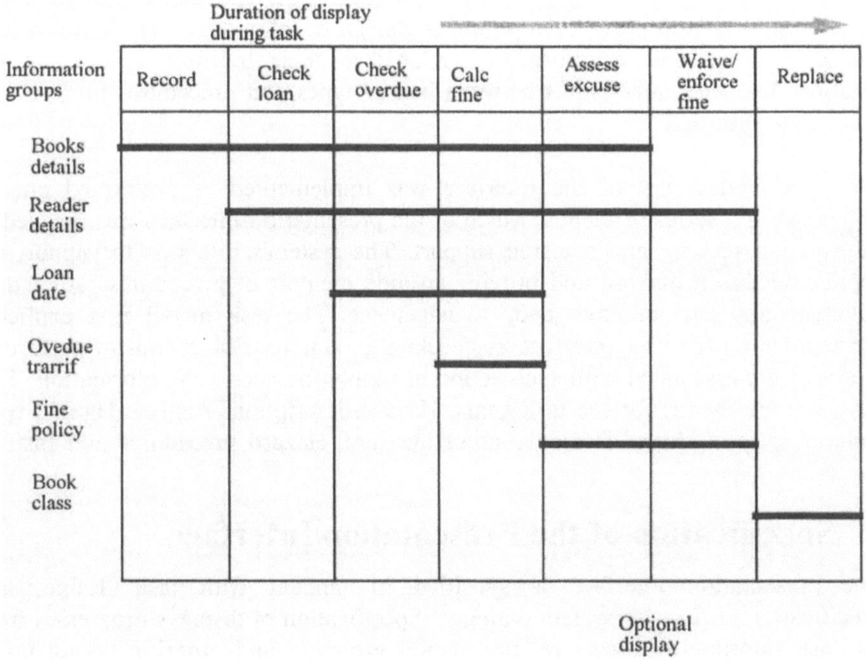

Figure 7. Display Bar chart cross referencing dialogue actions with the display duration of information

4.1 Planning Presentation Sequences

When several information needs are identified for one task action a considerable amount of information may have to be presented at once. This could exceed the available display real estate. While it is generally advisable to display more information rather than less; the designer has to solve the dilemma of displaying too much information which may cause 'can't see the wood for the trees' problem for users, while displaying too little may lead to increased search times by paging through windows.

Six principles of presentation design guide decision making:
(a) maximise visibility- all the necessary information required by users for their task should be immediately visible. This reduces search time and saves the user work by paging through many screens or windows.
(b) minimise search time- information should be made available to the user with the minimum of keystrokes. This has to be tempered by designing search mechanism for high usability, so for complex IR requirements usability may be more important than speed.
(c) structure and sequence displays - information should be grouped and ordered to help users find the parts they require and to suggest how the information is organised.
(d) focus user attention on key data- important information should be salient and easily comprehended by the user. This is achieved by highlighting, and positioning key data for prominence.
(e) provide only relevant information- the presentation should be adapted to the users needs so display of only the information relevant to a task step is advised, and when no strong task model is present, user configurable filters should be designed so displays can be customised.
(f) do not overload users' working memory- the presentation should not impose a memory burden which exceeds the users' limited working memory (Hitch 1987). This principle may be interpreted in several ways. Two examples are structuring and segmenting displays which reduces the access/search commands or cues the user has to remember. Making displays task sensitive reduces the quantity of information users need to remember when carrying out tasks.

The principles may conflict in many situations. Search time is a composite of time to access the appropriate display screen and search time within a screen. Hence, maximising visibility may hinder focusing user's attention on key data as there is more information on-screen to scan through. The alternative of placing less information/screen increase access time to the appropriate information. Although maximising visibility increases intra screen search time, it can be relieved by structuring.
The top level design objectives are to achieve balance between concurrent and sequential presentation, and to choose the optimal information grouping for structuring. The rationale for these decisions depends on the users' task needs. The principal point is whether the user has to cross reference different information groups. If so, then the burden on working memory should be reduced by concurrent presentation. Concurrent presentation is also advisable to save the user work. If all the necessary information is visible in a tiled display then it can be rapidly scanned, otherwise, the user has to swap between overlapping windows. Access controls have to be selected for scanning large presentations from UI components such as scroll bars, page controls, and sliders.

Case Study-Presentation Sequences

The main presentation requirement was for preformed queries and links as the data was too volatile for static displays. The quantity of information for most task steps was modest so concurrent presentation in tiled windows could be assumed. In some cases overlapping windows may be required when text procedures were displayed. A limited amount of information pathways were found from the user requirements and follow up questions, however, a full hypertext implementation did not appear to be warranted. Information pathways were linked to task stages e.g.

Task goal: Decide counter measures
basic information need-
Hazard type associate with appropriate emergency procedures
further information links-
Medical procedures appropriate to the hazard type

Task goal: Muster crew
basic information need-
Hazard location, crew location, compartments and pathway to hazard
further information links
Emergency appliance in relevant compartment
Crew composition and training details

Most information could be displayed within available screen sizes, however, text information on emergency and medical procedures was expected to exceed a single screen so sliders were specified with a dialogue command of skip to the next procedure. The length of information pathways was modest as a maximum of 2-3 entities or information items were associated in any one sequence. This and the volatility of the data did not justify a hypertext implementation, so information displays with 'link buttons' were chosen so the user could retrieve related information from a current display.

Hypertext and Information Links

If the information base is reasonably stable and the associations between information can be ascertained at design time then hypertext interfaces are appropriate.

Analysis of associations between information categories can employ standard software engineering models such as Entity Access Paths in SSADM which traces users' access needs across entity relationships. Information links may be suggested by the resources themselves, from indexes and cross references, while other associations can be discovered by observation of users' search paths and usage patterns. Information analysis may indicate links from task modelling or follow up questions. Hypertext specification combines both top down and bottom up techniques, starting with scenarios for pathways. This can be elaborated by conducting a walkthrough asking users to indicate possible links to and from each entity. The output from the specification stage is a data pathway model for hypertext design. The design question is how to transform information links into a hypertext like dialogue. Two main strategies are possible:

(i) when the pathway contains several information nodes a hypertext implementation is more appropriate. The design problem is to implement the pathways indicated in the analysis with other access routes which may be advisable for user navigation. Patterns of hypertext browsing (Belkin et al. 1985) can be used to refine the specification of pathways. Alternative search pathways can be cued by different colours or other means of highlighting. Another design possibility is to use 'guided tours' (Hammond & Allinson 1988) to lead the user though exploratory, task related or browsing style searches. Filtered views of links, history traces of visited nodes and mini-maps can deal with conceptual disorientation (Nielsen 1993). Information types and groups can be mapped to nodes. Anchors are specified with hotpsots or buttons as cue for links. Waymarks should be added as icons or book mark tags to label important nodes for the user's attention.

(ii) when simple links or shorter paths are specified preformed queries with links to related information are designed. More often the information types will be a network of different access paths. In this case cues for each query path have to be presented either on the retrieved resource or close by it. A small hypertext like interface may be designed as a panel of buttons placed close to the presented data. It may be possible to overlay hotspots directly on retrieved data, but this implies dynamic allocation of selectable objects, which may not be possible without a sophisticated graphical UI management system.

Case Study

Whereas a navigation type overview was not strictly necessary because a hypertext was not being used for this application, early user feedback suggested that it could prove useful to provide alternative views for information seeking. Hence a concrete metaphor of the ships architecture diagrams was used as well as presenting a more abstract conceptual view of the information . The early phase of the task had well known emergency needs hence the information displays could be designed in detail. Figure 8 illustrates the interface for supporting early phases in the emergency control task. Information links were designed between the emergency crews, appliances, access paths and location of the emergency.

Other presentation requirements were not concerned with location and consequently were implemented as a set of query lists linked to the task. Picking actions on the master task list displayed sub-menus of canned queries for the appropriate information. The user could pick the necessary information and customise the queries by adding details to the constraint clause. Preformed queries and links were cued on the interface metaphor by icons to represent important data such as fire fighting appliances, while compartments were all selectable for questions relating to contents, position and access paths.

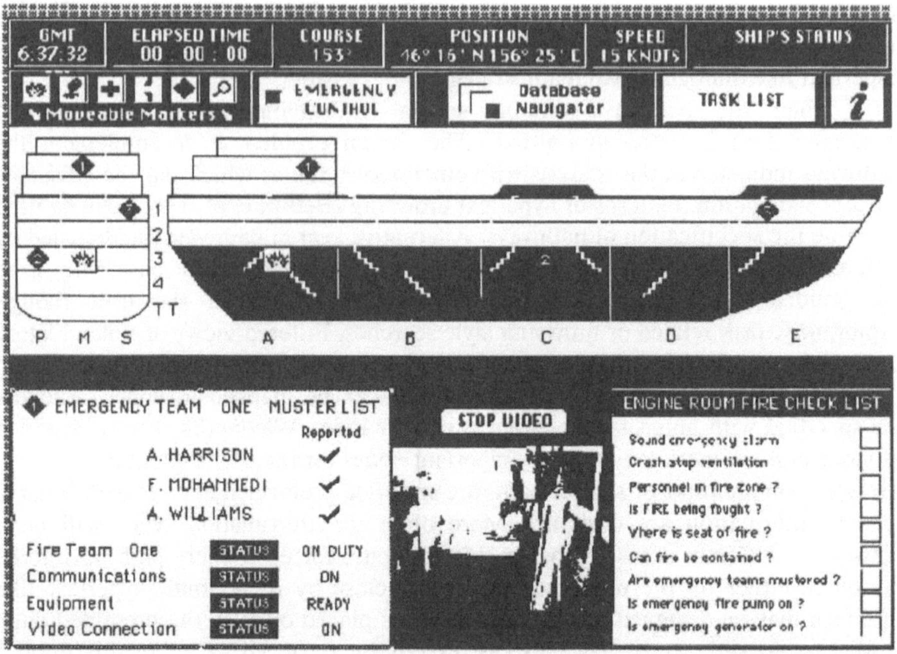

Figure 8. Illustration of the User Interface for early phases of the Emergency Control Task.

Although the task oriented view fitted the prime purpose of the system, i.e. decision support for emergency management, the system had a further requirement as a general shipboard information system. In the later stabilisation phases of the emergency task, information needs could not be determined beforehand. The users' need was far more open ended information retrieval to answer a series of questions about the state of the ship and its cargo with a browsing style interface. To support this need a more general information seeking interface was designed to give an overview of all the information categories as a conceptual map, as illustrated in Figure 9. An abstract metaphor of layers was used to suggest class hierarchies of information, organised in functional groups, e.g. crew related data, equipment, cargo; procedure manuals, etc.

As the users' categorisation of information did not fit the entity relationship model, sub-classes were defined to give categories more suited to the users view. For instance cargo was sub-divided into general, mixed, manufactured goods, organic, minerals, with another dimension for liquids, solids, and hazardous. These sub-categories formed the logical model from which an 'information map' display was designed.

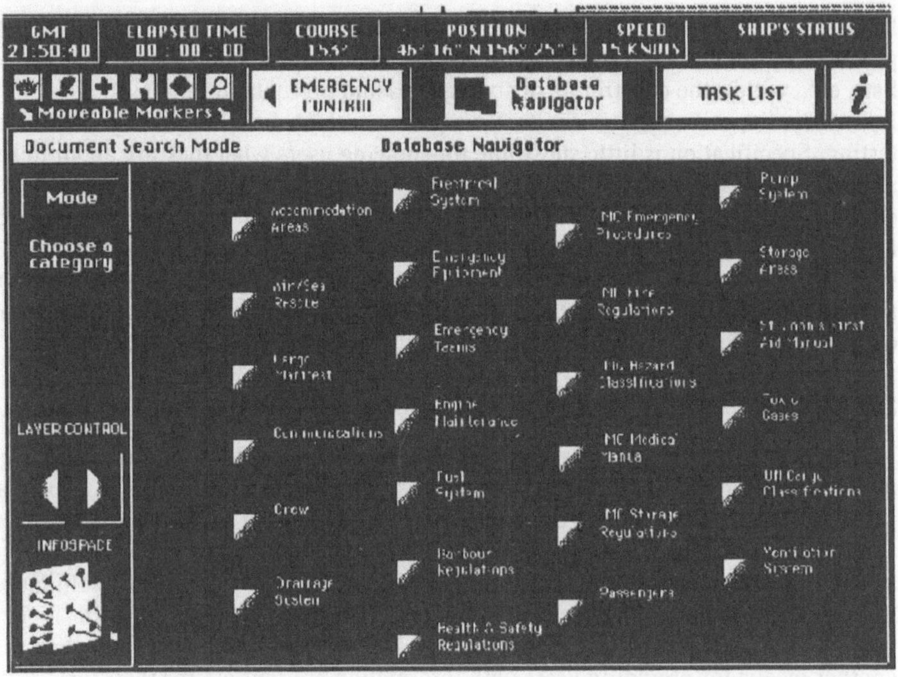

Figure 9. Navigator style of Interface showing a concept map of information categories.

Within each layer, entities relationships and sub-categories were placed in close proximity, as defined in the domain analysis. The map interface supported exploration of the databases, browsing and orientation towards the required information. The user could explore the map progressing through successive layers until the sub-class nodes which allowed query by pointing of the 'find all' type.

4.2 Transition to Detailed Design

Key data for important and safety critical actions should be highlighted following the requirements for user attention annotated onto the task model. Presentation layout is a matter of detailed design for which numerous guide-lines have been proposed (ISO 1994, Brown 1988, Tullis 1986, Galitz 1987), hence it is in not within scope of the TIM method.

At this stage the information specification contains:

(i) list of information types cross referenced to the task model

(ii) specification of information groups, listed in the data dictionary. These lists may be taken from the data analysis

(iii) specification of structure and organisation within information groups

(iv) diagrams cross referencing information presentation to the dialogue design using graphical notation or simple lists.

(v) high level design sketches of presentation layouts and screen metaphors.

Detailed design continues by mapping information groups to display widgets provided by the user interface design environment, e.g. windows, message boxes, lists, etc., within the constraints of style guides and presentation guidelines.
Information specification is an iterative process which benefits greatly from user testing. Specification is little substitute for showing users what they are about to see and story boarding, prototyping or Wizard of Oz techniques are invaluable ways of eliciting feedback (Gould 1987). Story boarding is one of the cheapest techniques for creating mock ups of screen designs. These can be explained to the user with a script for the task scenario and user-system dialogue. Prototypes and Wizard of Oz techniques give a more realistic feel to the use of information in an application. One or more of these techniques should be used to improve the design.

5. Discussion

The method presented in this paper has attempted to show that presentation design is not just part of dialogue design but a wider concern. Technologies such as hypertext and hypermedia are often considered to be distinct applications; however, as these technologies are used in more general applications, they should be seen as a means of information delivery in a task context rather than special techniques. Likewise information retrieval is not part of database technology, nor is it a specialised application limited to libraries and bibliographic databases, but just another means for providing users with information appropriate for their task.
Although hypertext systems are becoming easier to link with applications and SQL can be embedded within applications, the developer's job of creating a seamless presentation interface is often far from easy. However, with the advent of more general information access tools (e.g. Microsoft Access), and open hypertext environments (Hall et al. 1992), developers may have the necessary presentation and information access tools with which to build applications. Indeed the distinction between hypertext and data retrieval is becoming transparent in some hypertext environments such as Microcosm (Hall et al. 1992). A more comprehensive solution to this problem is being developed by the INTUITIVE project (Rosengren 1994) which is constructing an information retrieval toolkit which can be not only tailored to tasks, but also embedded in applications as part of the presentation interface, providing hypertext, standard displays or query facilities.
Information browsing has been a concern in hypertext systems , and these interfaces have been designed to guide users along paths of related information (Nielsen 1993). Other systems have produced overviews and map like interfaces to databases (Rosengren 1994, Larson & Wallick 1984); however, these designs have not portrayed a task-related view point. Indeed most hypertext design has concentrated on constructed pathways through an information space to support learning while few database interfaces have attempted to give high level conceptual views of data. Some advice on Hypertext wayfinding is given by Neilsen (1993) and in this paper, although further research is necessary on aide memoirs and visualisation metaphors. These approaches are necessary to deal with the well

known problems of conceptual disorientation (Conklin 1987) and information overloading.
User interface research on presentation of complex information, for instance the information visualiser project, has created 3D carousel views of information hierarchies and means of manipulating such views (Card et al. 1991). More recently browsing and more decision support approaches to information usage have been supported by 'sense making' (Russel et al. 1993), which is moving on the path towards a view of information within the context of its usage. These functionalities, and other metaphors for constructing information spaces, such as rooms (Halasz 1989), offered further design paradigms.
A further development of the methodology is to consider multimedia information resources. Although the analysis part of the method is suitable for data in any medium, the presentation opportunities are more diverse. We have proposed TIM method extensions to address multimedia database and presentations (Faraday & Sutcliffe 1993, Sutcliffe & Faraday 1994), although there is considerable work to be undertaken in planning effective multimedia presentation which relates to the user task and information needs.

Future work on the method will test its usability on further projects. The experience on the INTUITIVE project reported in this paper has demonstrated the feasibility of the method and ironed out some problems. One problem with methodical approaches to system development is that they consume resources. Even lean methods encounter user resistance. With this in mind part of our future work will be to devise a 'fast path' version of TIM which will carry out the essential parts of the process with limited resources. Integration with prototyping approaches will also be investigated. In conclusion, whatever the eventual merits of the TIM method in practice, there remains the prospect that the ideas and concepts will prove useful 'tools for thought' for software and information engineers. Even if only fragments of the method are incorporated into software development practice, a neglected part of HCI design may be improved.

Acknowledgements

This work was partially supported by the European Union's Esprit programme in Project 6593 INTUITIVE, whose partners are CAP Gemini Innovation, INRIA, IBERMATICA, SISU, BRAMEUR, Lloyds Register and City University.

Part II: Model-based User Interface design

There are a number of reasons why designers should take a model-based approach to user interface design. Dealing with the interface in terms of an abstract model allows designers to consider how the various components work together. If the model is well-specified it is possible to generate some or all of the interface automatically from that specification. The model can be used to provide support for users when interacting with the system. Mathematically-based 'formal' models can be used to prove how the system will operate under various conditions. This part of the book highlights the use of a number of different models and formalisms for the design of interactive systems.

Formal methods are a class of notations and tools that have been built in order to improve the reliability of the systems being designed. However in industrial software construction the use of formal methods during design is not widespread. This is due to the belief that it is easier to test than to prove. Each software component is considered as a transformational 'black-box'; accepting a set of inputs and producing a set of outputs. The inputs can be checked against the expected outputs for the component. The problem with this 'black-box' approach is that most modern user interfaces are 'event-driven'; their components remain passive until some event occurs at the interface (for example a mouse button is clicked) to which they are programmed to react. Due to their reactive behaviour, they cannot be considered as transformational components. Reactive systems are much more difficult to test because the outputs that are produced depend on the initial inputs, on the internal state of the components and on interaction that may occur during the calculation.

If the 'black-box' approach cannot be used, then the only practical solution to building a reliable system featuring an event-driven interface is to use a formal specification, or formal model, for the design of the dialogue and the interaction. Formal specifications lend themselves to mathematical analysis which can prove properties of the design without having recourse to testing.

In user interface systems engineering, the usability of the system is central. Accordingly, the work presented here focuses on modelling during design which focus on the both the user's and the system's actions. The work presented in this part deals with several ways of merging models of user tasks and models of software systems. Although relatively recent, this approach is likely to become an important trend in the design of interactive systems, as it allows designers to take advantage of a range of knowledge that has been recognised as critical within software design but has not been available in a unified approach.

Chapter 4 presents the advantages of the use of task models at the same time as system models. A formalism based on Petri-nets is extended to cover both the user side and the system side of HCI. This common framework clarifies the relationship between the task models and system models encountered in HCI design. Chapter 5 describes and criticises the Extended Task Action Grammar (ETAG) language, showing how it can be applied to the design of user interfaces. This chapter gives a clear view of the different formalisms and description languages that can be used

for task modelling and user interface design.
Chapter 6 presents a methodology which, starting from task analysis, ends up with a formal specification of the interactive system. This chapter shows how task modelling can be fruitfully used for the effective development of Interactive systems. The final chapter in this part shows how task analysis can be included within the ergonomic design of interactive systems. It describes how the requirements for user interface, ergonomics and functionality can be merged in order to increase the usability of interactive systems.

Chapter 4: Task Models - System Models: a Formal Bridge over the Gap

Philippe Palanque & Rémi Bastide

1. Introduction

Research in human-computer interaction abounds in various notations, formalisms and models that aim at capturing one or more aspects of a domain. One underlying problem is that various disciplines relating to HCI are complex in their own right, with no easy mechanism for transfer of results and expertise across diverse theories and models (Barnard 91, Kuuti & Bannone 1993). As HCI encompasses concerns ranging from human factors to software engineering and even device mechanics, it is necessary, for each of those approaches, to define a more or less crisp boundary, stating what belongs to the modelling domain, and what is exterior to it.

It is generally clear that, with respect to the HCI paradigm, certain approaches lend themselves towards the "human" side, while others are mainly devoted to the "system" side. For example (and without any pretence at exhaustivity) some approaches may be ranked among the "interface modelling" formalisms (Bass & Coutaz 1991, Jacob 1986, Van Biljon 1998). Several proposals attempt to include in their investigation domain not only the interface, but also a model of the internals of the application which constitute its functional kernel (Foley & Sukavirya 1993, Palanque et al. 1993). On the other hand, several formalisms focus on the description and the analysis of the users, either attempting to capture the essence of their goals and tasks (Hix and Hartson 1993, Moran 1981, Payne and Green 1986, Singley & Anderson 1987, Tauber 1990) or undertaking the modelling of their cognitive behaviour (Anderson 1993, Barnard et al. 1988, Bibby & Payne 1993, Card et al. 1983, Caroll & Olson 1988).

The fact that a formalism is dedicated to a given domain is generally considered as beneficial, since it allows for a straightforward mapping of concepts and notations, and allows for the building of concise and descriptive models. However, discrepancies between the approaches also make it difficult to achieve a coherent model encompassing the system, its interface and its potential users.

This paper is an attempt to provide an unified approach in which the same framework is used to describe the inner behaviour of a system (whether software or hardware), the interface it offers to users, and the behaviour of the system's users. The system and (one or more) user models may be built and analysed in isolation, while keeping within the same formal notation. System and user models may thus be merged, and useful results may be obtained by formal analysis of the *global* model resulting from the merger.

To describe the « system » part of the models, we have already proposed a Petri nets and object based formalism for the design of event-driven interfaces. The first presentation (Bastide & Palanque 1990) mainly focused on the use of this formalism for specification, another paper (Palanque & Bastide 1993a) being

devoted to the design methodology. This formalism, called Interactive Cooperative Objects (ICO) is mathematically founded, and allows for a formal verification of the models (Palanque & Bastide 1995).
As for the « user » part of the models, the use of task models in the design phase of the life cycle of interactive applications is now a relatively widespread practice. Despite this, it is not generally agreed on how those task models interact or relate with the models used in the design of the system itself (e.g. object models). The extend to which task models may help in designing models of the behaviour of the system itself is also unclear.

The main goal of this paper is to extend the ICO formalism to encompass task modelling as well as system modelling. We advocate a design life cycle where task and system models are tightly integrated, and produced together in an iterative process. The ICO formalism, which is used to convey both system and task notations, is briefly presented. We then demonstrate the approach by a simple example, where both task and system models are produced and analysed.

2. Design Life Cycle

Although it is generally agreed that both system and task modelling are needed to produce a satisfactory design result, the problem of the integration of task modelling in a conventional software engineering life cycle is rarely addressed. At first sight, it may seem that we are facing a « chicken and egg » problem with regards to the task and system models: Which of these is to be produced first ? On the first hand, many task modelling approaches describe tasks as combinations (sequences, alternatives, etc.) of system functions and relevant feedback. It is thus obvious that some functional model of the system must be available beforehand, at least to make precise the main functions afforded by the system. On the other hand, It seems difficult to produce any system model without the slightest idea on how this system will be used, and thus without a model (even informal) of the tasks of the future users.
To solve this apparent dilemma, we propose to start the design with some raw initial model of the system, which may originate from the existing situation (e.g. analysis of the paper documents in an information system analysis) or may be based on analogies with other similar systems. Task models are built in accordance with this early system model, and the complexity of these models is quantitatively analysed. The system designers propose modifications in the system models, in order to allow simpler and more efficient task models to be built. Task models are built in accordance to the new system, and analysed once again. This iteration will continue until satisfactory task models are produced.
This design loop may be undertaken successfully only if the analysis of the task models yields precise and quantitative results, that may be checked against pre-planned objectives. Our approach to this end is to use a sound and well established formal notation to support task modelling. We have chosen high-level Petri nets [3] because of their mathematical foundation, and of the huge amount of work devoted to their analysis, but more importantly because this allows us to relate task models

described by Petri nets to system models described within the ICO formalism, which is also based on Petri nets. We devise a set of metrics that can be applied to Petri net models. Those metrics are based on well known Petri net analysis techniques (e.g. the checking of place and transition invariants), but also on weightings applied to the various components of the net (places, transitions, arcs, inscriptions, functions), that will allow us to quantitatively assess the complexity of the analysed tasks.

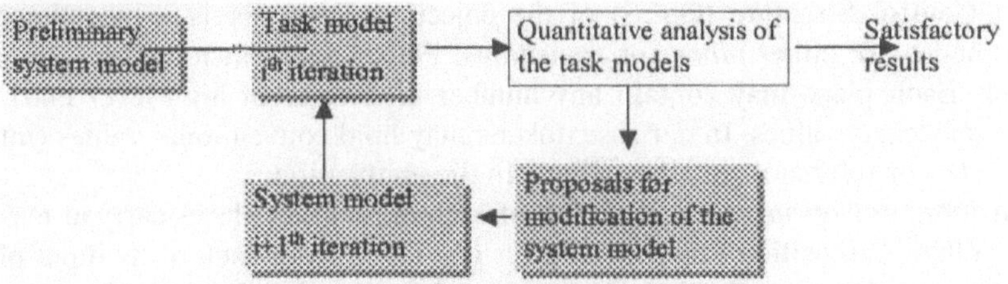

Figure 1 A task-oriented design life-cycle

The close integration of the models used to describe the task and the system permits an effective integration of task modelling and analysis in the system design life cycle.

3. Architecture of the Model

Our formal approach is based on the use of the ICO formalism. This formalism uses concepts borrowed from the object-oriented approach (classification, encapsulation, inheritance, client/server relationship) to describe the structural or static aspects of systems, and uses high-level Petri nets to describe their dynamic or behavioural aspects.

ICOs where originally devised for the modelling and implementation of event-driven interfaces. An ICO model of a system is made of several communicating objects, where the behaviour and communication protocol of the objects are described by Petri nets.

When we extend the use of the formalism to encompass task modelling as well, the task models themselves are encapsulated by object classes, thus providing the task description with a clearly defined state and behaviour description. The « task object » communicate with system objects in the same syntactical way as system objects communicate with one another.

When two objects communicate, one is in the position of a « client », requesting the execution of a service and waiting for a result, while the other is in the position a « server » whose role is to execute the service. In our modelling approach, task objects (which model the behaviour of an user interacting with the system) will most often be in the position of clients (thus modelling the fact that the user applies for a service offered by the system), whereas the system objects will most often be in the position of servers (because in modern event-driven software, the system is usually passive. waiting for the user to trigger an action).

In the ICO formalism, an object is an entity featuring four components: behaviour, services, state and presentation.

3.1 Behaviour

The behaviour of an ICO states how the object react to external stimuli according to its inner state. This behaviour is described by a high-level Petri net called the Object Control Structure (ObCS) of the object. A Petri net is a bipartite graph whose nodes are either *places* or *transitions*. Places and transitions are connected by arcs. Each place may contain any number of *tokens*. In high-level Petri nets, tokens may carry values. In our case, tokens may hold conventional values (integer, string, etc.) or references to other objects in the application.
A transition *may occur* (is enabled) only if each of its input places carry at least one token. When a transition occur, it removes one token from each of its input places, and sets one token in each of its output places. A transition features an action part, which may contain a service request of a token involved in the occurrence of the transition.

3.2 Services

An ICO offers a set of services. The services define the interface (in the programming language meaning) offered by the object to its environment. In the case of user-driven application, this environment may be either the user or other objects of the application. The behaviour of the object is tightly coupled with its services. Each service is related to a transition in the ObCS, and a service is only available when its related transition may occur. The services offered to the user, called *user services*, are represented in the ObCS by *user transitions*. The services required from other objects are stated in the ObCS by *invocation transitions*, whose action is a service request.

3.3 State

The state of an ICO is the distribution of tokens (called the *marking*) in the places of the ObCS. As services are related to transitions which may only occur if they are enabled, this allows to defined how the current state influences the available services, and conversely how the performance of a service influences the state of the object.

3.4 Presentation

The Presentation of an object states its external look. This Presentation is a structured set of *widgets*.
The user/system interaction will only take place through those components. Each user action on a widget triggers one of the ICO's user services. The relation between user services and widgets is fully stated by the *activation function* which associates to each couple (widget, user action) the service to be triggered.

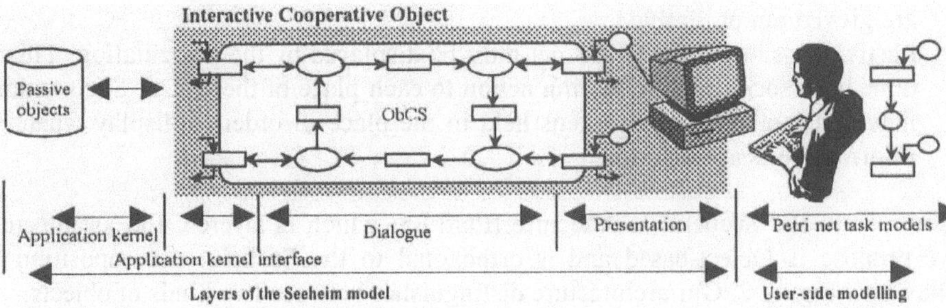

Figure 2 Architecture of an ICO-based design

Transitions relate to the object's services, stating their availability, and user services relate to widgets through the activation function. Thus the active or inactive state of the widgets may be known by looking at the ObCS's marking: The fact that no transition associated to a service is enabled by the current marking means that this service is not currently available to the user. This must be shown by greying out or otherwise inactivating the related widgets.

The ObCS plays the role of the *Dialogue* component in the Seeheim model. The *Application interface* and *Application kernel* are modelled by the classes of the tokens flowing in the net. The *Presentation* component is made of a set of interactors (widgets) that may display and edit data (for example text entry fields or radio buttons), or trigger events of interest to the application (for example menu items or buttons).

The communication between the *Dialogue* component and the *Application kernel* is thus described both by the flow of tokens in the net and by the calling of tokens methods in the transitions' actions.

The communication between the *Dialogue* component and the *Presentation* component is more complex to describe, since several aspects are to be taken into consideration :

- The *Presentation* component influences the dialogue through the occurrence of events. This occurrence is modelled in the ObCS by special places called event places. The *Presentation* component is able to deposit tokens in those event places after the occurrence of an event. A transition in the ObCS net may have at most one input event place. A transition with an input event place is called an event transition. The very notion of interface place is made necessary by the fact that a given incoming event may trigger different actions in the system, according to the system's inner state. This is modelled by two or more event transitions in the ObCS sharing a common event place. Those transitions are therefore in structural conflict, and this indeterminism has to be relieved by the structure of the ObCS.
- Conversely, the state of the *Dialogue* component (i.e. the marking of the ObCS net) influences the *Presentation* component : according to this state, several events may be disabled, and their associated interactor greyed out. This is described by associating event transitions to one or several interactors in the presentation : when a transition is not fireable, all of its associated interactors

are greyed out or disabled.

- Lastly, the state of the ObCS net must be displayed by the presentation. This is done by associating a rendering action to each place of the ObCS. Such actions may call methods of the tokens held in the place in order to display whatever information is appropriate.

Contrary to the Seeheim architecture [Pfaff 85] which is layered, the architecture we propose is Object-based and is orthogonal to the Seeheim decomposition as shown on Figure 2. Our architecture distinguishes between two kinds of objects:

- Passive objects bear the core semantics of the application, including the application's database, if any, functions for achieving the needed computations, and so on; they do not deal with user interaction and may be shared by all ICOs.
- Interactive Cooperative Objects (ICOs) support the application's user interface; they define the dialogue structure, and maintain the coherence between the state of the passive objects and what is shown to the user by the Presentation; each opened window in an application is associated to an instance of an ICO Class.

3.5 Inter-Objects Communication

In order to be able to execute a model made up of Cooperative Objects, the semantics of inter-objects communication must be defined : what actually happens when the action of a transition is a request to a server object ?

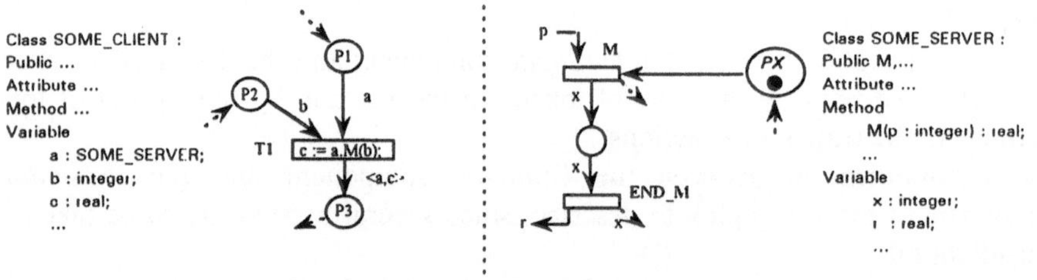

Figure 3 Excerpt of the definition of two cooperative Petri net classes.

Figure 3 illustrates at the syntactical level how two Cooperative Objects may communicate : The first one, acting as a client, requests the execution of method M on the object associated to the variable a. This variable references another Cooperative Object, of the class SOME_SERVER. In this class, the execution of the method M is represented by a subnet, starting from transition M and extending to transition END_M.

3.6 Semantics of a Request

The operational semantics of a request is defined by means of a simple communication mechanism. Any service request gives rise to an expansion of both client and server nets, as pictured on Figure 4.

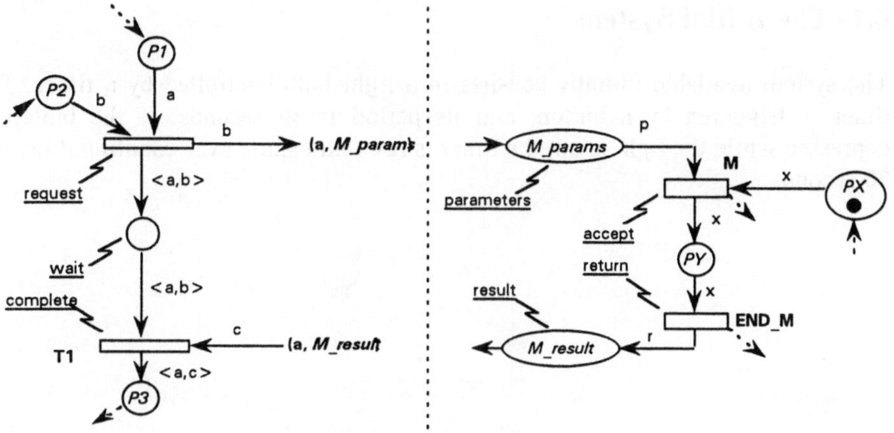

Figure 4 Semantics of an operation request.

The interface of a Petri net object, which offers services is made up of input/output places. At the end of a broken arrow, there is either an input place (called **parameter place**) if it represents the call parameter of a service or an output place (called **result place**) if it represents a service return parameter.

When an object Petri net requires services, its interface includes input/output transitions. A transition whose action is a service request is expanded as follows :

- the **request transition** loses its outgoing arcs; instead, it has an output arc which is labelled by the call parameter and refers to the server net and the parameter place of the requested service;
- a **waiting place** is introduced, with an arc from the request transition to it;
- a request **complete transition** is introduced; it has an arc coming from the waiting place, an input arc referring to the result place of the requested service, and the outgoing arcs of the initial transition.

The fact that the communication protocol as well as the objects' inner behaviour are both modelled in terms of Petri nets allows us to have a precise semantics for the behaviour of a system modelled by a set of communicating objects. We will make use of this feature in §5.

4. A Simple Case Study

To demonstrate our approach, we will present a very simple case study, where the system to be designed is hardware rather than software. However, the kind of problems studied in this case study are very common in software such as screen saver or other one where temporal aspects plays an important role. Our current work addresses scalability issues, in order to make this approach viable for real life software systems, but those concerns are not presented here for space reasons.

4.1 The Initial System

The system available initially consists in a light bulb controlled by a timer. The timer is triggered by a button, and its period is 30 seconds. If the button is depressed while the light is on, the timer is reset and starts over counting down for 30 seconds.

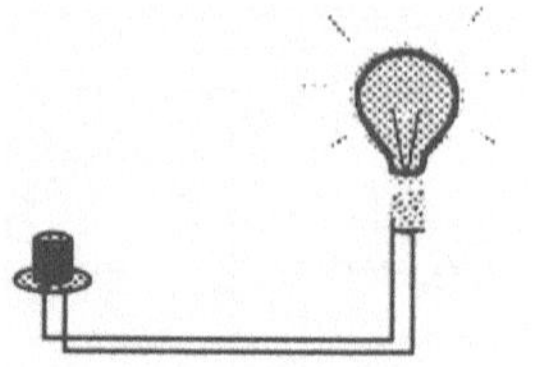

Figure 5 The initial system

Note that this presentation of the system is informal but that this information is absolutely necessary to start building a reasonably detailed model of the task. This information is the minimum that has to be provided to the task analyst in order to build a meaningful task model.

4.2 The System Model

The proposed system is straightforward to describe in terms of Petri nets, as shown in Figure 6. However, let's take some time in describing the Figure, in order to demonstrate various features of the ICO formalism.

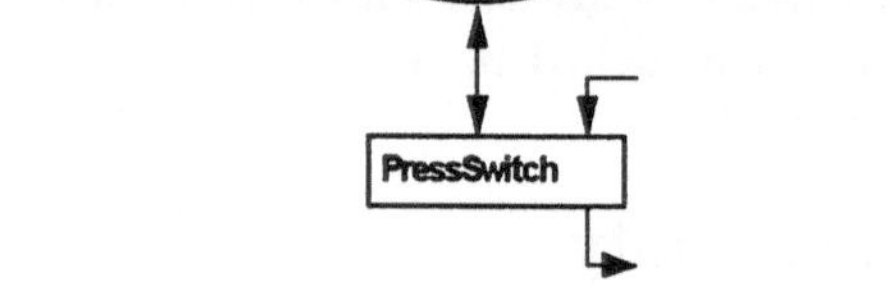

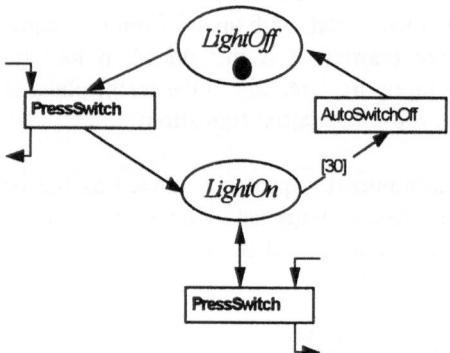

Figure 6 The model of the initial system

The timer controlled lamp offers only one affordance, a button allowing to turn it on. The model of this device also highlights other primitives of our modelling approach: The initial state of the system is the light off which is modelled by a token (a black dot) in the place *LightOff*. From that initial state the transition PressSwitch can be triggered by the user switching on the light bulb, removing the token from the input place *LightOff* and setting it in the output place *LightOn*.
The *AutoSwitchOff* transition is an *internal transition*, not related to any user action

(this is graphically represented as the transition does not feature broken arrows), and performed on the system's behalf as soon as it is enabled. The arc between place *LightOn* and transition *AutoSwitchOff* is labelled with the timing inscription [30]. This means that tokens staying in place *LightOn* are not available for the firing of transition *AutoSwitchOff* until they have stayed 30 seconds in the place. The second transition labelled *PressSwitch*, by removing the token from place *LightOn* and putting it back, resets the time for the token and thus accurately models the resetting of the timer each time the switch is pressed. Note that two different transitions are labelled PressSwitch, which means that the button allows to be pressed in two different states of the system.

4.3 The Task Description

To describe the task, we start by giving the high-level goal it aims to perform, and then detail the steps of the task in terms of primitive actions offered by the system. In this case, the user's goal is to maintain the light on without interruption for a period of at least 3 minutes. We want to minimise the number of actions performed by the user and thus the solution consisting in pushing and releasing the light switch all the time is not considered as relevant[1]. In order for the user not to press the light switch more than 7 times the system must be upgraded as it is impossible for the user to perform the desired task. In the following sections we will present two possible upgrades of the system, both of them supporting the requested task.

4.4 Upgrade 1: Adding a Stop Watch

The first possible upgrade is to provide the user with a stop watch. Thus the system is actually made up of two unconnected subsystems, the stop watch and the light bulb. In order to use this system, the user needs to use his/her hands to push the light and stop watch switches and the eyes in order to watch the elapsed time on the stop watch. Both user part and system part are represented on Figure 7.

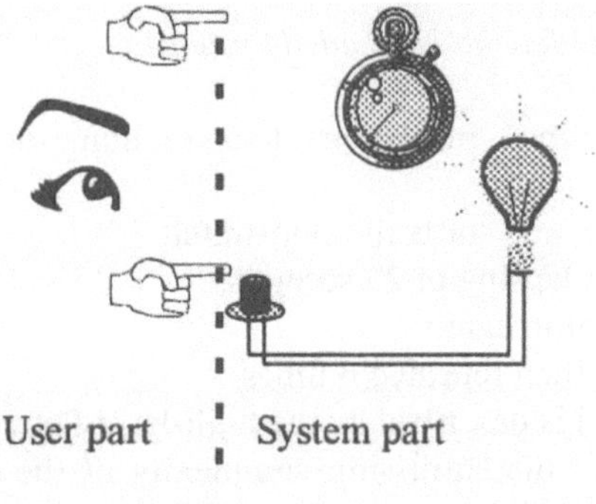

Figure 7 The first upgrade of the system

[1] Special thanks to Alan Dix for calling attention to this possible behaviour of the user

4.4.1 The System Model

The model of the upgraded system is presented on .

- the initial system described on Figure 5,
- the stop watch (right part of the picture) offers two affordances: one button allowing to toggle it on and off, and the watch face which allows the current time to be read, but only when the watch is on. The initial state of the system is described by the initial marking of the Petri net, in this case one single token in the place StopWatchOff. The watch affordances are modelled by transitions in the Petri net, labelled Press and CurrentTime. These transitions are related to user services, meaning that the user has a way to trigger the occurrence of the transition of the system through the associated input device. Graphically they are depicted with input and output unconnected broken arrows, which may eventually bear input or output parameters stating the data provided by the user of given back by the system. The transition CurrentTime, for example, provides of return value labelled <t>, the current time when the watch is read.

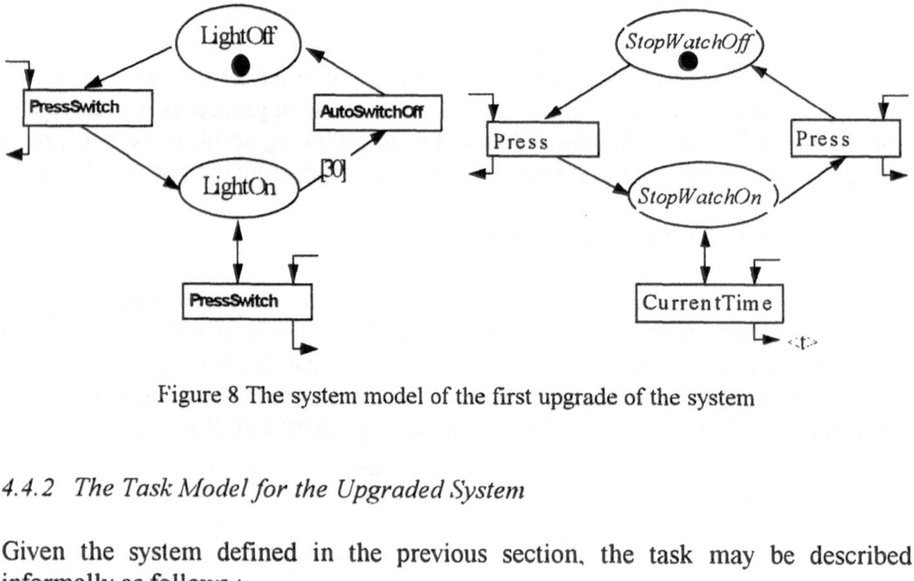

Figure 8 The system model of the first upgrade of the system

4.4.2 The Task Model for the Upgraded System

Given the system defined in the previous section, the task may be described informally as follows :

❶ User presses button, and starts the stop-watch,
❷ User measures the elapsing of 25 seconds,
❸ User presses the button again,
Actions ❷ and ❸ are then repeated 6 times.
The formal task model is described by the high-level Petri net in Figure 9.
Figure 9 demonstrates the surprising complexity of the task associated with this seemingly simple goal. This complexity mainly stems from the fact that the user has to perform a polling loop to consult the stop-watch, and then evaluate the value he has just read to decide whether he has to press the LightSwitch button once again. This can be seen on the model by the cycle made up of place

ReadyToReadTime, transition T3, place *CurrentTime* and transition T1.
From the initial state (modelled by one token in both *StartWatch* and *StartLight* places and seven tokens in *CountDown* place), the user can press both buttons in any order. After the firing of the corresponding transitions one token is removed form each input place and one token is set in *ReadyLight* and *ReadyWatch*. Then the internal transition StartCounting is triggered internally by the user meaning that from that state the user knows that the system is started and it is possible to see the current time on the watch (this is represented in the model by a token set in the place *ReadyToReadTime*).

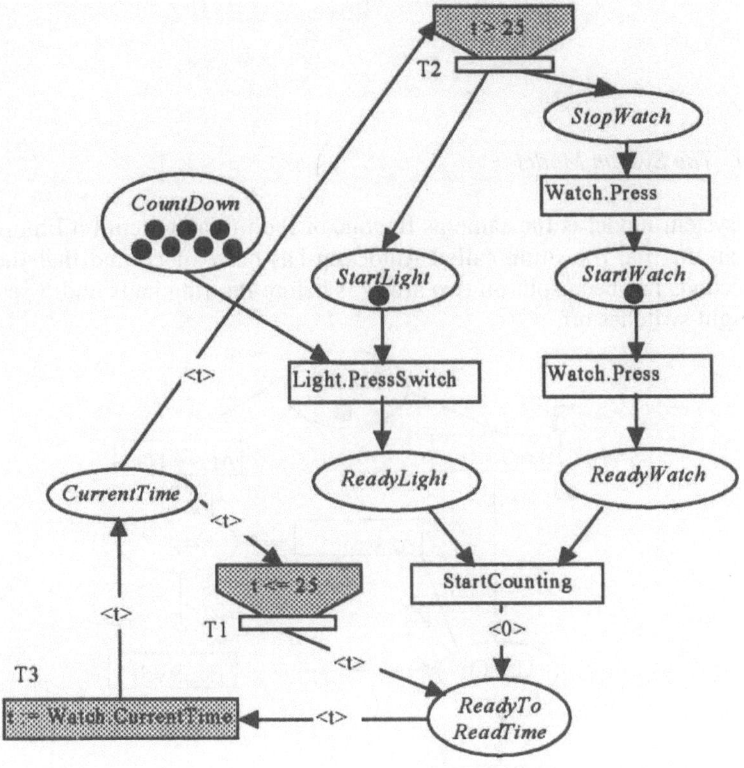

Figure 9 The task model corresponding to the first upgrade of the system

4.5 Upgrade 2: Adding a Bell

Faced with the complexity in the user's task presented in Figure 9, the designer might choose to improve the system, in order to reduce the user's workload. In this case, a solution might be to move the complexity out of the task and into the system, by ringing a bell 5 seconds before the timer expires. The user then only has to count down the number of chiming, which is significantly simpler than to compare several times the current time with the 25 seconds he/she has to wait before pressing the light switch. According to user activity with this system only the hearing and touch are used, the user can perform the task without using eyesight.

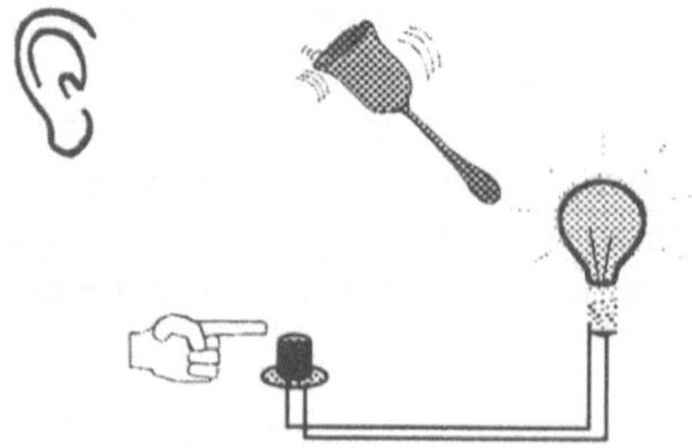

Figure 10 The second upgrade of the system

4.5.1 *The System Model*

The system model is the same as the one of the initial system (cf.Figure 6) except that an internal transition called AutoBeep has been added and that the timing of 30 seconds has been split on two arcs 25s before the ring bells and 5 second before the light switches off.

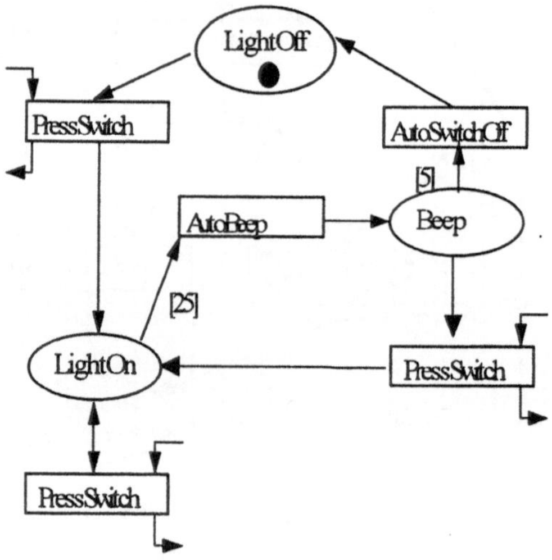

Figure 11 The System Model

4.5.2 *The Upgraded Task Model*

With this updated system specification, a new and significantly simpler task model may be built. The count down process is modelled by seven tokens in the CountDown place. The complexity of the task model, according to our metrics, is significantly smaller, which proves that the design decision was a good one. Indeed the only cycle of the net is the one corresponding to the repetitive task of pressing several times the light switch. It can be computed that the number of occurrence of the transition HearBeep is exactly seven thus stating that the task will correspond to the minimal number of actions requested by the goal.

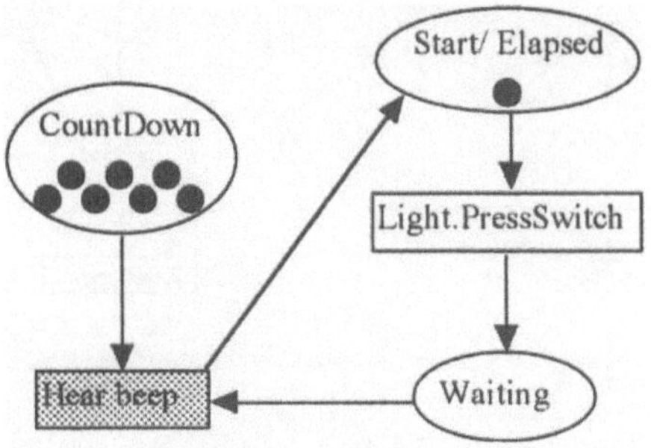

Figure 12 The upgraded task model

However, we have not demonstated that this task is actually supported by the system i.e. according to the system model given in Figure 11, the sequence of user actions embedded in this task model can be performed by the system. This is described in the next section.

5. Linking the Task Model and the System Model

We have just presented both a task model and a system model for the upgraded system, and we will now focus on how those models can be merged. This merging can be of several kind of help:

- it is possible to be sure that all the user's actions on the system described in the task model are available in the system model,
- it is possible to be sure that the sequencing of user's actions on the system described in the task model can be performed by the system (i.e. are supported by the system model).

This linking is done by merging the task model and the system model according to the client-server protocol presented in section 3.5.

Figure 13 presents the reconstruction of the global model, made by the combination of the task and system models. The transitions related to the operation of the switch (both on the user's and the system's side) have been processed. It is important to consider firstly that this global model may be constructed by completely automated means, and secondly that it is not meant to be read by humans, but merely to be processed by automatic tools, in order to perform analysis and prove properties. The result of this analysis on the reconstructed net allows to be sure that the models have been built in a that they can cooperate together without altering their inner behaviour. For example, using Petri net theory it can be automatically proved that the reconstructed net allows the place Countdown to be emptied and that there will be no token in place LightOff before the place CountDown is actually empty.

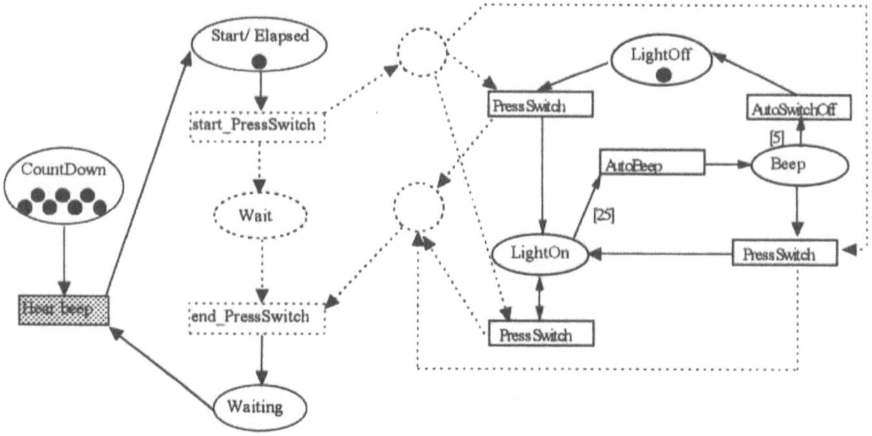

Figure 13 : Task and system models combined

6. Benefits of the Approach

6.1 Advantages of Using Formal System Modelling

The advantages of a formal model for system modelling has already been described in (Palanque & Bastide 1994), and we only summarise them here:

- the **absence of deadlock** is the possibility for the user to issue another system command whatever was the sequence of previous ones;
- the **predictability of a command** is the fact that the user must be able to foresee the effect of a command. That is, a command must always be processed in the same way in a given context;
- the **reinitiability** is the possibility for the user to reach the initial state of the system, or a given predefined state (this is very important when the system has to used several time for the same purpose e.g. an Automated Teller Machine);
- the **availability of a command** may take three different forms:
  - the command must be available at any moment, whatever state the application is in (e.g. a *help* command),
  - the command must be available for at least a specified number of times, eventually through any sequence of commands,
  - the command must always become available, that is the user may always issue a command sequence after which the command is available again;
- the **succession of commands** indicates in which order some commands may be issued; for instance a given command must or must not be followed by another one, immediately after or with some other commands in between;
- the **exclusion of commands** which must never be available at the same time (or on the contrary must always be available simultaneously);
- the **bound of a state variable** of the application corresponds to the fact that the number of elements of some resource handled by the application is restricted (or

is not);

- **integrity constraints** between the values of some application's state variables.

6.2 Advantages of Using Formal Task Modelling

The use of a formal model for task modelling result in the same advantages as formal system modelling but, as the task model describes the sequences of actions the user will have to perform in order to reach a given goal, it is very important to compute some performance evaluation on the model. This is very easy using Petri nets as they have been used for a long time for performance evaluation of systems and a lot of theoretical work is available in this area.

The kind of analysis results that can be done on the task model is:

- number of actions the user has to perform in order to reach the goal;
- the number and the length of cycles in the models;
- if some actions have to be performed by the user under temporal constraints (for example using an ATM you have to enter your pin number within 3 minutes) it is possible to compute the frequency of those actions and to prove that the temporal constraints are consistent i.e. they do not contradict each other

7. Conclusion and Perspectives

This paper demonstrates the possibility and the benefits of using a common formalism to describe both the system and the tasks of users interacting with it. To this end, we use a formal approach, based on the use of Petri nets and structured according to object-oriented concepts.

The ongoing work on this approach consists in extending the modelling to encompass user models as well as task and system models. We believe that, using a temporal representation of the human processor it will also be possible to evaluate the cognitive workload of the user.

Acknowledgments

The present work owes a lot to the working sessions held in the LIS laboratory in Toulouse, with the LIS CHI team and part of the PII team in the CENA, Toulouse. The authors are also involved in a related work, together with Tom Moher and Victor Dirda, from the University of Illinois at Chicago.

Chapter 5:ETAG-based Design: User Interface Design as User Mental Model Design

Geert de Haan

1. Introduction: ETAG

It is hard to expect that Human-Computer Interaction (HCI) or Cognitive Ergonomics will be taken as a serious candidate to contribute to the design of computer systems as long as it has little more to offer then a plea to consider "computer usability" and a huge collection of methods, tools and insights that rather seem organized around the concept of novelty (Newman 1993), instead of being organized in terms of the particular design questions they propose to answer. The focus of attention in HCI research, as we perceive it, is on multitude of activities that support computer system design, rather than constitute it, such as handling standards and guidelines, usability engineering, design rationale, and user interface analysis and evaluation. Even in the area of formal modelling, the subject matter of this paper, research has generally shifted away from design methods towards analysis of partial design aspects such as predicting user performance and measuring consistency of design products.
The continuing flux of new proposals, frameworks and approaches to yet other very interesting but relatively unimportant subproblems of HCI forms the background of the ETAG project. The project is meant as a step towards establishing HCI or Cognitive Ergonomics as a systematic design science and/or engineering practice.
Science and engineering disciplines are supposed to have three characteristic features: a body of basic knowledge, (based on) a set of generally accepted assumptions, and a collection of standard methods. ETAG-based design is a method to solve the basic question of the HCI: how to design user interfaces that are usable for human task performers. With respect to the engineering part, ETAG-based design is a systematic and fairly rigourous formal method for specifying the most important parts of most user interfaces. It is neither an empty framework that is applicable to all types of user interfaces and design problems, nor is it an overly restricted blueprint to completely solve one particular problem or type of user interface design. With respect to the scientific part, in ETAG-based design user interfaces are specified in terms of user competence knowledge, in the ETAG notation that derives from theoretical, psychological and psycholinguistic considerations. ETAG gives a fairly complete psychology of what users should know about user interfaces to perform tasks successfully, and thereby provides a theoretical framework for research into the questions that ETAG-based design does not account for.

At the basis of ETAG-based design is Norman's (Norman 1983) observation that users create mental models of computer systems in order to enable planning and executing commands, and interpreting the results with respect to the goals they should fulfill. Norman assumes that the completeness and correctness of mental models can explain the success or failure of using computer systems. To design computer systems such that user may indeed form and run appropriate mental models to attain successful task performance, Norman suggests to use a Conceptual or Design Model that considers user mental models as the basis for the complete design of the user interface, including its perceptual and training aspects, but he gives no details about how to do that.

In Software Engineering it is common to use design models to ensure among others the completeness and correctness of the computer code that implements a user interface. Unfortunately, software engineering models represent the structure and workings of computer programs in order to create them, and not the user interface as the task-environment or task-world that the user should get acquainted with. For the average user there is no such things as "the part of a computer program that handles the output to the display and the input from the person using the program" (Myers 1994; pg. 2).

For users who want to perform tasks with a computer system, the user interface simply is the computer system, or at least all the aspects of it that are relevant for task performance. When the user interface in the cognitive ergonomic sense is defined as "all aspects of a computer system that are relevant for performing tasks" it is something very different from the software engineering definition of the user interface (de Haan 1994).

First, whereas the user interface in the software engineering sense is a physical or functional object, what is relevant to perform tasks needs to be learned by users, via the information on the display, instructions or manuals, and as such it is a cognitive or knowledge object. Just like, for example, language understanding requires physical, lexical, syntactic, etc. knowledge, the user's "how-to-do-it" knowledge consists of knowledge at different levels of abstraction.

Secondly, whereas software engineering user interfaces exclude the workings of the computer system, to plan and evaluate actions users need to have "how-it-works" knowledge. To make use of Cut and Paste operations, for example, users have to know how a clipboard works (Payne et al. 1990). Likewise, to understand that deleted files are no longer available for viewing, users need to know how a delete command works. Since the user's understanding doesn't need to be similar to the exact workings of a computer system; only the input and output should correspond, what the user needs to know about the workings of the computer system is called the User's Virtual Machine (Oberquelle 1984).

User knowledge, both "how-to-do-it" and "how-it-works" is what ETAG represents and in ETAG-based design, design is specifying what a perfectly knowing user would know about performing tasks.

Specifying user interfaces in terms of user knowledge helps to keep focus on task performance aspects, rather than on technical software issues. Interface design in ETAG is formal to enable the use of the advantage of formality, such as precision and non-ambiguous communication. ETAG uses a layered representation of user interfaces since Human-Computer Interaction and user knowledge are layered along several levels of abstraction (conceptual, semantic, etc.), and to structure design into a number of discrete steps where each step aims at solving specific design questions, appropriate for the level of detail. Using one representation

throughout the design process instead of different design representations particular to each design step helps to keep the design process simple and manageable.
ETAG-based design is a loosely top-down structured design method. Design iterations will especially take place within design steps, and only where necessary between steps. Structuring the design process in discrete steps helps to make the design process manageable, it provides guidance for a timely use of supplementary HCI methods and tools (Lim & Long 1992), and it makes explicit where and how HCI and software engineering should communicate their respective results. The design structure of ETAG-based design is not very different from either the 'received view' of good HCI design practice or from software engineering design (de Haan 1994). What is very different, however, is the separation of concerns between HCI and Software Engineering design and the almost exclusive focus on user knowledge that in our view, should characterize the former.

2. ETAG: the Notation and Model

Specifying user interface design in terms of user knowledge puts requirements on the representation formalism with respect to the completeness of interface representations from the point of view of the user, the variety of design aspects the formalism may be applied to, the psychological validity of (the analyses and predictions of) the representation, and the usability of the model to designers. An evaluation study showed that most well-known formal models in HCI are not suitable for design representation. From the two models that turned out to be suitable; Moran's Command Language Grammar (Moran 1981) and ETAG, the latter was selected because of its better formalism (de Haan et al. 1991).
ETAG models consist of four parts. The top-most part is the Canonical Basis, which lists and defines the ontological concepts that will be used to describe the specific user interface. The User's Virtual Machine defines the specific concept types of the interface and uses these to describe how the interface works when a task is invoked. The Dictionary of Basic Tasks lists the tasks the interface provides for and connects the higher level descriptions with the Production Rules. The Production Rules describe how the commands for each Basic Task should be specified in terms of command element order, reference, naming and physical actions.

ETAG has been developed out of Task-Action Grammar (TAG) (Payne & Green 1986) which aims at giving a psychological account of the ease of use of interaction languages. In a sense, TAG covers ETAG's production rules and dictionary of basic tasks, but since ETAG is meant for user interface (knowledge) representation it uses TAG's interaction language description for specification purposes and it has the user's virtual machine description added on top of the TAG representation.
TAG uses a feature grammar (a BNF extension) in which the rewrite rules describe how to derive the appropriate command actions from tasks. Task are "tagged" with semantic features which are assumed to be used by the "Grammar in the Head" to distinguishing tasks from one another on the basis of their (psychological) meanings. Since TAG's feature grammar allows similar tasks to be represented in a

similar way, it is also a very efficient representation scheme. For example, to represent character movements of a cursor BNF representations would need four rules (up, down, left, and right) whereas TAG would need only one:

Move_Cursor[Direction] ::= Cursor_Key[Direction]

Feature grammars allow a user interface to be described in different ways, most of which will not be valid in a psychological respect.

2.1 The Canonical Basis

The Canonical Basis is used to standardise ETAG representations and ensures that they are psychologically valid by insisting that all ETAG concepts derive from a restricted set of analytic or canonical categories that may be assumed to underlie all human knowledge. The Canonical Basis uses the analytic categories and an existential logic system (Jackenoff 1983, Sowa 1984) to describe which real-world knowledge is required to understand the user interface in terms of Events, States, Attributes, Relations, Places, Objects and perhaps others, without referring to the specific interface.

Existential logic makes it relatively easy to describe how objects (e.g. files) start or cease to exist and because of its seamless connection with feature grammars, it allows an ETAG representation to be regarded as a uniform set of definitions (de Haan 1995). The combination of existential logic and canonical concepts allows modelling of parts of the real world as well as artificial worlds such as user interfaces in a formal but easy-to-grasp visual-spatial language, wherein, for instance, Events move Objects between Places or move from one State into another by changing Attributes or Relations.

```
CONCEPT ::= OBJECT | PLACE | EVENT | ATTRIBUTE | STATE
[PLACE] ::= place.IN [OBJECT] |
              place.ON_TOP [OBJECT] | place.ON_END [OBJECT]
[STATE] ::= state.IS_AT [OBJECT, PLACE] |
              state.IS_ON [OBJECT, PLACE] | state.HAS_VAL [ATTRIBUTE]
[EVENT] ::= event.CREATE [OBJECT, PLACE] |
              event.COPY_TO [OBJECT, PLACE] | ....
type[EVENT = event.MOVE_TO[OBJECT: *o, PLACE: *p]]
   precondition:  state.IS_AT [OBJECT: *o, PLACE: *p0]
   clears:        state.IS_AT [OBJECT: *o, PLACE: *p0]
   postcondition: state.IS_AT [OBJECT: *o, PLACE: *p1]
end
```

2.2 The User's Virtual Machine

The User's Virtual Machine describes what a user needs to know about the internal workings of the computer system when performing tasks: the "how-it-works" knowledge. It is called the User's Virtual Machine because it is a description in

terms of the user's task concepts, which may be substantially different from the actual workings of the machine.
The Objects, Places, etc. are hierarchically derived (by inheritance) from the types in the Canonical Basis. For example, the event of moving an object as defined in the Canonical Basis may be used to describe what happens when a file is moved between directories. Object-type inheritance and the use of Events make ETAG representations rather similar to Object-Oriented Models of Software Engineering. Although this similarity is largely accidental, it does promise a smooth transition with those Analysis, Design and Programming approaches.
In the aforementioned evaluation study of formal models in HCI, Command Language Grammar (CLG) (Moran 1981) was apart from ETAG the only model that allows for conceptual descriptions of user interfaces. A problem of CLG is that at each level of abstraction a complete definition of the interface is given. Consequently, CLG representations are much larger and complex than their ETAG counterparts.
User interface descriptions in terms of what users need to know to perform tasks go well beyond most (common) definitions of what a user interface is (de Haan 1994). ETAG's description of the "how-it-works" knowledge of the interface describes part of the application's functionality, although the description is in terms of user tasks instead of software processes.

```
type [OBJECT = CLIPBOARD]
        supertype:      [SINGLE_OBJECT_BOARD]
        themes:         [STRING: *s] | [PICTURE: *p] | ...
        instances:      [CLIPBOARD: #clipboard]
end
type [EVENT = CUT_STRING]
        description:
                event.MOVE_TO [STRING: *s, OBJECT: #clipboard]
        precondition:
                state.IS_AT [STRING: *s, OBJECT: #document]
                state.HAS_VAL [STRING: *s, ATTRIBUTE: selected]
        clears: state.IS_AT [STRING: *s, OBJECT: #document]
        postcondition:
                state.IS_AT [STRING: *s, OBJECT: #clipboard]
                state.HAS_VAL [STRING: *s, ATTRIBUTE: purgeable]
        comments: "move string from document to clipboard"
end
```

2.3 The Dictionary of Basic Tasks

The Dictionary of Basic Tasks describes the functionality of the interface in terms of the available commands and links the Production Rules to the higher levels of the ETAG specification. To avoid intuitive decisions about what constitutes a task for a user, Basic Tasks are defined as the elementary commands of the user interface rather than as psychological tasks, such as "simple tasks" in TAG (Payne

& Green 1986) or "unit tasks" in the GOMS model (Card et al. 1983). ETAG is a strict competence model of user knowledge, and thereby avoids imposing planning and decision structures upon users as in the GOMS model and Cognitive Complexity Theory (Kieras & Polson 1985).

ENTRY 1: TASK = CUT_STRING
T1 [EVENT = CUT_STRING, OBJECT = STRING: *s, ATTRIBUTE = selected]
comment: "move string from document to clipboard"
ENTRY 3: TASK = PASTE_STRING
T3 [EVENT = PASTE_CLIP, PLACE = EDIT_SPOT: *p]
comment: "copy clipboard content to document"

2.4 The Production Rules

In order to reflect the main design decisions of the interaction language ETAG's Production Rules are organized along four levels to describe the ordering of commands (action-object or object-action), the way of referring to command elements (pointing, naming, knobbing), the lexical entries of command elements (names, labels), and the physical actions. The use of four levels of description also allows ETAG to be applied to a variety of interfaces, such as VCR's, radios, cars, etc. and in particular when it is undesirable or impossible to design the interaction language at once, or when more than one interaction language should be used.

Specification level:
T2 [EVENT = CUT_STRING, OBJECT = STRING: *s, ATTRIBUTE = selected] ::=
specify[OBJECT = STRING: *s, ATTRIBUTE = selected] + specify[EVENT = CUT_STRING]
Reference level:
specify[OBJECT = STRING: *s, ATTRIBUTE = selected] ::= object_select[STRING: *s]
specify[EVENT = CUT_STRING] ::= menu_select[EVENT = CUT] | key_name [EVENT = CUT]
Lexical level:
object_select[STRING: *s] ::= click[STRING: *s] + drag_over[STRING: *s]
menu_select[EVENT = CUT] ::= click[MENU: "Edit"] + drag_to[Item: "Cut"]
key_name[EVENT = CUT] ::= symbol[EVENT = CUT]
Physical level:
click[ANY] ::= press_mouse_button[ANY]
drag_over[OBJECT] ::= drag_mouse_to_end[OBJECT] + release_mouse_button
drag_to[OBJECT] ::= drag_mouse_on[OBJECT] + release_mouse_button
symbol[EVENT = CUT] ::= press_key["key-for-cutting"]

3. ETAG-Based Design

ETAG-based design (de Haan 1994) is best viewed as a skeleton method for the design of user interfaces. It enforces, or, at least stimulates a focus on the user's needs, provides a structured method to yield timely and communicable results, but leaves it to the preferences of the designer and the demands of the situation which faculties, tools or techniques, etc. are used. A basic idea underlying ETAG-based design is to divide the design process into discrete design steps, each asking a specific set of questions according to the part of the ETAG representation being worked on. As such, the design specification (the ETAG representation) provides the structure to the design process to proceed in an orderly and timely manner. In addition, the different parts of ETAG are structures in such a way as to require few iterations required between design steps, and many within. Within each design step, it is completely up to designers to decide how to proceed. Figure 1 presents the structure of ETAG-based design

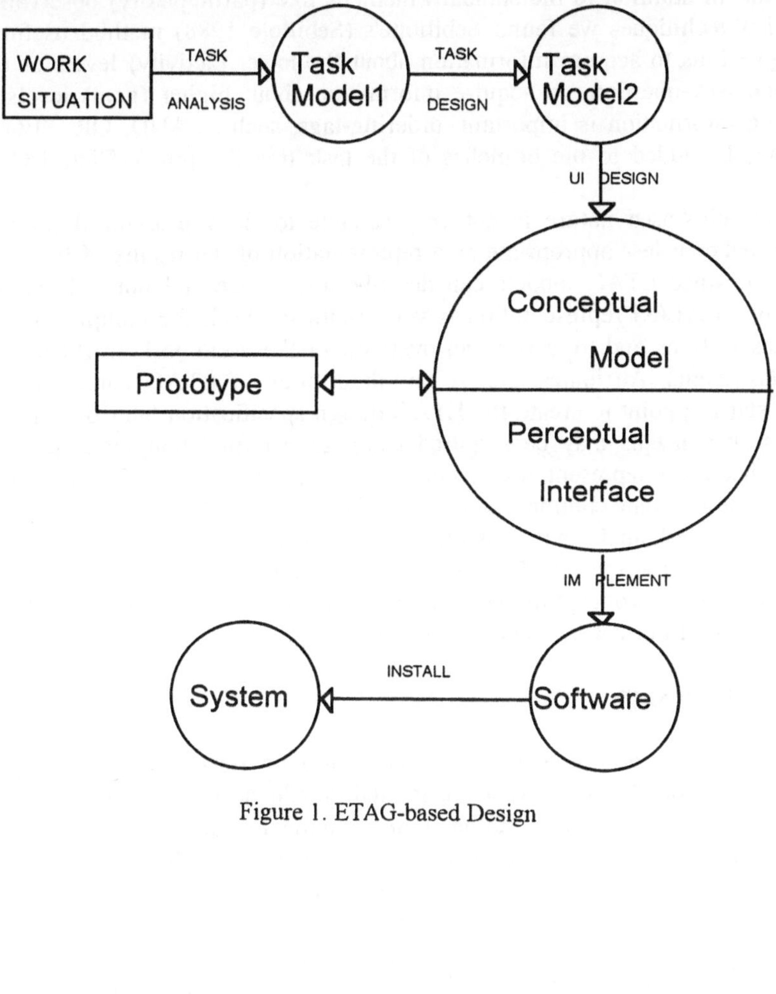

Figure 1. ETAG-based Design

3.1 Task and Context Analysis

A first step in any user interface design project is to acquire sufficient understanding of the use of the interface within the context of the user group, the user's tasks and the work organization. It may not always be necessary to perform a full blown task analysis, but it should be noted that task-analysis is the only systematic method available to guard against uncontrolled design conservatism; keeping things as they are and merely changing details. The purpose of task analysis is to describe how tasks are performed in a current situation to enable argumentation about improving the work situation in general as well as improving task performance at the user interface.

The main results of task analysis are task diagrams: task trees that show the recurrent decomposition of the tasks associated with jobs and roles into subtasks. ETAG does not specify which methods should be used to acquire task trees. However, in addition to the standard methods like (participatory) observation and interview techniques we found Sebillotte's (Sebillote 1988) method useful to ask how-questions to acquire information about the lower (activity) levels of the task tree and why-questions to acquire information about higher (goal) levels. When ordering information is important, ordering-tags, such as AND, OR, SEQuential, etc. may be added to the branches of the task tree (Scapin & Pierret-Golbreich 1989).

ETAG's rule-based nature is not very suitable to show procedural information, which makes it less appropriate as a representation of the results of task analysis. However, since ETAG models can describe any device and not only computers, creating an ETAG representation is very useful to check the completeness of the task descriptions and to acquire an overview of the user's task world in terms of Objects, Events, Attributes, etc. A raw description of ETAG concepts is also a useful starting point to create the ETAG design specification later on. Information about task concepts may be acquired using semi-formal templates: paper fill-in forms that each represent an instance of an ETAG-concept described in plain language to facilitate communication with users.

The result of task analysis is called the Task Model(1) which consists of all the task information that is relevant for further design: procedural and timing information in the task tree(s), concept information in the concept specifications and hierarchies and any other information, such as comments.

3.2 Task Design

Task Design as a design stage before actual user interface design is a response to the phenomenon that user interface is, and should be used as an opportunity to improve the work situation. Rather than noticing too late how a new computer system does not fit in or leads to unexpected changes in the old work situation, design should start with redesigning the work situation on the basis of user preferences with respect to the situation of Task Model(1), opportunities of new technology, and improvements in the organization of work through new combinations of responsibilities and low-level tasks into roles and jobs. Similar to task and context analysis, it may not be necessary to perform a full blown task (re-) design, but if it is necessary, it should be done in advance of user interface design. Task design involves two parts: a reshuffle of jobs, responsibilities and roles among users, and based on that, a new high-level task allocation between users and the computer system(s). The result of task design is put down into a Task Model(2), which is identical to Task Model(1) except that it is the result of design rather then analysis.

3.3 Conceptual Design

Conceptual design is the first stage of user interface design proper. It consists of specifying the Canonical Basis, the UVM and the Dictionary of Basic Tasks: the user's view of the workings of the computer system. It is easiest to start Conceptual Design with a list of user tasks. A main part of the Dictionary of Basic Tasks, the primary tasks, follows from Task Model(2) and a low-level task allocation between user and the computer system. Part of the UVM can be specified by abstraction from the objects, relations, etc. of Task Model(2). The Canonical Basis can be specified by subsequently choosing from among the standard Canonical Basis concepts those that are required for the concepts of the UVM. In this way, the parts of the Canonical Basis, the UVM and the Dictionary of Basic Tasks can be specified that are required for the tasks for which the computer system is actually designed. This is a specification of a minimal interface (Neerincx & de Greef 1993): a service hatch, that does not yet provide an integrated view on the user's task world. Creative design is now necessary to add the tasks and task concepts which enable the user to perform the tasks of the minimal interface in a uniform, consistent and intuitive way. As an example, when a minimal interface has a task to Query a Database, the full interface might have a task to select a database, a window object to present the results and possibly additional tasks to manage window objects in general.

The Canonical Basis, UVM and Dictionary of Basic Tasks at specified in one step to help establish a coherent underlying task world for the user interface, first as a clear starting point for subsequent perceptual design, and secondly, as the point whereafter HCI and software engineering should take their own separate responsibilities without the need for major redesigns or having to patch up usability problems.

During Conceptual Design ETAG is as specification language and in its role as an early applicable tool for formal analysis of the size, complexity and consistency of the user interface.

3.4 Perceptual Design

The System Image (Norman 1983) or 'everything the user comes into contact with' is the object of perceptual design. The perceptual interface consists of the presentation interface, the interaction language, and the metacommunication facilities (eg. user documentation, on-line help). The presentation interface can not be specified in ETAG, because suitable grammars for information presentation have not been available and because it is not very urgent, given the number and quality of user interface (screen) builders and eg. windowing standards. The ETAG specification does provide a good starting point to design a presentation interface that is compatible with and supports the Conceptual Design model. The interaction language can be specified in ETAG's Production Rules by subsequently specifying the ordering, manner of reference, lexical access, and physical actions associated with each Basic Task. The Production Rule specification may be sizable, though also a very useful vehicle for formal analysis of the consistency and complexity of the interaction language. For the design of metacommunication, the ETAG representation may serve as a source of exact information about a computer system. In addition, ETAG representations have been used to automatically generate user documentation drafts, on-line help, and rough prototypes, which helps keep design and metacommunication mutually compatible (de Haan & van der Veer 1992).

3.5 Implementation, Installation and Usage

ETAG has not been explicitly developed as an object-oriented representation in the software engineering sense. Nevertheless, the resemblances between ETAG and object-oriented representations for analysis and design (Monarchi & Puhr 1992), and for interactive system development (de Bruin et al. 1994) support our observation from students' work that translating between ETAG and object-oriented program code is relatively easy. The transition between ETAG and procedural programming languages is less straightforward but facilitated by the fact that at least part of the input and output behaviour and the functionality are formalized. Using standard Unix tools such as Lex and Yacc, and a BNF representation of the ETAG notation it was possible to create a user interface simulator or prototyper that, apart from the graphics, behaved according to the ETAG representation that it used as input (de Haan & van der Veer 1992).
After the implementation or coding phase there are no principal differences between ETAG-based design and software engineering design methods, except that since a task-oriented design representation remains available it may be more difficult to "maintain away" the usability of a computer system.

4. Discussion

4.1 Related Approaches

There are few traditional formal models in HCI that come close to the completeness with which ETAG is able to describe user interfaces. Most formal models are limited to describing the interaction language to analyze cognitive complexity aspects (Payne & Green 1986, Kieras & Polson 1985) or to predict performance times in restricted circumstances (Card et al. 1983, Kieras & Polson 1985). Command Language Grammar (Moran 1981) is quite similar to ETAG. Both describe user competence knowledge for design purposes and use more or less the same levels of description. A main difference between CLG and ETAG is that each level of a CLG representation is meant to be a complete representation of the user interface, at that level, whereas in ETAG, the higher levels are build upon the lower ones. As a result, CLG models are notably large and complex, and as a consequence difficult to change and keep consistent (Sharratt 1987).

ETAG-based design is not the only structured design method. Here, the main question is the relation between HCI and Software Engineering. At one end of the scale, there are software engineering methods with HCI extensions. Summersgill and Browne (1989) propose to add various "things to do" to SSADM stages, as well as a few specific HCI oriented deliverables. Apart from the fact that this proposal results in an even more complex method than SSADM already is, the input from HCI and the usability of systems is still regarded as an add-on to design from a Software Engineering point of view.

MUSE*/JSD (Lim & Long 1992) also uses a software engineering method (JSD), in order not to deviate from common practice. In MUSE*/JSD HCI design proceeds parallel to software design, and JSD is used to structure the design process as a whole, and enforce well-defined and timely HCI inputs as a means to promote system usability. MUSE*/JSD will probably facilitate the acceptance of system usability in the software design community, but there is still no guarantee what will happens when Muse*/JSD is used in a team without any HCI expertise.

ADEPT (Wilson et al. 1993) is a design method, an environment and a set of prototypical tools. ADEPT makes use of SSADM, but also of the TKS (Task Knowledge Structures) family of HCI formalisms. TKS models derive from research on task analysis, and as such they are most appropriate for modelling work procedures, objects and roles. TKS methods are not extremely formal and thereby exclude the use of formal techniques. On the other hand, ADEPT offers some graphical design tools which make life for the designer more pleasant.

DIGIS system (de Bruin et al. 1994) offers an object-oriented software method and environment, specially created for user interface or interactive system design. DIGIS shares ETAG's focus on the user's task world, which may explain the similarity between ETAG UVM and DIGIS's Domain Application Model (DAM). Whereas ETAG does not specify a Software Engineering design representation, DIGIS uses one for both HCI and Software Engineering. In applying ETAG in small to moderate size projects, we found that one (HCI) representation could do, but it is yet unclear what happens in sizeable projects with ETAG or DIGIS. Finally, DIGIS also offers some prototyping design tools.

It is too early to say anything definite about the ETAG and ETAG-based design in comparison to the models and methods mentioned above. In our opinion, ETAG-based design has a superior formalism, but in practice, the formalism is not the only relevant determinant of success. To this may be added that in terms of design steps, ETAG, MUSE*/JSD, ADEPT, and DIGIS have more commonalities than differences. All four methods focus on the user's knowledge of the task world, and structure design in levels of abstraction from task analysis to detailed interface design. As a result, they also distinguish very similar representation models for intermediate results, such as a Task Model, an Abstract Interface Model and a Concrete or Specific Interface Model.

What seems most important about these four models is that they present, in combination, a generalized systematic method of how user interface design should take place to ensure usable systems. In providing the requirements for usability from the level of task concepts down to low level details, these methods are likely complements, and perhaps even replacements for the Software Engineering user interfaces tools and design methods.

4.2 Conclusions

This paper described ETAG-based design as a structured method for user interface design, build upon a formal model of a perfect user's competence knowledge. As a user interface representation tool for designers, ETAG is functional in its ability to represent conceptual models of user interfaces in a psychologically valid way. As such, the feasibility of ETAG and ETAG-based design do not need further support (de Haan & van der Veer 1992).

With respect to completeness and ease of use, there is room for improvement. ETAG is not able to model the presentation interface. This is not a main problem: given that the presentation interface to help users develop the appropriate conceptual model of the design, it may be both faster as well as easier to use an ETAG representation and one of the graphical design tools to design the presentation interface, rather than to solve the problem of visual grammar. For prototyping purposes tools like, Visual Basic and HyperCard are fine for educational purposes, but too slow for professional use. Advanced software engineering interface builders are powerful, but they seem to be especially suitable for bottom-up creation of interactive systems from scratch, rather than a top-down creation on the basis of HCI specifications.

More serious is the problem that it is difficult to create and change ETAG representations. To make ETAG usable for designers, a graphical editor is needed to hide away the formalism and its syntactic details. Research to develop (or find) such a tool is underway, but thus far, without tangible results. Presentation Interface builders are also investigated, as a secondary requirement for an integrated ETAG-based design environment.

Perhaps the most important conclusion of this paper is that ETAG-based design is the only integrated design method that is based on a specification of user knowledge. We have argued that model-based design methods both organize the HCI knowledge-base as well as provide the best guarantees that HCI's design products will be usable. As such, we may only hope that ETAG-based design, or more in general, model-based design will become a new standard in HCI.

Acknowledgement

I would like to thank Michael Tauber for initially proposing ETAG, Gerrit van der Veer for putting ETAG to the test in teaching student and designers courses, and numerous students adding their bits and pieces to the subject of this paper.

Chapter 6: A Methodology for a Task-driven Modelling of Interactive Systems Architectures

Fabio Paterno'

1. Introduction

Making systems easier to use es an ever increasing complexity in the part dedicated to managing commu-------on between users and applications. In fact a large part of the code is devoted to the user interface portion. In order to manage this complexity, it is very important to have a structured methodology which supports the designer's work during the refinement process from requirements specification to implementation.

We consider an *Interactive System* (Carlsen et al. 1991) as a system which the user interacts with in order to fulfil a specific goal. In order to design and evaluate these systems, formal specifications play a key role thus giving precise and unambiguous descriptions which we can reason about in order to check the results of the design. They also provide a more compact and manageable documentation with respect to long and ambiguous descriptions in natural language.

Some well-known problems in the formal specification of user interfaces are: "scaling up" specifications for large and complex user interfaces, describing concurrency, developing the appropriate set of abstractions for various kinds of user interfaces. These are still open issues and in this work we try to provide one possible solution which is based on five elements:

- We focus on interactive aspects because we think (Hartson & Gray 1992) that a user-centred design entails focusing on the actions of the user and what the user perceives while performing tasks with the computer. Furthermore we agree that requirements that involve the usability of systems can be properties of interactions rather than system alone (Harrison & Barnard 1992).
- We want to identify a methodology which allows designers to structure their specifications in a systematic way and to reason on them at different abstraction levels depending on the aspect they want to investigate in the various phases of the refinement process. For example in (Wright et al. 1994) there is an approach for evaluating human-error tolerance aspects from formal specification of user tasks, while here we want to use tasks specification for driving the modelling of a corresponding architectural specification able to support the given tasks. Specifications of different abstraction levels of an Interactive Systems should be equivalent.
- In order to have more usable software its functionality needs to be organised in a user-oriented way rather than a system-oriented way. This means that the task analysis and organisation which users perform in order to logically structure their activity should be used as requirements for the software specification.
- It is important to use a concurrent notation which allows us to describe the functionality that can be active in parallel, their dynamic activation and

deactivation, and the temporal ordering of actions at both the task and the system levels.
- Another important element is the use of formal notations because they constrain designers to be precise and clarify their specifications since the first steps of the refinement process.

The current trend is to design Interactive Systems in a parallel approach in order to make them able to support parallel users' tasks which can be performed by reacting to parallel user-generated input and by supporting parallel dialogues, multiple processing levels and multiple feedback levels. In fact, several programming languages and notations influenced by CSP (Hoare 1985) (such as ERL (Hill 1986) and Squeak (Cardelli & Pike 1985)) were developed to specify user interfaces.
Process algebras rely on a small set of basic operators and on one or more notions of equivalences. They can be very useful in the design of Interactive Systems because they provide a solid formal base for describing their dynamic behaviour, and a generation of tools for computer aided verification are being developed thus making it possible to reason about the specification performed.
This means that a process-oriented descrip ı of Interactive Systems makes it possible to reason on their dynamic behaviour, which is mainly driven by user-generated events, at an abstract level before implementing them. We use LOTOS (ISO, 1989), a formal notation which combines process and data algebra. Several automatic tools for automatic analysis and verification of LOTOS specifications are currently available. In a previous work (Paterno' & Faconti 1992) LOTOS was used to specify small examples of interactions, now we need a methodology to structure specifications of complex Interactive Systems. In fact having a language with concurrent constructs is not enough: information and approaches for structuring the design are also needed to support the designer's work in this specific field. For this purpose we propose to use the result of task decomposition. We can thus obtain a software organisation which better reflects the users' view of its functionality and we can overcome one typical error i.e. waiting for an action which is not possible (Sutcliffe & Springett 1992), when users attempt to perform an action which is not supported by the interface. This type of error is typically a result of a model mismatch between the user and the system. An action is present in the user's model of the task but absent in the system model. This means that the dynamic behaviour of the Interactive System is not clear enough for the user, probably because the software organisation does not reflect how the user organises his tasks.
LOTOS was developed for a different application area (network protocols) but as we said new trends in Interactive Systems design indicate that their features are very similar to those of distributed systems. This notation is being used in industrial sites other than universities and public research centres. Specific user interface properties expressed in Action-Based Temporal Logic can be automatically checked on the system's LOTOS specification (Paterno' & Mezzanotte 1994).

This paper is organised as follows: firstly, we describe the architectural model for user interactions which we use for modelling Interactive Systems. Next, operators for composition and refinement of interaction objects are defined. Then, we show a methodology to refine task descriptions into interactor-based Interactive Systems. We describe relationships between architectural and interactional descriptions of Interactive Systems. Finally, an example of application of the proposed methodology is provided.

2. An Architecture for Basic Graphical Interaction

A User Interface System (UIS), the part of an Interactive System dedicated to the management of the communication between users and applications, can be described by composing interaction objects or interactors which are defined following a common general architectural model. Its choice affects how the entire system is modelled because each architectural model has its specific basic components and composition operators. An interactor can be considered as a building block to structure the design of Interactive Systems. There are several proposals for the architecture of interaction objects which have to interact with users, for example (Coutaz 1987, Duke & Harrison 1993, Goldberg & Robson 1983, Myers 1990).

In our case the purpose of an interactor is to identify and encapsulate in a unique way the general dynamic behaviour of an interaction object. We start from the assumption that at a very abstract level we can view an interaction object as a black box which can receive information from the user or the application side, perform its processing and return related results to the application or user side (Figure 2). It also should be able to support feedback of the user-generated input. This is valid whatever modality of interaction we are considering.

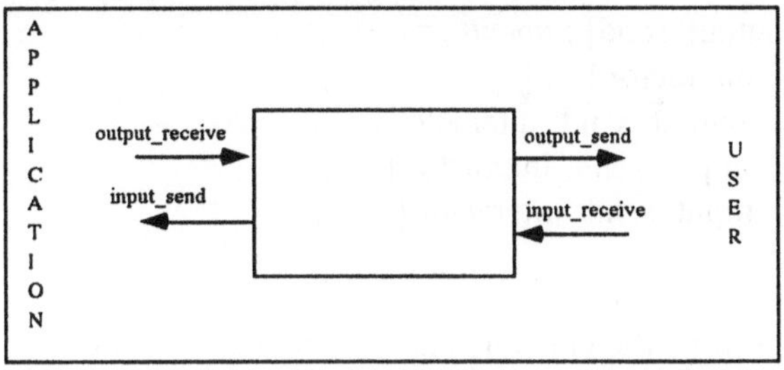

Figure 1: An Interaction Object.

Now we want to give a formal specification of our architectural model. We begin with the specification of its dynamic behaviour. Then in order to obtain a specific instance of interactor, further processing is necessary: to indicate the data types which it can receive or produce, and those which define their internal state; and to indicate further constraints in the dynamic behaviour. This can be done by indicating specific policies in enabling and disabling input and output gates.

Different styles of specification are possible in the LOTOS notation. In (Vissers et al. 1991) they are classified as *extensional*, where the architecture is defined in terms of observable behaviour like a black box (monolithic and constraint-oriented), and *intensional* where information about the internal organisation is provided (state-oriented and resource-oriented).

The specification provided in (Paterno' & Faconti 1992) is an example of a resource-oriented specification because both observable interactions and interactions among the internal components are described: the behaviour in terms of the observable interaction is defined by a composition of separate resources (collection, feedback, measure, and control in that case). As mentioned before, that type of specification is oriented to providing indications for implementation, in that case in a graphic environment. In order to reason on networks of interactors, a more abstract specification of the general model is needed. We chose the monolithic style where only observable interactions are presented and where no hints concerning internal structure and implementation-oriented aspects can be given. Before we want to introduce a distinction among the communication channels of an interactor thus refining the representation provided in Figure 1: we want to distinguish between gates used for transmitting/receiving information data (*input_receive*, *input_send*, *output_receive*, *output_send* types) and those used for control purposes (*triggers*). The reason being that when an interactor receives an input both from the application and the user side, this does not mean that immediately after an output is produced on the opposite side. To indicate when to generate a data toward the user or the application, an input trigger or an output trigger, respectively, may have to occur. Both input and output triggers can be generated by the user or the application (obtaining a user-driven or application-driven behaviour). We obtained the following specification in Basic LOTOS of the dynamic behaviour of a general interaction object (we use ... to abbreviate the repetition of the event gate names in the header):

process interactor [input_receive, input_trigger, input_send, output_receive, output_trigger, output_send] : *noexit* :=
(output_receive; interactor [...]
[] output_trigger; output_send; interactor [...]
[] input_receive; output_send; interactor [...]
[] input_trigger; input_send; interactor [...])
endproc

Once we have specified the general behaviour of an interactor then we can think to describe specific instances of it by just replacing the names of the actions with those related to the instances of interactors considered. An example of concrete instance of an interaction object obtained by the specification of the general model by gate instanciation is the popup menu:

process pop_up-menu [mouse_position, button_release, selected_menu_element, description_menu_elements, button_press, update_menu_appearance] : *noexit* :=
(description_menu_elements; interactor [...]
[] button_press; update_menu_appearance; interactor [...]
[] mouse_position; update_menu_appearance; interactor [...]
[] button_release; selected_menu_element; interactor [...])
endproc

Here the input trigger is the button release and the output trigger is the button press. In fact when the button of the mouse is pressed the menu appears (the description of the visual appearance is interpreted and the result is visualised on the screen), and when it is released the current selected menu element is delivered to the application (if fact at that time the input processing is applied and the result is sent to the application). The appearance of the menu is updated by the interactor, also when a new cursor position is received in order to provide graphical feedback of the current selected element.

If we want to provide a more concrete description, it is straightforward to pass from a monolithic style to a state-oriented style. LOTOS supports this style of specification because it provides a combination of process and data algebra which makes it possible to describe the state and behaviour of a system (in our case of the components of a User Interface System).

The state is described by three elements: the *collection* which contains the description of the primitives to visualise, the *last input data received* from the user side and the *last input data produced* toward the application side. In some specific instances of interactors one of these state components may be missing.

We thus obtain:

process interactor [input_receive, input_trigger, input_send, output_receive, output_trigger, output_send] (collection :collect, input_data_received :input_data, input_data_produced :input_data): *noexit* :=
(output_receive?od:output_data; interactor [...] (add(od, collection), input_data_received, input_data_produced)
[] output_trigger!True; output_send!update(collection); interactor [..](collection, input_data_received, input_data_produced)
[] input_receive?id:input_data; output_send!feedback(id, collection); interactor [...] (collection, id, input_data_produced)
[] input_trigger!True; input_send!measure(input_data_received); interactor [...] (collection, input_data_received, measure(input_data_received)))
endproc

Thus we can have a specification which indicates clearly the behaviour of an interactor even in terms of its state modification. When the output trigger event occurs then the collection is updated and the result (which is the description of the current presentation of the interactor) is transmitted on the *output_send* gate. When a new input data is received (*id* in the specification), the feedback of it, which is a function depending on the data received and the current collection, is transmitted on the *output_send* gate and then the input data received is stored in the state of the interactor. Finally when an input trigger is received the result of the input function (*measure*) is transmitted on the *input_send* gate and it is stored in the state of the interactor (in the field *input_data_produced*).

We have shown the general model of the dynamic behaviour of an interactor. With a few modifications we can refine it into a wide spectrum of interactions:

- We can have interactors with only the input or the output components.
- We can have interactors without distinctions between the receiving data and the trigger event to indicate when the result of the related processing has to be delivered in the opposite direction. In these cases the are no triggers and

whenever new data is received from a side then automatically the result of the interactor's processing is generated in the opposite site.

- When we present the interactor model, for the sake of simplicity we always only show one gate for each of the six possible types of gates (*input_receive*, *input_send*, *output_receive*, *output_send*, *input_trigger*, *output_trigger*). Actually, a specific interactor can have zero or one or more instances of gates for each possible type. We thus define the arity of an interactor. The *arity* of an interactor is given by six integers, each one indicating the number of gates for the related type used by the interactor to communicate with the outside.
- We can have interactors which are continuously reacting to the user or application-generated events, or interactors which after generated one input data toward the application deactivates themselves.

3. A Task-driven Approach for Modelling Interactor-based Interactive Systems

Now in order to provide a meaningful formal specification of an Interactive System, some phases have to be introduced:

- *A task analysis*, it is important to identify the task which the user has to perform independently from the specific functionality supported by the available systems.
- *A methodology to model the entire Interactive System*, because of their generality, architecture models are often difficult to apply: for example developers often have problems identifying the agents of their systems. This means that indications on how to apply architectural models have to be provided. Our approach is to use the results of task analysis for this purpose, so that we can also ensure that user-related considerations are incorporated into the system.

Figure 2 shows which are the main phases of our approach. We can specify Interactive Systems by a methodology which allows us to perform task-to-interactor associations. This methodology should be defined bearing in mind the architectural model we use and the related operators. Formal specifications of user tasks and corresponding architectural descriptions can be simulated and verified in order to evaluate them. As a result of the evaluation some modifications to the specifications can be performed. The result of the task specification and the architectural model provide the information needed to build the network of interactors which defines the Interactive System at the abstraction level which we are considering. This network can be translated into a programming language for prototyping the user interface.

There are several studies which stress the need to refine complex tasks into smaller tasks, examples are: GOMS (Card et al. 1983), ETAG (Tauber 1990) and TKS (Johnson et al. 1992) approaches. We want to use information produced in the task decomposition for modelling the Interactive System.

The association tasks/interactors can be done either by following in parallel the task decomposition (associating more abstract interactors to more abstract tasks and refining them similarly) or by starting from the final basic tasks, associating them with basic interactors that then have to be composed in order to obtain the entire

Interactive System. We prefer the first approach because in the second case starting with basic interactors (especially when they are in a large number) it is then difficult to identify the best solution for their composition.

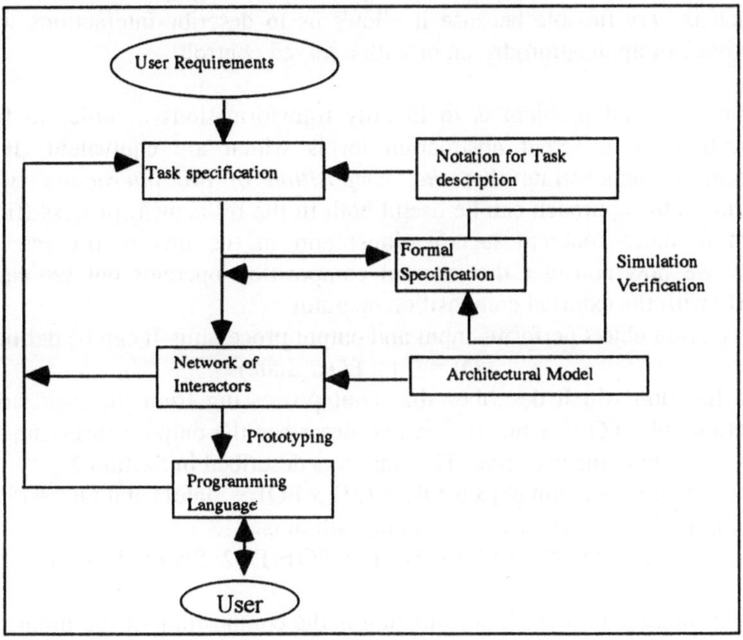

Figure 2: The proposed methodology for designing Interactive Systems.

A first element in the correspondence between tasks and interactors is that *if a temporal ordering is defined among a set of tasks, the same ordering has to be respected by the corresponding interactors.*

In the modelling work one problem is to identify the upper and lower bounds of the possible abstraction levels:

- The lowest abstraction level for interactors is the one where we associate one interactor for each individual physical event which can be generated by the user.
- The highest abstraction level is obtained when we consider the entire system as a unique interactor.

This means that the interactor concept is valid at all the possible abstraction levels.

Among the set of composition operators which have been defined (Paterno' 1994), the two most important are: the external and the internal composition operators. In the former case they allow to describe the global flow of data in the UIS from the application towards the user, in the latter case they allow the description in the inverse way.

The *external composition* allows the result (transmitted by the output_send gate) of the output part of an interactor to be passed to the output part (received by the output_receive gate) of another one, and the *internal composition* which behaves similarly but in the case of the input side of two interactors. At a given time an interactor can be externally or internally composed with several interactors.

The resulting systems are logically organised as a graph of interactors. This approach is very flexible because it allows us to describe interactions which are user-driven, or application-driven or with a mixed control.

Another important problem is to identify transformations in order to transform specifications at different abstraction levels which are equivalent. It is thus important to demonstrate that *the composition of two interactors is still an interactor*. This approach can be useful both in the refinement process (from more abstract to more concrete specifications) and in the inverse process. For this purpose we now consider the internal composition operator but we can reason similarly with the external composition operator.
An Interaction object performs input and output processing. It can be defined as:

$$OI = (FI \times FO \times State)$$

FI is a function which describes the input processing from the user side to the application side. FO is a function which describes the output processing from the application side to the user side. The state was described in Section 2.
If we have two interaction objects $OI1 = (FI1 \times FO1 \times State1)$ and $OI2 = (FI2 \times FO2 \times State2)$, the result of their internal composition is:

$$OI3 = OI1 \circ_{int} OI2 = (FI1 \circ FI2, FO1+FO2, State1+State2)$$

OI3 is an interactor whose input function is the composition of the input functions of the component interactors, and the appearance and state are the sum of the appearance and state of the component interactors. The $\circ$int symbol means that we simply apply the standard function composition between the two functions describing the input parts of the two interactors. For example, let us consider a menu interactor and a cursor interactor. Their internal composition means that the cursor position is passed to the menu which uses this information to select an element, while the appearance is the sum of the menu's appearance (the echoing of the current selected elements) and the cursor's appearance. The appearance of the interactor at the lower level (the cursor) occludes the other (the menu) when they overlap.
This composition of interactors means that at a higher level of abstraction it is possible to see them as a unique interactor receiving the mouse movements and producing the menu-element selected.

This type of transformation can be used recursively in refining an Interactive System in a top-down approach.
Note that the arity of an interactor depends on the abstraction level considered: for example if we consider the level of user-generated events then an interactor (which moves an object by pressing and moving the cursor) has 2 as input_receive arity, but if we consider a more abstract level we can say that the interactor has the drag event as input which is an abstraction for the two lower level events.

4. Relationships between Interactional and Architectural Descriptions

An *Interactional* description of an Interactive System is a description in terms of possible user actions and system feedback. An *Architectural* description indicates also what are the possible basic components of the part controlling the user interface. An interesting notation for the specification of user interfaces is the UAN notation (Hartson & Gray 1992). UAN is a task-oriented notation which focuses on the dynamic behaviour of the user interface but it does not indicate how to model the underlying software system which has to support the indicated human-computer interactions. In UAN more complex tasks are built up by using basic tasks. A basic task is described by user actions, the interface feedback and, where necessary, the interface state and the connections to computation.

We can analyse UAN by considering how the generic interactor can be codified in the UAN notation (Table 1) and thus we can also show how the UAN approach can be linked to our architectural model. The task supported by an interactor is mainly identified by the data produced in the *input_send* gate because on this gate the information for modifying the application state in order to perform the task is transmitted.

Actually we use a modified version of UAN as in the notation the rows should be read in a sequential way from top to bottom while in our description they should be read in an alternative way in the sense that there is a continuous possible choice among the initial events belonging to different rows. When a row is started to be executed then it has to be finished and then all the rows are newly available.

Usually user actions are divided into *input_trigger* and *input_receive* (sometimes the *output_trigger* can be generated by a user's action as well, for example in a pop-up menu). Even if the input trigger may be generated by the application in a polling behaviour. The interface feedback is used to visualise echoing of the input data received and the modifications of the state of the output part and the state of the input part (for example in a menu the element currently indicated by the last position of the cursor is highlighted by inverting foreground and background colours; the state of the output part is information used for the visualisation of the menu; and the state of the input part is indicated by putting a symbol beside the last element transmitted toward the application). While in UAN rows have to be read from left to right (which means they describe before the user actions and then their effects) in our case we accept exceptions as in the last row of Table 1 and 2 which have to be read from right to left because describe an interaction which is application-driven. In Tables 1 and 2 we consider the case where triggers are generated by the users.

If we consider a specific interactor such as a pop-up menu, obtained from the general model by providing actual gates, this description becomes:

TASK Generic Basic Task			
USER ACTIONS	INTERFACE FEEDBACK	INTERFACE STATE	CONNECTION TO COMPUTATION
Input_receive	Output_send	New_input_data	
Input_trigger	Output_send	New_input_result	Input_send
Ouput_trigger	Output_send		
		New_collection	Output_receive

Table 1: The UAN description of the general model of an interactor.

The UAN approach is interesting but it only aims to derive an interactional description of a user interface (a description in terms of user actions and system feedback) from task decomposition. This is useful especially as documentation of existing software in order to understand how to interact with it and for communication between designers and developers. But if the current goal is to develop new software then an architectural description is needed in order to indicate how to model the Interactive System terms of basic components and how to connect them.

TASK Select_element_from_a_list_of_elements of_the_same_class			
USER ACTIONS	INTERFACE FEEDBACK	INTERFACE STATE	CONNECTION TO COMPUTATION
Move_cursor	Echo_current_element	New_current_element	
Button_release	Echo_selected_element	New_selected_element	Generate_new_data
Button_press	Visualise interactor		
		New_menu description	Receive_menu

Table 2: A UAN Description of a pop-up menu described by the interactor model.

From this architectural description it is then possible to obtain an interactional description similar to that obtained in the UAN approach by indicating the user actions and the system feedback related to performing the tasks considered.

5. An Example of Application of the Proposed Methodology

Now we discuss an example in order to show our methodology to build a user interface based on interactors following a top-down approach. We start by considering the goal of managing a document with a word processor. At this more abstract level a complex task needs to be decomposed into smaller tasks by trying to identify their temporal ordering: selecting file; editing; printing; saving. Each of these sub-tasks can be further refined. For example selecting a file entails providing the related command and, if the file already exists, indicating its name; editing is done by adding and deleting text (using the keyboard or the mouse) and so on.

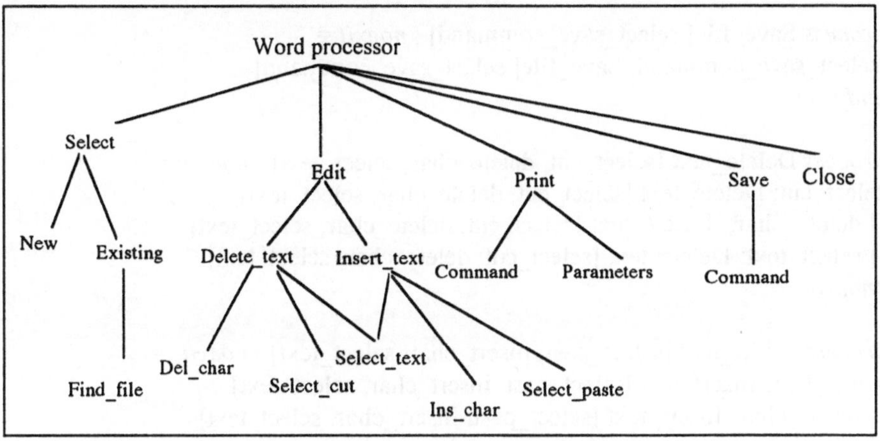

Figure 3: A possible task decomposition in the word processor example.

Figure 3 shows how in the example we can have task decomposition in the word processor example but it does not show the temporal relationships among tasks which are indicated in the specification. In the tree-like organisation of tasks, a subtask is child of another task when it is present in the father's definition. More precisely, the specification of the word processor task (Figure 3) in LOTOS is:

Select_file[...] >> (Edit_file[...] ||| Print_file[...] ||| Save_file[...]) [> Close [...]
where
process Select_file[select_selection_file, select_new_file, select_existing_file, find_ex_file] : *exit*:=
select_selection_file; (select_new_file; *exit*
[] select_existing_file; *exit* >> Find_file[find_ex_file])
endproc

process Find_file[find_ex_file] : *exit* :=
find_ex_file; *exit*
endproc

process Edit_file[select_cut, select_past, select_text, delete_char, insert_char] : *noexit*:=
Delete_text [select_cut, delete_char, select_text] ||| Insert_text [select_past, insert_char, select_text]
endproc

process Print_file[select_print_command, select_parameters, send_command] : *noexit* :=
select_print_command; select_parameters; send_command; Print_file[...]
endproc

process Save_file[select_save_command] : *noexit*:=
select_save_command; Save_file[select_save_command]
endproc

process Delete_text [select_cut, delete_char, select_text] : *noexit*:=
select_cut; Delete_text [select_cut, delete_char, select_text]
[] delete_char; Delete_text [select_cut, delete_char, select_text]
[] select_text; Delete_text [select_cut, delete_char, select_text]
endproc

process Insert_text [select_past, insert_char, select_text] : *noexit* :=
select_text; Insert_text [select_past, insert_char, select_text]
[] insert_char; Insert_text [select_past, insert_char, select_text]
[] select_past; Insert_text [select_past, insert_char, select_text]
endproc

process Close [quit_wp] : *exit* :=
quit_wp; *exit*
endproc

This specification indicates that the general task of managing a document is performed by firstly selecting a file. When the selection task is completed we can continuously edit, print and save it until the user wishes to close the session. The actions which define the editing, the printing and the saving tasks can be performed in interleaving mode (any ordering among these actions is allowed). We can notice that the Select_text task is used within both the Delete_text and the Insert_text tasks. In fact tasks can be considered as abstract modules which can be used within other tasks.

Then we take the specification of the more abstract tasks (select file, edit file, print file, save_file), we can consider it as the requirements for identifying the interactors needed to perform the given tasks and the dynamic relationships among these interactors and we obtain the following abstract architectural specification graphically represented in Figure 4. The interactor associated with the selection of a file allows the user to provide a request to the functional core which returns the selected file to the interactor dedicated to editing the file which has been activated in the meanwhile. This interactor receives requests from the user in order to modify the current text. When the print command is selected the state of the interactor with the text is transmitted to the printer (the result of the Print interactor can be considered as an output trigger for the edit interactor). Similarly when the save command is selected the content of the file is transmitted to the functional core for storing in the file system (the result of the save interactor can be considered as an input trigger for the Edit interactor).

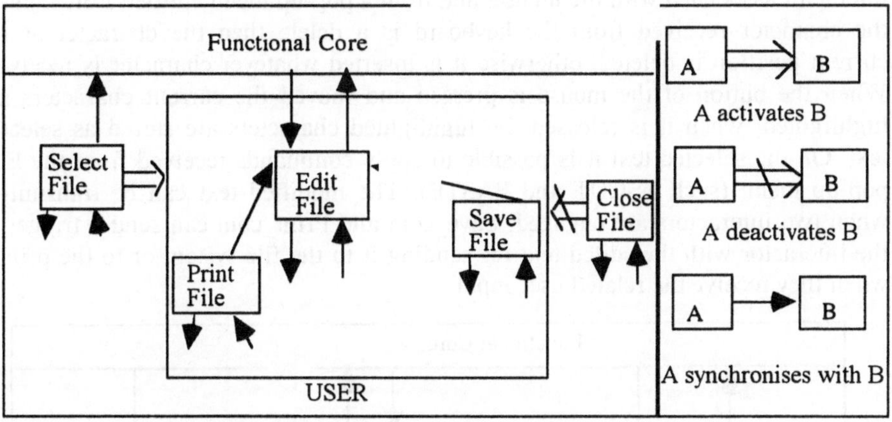

Figure 4: The refinement in Interactors of the first levels of tasks.

At this level we have transformed the specification of the tasks into a corresponding specification of interactors where the interactors are used to indicate an abstract architecture following our model but without indicating how to implement these interactors.
One element introduced in this level of the system specification, which was not present in the task specification, is the need to explicitly indicate on which gates processes synchronise in order to describe the information flow among the related software components.
The specification of each specific interactor is obtained by providing the actual gates of the considered interactors which replace those in the general definition or in one of its possible small variations.

Then we can refine the specification of the architectural description of a text processing following the task refinement by identifying specific instances of interactors supporting the basic tasks. Each abstract interactor which was previously identified is refined into one or more interactors specifying specific interaction techniques. As given a basic task we can have different interactors able to support it, at this time the designer has to make a choice from sets of task-equivalent interaction objects to support the current basic tasks. Each task-oriented class of equivalence among interactors is identified by the information which is required to be delivered towards the application for modifying its state in order to fulfil the task.
In our example the association among basic tasks and interactors can be performed as follows (see Figure 5). There is a pop-up menu entitled File by which the user can indicate whether the file to open is new or not. If it is not new the name of the file to edit is provided by a dialogue interactor which communicates with the file system in order to require the current version of the file with the given name and

this is then passed to the interactor which manages the editing of the file. This can receive input data from the interactor associated with the keyboard, from the interactor associated with the mouse, and from a pop-up menu entitled Edit_com. If the character received from the keyboard is a delete then the character at the current position is deleted, otherwise it is inserted whatever character is received. When the button of the mouse is pressed and moved the current characters are highlighted, when it is released the highlighted characters are stored as selected text. On the selected text it is possible to apply commands received from the Edit pop-up menu (such as CUT and PASTE). The modified text can be transmitted when two interactors are engaged: Save_com and Print_com can send a trigger to the interactor with the edited text for sending it to the file system or to the printer when they receive the related user input.

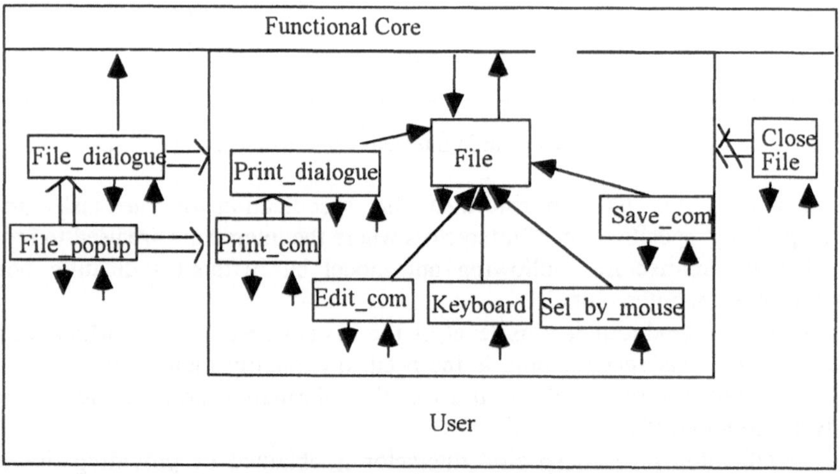

Figure 5: The architecture of the resulting Interactor-based implementation.

We have thus obtained the specification of the implementation of a word processor. You can note that the temporal constraints indicated in the LOTOS specification of the user tasks are maintained in the corresponding architectural specification graphically represented in Figure 5. In fact, for example at the end of the interaction for selecting a file the set of interactors used for editing it are activated, and they remain active until the user interacts with the close interactor. In the meanwhile interactors allow the user to edit, print or save the file without any restriction in the ordering of the actions.

As users can find the LOTOS descriptions difficult to interpret and they usually want to understand how the system behaves in terms of user actions and system feedback we can extract the information needed to obtain a UAN-like description of the user interface: Table 3 shows an example for the task of editing a file from the LOTOS specification of the specific interactors which make up the system. The elements in Table 3 are obtained by using the approach shown in Table 1.

TASK	Editing Document		
USER ACTIONS	INTERFACE FEEDBACK	INTERFACE STATE	CONNECTION TO COMPUTATION
Press_delete_key	Delete_last_char	Delete_last_char	
Press_key	Insert_new_char	Insert_new_char	
Button_down	Echo_current_text		
Button_up		Set_selected_text	
Select_Cut	Cut_selected_text	Cut_selected_text	
Select_Paste	Paste_selected_text	Paste_selected_text	
Select_Print	Print_file		
Select_Save			Send_to_file-system

Table 3: The description of the interactor performing editing of text.

6. Conclusions

This paper introduces a methodology for designing architectures of Interactive Systems based on requirements provided by task decomposition. We introduce a more abstract description of the interactor model in order to reason better on networks of interactors. We also define transformations in order to compose and refine interactors. This provides a way to pass through different but equivalent abstraction levels.

We show how it is possible to obtain specifications of systems which reflect the users' view of the application functionality starting from a task analysis and specification, and using it for driving the modelling of the basic components in order to obtain the specification of the corresponding abstract architecture and implementation. All the different levels of specifications are performed by using the same formal notation (LOTOS).

Relationships among interactional and architectural descriptions of Interactive Systems are described as these two types of descriptions are both important and useful but for different purposes.

Finally, we provide an example of this methodology to specify a word processor at three levels: tasks, abstract interactors, and concrete interactors.

We think that this methodology can improve the practice in software development of Interactive Systems because it can help designers and developers to structure the specification of their systems, to identify basic components and to specify temporal ordering among them.

We can also obtain software easier to use for final users because it is modelled following their view of the logical organisation of the functionality to support.

The methodology has also been used for more large-scale examples such as a Geographical Information System, a Multimodal Interactive System for providing requests to a flights data base (Paterno' & Mezzanotte, 1994) and the user interface for an air traffic controller (Paterno' & Mezzanotte, 1995). Further work will be dedicated to identify precisely the rules to transform task specifications into architectural specifications in order to make the methodology proposed more easy to apply for developers and designers.

Acknowledgements

I wish to thank colleagues from the Esprit BRA 7040 Amodeus II, System Modelling Research Package, for helpful discussions. Many thanks also to British Council and C.N.R. for their support to the visit at the Department of Computer Science of University of York during which this work has been completed.

Chapter 7: Key Activities for a Development Methodology of Interactive Applications

François Bodar, Anne-Marie Hennebert,
Jean-Marie Leheureux, Isabelle Provot,
Jean Vanderdonckt & Giovanni Zucchinetti

1. Introduction

User Interface (UI) development tools (e.g., toolboxes, user interface management systems), design guides and guidelines provide essential support for interactive systems development, but they are not enough in isolation, since no fruitful outcome of an interactive application development process can be guaranteed. Ideally, development methodologies for interactive business applications should combine searching analyses of business processes, with design models and appropriate development tools that impose structure on development and guarantee high quality solutions, in both their technical and ergonomic aspects. This ideal may be utopian. A more feasible and profitable goal is for a methodology's phases to satisfy some minimal properties. Such properties require key activities to be integrated into development methodologies for interactive systems. Each activity can ensure coherent integration of the outputs of different phases, preserving these through subsequent phases without loss of information, yet entailing no further work. Each activity supports the convergence of development phases at a satisfactory solution.

2. A Methodological Framework

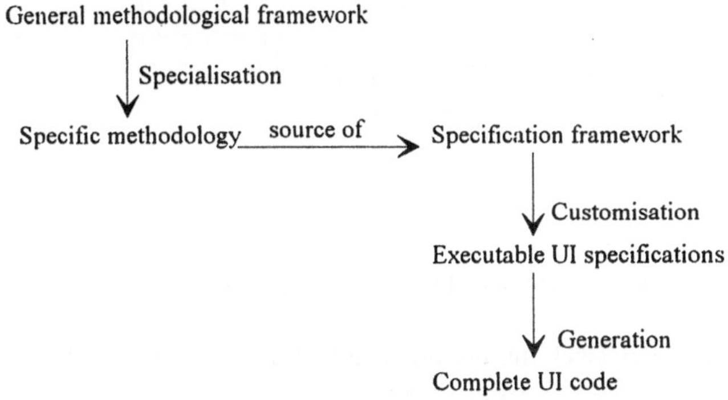

Figure 1. Structure of TRIDENT methodology.

The methodological framework developed on the TRIDENT project had to be informal. Task analysis, model specification and tool use are all overlapped within the framework of a methodology that supports a wide range of design situations and also provides a design space. The aim is to provide a general framework that covers various interaction styles (e.g., menu selection, form filling, command language, direct manipulation, multi-windowing) and dialogue structures (e.g., synchronous, asynchronous, multi-threaded dialogues).

This general framework can be specialised to produce a specific methodological framework. The specialisation produces a design space that is specific to a given class of problems. This design space replaces the full range of different groups of user interface design options with the narrower choice of one group of option (Figure 1). The specific methodology can also be used to generate a specification framework. This in turn can be customised to produce executable UI specifications allowing to generate the code of the interactive application (Figure 1).

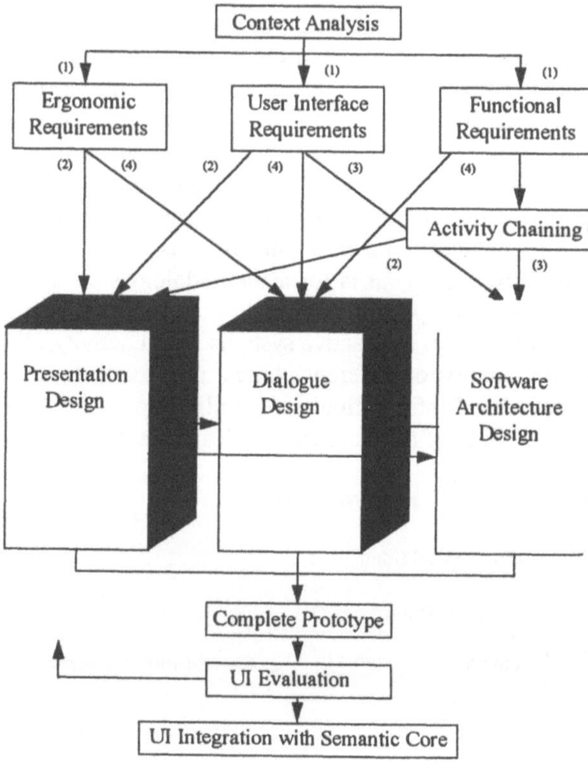

Figure 2. Structure of TRIDENT methodological framework.

The structure of TRIDENT methodological framework is due to five key activities. Each is described in the following sections :

1. forming UI specifications from the output of task analysis (section 3);
2. guiding presentation design using ergonomic rules (section 4);
3. deriving a software architecture from task analysis and presentation components (section 5);
4. forming high level dialogue specification from the output of task analysis (section 6);
5. transforming the methodological framework into a specification framework (section 7);

Figure 2 outlines the main parts of TRIDENT methodology. We will show throughout this paper how suggested key activities are set along this general structure.

3. Activity 1: Forming User Interface Specifications from the Output of Task Analysis

Starting from an extensive context analysis (task analysis, user stereotypes and workplace description) (MacLeod & Bevan 1993), our goal is to define a systematic approach for specifying UI components from this contextual information (see « 1 » arrows on Figure 2). Such a systematic approach should ensure preservation of information between development phases, and thus we express contextual information using concepts and formalisms that are appropriate for UI designers.

3.1 Task Analysis

A *task* is defined as any activity carried out by an operator (often named user) that results into a significant state change in a given activity domain in a given contextual situation. Hierarchical task analysis (Shepherd 1989) could be appropriate for highly-structured tasks, but event-driven analysis (Frese & Zapf 1994) or constraint-based approaches (Figarol & Javaux 1993) may be more effective for weakly structured tasks, whether they are simple or complex.

Though we will limit the scope of this paper to hierarchical task analysis (we currently use TKS (Johnson 1991) method for this type of task), weakly structured tasks will be addressed in future work since such tasks dominate interaction with decision support systems. Task analysis will therefore be expanded to event-driven analysis and constraint-based approach in order to compare both their outputs and the UI components that are derived from these outputs.

In hierarchical task analysis, the significant state change of domain activity is related to a main goal. A *goal* is a particular state of the domain to be fulfilled. A goal explains why a particular task should be carried out. Any goal could be decomposed recursively into smaller units called *sub-goals*. Each sub-goal consists of any intermediary state of the main goal through which the user should pass. This approach includes three steps :

1. *identifying goals and sub-goals*: this identification is achieved by asking specific questions, by examining documents produced by the organisation, by interview, by basic protocol,...
   This step produces a hierarchical decomposition of the task into sub-goals.
2. *identifying procedures*: a task is decomposed into *procedures*, too. A *procedure* establishes an observable and executable behaviour which is the combination of actions on objects resulting from a particular state of the domain activity. Some procedures are qualified according to the level of their constituting actions: *sub-task*, *intermediary*, or *action*. A set of identification criteria is to be considered for this purpose. The action level is the last level in

the hierarchy, leading to only one action. The sub-task level is a privileged level in the hierarchy since it satisfies special properties resulting from the action combination. Other levels (between task and sub-task, between sub-task and action) are the intermediary levels ; they do not have any special status.

This identification is achieved by asking specific questions, by filling questionnaires, by card sorting, by observation, by basic protocol,... (Shepherd 1989)

This step produces a hierarchical decomposition of an interactive task into procedures, a definition of inter-procedure relationships (e.g., sequence, iteration, parallelism, concurrence) with the links between procedures and sub-goals.

3. *identifying objects and actions related to the task*: each action handles one or several *objects*. An object designates any abstract or concrete entity belonging to the domain activity, which is related to one or many actions within one or many procedures. Each object possesses a predefined set of properties depending on the activity domain.

   This step produces a list of task objects linked with their relationships and their actions.

3.2 Expressing the Product of Task Analysis

3.2.1 Writing an Object-Oriented Entity-Relationship Model

Task analysis not only produces task objects and actions (as in TKS (Johnson 1991)), but also identifies relationships between objects (e.g., is-a, is-member-of, has-a, is-used-by, is-a-group) and relationships between actions (e.g., sequential, parallel, deterministic or non-deterministic alternative, interleaved, repetition, disable). Objects produced by task analysis and their relationships are further specified in a schema based on an object-oriented entity-relationship model (Rumbaugh et al. 1991). It describes not only simple entities and semantic n-ary relationships with attributes, but also complex entities defined as aggregates of entities and/or semantic relationships between entities. Similarly, any attribute from any entity or relationship can itself form a new entity. This schema is supposed to fill the gap between the cognitive universe of the task analyst and the conceptual world of the software engineer. This schema can be obtained as follows :

- entities and attributes come from the list of task objects with their relationships;
- relationships come from object relationships: they include inheritance, aggregation, and semantic relationships of the activity domain.

3.2.2 Identification of Semantic Functions of the Application

Task analysis produces actions that deal with task objects. These task concepts should be transformed into concepts that are relevant to software engineering (i.e., functions that deal with entities/relationships attributes. For this purpose, actions

identified during task analysis are modified in accordance with software properties (e.g., precision, completeness, consistency, redundancy, generalisation) in order to get functional specifications of the application.
This critical process transforms actions into functions by abstraction mechanism based on both generalisation and consolidation (Figure 3). For example, actions that are performed on objects possessing common slots can become a more general function dealing with two entities. These functions will become methods attached to the application objects according to object-oriented programming.

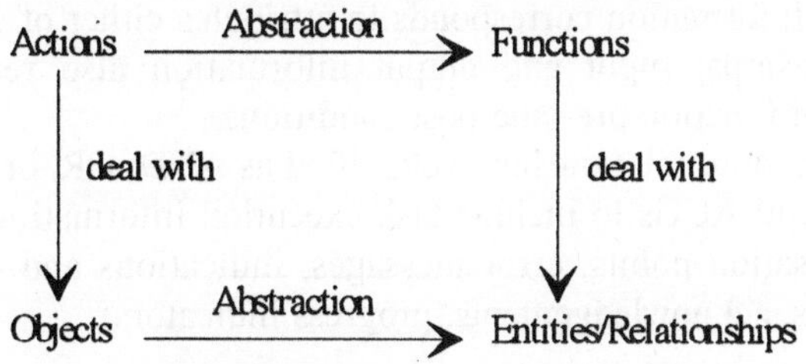

Figure 3. The abstraction mechanism.

3.2.3 Constructing an Activity Chaining Graph

After having described static task aspects, dynamic aspects remain to be further detailed. This task behaviour model can be graphically represented with an *activity chaining graph* (ACG). This ACG institutes a contract between the programmer who is responsible for the semantic functions of the application and the designer who is responsible of the UI (Petoud & Pigneur 1989a, Petoud & Pigneur 1989b, Petoud 1990, Provot 1993).
It expresses the information flow between functions to be executed for achieving the main goal associated with an interactive task. From the graph theory viewpoint, this graph is a 1-graph without loops, that is simple.

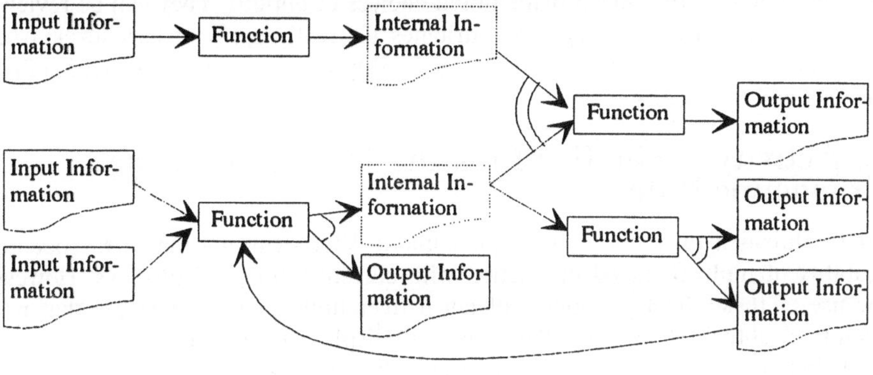

Figure 4. Example of Activity Chaining Graph.

The ACG is exemplified in Figure 4. Each function receives input information, representing data required for the good execution of the function. Each function receives input information, produces output information which are either external (to the user) or internal (to another function). External information input to a function must come from an interactive dialogue. External information output from a function must go to an interactive display. Input and output information can be related using OR (no arc of a circle), AND (simple arc) or XOR (double arc) links.

An ACG is constructed as follows:

- the elementary input and output information is determined for each identified function: this information corresponds to attributes either of entities or of associated relationships; input and output information also respectively support specification of function pre- and post-conditions.
- each inter-procedure relationship is classified as AND, OR, or XOR;

We intend to extend ACGs to include task execution information such as decision points, synchronisation points, error messages, indications and dialogue information (e.g., prompts, acknowledgements, progress indicators).

3.2.4 Derivation of Dialogue Attributes

For each interactive task, an appropriate (hybrid) dialogue style should be selected. This choice could be guided by a table that mapped task, user and workplace characteristics to a (hybrid) dialogue style.

(Hybrid) dialogue styles are examples of design options and their principled selection is the first example of restricted choice within our methodological framework.

For each interactive task, four dialogue attributes are derived from these interaction styles: a dialogue mode (sequential, asynchronous, or mixed), a dialogue control (internal, external, or mixed), a function triggering mode (automatic, implicit or explicit manual, displayed or not) and a metaphor (conversation based, universe based or both). These four attributes are introducing four new design options to be considered. They usually have their own default value according to the chosen interaction styles.

Default dialogue attributes provide initial choices of options. They can be reviewed for specific subtasks, although the attributes for really apply at task level, where they can provide UI consistency and compatibility with the ergonomic needs of both the user and their tasks.

4. Activity 2: Guiding Presentation Design Using Ergonomic Rules

Single threaded interaction with alphanumeric VDUs can not match the potential usability of multi-threaded interaction with current bitmapped displays. However, the use of these displays alone will not deliver high quality interfaces that users want to be able do their work. This is why all display layouts must be considered by the judicious use of ergonomic rules (or guidelines).

The ergonomic rules that guide the design of display layouts must not be restricted to considerations of the physics of human perception. However, the many advantages of such guidelines are dependent on intelligent interpretation of cognitive

psychology principles (Miyata & Norman 1986), in order to adjust them for specific task contexts and design situations.
To address this shortcoming, a pre-defined set of domain relevant ergonomic rules should be extracted: here, the area of business applications is considered.
The goal of this activity is to find a systematic approach for specifying UI presentation components on a pre-defined set of ergonomic rules in order

- to meet ergonomic criteria that are relevant to the task;
- to drive this process with computer-aided active and intelligent tools (see « 2 » arrows on Figure 2).

4.1 Presentation Content

UI presentation can be decomposed using the following four concepts:

- *concrete interaction object* (CIO): this is a real object belonging to the UI world that any user can manipulate such as a push button, a list box, a check box. A CIO is simple if it cannot be decomposed into smaller CIOs. A CIO is composite if it can de decomposed into smaller units;
- *abstract interaction object* (AIO): this consists of an abstraction of all CIOs from both presentation and behavioural viewpoints that are independent of target environments;
- *window*: this is a root window either considered as a logical window for AIOs or corresponding to a physical window, a dialogue box or a panel for CIOs. Every window is itself a composite AIO at logical level or CIO at physical level, composed of other simple or composite AIOs/CIOs. All windows are geographically delimited on the user's screen;
- *presentation unit* (PU): this comprises of an input/output facilities required for execution of specific sub-tasks. Each presentation unit can be decomposed into one or many windows which may not be all displayed on the screen simultaneously. Each PU is composed by at least one window called the *basic window* from which other windows are chained.

4.2 Systematic Approach for Specifying Presentation

The approach here defines a presentation by iterative refinement starting from global objects to end with simple objects according to the structure reproduced in Figure 5.
The steps of this approach are the following :

- *Identification of PUs*: each sub-task of the interactive task is mapped onto a PU. This mapping is achieved by a series of sub-task identification criteria (for instance, a different work skill). Since the ACG graphically represents the function chaining within a particular task, a PU can correspond to a sub-graph of the ACG that can be drawn graphically distinguished on the ACG (Figure 6).
- *Identification of windows*: for each sub-graph associated with a PU, partitioning into sub-sub-graphs identifies windows of the PU. Correct identification of these windows requires the application of precise ergonomic rules to ensure satisfaction of several ergonomic criteria (e.g., compatibility, work load, guidance)

(Vanderdonckt 1994). With this done, designers then know which functions will be triggered from the window, and thus which inputs and outputs must be associated with the window. Like PUs, windows correspond to sub-graphs of the ACG and can again be graphically distinguished (Figure 6).

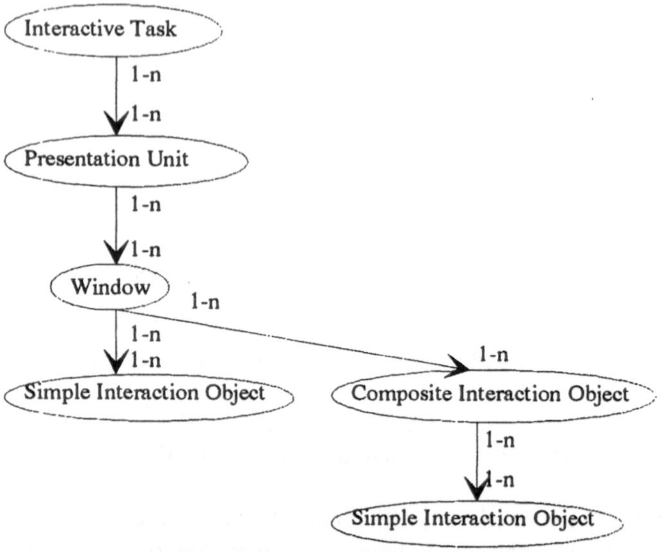

Figure 5. Structure of presentation.

- *Selection of AIOs*: each identified window can be associated with a physical window, a dialogue box or a panel ; within each window, each piece of input and output information is mapped to a simple or composite AIO (e.g., a text widget), as are functions (e.g., to push buttons or icons). Elementary information is always mapped onto a simple AIO. Composite information is mapped onto a composite AIO resulting in a hierarchy of simple AIOs. Similarly, a PU is completely defined by a hierarchy of windows.

  Selection of AIOs is supported by a set of selection rules with a scope exceeding the simple physical emphasis of style guides (Shneiderman 1992). The rules are initially based on empirically validated cognitive principles. They are subsequently specialised in accordance with user's habits and established conventions. Within the scope of TRIDENT project methodology, the process of selecting AIOs consists of:
  - an initial proposed set of AIOs is generated automatically from the specification contained in the object-oriented entity-relationship model (Siochi & Hartson 1989): for example, an edit box is selected for two digit positive integer;
  - a second step extends the initially proposed AIOs on the basis of information attributes: for example, a scale is preferred when this integer is a value bounded in a specific range;
  - a third step modifies the extended AIOs on the basis of user and domain

preference (e.g., a thermometer is useful in medicine).

This selection process is supported by an expert system containing about 300 rules (Bodart & Vanderdonckt 1994). The expert system is:

- interactive because one or many AIOs are presented to the user within the scope of the three steps mentioned above;
- visual because the different alternatives are visually displayed on the screen to develop the developer's understanding;
- able to explain choices with full reference to benefits/shortcomings, enabling the designer to refine the decision by enlarging his/her own knowledge.

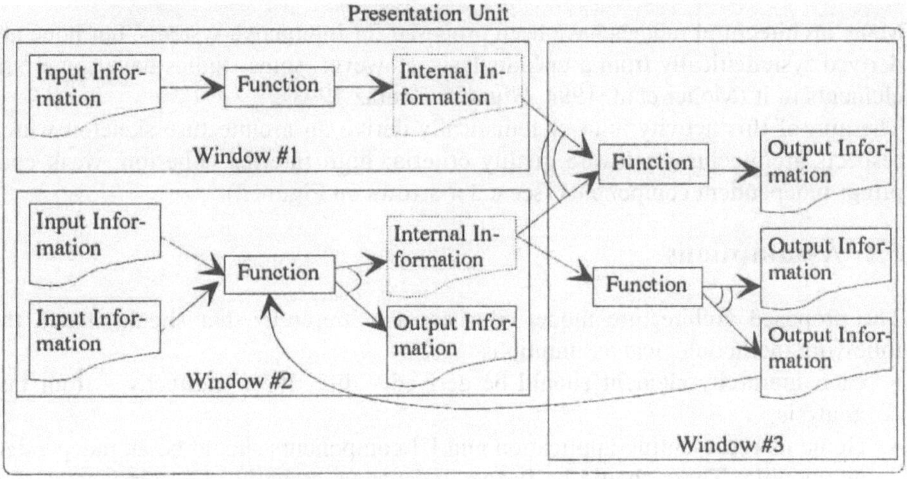

Figure 6. Overlapping of a PU with its three windows onto the ACG.

- Transformation of AIOs into CIOs: the complete PU hierarchy is automatically transformed into a hierarchy of CIOs depending on the particular target environment in which the designer is working. Simple and composite AIOs are mapped respectively to simple and composite CIOs.
- *Placement of CIOs*: the co-ordinates of CIOs are calculated precisely for each window by applying placement strategies (Bodart & al. 1994a). These strategies include visual design principles for three aspects: localisation, scaling, and arrangement. At the end of this step, each PU hierarchy is completed with relevant positions.

  Within the scope of the TRIDENT project methodology, the process of placing CIOs is computer-aided by two placement strategies :

  1. a static strategy that places CIOs according to a predefined layout grid (Bodart & al. 1994a); this strategy allows a completely automatic generation of placement within each window;
  2. a dynamic strategy that places CIOs according to heuristics (Bodart & al. 1994a) that let visual designers control the generated layout of each window.

  Using ergonomic rules is believed to encourage presentation aesthetics, but does not lead inevitably to a perfect result under every circumstances. We claim that only a multiple-strategy approach is useful in the long-term. Other placement strategies, whether they are automatic or computer-aided, can also be investigated.

- *Editing presentation*: once all CIOs have been placed into composite CIOs, they can be read into a graphical presentation editor. Direct manipulation of CIOs lets designer tailor the presentation to user's needs, in part by attending aspects ignored during the above selection and placement.

5. Activity 3: Deriving a Software Architecture from Task Analysis and Presentation Components

Many architectural models have been proposed for interactive systems, but none are derived systematically from a task analysis. However, some studies have some task elements in it (Moher et al. 1994, Nigay & Coutaz 1993).
The aim of this activity is to systematically derive an architecture skeleton which respects architectural software quality criteria: high internal cohesion; weak coupling; independent components (see « 3 » arrows on Figure 2).

5.1 Assumptions

The proposed architecture model consists of a hierarchy that should match the following methodological assumptions :

- each hierarchy element should be derived - directly or indirectly - from task analysis;
- elements representing application and UI components should be as independent as possible. There should be further independence within UI components, i.e., between dialogue subcomponents (which realise behaviour) and presentation subcomponents (which realise appearance) (Bodart & Pigneur 1989, Petoud 1990).

The latter assumptions are possible for business oriented applications, since generally there is no semantic role for the interaction objects.

5.2 Content of the Model

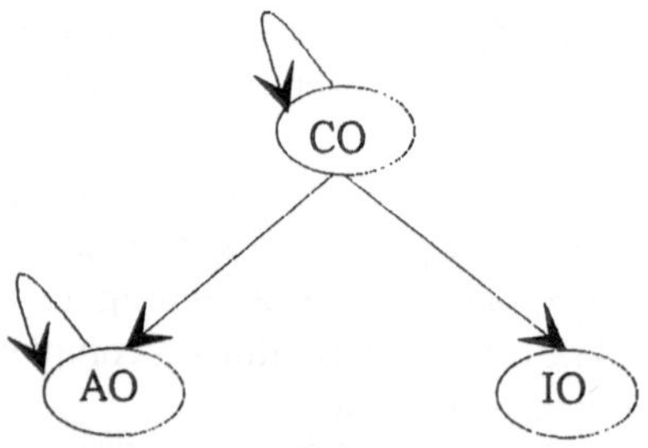

Figure 7. Generic scheme of the architecture model.

The proposed architecture model (Bodart & Provot 1989, Bodart et al. 1993) consists of a hierarchy of generic elements illustrated in Figure 7.

There are three classes of object in this architectural model. Each is distinguished, as follows :

1. The *Control Objects* (CO) class is generic with instances decomposed into COs of different types that both manage dialogue and preserve the correspondence between application data and the presentation. Each CO has a specific behaviour that combines management of a portion of the dialogue and some application-presentation correspondences. A rule-based language (Bodart & Provot 1989, Bodart et al. 1993) configures CO behaviour in *scripts* that have a partial graphical representation as state transition diagrams.
2. The *Application Objects* (AO) class is not generic: instances cannot be decomposed, since they represent the application functions.
3. The *Interaction Objects* (IO) class is generic and provides two types of CIOs: application-dependent CIOs that translate input and output information for functions; and application-independent CIOs that are required for a dialogue (e.g., command buttons that trigger functions).

Identical rules for behaviour and interaction apply to all these three object classes. Similarly, identical relationships link any pair of these from these three objects: each object is an *agent* (Baecker & Buxton 1987, Bodart & Provot 1989).
Objects are composed in a hierarchy where parent objects "use" child objects, as follows:

- child objects send events related to signal behaviour states to their parent;
- parent objects obtain the information needed for the next interaction step by calling a child object's primitive methods.

5.2.1 Application Objects (AO)

Each function in the ACG has a single corresponding AO. Where an existing function is to be re-used, but is not implemented in an object-oriented language, it must be encapsulated in a AO, when it becomes one of the AO's methods. Otherwise, the AO should be implemented in an object-oriented language. Every AO should be the child of one (and only one) CO (i.e., the CO-Fc as we will see in next subsection), which becomes responsible for the execution of the corresponding function.

5.2.2 Control Objects (CO)

There should be a CO in the hierarchy for every composition in the presentation. The composition of the presentation encourages autonomy for windows, which are linked dynamically into PUs. These PUs realise the context for execution of an interactive task. The CO hierarchy is thus built according to our presentation structure (Figure 5), and thus four types of CO result (Hennebert 1994):

- CO-IT: the lonely control object corresponding to the interactive task;
- CO-PU: the control objects corresponding to the presentation units;
- CO-W: the control objects corresponding to the windows;
- CO-Fc: the control objects corresponding to the application functions.

The resulting structure is shown in Figure 8.

Every CO corresponding to an application function (CO-Fc) is a child object of the window control object (CO-W) that holds all CIOs required to trigger the function from the functional machine. The set of AOs and corresponding CO-Fc's forms the *functional machine* (Petoud & Pigneur 1989a), where Co-Fc's mirror the business activities represented in the ACG by the way they chain functions.

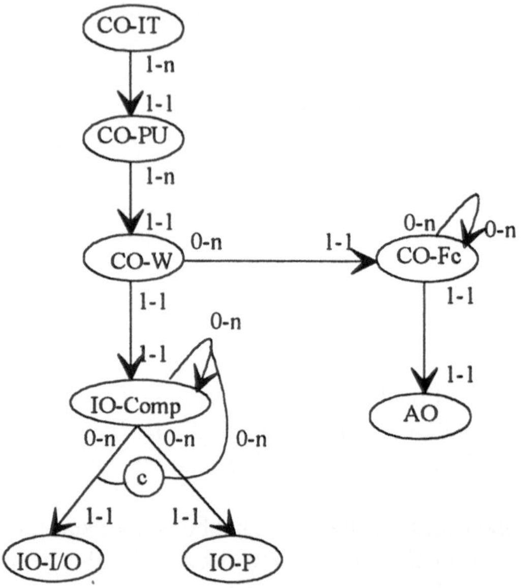

Figure 8. Structure of Control Objects.

5.2.3 *Interaction Objects (IO)*

According to Figure 5, presentation is structured into simple and composite IOs. *Composite IOs* (IO-Comp) are all IOs corresponding to logical windows (e.g., dialogue boxes, physical windows, panels) or any grouping of simple IOs (e.g., child dialogue boxes, group boxes). IO-Comp use simple IOs for creating the UI's presentation: as *input-output interaction objects* (IO-I/O, e.g., an edit box, radio button, check box); or as *presentation interaction objects* (P-IO, e.g., push buttons, icons). IOs are selected by an expert system on the basis of several parameters. They correspond to specific toolkit CIOs in physical environments like Ms-Windows, OSF/Motif. IOs are always children of CO-W control objects, to which they send events representing significant state changes. Primitive IO methods pass relevant values to parent objects. These primitive methods tend to be native to specific toolkits.

5.2.4 *Inter-Object Relations*

- In CO-IT→CO-PU interactions, the dynamic chaining of PUs is managed by the CO-IT, which loads and unloads - sequentially or concurrently - a particular PU_i

according to events received from a PU_j.

- In CO-PU→CO-W interactions, the dynamic chaining of windows is managed by the CO-PU, which displays and undisplays - with tiling or overlapping - a particular window W_i according to events received from another window W_j.
- In CO-W→CO-Fc interactions, the CO-W calls the CO-Fc in order to call a semantic function, when all data required by the function to be performed are available in the child objects of the CO-W. The CO-Fc is the control object which is responsible for the final call of function contained in AO. On completion of processing, CO-Fc's send an event to their CO-W.
- In CO-Fc→AO interactions, the CO-Fc are responsible for the final triggering of functions contained in AOs. A CO-W object calls a function when all required information is input, but the final triggering will be effective only if all triggering conditions expressed in the ACG are fulfilled, that is if all termination events have been sent and internal information has been transmitted. The corresponding CO-Fc only verifies the complete pre-condition before executing the function.
- In recursive CO-Fc interactions, CO-Fc's exchange events to maintain ACG dynamics and to exchange information by calling on each others services.
- In IO (for IO-I/O or IO-P) and CO-W interactions, the parent object polls children to find out what users have input, and in turn send events to their parents that indicate their contents.

5.3 Systematic Approach to Hierarchy Building

We assume that task analysis (subsection 3.1), constructing an ACG (sub-subsection 3.2.3), the development of the functional machine (sub-subsection 5.2.1) and the definition of presentation (sub-subsection 5.2.3) are all completed (Hennebert 1994).

5.3.1 List of Hierarchy Objects

Here, we summarize the complete list of objects of the three kinds. It holds:

- a control object corresponding to the interactive task (CO-IT);
- a control object corresponding to each presentation unit ($CO\text{-}PU_1,\ldots,CO\text{-}PU_n$);
- a control object corresponding to each window of each presentation unit ($CO\text{-}PU_1F_1,\ldots, CO\text{-}PU_1F_m,\ldots,CO\text{-}PU_nF_1,\ldots CO\text{-}PU_nF_p$);
- a control object for each function in the ACG (CO-Fc);
- an interaction object for each input/output information for all functions (IO-I/O);
- an interaction object for each object induced by the presentation (IO-P).

5.3.2 Relationships Between Hierarchy Objects

"Uses" relationships linking the different objects can be systematically created as follows:

- connect any control object corresponding to a presentation unit to the control object corresponding to the interactive task from which it depends (CO-IT→CO-

PU);

- connect any control object corresponding to a window to the control object corresponding to the presentation unit which contains this window (CO-PU→CO-W);
- connect any interaction object corresponding to an input/output information to the window that uses the function with this information as parameter (CO-W→ IO-I/O);
- connect any interaction object corresponding to an information induced by the presentation to the window where it appears (CO-W→IO-P);
- connect any object control corresponding to an application function to the control object corresponding to the window in which this function is represented (CO-W→CO-Fc).

6. Activity 4: Forming High Level Dialogue Specifications from the Output of Task Analysis

Normally, each dialogue layer should be specified in a notation that task analysts can understand, but can also be executed by some software tools. Multiple formalisms could be avoided by using ACG constructs. Most current approaches do not use common specifications: task analysts tend to use natural language descriptions for dialogue or task-related notations; construction tools that execute (or generate) dialogues use formal languages (e.g., Petri nets, rule languages (Bodart & Provot 1989), attributed grammars), although they are unfamiliar to task analysts.

In this section, we will investigate some perspectives for modelling the dialogue in order to fill this important gap (see « 4 » arrows in Figure 2).
We retain the need for independence between the dialogue and the application functions. Such independence is easy to achieve for the presentation components, since control objects guarantee correspondence between these and the application functions (Cockton 1987). Control objects thus can guarantee the separation of the presentation and application objects (Cockton 1987 ,Cockton 1991). However, separation between dialogue is more critical: the functional logic of the ACG should not govern the progress of the dialogue, but the dialogue should be compatible with it, and clearly the ACG cannot be achieved.

6.1 Dialogue Content

Dialogue is related to four types of element (i.e., PU, window, CIO, and function) and can be described at three levels of abstraction (Figure 9):

1. *inter-PU level*: the triggering of sub-tasks represented by PUs at the interactive task level;
2. *intra-PU level* (or inter-window level): the chaining of windows at the PU level;
3. *intra-window level*: the behavioural dependencies among CIOs in the same window.

CIOs linked by a bi-directional link (arrow) in Figure 9 become involved in the same dialogue at the inter-window level; similarly, windows linked by a bi-directional arrow are involved in intra-PU dialogue, just as PUs involved at the inter-PU level are linked by such arrows.

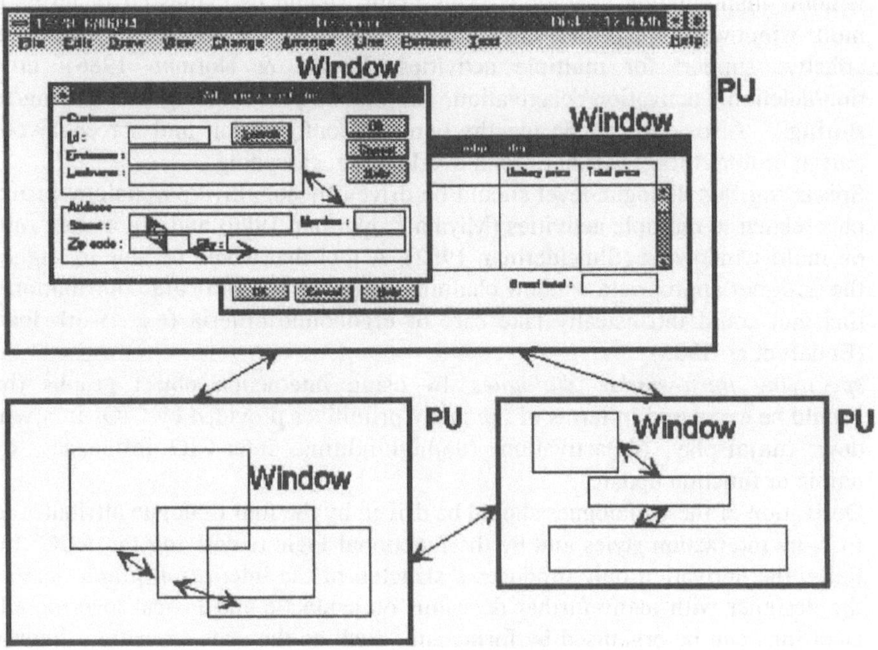

Figure 9. The dialogue levels.

6.2 Systematic Approach for Specifying a Dialogue

Initially, the approach should be driven by task analysis:

- a list of dialogue states (e.g., default, display, history, object, initial, final, related/alternative) can be derived from the decomposition of a task into goals and sub-goals;
- a list of dialogue transitions (e.g., triggers, actions, constraints) can be derived from the relationships between procedures implied by associated (sub-)task goals.

The approach iteratively refines dialogues, starting with high-level dialogues and ending with low-level ones. The following steps will achieve this refinement:

- *specifying inter-PU dialogues*, by using *presentation unit chaining graphs* that specify the conditions under which PUs are initialised, activated, and terminated (Provot 1993). This graph should be expressed in terms of activation/deactivation of PU, serialisation/parallelism, foreground/background, suspend/restore,...

  The graph can be derived from the PU's definition and from the decomposition of the interactive task into subtasks. Further support comes from dialogue ergonomic rules and from constructs for sequence and concurrency.

- *specifying intra-PU dialogues*, by using *window chaining graphs* that specify window manipulation operations. This graph should be expressed in terms of multi-windowing operations since multi-windowing is widely recognised as an effective support for multiple activities (Miyata & Norman 1986): creation/deletion, activation/deactivation, minimising/maximising, iconifying/restoring,... Also, one can decide the window configuration and screen layout: partial or total tiling, partial or total overlapping, cascading.
  Specifying this dialogue level should be driven by cognitive psychology principles related to multiple activities (Miyata & Norman 1986) and ergonomic rules on multi-windowing (Shneiderman 1992). A tool that would be able to suggest the designer appropriate window chaining would be a significant contribution if this tool could intrinsically take care of ergonomic criteria (e.g., work load) (Bodart et al. 1995).
- *specifying intra-window dialogues*, by using interaction object graphs that should be expressed in terms of the many primitives provided by CIOs in a window: (un)display, (de)activation, (de)highlighting, inter-CIO influences, dynamic or function update,...
  Derivation of these dialogues should be driven by the four dialogue attributes for PUs, by interaction styles and by the functional logic underlying the ACG. Initially, the derivation only produces a skeleton of the interaction graph, leaving the designer with many further decisions on syntactic and lexical level details. Decisions can be organised by formalisms such as the state transition diagram (Wasserman 1985) and the interaction object graph (Carr 1994) UAN (Provot 1993) can also specify this detail.

One problem is the diversity of formalisms used across the different levels of dialogue specification.

7. Activity 5: Transforming the Methodological Framework into a Specification Framework

7.1 A Specification Framework Based on the TRIDENT Methodology

General assumptions in the TRIDENT methodology can be satisfied by the detail of concrete specification frameworks. Once these frameworks are specialised for a specific problem, they can support automatic UI generation. In their general form, they can underpin industrial approaches to UI development that are based on current technologies (e.g., bitmap asynchronous screens, pull-down menus, multi-windowing techniques); these approaches should be similar to previous prevailing approaches (e.g., for text screens).

Several approaches can be envisaged for defining specification frameworks. They could be domain-specific: bank, insurance, hospital,... 4GL environments, objects

librairies (e.g. Microsoft Foundations Classes) could also be considered as implementation environments. A specification framework could be based on restricted UI functions: interaction style, dialogue mode, choose of interaction objects,...
This third alternative is illustrated by an extension of MacIDA project developed at University of Lausanne and lead by I. Petoud and Y. Pigneur (Petoud & Pigneur 1989a, Petoud & Pigneur 1989b, Petoud 1990). MacIDA's aim is to allow a quasi automatic derivation of a UI from a task's entity-relationship model, from attached functions and their activity chaining graph (cfr. supra 3.2.1, 3.2.2 and 3.2.3). In terms of the general methodological framework presented above, the framework based on this third approach involves three restrictions which are described below.

7.1.1 Supported Applications

This framework supports highly interactive business oriented applications that enable the user to follow multiple dialogue threads, in contrast to previous applications that were purely transactional and did not allow any user freedom.

7.1.2 Interaction Style

MacIDA supports forms filling for graphical UI. Therefore, control is basically external (i.e., user-driven), although mixed input information is also possible. The dialogue mode is asynchronous, letting users enter data in any convenient order, entering or modifying input information at any time. Functions are triggered by explicit user interaction with display objects. A menu bar is displayed in the upper part of the screen letting users select general items (e.g., quit the application, cut/paste information). A pull-down menu lets users navigate between the different windows containing the information.

7.1.3 Assumptions Made

MacIDA uses an entity-relationship model with an ACG without AND, OR, XOR links. The entity-relationship model is not object oriented, although it could be extended to become one. The main goal of MacIDA is to permit automated UI generation. This approach is grounded on two basic assumptions :

1. **Assumption 1: each entity and each relationship appearing in the entity-relationship model, that has attributes and/or is attached to at least one function, should be mapped onto a UI root window.**
   The generated root window contains consequently all the CIOs required for the input/display of elementary data used in this task. The set of these windows, which contains the set of all input/output information for the task, is therefore required for carrying out the task efficiently. This set is automatically created when the task is initiated. Each window, containing the required CIOs, is always present on the screen during run-time, but not necessarily visible nor active. This is why each window is associated with an item in the pull-down menu that lets the window be activated. We have to point out that the activation of a window does not imply the activation of the contained CIOs. The two mecha-

nisms responsible for this activation are described later.

2. **Assumption 2: dialogue aspects are completely subordinated to functional aspects.**
As soon as information is input or modified, the conversation management system is able to evaluate the current input state. This evaluation is instantly applied to particular CIOs, called *action CIOs*, such as a push button, an icon, a drawn button. When conditions required for triggering a typical application function are fulfilled, the user is warned by a presentation change of action CIOs: its activation alerts the user to their ability to trigger the function. As soon as the user pushes on that action CIO, the function is triggered and executed: for instance, if a user pushes on a (Save) button, then the associated information will be stored in the database. Action CIOs are included in the IO-P (Figure 8) part since they are implied by the presentation.
This choice is compatible with the function triggering mode (explicit manual displayed, i.e. explicit user interaction with display objects, sub-subsection 7.1.2 above). If an implicit mode has been used instead (e.g., when the cursor is leaving an information field) or explicit manual undisplayed, i.e. user interaction with invisible objects (e.g., when pressing a function key such as [F10]), then action CIOs would have been replaced by control objects responsible for receiving these events to trigger the same function.
As the user proceeds to input new information and to trigger new functions, the main goal assigned to the task becomes closer. But the user can be forced to modify previously input information to satisfy validation rules. For example, when recording an order, a customer whose credit is no longer sufficient may be forced to reduce the ordered quantity or to forego making as many purchases. As indicated, the user has to modify the related information. The user does not need to specify this value change. Any information can be accessed or modified at any time. The only thing the user has to do is to locate the related information and to modify it. The system again automatically evaluates the input state, as existing validations may not now hold. The system then responds to the new value.
Two mechanisms can ensure that dialogues will be determined by functionality: firing/disabling action CIOs; consistency control between UI and functional machine. Details of these mechanisms will be given later. They have to allow designers a free choice of:
   - the nature of events required for triggering functions: here, pushing on an action CIO is the only option because of the second assumption and because of the choice of function triggering mode (explicit manual displayed);
   - the scope of triggering: e.g., a combined push button PB_1 for triggering functions Fc_1, Fc_2, and Fc_3 or a single push button PB_1 for triggering Fc_1, another one PB_2 for triggering Fc_2 and a last one PB_3 for triggering Fc_3.

   Choices here are however constrainted by the ACG and the associated temporal relations (e.g., sequence, parallelism, condition).

The scope of MacIDA and its associated interaction styles are more restrictive than the general TRIDENT methodological framework. However, the above two restrictions, coupled with new specification constructs, allows complete automatic generation of the UI from the entity-relationship model. UI presentation design is computer-aided, whereas UI dialogue generation is fully automated.

7.2 Impact of the Restrictions on Specifying and Generating a Presentation

From hypothesis 1, one can deduce that UI presentation is derived from ACG and described by screen masks basically made up of CIOs for input/display information and actions CIOs. CIOs displaying error and help messages, pure static CIOs (e.g., a group box) can also be included.

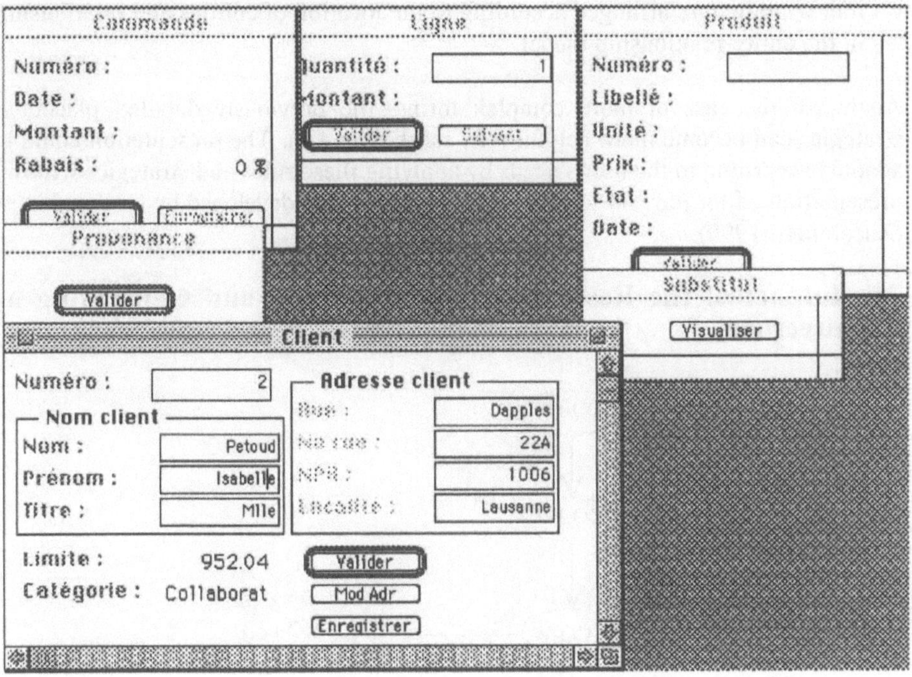

Figure 10. UI generation.

The first hypothesis constraints AIO selection and AIO→CIO transformation steps (cfr. activity 2 introduced in section 4) to the applicability of the following selection rules :

- each entity is mapped onto a root window;
- each relationship is mapped onto a root window;
- each simple attribute is mapped onto a single-line edit box;
- each repetitive attribute is mapped onto a table;
- each multiple attribute is mapped onto a group box surrounding CIOs resulting from composing the multiple attribute (into edit boxes and/or tables);
- each function is mapped onto an action CIO, most of the time onto a push button.

However, in the case of more complex forms, the previously introduced expert

system can become more helpful (cfr. subsection 4.2).
The first hypothesis can also constraint the CIO placement step to the applicability of the following placement rules (Figure 10):

- single-line edit boxes, tables and group boxes are arranged in a single vertical column, are left justified in the root window to which they belong;
- identification labels of previous CIOs are placed in a single vertical column, are left justified between themselves and are bottom justified with respect to the CIOs they identify in the root window;
- action CIOs are vertically or horizontally justified at the bottom of each root window;
- root windows are arranged according to the location of entities and relationships in the entity-relationship model.

Again, in the case of more complex forms, the previously detailed placement strategies can become more helpful (cfr. subsection 4.2). The presentation could be adapted according to the user's needs by applying these rules and strategies within a presentation editor (cfr. subsection 4.1) such as the one developed by G. Zucchinetti (Zucchinetti 1990).

7.3 Impact of the Restrictions on Specifying and Generating an Architecture

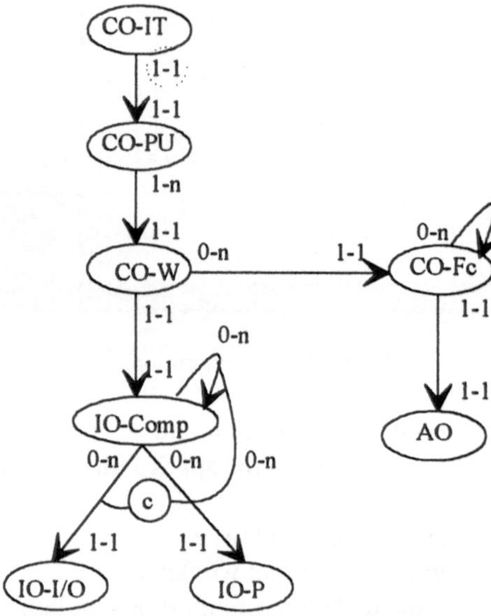

Figure 11. Structure of Control Objects in MacIDA.

Constant presence of all root windows on the screen, resulting from the first assumption, entails that the interactive task only consists of one PU composed of these windows. Task decomposition into sub-tasks is no longer indispensable in this case. The resulting architecture (Figure 11) still conforms to the generic schema of architecture model (Figure 7), but the object structure is far simplified with respect to Figure 8 since only one CO-PU remains.

7.4 Impact of the Restrictions on Specifying and Generating a Dialogue

From first assumption, one can deduce that specifying a dialogue is largely simplified at the three levels defined in sub-section 6.2 :

1. inter-PU level dialogue is shrinked to a simple triggering of the only PU remaining. The behaviour of CO-IT therefore consists of only one rule for triggering the PU;
2. intra-PU level dialogue enables the user to browse freely between the PU's windows. The behaviour of the unique CO-PU is confined to one rule for creating all windows when initiating the interactive task and to the management rules for pull down menus required to activate windows;
3. intra-window level dialogue is reduced to an asynchronous conversation for the set of all CIOs in each window and for each action CIO. This total asynchronism results from the miss of links in MacIDA.

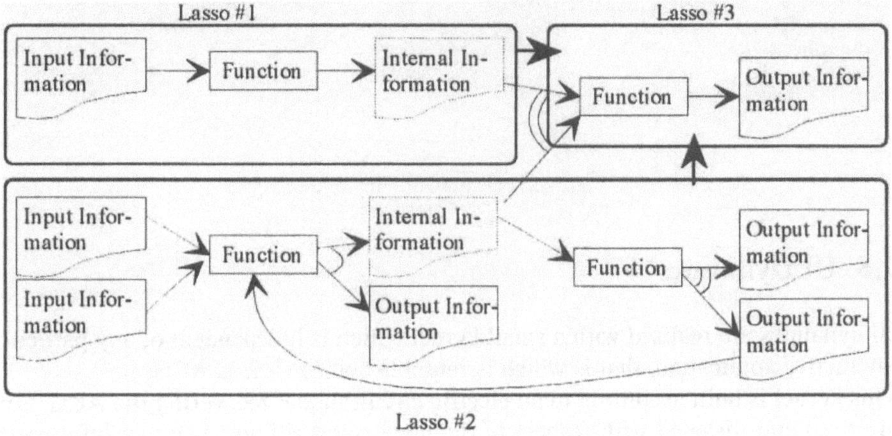

Figure 12. Lasso technique.

From second assumption, one can deduce that intra-PU level (for menu items only) and intra-window level dialogues still allow some freedom constrainted by functional machine: these dialogue constraints are specified by ACG extensions that enables us to make the economy of state transition diagrams and specification rules. The so-restricted CO behaviour can be entirely pre-programmed. We now show these extensions. Specifying a dialogue is a matter of enriching ACG with two techniques :

1. *defining the nature and scope of events for triggering functions*: this definition is achieved by a "lasso" metaphor grouping triggering of several functions into one event attached to a single action CIO (Figure 12). This metaphor decreases

the amount of action CIOs by concentrating into one or many CIOs the set of all function triggerings in an interactive task. When functions are no longer triggered by their original action CIO, but by an action CIO resulting from a lasso, the function triggering mode becomes implicit.

2. *sequencing asynchronous inputs*: a sequence of input is forced (Figure 13). This sequence is specified by annotating the ACG with precedence links between information. These links are graphically represented by vertical bold arrows. A more directive conversation with a strict information ordering is gained.

Extensions reported on the ACG should be consistent with the functional specifications. To insure this property, an extended ACG editor, called *dialogue editor*, will perform specific validations. For instance, it will check that a particular lasso surrounds all input information of a specific function.

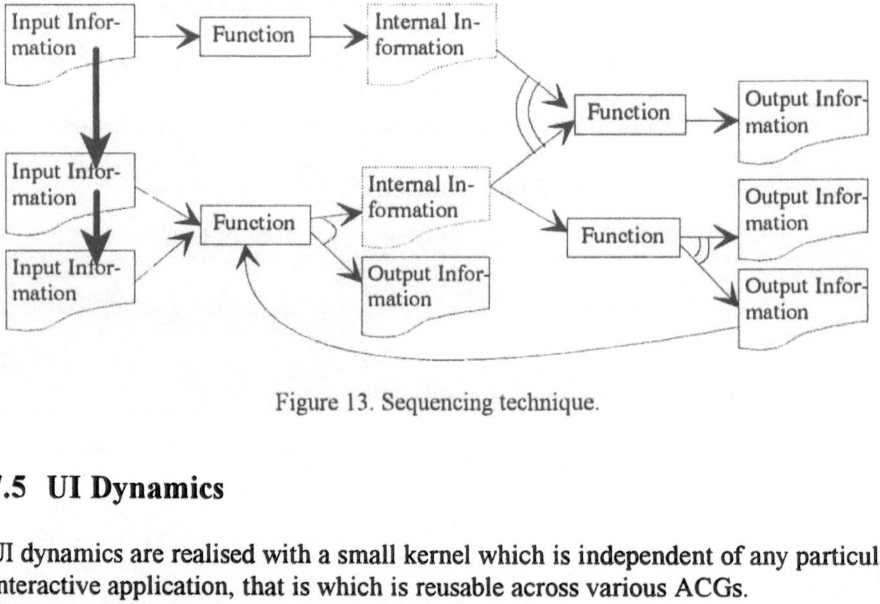

Figure 13. Sequencing technique.

7.5 UI Dynamics

UI dynamics are realised with a small kernel which is independent of any particular interactive application, that is which is reusable across various ACGs.

This kernel is built according to an electric circuit model recovering the ACG. Arcs are fired and disabled with respect to the node states (Figure 14): any information input or function triggering will fire the corresponding symbol in the circuit.

This firing proceeds in a parallel direction with the triggering of authorised functions. The role played by this kernel is double: on one hand, it insures a consistent information display with task's progression and, on the other hand, it restricts user's actions to the one which are functionally allowed. Two techniques ensure a correct execution :

1. the firing/disabling of action CIOs: action CIOs are activated whenever information input or function triggering requires it. This activation occurs when the pre-condition of related function, expressed in terms of input information, is verified. Similarly, action CIOs which are related to functions whose triggering is not valid are deactivated. This deactivation occurs when the precondition of related function is not satisfied. For example, the input of a customer identifica-

tion number provokes the activation of a push button for searching this customer;

2. the maintenance of consistency between UI and functional machine: this mechanism supports new information input by forgetting (deactivating) all information dependent of old values. Let us suppose that a customer id. has been provided and searched. The user becomes conscious that this customer is a wrong one. As early as the user provides a new id., all old information are forgotten to insure application consistency.

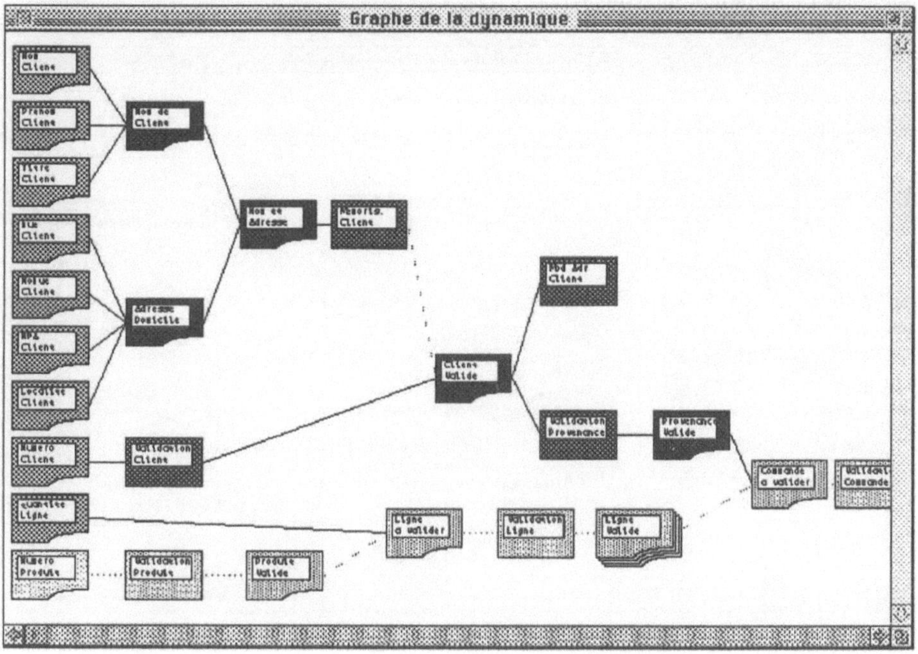

Figure 14. The Activity Chaining Graph considered as an electric circuit.

7.6 Original Ergonomic Contribution for an Interactive Application

MacIDA provides guidance and contextual help as a control panel with two windows :

- the first window of the control panel reflect graphically the state of the electric circuit (Figure 14). The user is then able to clearly visualise where (s)he is in the task progression, that is what (s)he has already done and what is remaining to do;
- the second window depicts the same information, but according to a natural language format with respect to the input context (Figure 15). In this example, the radio button highlighted on "+" for the product quantity means that the related information has already been provided and is correct ; conversely, the ra-

dio button highlighted on "?" for a product identification number indicates that this piece of information has already been provided, but not validated. Therefore, the current state is not yet correct.

These guidance features are automatically derived from the ACG. No extraneous specification effort is required from the human factors expert. Automated generation of such a control panel from the ACG as a contextual help and guidance for task's accomplishment is very worth and can be expanded easily to build a new key activity: the automatic derivation of a help and guidance system from task analysis (Moriyon et al. 1994).

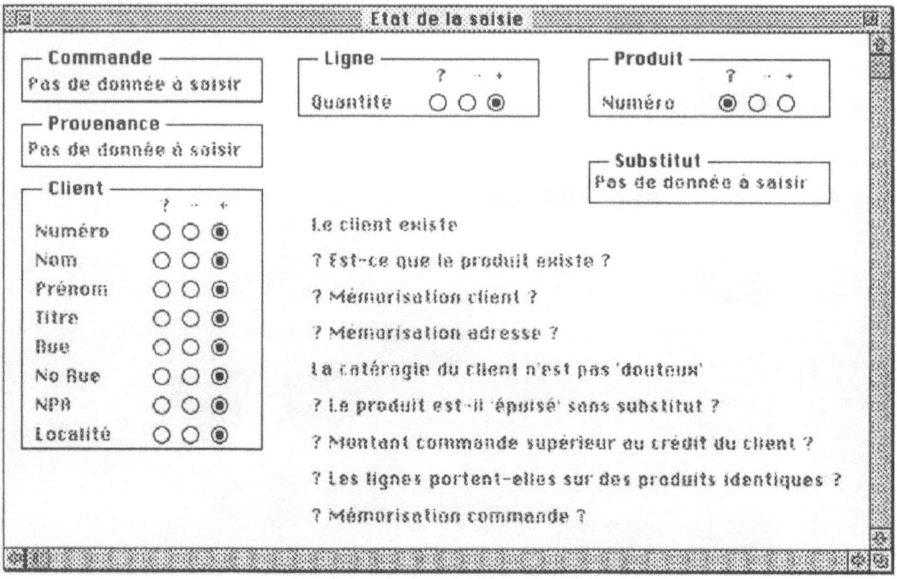

Figure 15. Guidance Control Panel.

8. Conclusion

Five key activities have been examined and illustrated within a particular framework. Lessons learned show several benefits that have already been emphasised. A positive evaluation can be drawn for at least three issues:

- a better understanding of relationships between the different actors of the development life cycle of the interactive application;
- a highlighting of a precise set of design options to be defined for any particular design situation;
- an inducement to consider other key activities not only for business oriented applications but also for other domain areas.

8.1 Relationships Between Actors

Different actors in the complete development life cycle of an interactive application have been identified. We show here a supplemental advantage of the key activities: to recognise the relationships between those actors and to encourage them. Forming UI specification from the output of task analysis (activity 1 introduced in section 3) promotes a better communicability of the work done by task analyst, psychologist and usability engineer towards the software engineer.

Guiding presentation design by ergonomic rules (activity 2 introduced in section 4) helps the graphical artist who is responsible for the graphical appearance of the UI. Deriving an architecture from task analysis and presentation components (activity 3 introduced in section 5) is particularly well suited for the software engineer and/or the system engineer. The proposed systematic approach provides guidance grounded on the work of task analyst without forgetting specific goals of the information system.

Specifying a high level conversation from task analysis (activity 4 introduced in section 6) should offer to the dialogue designer the faculty of conversation prototyping more rapidly and easily than with empirical manual methods. Specialising the methodological framework into a specification framework (activity 5 introduced in section 7) is more aimed at software engineers. This activity shows how important and affordable it could be to particularise a methodological framework into a specification framework.

8.2 Design Options for a Design Situation

Each specification framework actually defines *a particular design situation*, characterised by a set of design options chosen among different alternatives. The clear identification of the five activities has collaborated to determining such options which are here summarised :

- a definition of activity domain: process control, office automation, information systems (e.g., accounting departments, selling, pharmaceutical area, medical area,...), information system level (operational, driving, decision);
- a task analysis method: by hierarchical decomposition, by constraints, by space-problems, by cognitive analysis,...
- a physical environment: availability of a screen editor, fourth generation language, library of custom widgets,...
- a selection of interaction style: command language, query language, natural language, questions & answers, menu selection, direct manipulation, form filling, function keys, iconic interaction, multi-windowing, multimedia interaction;
- a selection of dialogue attributes: dialogue control (i.e., internal, external, mixed), dialogue mode (i.e., sequential, asynchronous, mixed), function triggering mode (i.e., automatic, manual, implicit or explicit, displayed or undisplayed), metaphor (i.e., conversation based or universe based, navigation based);
- selection rules for choosing interaction objects: complete selection, customised selection, standardised selection (e.g., IBM CUA, Ms-Windows, Open Look, Humanoïd (Moriyon et al. 1994);
- rules for placing interaction objects: complete placement, customised placement,

standardised placement, column oriented (single, double, balanced double, multiple), form oriented, frequency oriented, conforming to the entity-relationship model's configuration, visual continuity,...

Other design options can also be investigated such as window selection type within a PU (maximal, minimal, functional, input/output, typed, grouped, or free (Bodart et al. 1995)). Any design situation can be completely determined by choosing a particular value for all design options.

8.3 Completeness of Key Activities

Discovering and investigating the five activities has been confined in the beginning to business oriented applications. This should not mean that these activities are to be neglected when another domain area is concerned (e.g., graphical applications, multimedia services). They are likely to be revisited, but not forgotten. This should not also mean that these five activities are sufficient, whether for business oriented applications or not.

For instance, a desirable activity seems to be the systematic derivation of ergonomic criteria (e.g., compatibility, consistency, adaptability, work load) according to parameters of a task analysis. As a matter of fact, deciding that a particular criteria is more important than another can only be achieved by considering the whole task structure. For a given task in a known context, explicit control might be appropriate. For the same task to be carried out in another context, with another user population, this criteria might become obsolete and should be changed by an implicit control.

Acknowledgements

The authors would like to greatly thank Gilbert Cockton for comments on earlier versions of this manuscript.

Part III: Methodologies and Communication throughout the Life Cycle

User interface systems engineering is not just concerned with the products of systems design. It is also concerned with the process. In Part III the emphasis shifts from details of the products — the formal models and other representations which are produced during the design process — to details of the processes which are needed. The wide scope of UISE means that there must be successful communication between members of the design team (e.g. HCI specialists and software engineers), between the developers and the users and between the activities at various stages of the project. The methodology which is adopted must be able to accommodate these differing communication needs. Although the emphasis of this part is on the process, this does not mean that representations are ignored. Indeed all three chapters review and discuss the suitability of different representations at different stages of user interface software development. As with the other parts of this book, the methods and techniques are applied to very different domains: cooperative working, consumer products and complex systems.

Chapter 8 focuses on the development of computer supported cooperative work systems and introduces the idea of work scenario graphs. These are graphical representations of the system which are aimed to build bridges between users and designers primarily in the area of understanding and representing user requirements. These graphs form part of a user-centred method for software development which adopts a 'middle-out' approach. The approach and related representations are described in the context of developing systems which support cooperative working.

Chapter 9 provides a wide ranging review of current practise in UISE. The focus of this chapter is on where and when communication between members of the design team is most important and how it can be effectively achieved. Techniques, software tools and methods for achieving this integration are summarised from the perspective of the vital need for communication; between all the people involved in software development and between the phases of software development. The chapter introduces the idea that there must be 'handshaking' at several points — verifying and explaining design decisions. The chapter provides a 'document-oriented' perspective on this and concludes with an agenda of activities which are needed if this communication problem is to be successfully overcome.

The final chapter in this part looks in particular at the development of highly complex systems and at the range of methods and tools which are needed for the effective development of such systems. This chapter focuses more on strategy than methodology where prototyping and evaluation is central. Traditional methods are shown to be inadequate for this type of system. Instead, existing tools and techniques must be brought together and enhanced to provide the necessary degree of user involvement and project management necessary to build successful complex systems. A strategy known as FOCUS is described and related to other methods.

Chapter 8: Design of Workplace-Integrating User Interfaces based on Work Scenario Graphs

Hans-W. Gellersen & Max Mühlhäuser

1. Introduction

People use computers to accomplish work. Traditionally, computers support monolithic applications in which single users perform isolated tasks. Applications in this context can be viewed as tools regarding a specific task. User interface design methods have concentrated on support for three types of human-computer interfaces according to Dzida's taxonomy (Dzida 1987): the I/O-interface describing the usage surface of the tool, the dialogue interface describing the interaction dynamics, and the tool interface describing supported functions (Figure 1). Although human work spans a complex network of interaction with other humans and with many different tools, the organizational interface, which is concerned with relating humans and tools in the context of their work environment, is usually hardly taken into account in user interface design (Viereck et. al. 1991). In other words, user interface design is tool-centred and not work-centred, as criticized by work psychologists: "Not the machine, but the organization and design of work places is the essential task in the centre of informatics. The design of machines, hardware, and software is subordinate to this task" (Coy 1989).

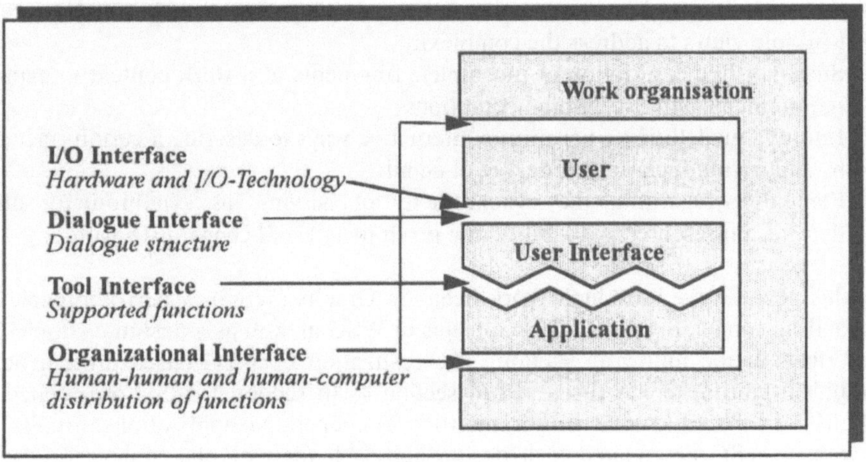

Figure 1: Human-Computer Interfaces.

Support for cooperative work is currently investigated by two research communities with traditionally diverging views of cooperation support. In the CSCW community, which is mostly influenced by human factors specialists, the problem of coordinating cooperative work is approached by providing specialized tools containing rich communication paths for the cooperating humans. These tools for teams, so-called groupware, support isolated tasks performed by a tightly coupled team, but they do not relate to a more general work context.

In the workflow community, which has its roots in information systems, coordination of cooperative work is approached by routing documents from one person to the next. Workflows assume well-defined tasks that are decomposable into single-user steps. The major problem with the workflow model is that it assumes highly regulated work procedures, whereas work in the real world is characterized by large amounts of exceptional conditions (Swenson 1993). Rule-based workflow models reflect the need for expressing exceptional conditions, yet they suffer from two problems. First, rules are very hard to elicit as they are embodied in the implicit knowledge of workers. Secondly, the complexity in work organisations leads to large rule sets which tend to be unmanageable.

In summary, both groupware and workflows address extremes of cooperative work (Gellersen et. al. 1994). For example, groupware commonly assumes synchronous collaboration of a team while workflows commonly assume asynchronous collaboration. Yet, in the real world teams do not only switch frequently between these two styles of collaboration, they also work in mixed modes.

The deficiencies of the workflow model for describing cooperative work lead us to a list of requirements for a more adequate model of cooperative work:

- Support for the full spectrum of cooperative work, harmonizing groupware and workflow approaches
- Graphical notation instead of textually represented rule sets to ease understanding and communication (among developers, and with users)
- Multiple views to address the complexity
- Snapshot-like description of incomplete fragments of a work context to capture requirements and exceptional conditions
- Intuitive modelling by permitting alternative ways to describe a certain fact and by supporting inconsistent degree of detail
- Flexibility regarding the synchronicity of actions, as synchronicity often depends on resource availability in a given instance of cooperative work.

In this chapter, we introduce Work Scenario Graphs (WSG), a new approach for modelling cooperative work. The concepts of WSG as well as a design example are described in the following section. The realization of WSG based on a generic graphical editing tool is discussed in section 4. In section 5 WSG are related to ITEMS, a software engineering framework for cooperative applications. Finally, in section 6 WSG are related to a design approach for workplace-integrating user interfaces.

2. Work Scenario Graphs

Work Scenario Graphs are a new approach for modelling cooperative work. WSG evolved in our research group out of the need for an easy-to-understand model of cooperative work that would enable us to discuss issues of software technology for cooperative work (among ourselves and with users of our technology). WSG are much inspired by whiteboard sketches as typically used in very early design for capturing ideas.

WSG are snapshot-like graphical views of cooperative work that are comprehensive in the sense that they include people, processes and information involved as well as different types and patterns of connectivity. However, they do not intend to describe a cooperative application *completely* at any level of abstraction. Rather, WSG represent *one* out of five interrelated graphical notations which are used to describe cooperative software systems, as described in section 4. WSG can be related to one another in various ways, thereby contributing to a more complete picture of the system described. In this sense, WSG can be understood as a requirements capture technique.

2.1 Elementary Concepts of WSG

The elements of WSG are summarized in Figure 2 and will be described below with basic syntactic and semantic rules.
One basic design rule for WSG is called "omit trivial things, express the essential". Reference to this rule will in the remainder be indicated with the flag (OTEE). WSG design is supposed to be very simple and intuitive in the beginning, but to allow more detailed specification of scenarios as a design process proceeds. In the beginning, a WSG designer has to understand not much more than the intuitive meaning of WSG node types.

Nodes: WSG are composed of only three types of nodes.
Agent nodes describe "substantial" (cf. OTEE) self-contained software components. Such components may in themselves represent distributed, multi-threaded software. Agents are supposed to act largely "on-their own" as opposed to merely user-driven software which would usually be identified as a subpart of one of the other two node types, see below.
Archive nodes depict collections of documents, stored in single or replicated files or databases. As such, they model persistent information and abstract from the actual document types served. According to the OTEE rule, "access tools" for archives like editors, browsers, database interfaces, or TP monitors are assumed to be part of an archive. An exception would be an autonomous information filter agent which browses different archives without user interception and delivers a compiled selection of information – such a component would be modeled as an agent of its own.
User nodes represent *user access points* rather than physical users or self-contained user interfaces. A user node may be viewed as the "end-point" of a connection to another user (another user node, more precisely), to an agent or to an archive. Both by filling out a specific "role" and by performing a specific task, a user may use several user access points simultaneously. It is the task of a workplace-integrating user interface to offer and coordinate the right selection of

user access points in a timely fashion, according to the tasks and roles which the user actually fulfils.

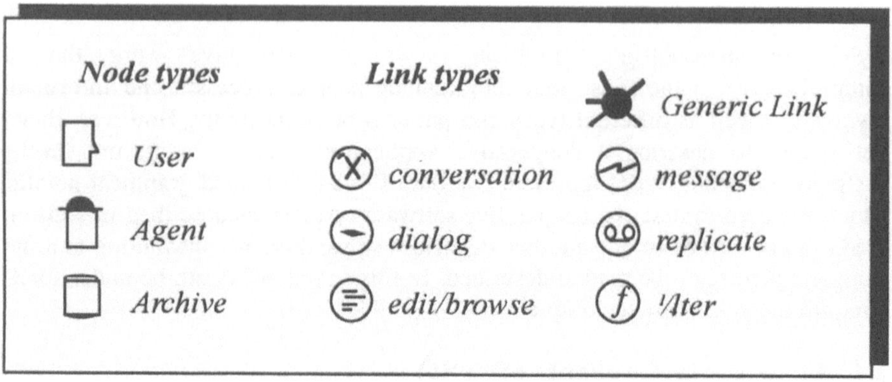

Figure 2: Node and link types of Work Scenario Graphs

Links: WSG nodes are linked by undirected typed multi-party connections (two-party connections thus represent one possible case). Link types are fully determined by the types of nodes they connect, a link may connect either nodes of one type or nodes of two different types. In the simplest case, links are denoted as spiders with a black circle in the centre.

At a deeper level of detail (e.g., when a designer zooms into a WSG), link depiction is changed from a black circle to a circle with an icon according to the link type (note that the link type is automatically derived from the interconnected node types). Obviously, there are six different link types, with the following depiction and meaning:

Conversation: synchronous or asynchronous connections between user nodes ("switch" icon)

Dialog: connection between users and agents (the icon alludes to the fact that two "sides", humans and computers, interact)

Edit/browse: user access to archives for document editing or information acquisition purposes ("document" icon)

Message (agent-agent), *replicate* (archive-archive) and *filter* (agent-archive) denote agent inter-process communication ("wired connection" icon), document update / interchange / replication ("recording" icon), and autonomous access of agents to archives ("formula" icon), respectively. At the current stage of our project, links with equal participation of all three kinds of nodes are not yet supported (mainly since we do not yet understand the semantics of such a link well enough). There are, however, link types which relate all three node types in a non-equal manner, see below.

Further levels of detail: Link icons may be complemented by an archive icon if the corresponding "transient" communication is to be recorded and stored. Link configuration and management is assumed to be a natural part of the link. Thus, according to the OTEE rule, there is no separate depiction of, for instance, the

configuration management software included in teleconferencing systems (which in turn represent a "conversation" link).
Of course, much of the "meaning" of a graphical design stems from the mnemonics associated. Accordingly, WSG are supposed to be augmented by identifiers for the nodes sketched.
In addition, the instantiation of WSG elements can be determined by adding a corresponding symbol. Three possibilities exist: a "0" node is optional, it may or may not exist in a concrete instantiation of the WSG; a "1" node is mandatory, and a "*" node may be instantiate arbitrarily often, the number of instances may even change at run time. This relates to the observation that practical cooperative work often involves unknown and dynamically changing numbers of participants. Unlike programming languages, WSG allow multiple use of identifiers within the same scope. A common example is the one in which, for one aspect, there is a number of equal participants in a cooperative setup (represented by a "*"-labelled user node), for another aspect, one of these "stands out": this fact can be denoted by drawing another user node with the *same identifier* but a "1"-label (cf. the example below).
There exist even more possibilities to add information to a WSG, for example, about the concrete meshing of nodes associated with a multi-party link. Such further levels of detail will be omitted for the sake of space.

2.2 Design Example: Electronic Meeting Assistance

In the following, the basic concepts of WSG design will be illustrated with a fragmentary example design of a software system for electronic meeting assistance.

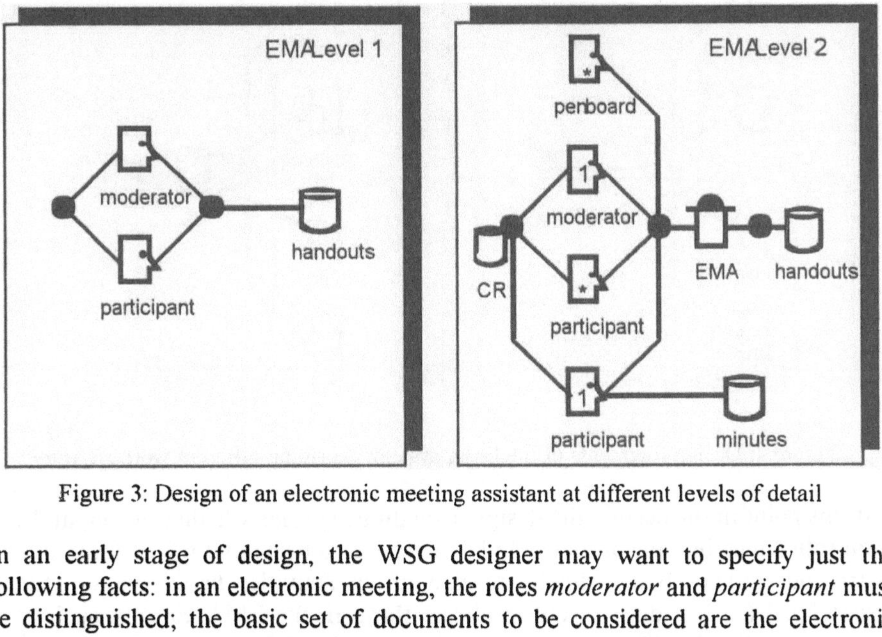

Figure 3: Design of an electronic meeting assistant at different levels of detail

In an early stage of design, the WSG designer may want to specify just the following facts: in an electronic meeting, the roles *moderator* and *participant* must be distinguished; the basic set of documents to be considered are the electronic *handouts*; everybody must be able to communicate and to access the handouts. The

resulting basic WSG is depicted in the left of Figure 3 (*EMA Level 1*).
A more detailed WSG adds design decisions and introduces both a change in the topology and additional labels as follows (cf. Figure 3, *EMA Level 2*): electronic meeting assistance is found to require substantial software support by an autonomous component which dynamically manages the topic list, supports computer-based discussions and decisions for each topic, organizes time management, and so on, all in cooperation with the moderator. Therefore, an agent called EMA (*electronic meeting agent*) is introduced; due to EMA control, direct user access to the handouts is excluded. One user who "from the perspective of EMA" behaves like any other participant, is appointed for taking the minutes. This particular participant is denoted as "singular-instance" and separated from the "multiple-instance" (further) participants.
All conversation is recorded in an archive "conversation recording (CR)". Note that the decision about asynchronous or synchronous conversation – which may be based on, for instance, audio-video conferencing or electronic mail, respectively – is not taken here. Accordingly, CR may represent, for example, a folder for "carbon copies" of mails, or an audio-video store.
The detailed WSG also shows that the EMA supports interaction via an electronic whiteboard (node "penboard"). Such penboards are supposed to be available at each physical location which participates in the electronic meeting. Activities during a meeting which would normally occur at a traditional whiteboard can thus be propagated to all locations involved in the meeting.

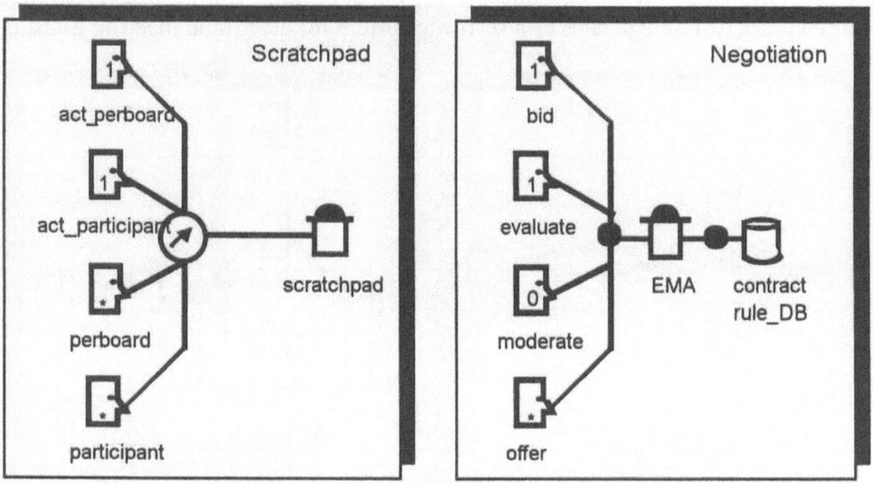

Figure 4: Design fragments of the EMA system, decribing different work *situations*

At this point in the design, the designer might be curious whether during an EMA-controlled meeting, the users would be interested in bypassing the EMA in order to carry out rather "free" whiteboard-type group activities based on a replicated scratchpad (such a desire would indicate flaws in the EMA concept such as too rigid control). Considering the above-described WSG "complicated enough", the

designer may want to sketch the liveboard-based scratchpad in a separate design, as shown in the design fragment WSG *Scratchpad* in Figure 4. The expanded "dialogue" icon indicates that the communication links are grouped: for example, the link to the participant who provides input to the scratchpad at a given time (act_participant) is grouped with the link to the penboard at the location of this participant (act_penboard). Details of this grouping could be inspected by zooming furher into the dialogue icon.
The WSGs *EMA Level 2* in Figure 3 and *Scratchpad* in Figure 4 showed different details of the same software at the same time, making them two "fragments" of the same scenario. The WSG *Negotiation* in Figure 4 shows the same software under different conditions (in a different "situation"). Take for example a project meeting for an ongoing project in which the telecooperating partners belong to different companies or cost centres. At any time during such a meeting, we want to foresee the possibility for partners to instantaneously enter a phase of formal negotiations (e.g., when the electronic meeting raises the need for a new work package within the project). The participants would then take on new roles in a bidding process (bid, offer, evaluate), except for the moderator: it might be decided that the meeting moderator should moderate the negotiations, too. Note that in this WSG, the "moderator" node is optional! The EMA would assist in the negotiation based on commonly agreed "contract" rules (stored in an archive); direct conversation between users would be excluded. Note that this negotiation situation is related to the situation described by the fragments *EMA Level 2* and *Scratchpad* via an event-based transition (in this case, a user-triggered event).

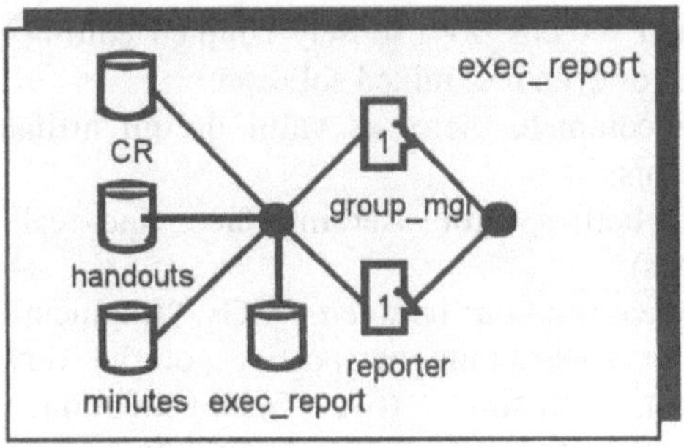

Figure 5: A design fragment of the EMA system describing a *step* in a work process

Finally, one may think of a follow-on activity to a meeting, in which the minute-taking participant ("reporter") and the group manager have to prepare an executive summary based on all documents collected up to then. Such a scenario represents a different step in the cooperation, very much according to the understanding of steps common to workflow management systems. Figure 5 depicts the "exec_report" step which might follow an EMA-based meeting. Note that in this scenario, an organizational role (group manager) is used to describe one of the user nodes. This relates to the fact that an organizational role often implies task-related behaviour (cf. section 5).
The example described in this section could be refined step by step to include more

details. Both these steps and the necessary "next level" of semantics have been omitted here for brevity. Note that a designer, too, does not need to know more about WSG semantics than described above in order to carry out early design as exemplified in this section. Instead of adding more detail to the WSG-based design, a software engineer may also relate WSG to other aspects of the software under development (cf. section 4), for example user interface design (cf. section 5).

2.3 Summary of Key Ideas

The above example ought to have motivated the essential rules and concepts of WSG. To summarize, these comprise:

- the OTEE rule and a maximum of freedom in the sequence of design steps. The steps proposed above allow to get a rough idea of the underlying design method, yet the essence of this method is freedom of choice.
- means to express optionality and multiplicity (cf. the "0/1/*" notation as explained for "nodes") as required for description of dynamic cooperative work.
- ways to specify peculiarities for "one of a group" when it is the intent of the designer not to distinguish this "one" via a different role (cf. reuse of identifier within WSG).
- support for task-specific roles v[illegible]us organizational roles (cf. section 5)
- deferring of decisions to run time. For example, a "conversation" may be instantiated as synchronous phone or "screen-to-screen" conversation or as asynchronous (email, voice_mail, ...) conversation, the decision may even be different for different branches of a conversation; "edit/browse" may lead joint editing via shared screens, to a loosely coupled editing process followed by a merging process, or even to a mixed solution.
- acceptance of incomplete views as valid design artifacts by supporting the notion of fragments.
- abstraction from both specific user interfaces and real users via user access points (user nodes).
- support for different relations between WSGs: "fragment" (two WSG fragments show different or overlapping perspectives of the very same situation of a software system), "situation" (two WSG situations are interrelated via spontaneous events), and "step" (the beginning and end of WSG steps are usually marked by either the availability of specific artifacts or the beginning or end of another WSG step, i.e. document flow or control flow).

For the sake of brevity, we have also omitted details about the procedure by which WSG are related to one another as fragments, situations, or steps. This procedure creates hierarchies of WSG and identifies different "flow" types (role flow, document flow, etc.). The corresponding design procedure relates WSG to "scenario flow graphs" which represent a higher level of design abstraction, see section 4.

3. Implementation of a WSG Editor

3.1 Tool Support for Design Methods

In the previous section, the WSG approach for modelling cooperative work was described rather informally to stress the intuitive usage. More formally, the WSG method can be specified as a system consisting of a set of design elements, a set of design steps, a set of design rules and a design procedure (Rösch et. al. 1992). In the previous section, the method was motivated in a graphical way to visualize the concepts, however it is important to distinguish the design elements, steps and rules from graphical elements, steps and rules defining a graphical editing tool.

Obvious WSG design elements are the node and arc categories and their interrelations, but also hole graphs and graph inter-relations. Design steps are the operations that can be performed on design elements (creation, modification, deletion), for instance the assertion of a relation among WSG nodes. Design rules are predefined constraints which apply to design steps, for example the rule that no connection can be established among nodes of all three categories. Finally, the design procedure specifies the process of design reasoning and decision making. In the context of WSG, the use of the term design procedure is rather misleading, as the design process does not follow a strict protocol, as described in the previous section.

In order to effectively support a design method by a graphical tool, a good mapping of design elements, steps and rules to graphical elements, steps and rules has to be achieved. Mapping of design elements should be straightforward. Note that this is a mapping between classes of elements: each class of design elements is represented by a single graphical class. In a concrete design, a single instance of a design element may still be represented by multiple graphical instances of the related graphical class, thereby supporting multiple overlapping views of a design. Mapping of design steps to graphical steps should aim at providing short-cuts in design, so related sequential design steps should be considered for representation by a single graphical step. Finally, design rules should be enforced by related graphical rules. such as context-sensitive enabling of graphical steps. In addition to the mapping of design rules, human factors in visual languages have to be considered for identification of graphical rules, such as maximum number of nodes in a graph.

3.2 WSG Implementation

The implementation of a graphical editor for WSG is based on TNO1(Leidig 1994), a tool-building-tool for graphical editors. TNO comprises an interpreter for EXL (an extension of Scheme), and a number of libraries for visual techniques (various WIMP platforms, graphs, automatic layout) and integration with other tools (IPC, tuplespace). EXL implements an object-oriented prototype-instance

---

1*The New ODE*, a re-engineered and enhanced successor of ODE (Object Design Editor) (Rösch et. al. 1992)

model on top of Scheme. Within this model, relation types are supported by generic methods such as 'build transitive closure' and 'traverse graph'. This feature supports straightforward implementation of design models expressed in terms of objects and relations. For implementation of graphical elements, EXL provides convenient types abstracting from low-level toolkits such as X. Further, EXL embodies handling of one-way constraints based on the Lisp concept of active values. This constraint handling mechanism is ideally suited for establishing consistency between the internal representation of design elements and their graphical representatives, based on an architecture strictly separating model and view. Constraints can also be customized for implementation of graphical rules.

4. Embedding in Software Technology

4.1 ITEMS: Software Technology for Advanced Cooperative Applications

The present document concentrates on the idea of WSG as a particular approach to scenario-based design. However, WSG owe much of their power to the fact that they do not represent an isolated, self-contained concept, but an integral part of a multi-faceted graphical design approach for cooperative multimedia applications, called ITEMS (Gellersen et. al. 1994).

In ITEMS, software technology for cooperative applications is developed with respect to three key aspects:

- *synergy*, promoting synergy of cooperating humans based on workflow management and groupware approaches,
- *ubiquity*, providing mobile humans with "application access virtually anytime anywhere", based on mobile software objects,
- *modality*, promoting effective human-computer interaction based on integration of multiple media and modalities.

Detailed design of complex software under many aspects needs exhaustive design documents, even if compact graphical depiction is stressed. In order to keep designs as simple as possible despite size and complexity, ITEMS introduces five different yet closely interrelated (types of) views, as described below.

4.2 ITEMS Views

Figure 6 depicts the five view types supported in ITEMS, and their interrelation. "Work Scenarios" are supported by WSG, and the other view types are similarly supported by graphical design notations, methods, and detailed semantics.
ITEMS promotes a middle-out design approach (though, top-down and bottom-up approaches are not ruled out), in which a designer starts out with scenario description using WSG. These scenarios form the basis for development of both more general views and more specific views of an application, thus the term

middle-out design. We implemented middle-out design based on scenarios in an earlier project and found that it was accepted as more intuitive than strict top-down or bottom-up approaches (Gellersen 1993).

Relating WSG to one another as fragments, situations, or steps, the designer can move on to *scenario flows*. Within scenario flow graphs, individual WSG are shrunk to atomic nodes called "cooperation description unit" (CDU). Scenario flow graphs describe the hierarchical and planar arrangement of CDU as well as different flow types (document flow, role flow, control flow).

Document networks are used to describe the contents of archives. Any particular type of document is specified as a document network; such networks represent in essence a type definition of a hypertext, with read-only, revisable, executable, and blank parts. Like with WSG, there are ways to express multiplicity and optionality to support flexibility.

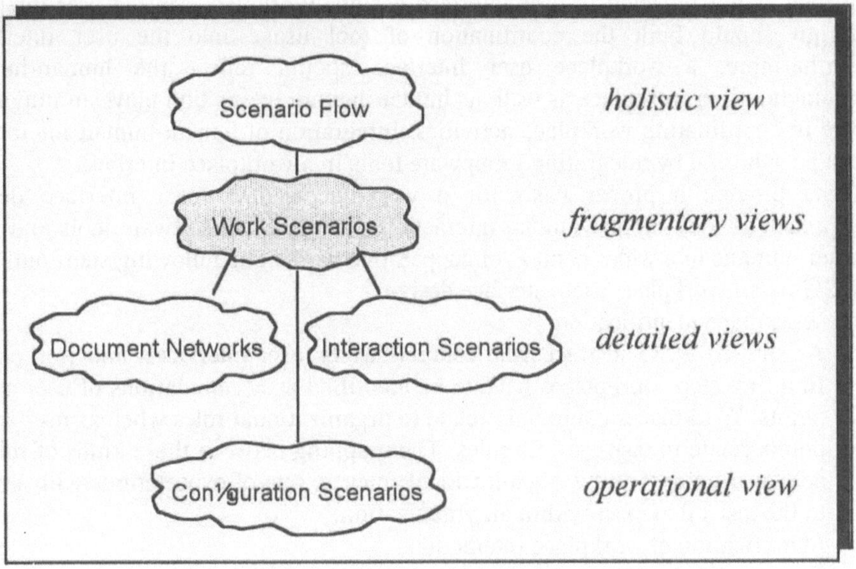

Figure 6: The five view types of ITEMS

Mobility scenarios cover the "ubiquity" aspect of ITEMS-based applications. The corresponding graphs are used both for defining the physical architecture of a hardware environment which supports mobile computing, and for describing the mapping of the "logical" software architecture (as specified in the four other views) onto this physical architecture. Mobility scenarios are primarily concerned with mapping the three "dimensions" of mobile users, mobile devices, and mobile information.

Finally, interaction scenarios are a graphical notation for modality-independent dialogue design. Interaction scenarios model dialogues based on abstract interaction objects which abstract from media and modalities, yet embody semantics to support modality allocation (Gellersen 1995). Work scenarios and interaction scenarios are related by a WSG-based approach for identification of workplace-integrating user interfaces. This approach is described below.

5. Workplace-integrating User Interfaces

User interface design methods traditionally focus on isolated interactive applications. As argued in the introduction, these applications can be viewed as tools for a limited range of tasks, and current user interface design can be classified as tool-centred. We argue that user interface design instead should be workplace-centred. By workplace, we mean a surrogate for a particular user in a work organization. Intuitively, a workplace relates to a physical work place, but with emergence of remote and mobile computing a more flexible notion is required.

In a workplace, usually a number of software tools are used in parallel to support workplace-related tasks. Users switch very frequently among tools, yet the interplay of tools is not reflected in user interface design. Workplace-centred user interface design should built the coordination of tool usage into the user interface. Furthermore, a workplace user interface should reflect the human-human interaction in a workplace as well, as human-human interaction plays an important role in coordinating workplace activities. Integration of human-human interaction can be achieved by integrating groupware tools in a workplace interface.

WSG provide a proper basis for a workplace-centred user interface design approach as they capture human interaction with different software tools and with other humans in a wider context of cooperative work. The following steps outline a WSG-based workplace user interface design:

- Workplace identification
  As shown, WSG abstract from concrete users, user interfaces, and workplaces. In a first step, workplaces have to be identified as accumulations of user access points. Workplaces commonly relate to organizational roles whereas user access points relate to task-specific roles. The mapping between these kinds of roles is achieved by describing organizational roles as sets of expectations with respect to the tasks that exist within an organization.
- Identification of workplace interactions
  The set of interactions related to a workplace comprises all interactions associated with the user access points related to a workplace. In addition, those interactions required for management of user access points have to be identified. For instance, in order to be able to switch from one task A to task B, the user access point to task A needs to be augmented with an interaction link to activate task B.
- Modelling of workplace interactions
  Based on WSG, workplace interaction can be categorized as conversation, dialogue, and edit/browse. For each of these interactions two aspects have to be modelled: first, the task-specific interaction with user, agent, or archive; secondly, the human-computer interaction required for handling the interaction. For example, for an edit/browse-link to an archive the actual editing and browsing of information has to be described, but also the management and customization of the link.

6. Conclusion

In their work places, humans interact with different software tools and with other humans, possibly computer-mediated. Currently, software design in general and user interface design in particular are tool-centred. The fact, that usage of different tools ought to be coordinated is not reflected in current design practice. A prerequisite for a more work-centred approach is a model of cooperative work capturing the roles of tools and humans with respect to the tasks that exist within a work organization.

In this chapter, we proposed WSG for modelling cooperative work. WSG are designed to support intuitive modelling of cooperative work settings based on scenarios. In WSG, the interrelation of humans and software tools with respect to task-based work situations is depicted in a comprehensive way. A key feature of the WSG approach is, that it does not require a deep understanding of underlying semantics to develop or communicate a first sketch of a cooperative application. Nevertheless, we aim at refining the semantics to provide a proper basis for reasoning about WSG designs, and for automatic code generation.

Chapter 9: Methods & Tools for Supporting the User Interface Design Process

David Bell, Ashok Gupta, Raghu Kolli & Martina Manhartsberger

1. Introduction

Users increasingly base their judgement of the functionality and quality of a product on their perception of its interface. The identification of techniques that improve the interface are therefore of great interest to developers of software and other products alike. By addressing issues early in the design cycle, redesign and maintenance costs can be reduced. By improving the integration between human factors on the one hand and the software engineering and product development team on the other, good human factors practice can be incorporated in our products. This suggests that we need a methodology that supports the interface design process and that enables it to be coupled with a concurrent product development activity.
Developing user interfaces today is a complex process that involves experts from various fields who design, prototype, evaluate and implement a product. In software user interfaces where a large amount of functionality may be presented to a user, developers have to deal with lots of detail that can amount to 2500 widgets for one application (Myers & Rosson 1992). Many aspects have to be considered from many different viewpoints. These considerations necessitate that to be successful, methods have to incorporate tools to support the developer in organising the development process.
Based on an analysis of the information collected from real design situations and our own insights into the problem domain, we conclude that there is no one solution to the many problems faced by designers. Both methods and tools are urgently needed and these must have a basis in the cognitive processes involved during design.
Three levels are suggested at which new methods and tools are required: to support the cognitive tasks involved in designing dynamic structures; to support the communication of design concepts between team members; and to support the accurate specification of the design in readiness for production.
The chapter is divided into sections. We begin in Section 2 by looking at the design problem, tools are examined in Section 3 and in Section 4 we describe actual design practice. In Section 5 the issue of human factors and software process integration is examined. Finally in Sections 6 & 7 we identify requirements for future methods and tools, respectively. It is hoped this paper will be of help to other researchers in formulating their own unique approaches for finding appropriate solutions and tools.

2. Problem Statement

Since the early 80s, much research has been done in the area of Human-Computer Interaction. Considering the number of international scientific conferences held today (an average of ten a year) and the number of journals (at least eight), a substantial body of knowledge has been built-up over the years. A closer look at the published literature will reveal that most of the studies are concentrated in few directions like cognitive psychology and computer science, in spite of the inter-disciplinary nature of the subject (i.e. very little in published form from a designer's perspective). Also, most of the research is directly related to the application of graphical user interfaces and refers primarily to a user working with screen based computer e.g. (Rosson, Maas & Kellogg 1987) and (Hakiel 1991). There are at most a handful of studies that are based on smart products, though some literature exists on design methodologies and conceptual design process as applied to the industrial design domain (Cross 1992). Recently several design magazines have started reporting case studies and design processes related to digital products (Aldersey-Williams 1994), (Patton 1992) and (Harada 1992).

Therefore, the following research problem is formulated mainly from an understanding of the scenarios from real life practices, a review of available tools and problems stated by designers during discussions and researchers (Bekker & Vermeeren 1992), (Manhartsberger & Tscheligi 1994) and (Rosson, Maas & Kellogg 1987).

The main problem facing interaction designers for example, seems to be the task of visualising a dynamic process as opposed to static forms or objects. (Sato 1992), states that the design object in the case of user interface design is the dynamic interaction process between object and user. He argues that representation forms like drawings made by industrial designers contain only static form-related information of the object and not the functionality. He suggests providing appropriate representation methods for the dynamic processes which are difficult to recreate mentally or represent on paper.

The simplest and most common representation method used at the moment is a storyboard which is a linear narrative with visuals and accompanied text. In the conceptual phase, storyboards are the dynamic equivalents of the sketches industrial designers make. Many of the authoring tools available today are neither suitable for quick sketching nor do they provide any special features for quick and dirty representations (Landay 1994). For lack of supporting techniques and tools, designers pin up large sheets of paper on the wall and mark flow structures with marker pens. This technique gives an overview of information space but does not really help in manipulating structures to look at alternatives.

It is informative to look at other creative professions who deal with dynamic processes namely, choreographers, music composers and film-makers. A preliminary survey shows that these professions have established notations that are extensively used in making new compositions and which eventually serve as reliable documentation of an event. However these notations have developed gradually over a long period of time. For example, the music notation that is widely used today to represent western classical music was developed from 900 to 1600 A.D. (Brown et. al 1978). On the other hand, Labanotation, a system used by modern choreographers to represent dance movements is relatively new, dating from 1928, and was developed by the architect Rudolf Laban (Guest 1990). There were even some attempts to represent how operators work with machines in 1947 which was termed as effort diagrams (Preston-Dunlop 1969). Film makers evolved their own make-shift notations for planning camera movements and set lighting (Katz 1991). In behavioural studies, researchers formulated several notation systems to represent dynamic behaviour of human beings and animals in interactive situations (van Hoff 1982). In addition to these fields, software engineering and cognitive science have numerous notation systems to describe user actions (Hartson & Gray 1992), (Jacob 1986) and (Windsor & Storrs 1993), but these are not popular among interaction designers because of their complexity. Chemical process control systems, traffic control patterns and similar areas could also offer insights into how dynamic variables are represented on paper in a diagrammatic fashion.

Perhaps, by examining such systems from other fields, it may be possible to draw on their characteristics and develop a similar system for interaction design. Once a practical technique is formulated with an easy to understand visual grammar, computer support can be incorporated, if necessary at a later stage. Let us now look at the area of tooling *per se*.

3. Elaboration of Existing User Interface Tools

Much effort has been put into the design and development of user interface software tools in the last years. Today there exist around 260 software tools to support various aspects of user interface development. Although they are intended to support the usability engineering process, many of these tools are themselves rather difficult to use. Also most of them are intended for implementing a user interface. Only a few of the various representation techniques can be used to support the design part of the user interface development process. For this phase a technique is needed that enables creation of a prototype of the design solution. Prototypes are not only needed for evaluating design choices but to also represent the best possible specification of the design.
Due to the lack of suitable tools, the whole life cycle often deviates from the "ideal" life cycle which includes prototyping as a substantial part, to a life cycle that is oriented towards available tools and less suited to user interface development. There is still no common view on what the precise usability engineering life cycle should be. The approaches described in (Bass & Coutaz 1991), (Nielsen 1993), (Hix & Hartson 1993) and (Lewis & Rieman 1995), together form a life cycle standard of which prototyping is the most important aspect. This is emphasised by the fact that there is no tool support for an integrated life cycle. State of the art software engineering methods and CASE tools only pay lip service to user interface design and evaluation. A lack of suitable tools can result in *communication* problems between the designers, managers, marketing people, software engineers etc. who have difficulties in expressing their product ideas. These communication problems can result in bad user interfaces due to changes in late phases of the life cycle which are very expensive and prolong the time to market.
Existing tools for prototyping and development incorporate several shortcomings. The most important one is a trade-off that exists between fast creation and high

expressivity of a prototype (Szekely, Luo & Neches 1993). Tools like interface builders allow fast prototyping at a high level of abstraction but are very limited in expressivity. Many so called prototyping tools claim to support graphical user interfaces but in fact their possibilities are restricted to selecting pre-defined interaction techniques like scrollbars or buttons from palettes to build screens. The designer has the possibility to work at a high abstraction level but the possible user interfaces that may be created are rather strictly limited.
Designers may want more than a standard WIMP user interface and even if they want to comply with a certain standard, there is no tool support for the contents of the window. The designer is constrained by the usual WIMP oriented standard widgets that the interface builder provides. Although it should be possible to support standards, they should not be a constraint. When using standard tools, non standard objects for representing new metaphors have to be dispensed with or they have to be programmed at a low level of abstraction which is too time consuming for prototyping.
Authoring tools and animation tools can help one design non-standard software user interfaces but have other shortcomings. The inherent behaviour of the user interface is often neglected in higher level tools. Modelling static objects of the user interface is easy and has been successfully managed by most user interface development systems. To the prejudice of the user interface designers, the more complex task of modelling the behaviour at an abstract level has not been accomplished satisfactorily and making a working user interface still requires programming skills. (This is adequately discussed elsewhere in this paper).
Recently created prototyping and development tools already use sophisticated techniques like programming by demonstration (Myers & Rosson 1992), programming by example (Miyashita, Matsuoka & Takahashi 1992) and visual programming (Singh, Kok & Ngan 1990). These are steps in the right direction, but still the systems do not support creation of whole user interfaces and lack user interface builders that let the developer work in an interactive way to add behaviour to static parts (graphical objects) of the user interface.

Other tools try to cope with complexity by limiting the application domain they support (e.g. application frameworks). This is not really a feasible solution because at the time of tool development it need not be clear which applications are needed in the future and which functionalities will be suitable in which application domain. Although application frameworks are limited in functionality, they are still much too complex to be used in design.

A regrettable trade-off exists between the usability of a tool and the performance of the output prototype. High level tools are prone to produce slow code. This may not be a problem when throwaway prototyping is being deployed. Evolutionary prototyping, which would be the ideal development process is not implementable due to lack of tools that can be used during the whole product life cycle i.e. produce prototypes as well as the final software package.

4. Observations of Design Practice

It is rather a difficult task to embody the user interface design process into a specific framework because of the many diversities involved at various levels. The nature of each project is different, team composition changes over time, the duration of a project is highly variable and the project management structure differs depending on role of external consultants, for example. Even, the design techniques used differ from case to case depending on the product. This multiplicity factor of the design process is stressed in the summaries of design practices described below:

4.1 Product Range

Depending on its nature, each project has a specific orientation and priority. Development efforts usually tend to evolve around this aspect. External consultants and small independent design studios deal with a wide variety of projects compared to in-house design departments which more or less limit themselves to their company's products. Very few designers tend to specialise in a product.

4.2 Management Structure

The way a design project is administered depends on the project and the established practices within the manufacturing company. In-house design departments tend to have design methods and procedures that integrate into the overall manufacturing procedures. Such methods and procedures are drawn up by specialists in the company. Making changes to these established methods involves seeking consensus from several of the involved departments.

4.3 Team Composition

The team composition varies completely from one project to another and is also likely to change over time within the same project. For designing a user interface for a database front-end, a team may consist of a software engineer and a domain expert while the team for a CD-ROM production may, in addition, consist of a graphic designer, illustrator, interaction designer, writer and a publishing executive. Specialists may be brought in at certain stages of the project while a set of core members can be found from inception to completion of the project. Multi-disciplinary teams often cause *communication* problems because the many specialists involved have their own jargon and styles of working. The notations used by a practitioner in one discipline may not be understood by one from another discipline. For example, notations like state transition diagrams or User Action Notations (UAN) (Hix & Hartson 1993) produced by a human factors specialist, make little sense to an industrial designer. Similarly, a virtual mock-up made by a designer cannot be directly used by a software engineer because of the incompatibility of tools and the incompleteness of a mock-up as a software specification. Numerous face-to-face meetings must therefore be frequently held to resolve various design issues. Team members use various artefacts like sketches, mock-ups, models etc., to aid discussion and rely on note taking or quick annotations to capture the highlights of discussions. There are no specific aids for tracking continuity from one meeting to another and new members take a while to get into the flow of discussions.

4.4 Project Duration

The duration of a project may vary from, say, two weeks to a year or more. There are no definite time estimates for even the same categories of products. A CD-ROM title could be made in one month or one year depending on the contents and complexity of design. It is not uncommon for a designer to handle three or four projects simultaneously.

4.5 Design Activities

While there are some broad phases of design, often there are no clear milestones as many activities flow one phase to another in a seamless manner. Also some activities may take place simultaneously. Projects are usually scheduled according to deliverables which are in the form of reports, prototypes, videos or models. The tools and techniques used differ from one activity to another.

4.6 Using Tools and Techniques

Interface designers use several tools depending on the task on hand. In the initial stages of project, they collect information in various forms: reports, clippings, product samples, brochures, videos, demos and so on. Organising such diverse formats into an easily retrievable form is a cumbersome task.

Designers don't generally use any formal, creative idea generation methods except for brainstorming sessions with colleagues. To analyse the structure of the user interface, they often pin-up sheets of paper on large areas of walls and use marker pens to draw links and flows. There do not seem to be any tools to support this activity. It is also becoming common practice to make user scenarios and story-boards in a cartoon style narrative structure. For this, they use pen and paper or the paint tools in a software program. At a later stage, they start making detailed sketches and screen mock-ups. Existing paint tools (Adobe Illustrator, Coral Draw, Macromedia Freehand, for example) or animation programs are used for these tasks. For simulating user interfaces, multimedia authoring tools (Asymmetrix Tool Book, Macromedia Director and Allegiant SuperCard, for example) are very popular. In addition, multimedia tools themselves require the use of several other supplementary tools for preparing images (Adobe Photoshop), sound (Macromedia SoundEdit) and video clips (Adobe Premiere). At the final stages of prototyping, tools such as Philips' Rapro-T and Emultek's Rapid may be used. There are no standard practices for making specifications of user interfaces other than writing detailed reports and including bitmaps. Many of the tools designers use are not well-integrated and many difficulties arise when there is a need to exchange data (a CAD model cannot be imported and used interactively in an authoring program, for instance). Current tools are rather general purpose and production oriented, and are not well suited for conceptualisation of interaction design. Therefore many interaction design specific tasks like organising information, analysing structures or making scenarios remain unsupported to a large extent.

4.7 General Issues

The user interface is one component of the overall product development process; it therefore enjoys only limited importance. Due to the lack of documented practical design techniques, designers seem to be constantly improvising new techniques on a trial and error basis which draws subjective criticism from other team members. They also lack support for making decisions (When and how to use sound for instance). Sometimes, quick and dirty user trials determine the design decisions. Many designers emphasise the evolutionary nature of the field and state that it is too early to form rigid guidelines or structures for the evolving process.
Interaction design is a highly variable process that differs from one context to another. The following section contains an analysis of problem areas.

4.8 Analysis

The task of the interaction designer is to make user interfaces that are not only pleasing to the eye but also easy to understand. In ideal situations, interaction design professionals introduce user interface concepts in the early stages of product design and thereafter iteratively develop detailed specifications through user testing. However, in actual practice, interaction designers are often brought into the picture when the project is in an advanced stage of development and when it is too late to make changes to user-interface features which are deep-rooted. In any case, the process of interaction design involves communicating conceptual ideas, suggesting alternative designs and iteratively developing ideas into precise specifications for implementation. The following section describes the interaction design practices in more detail .
Interaction design has one aspect which is unique. A graphic designer deals with two dimensional visual images; an architect deals with three dimensional space; a film-maker deals with linear narrative and an industrial designer with product forms. Additionally, the interaction designer deals with dynamic and non linear processes; in other words, conditional events that occur in response to several parameters. Anticipating the dynamic changes in parameters and visualising the ensuing event structure is indeed a formidable task. Considering this as fundamental to design thinking, a simple frame-work suggests multiple levels of support. (An alternative is proposed by (Marmolin 1992) who suggests how the use of different media may be best matched to the different phases of information understanding).
In the *incubation* phase, the perceptual and cognitive skills of the designer play a dominant role. These skills are primarily obtained through design training and education over a prolonged period of time. However, few design schools impart skills for visualising dynamic structures. New techniques must be developed to

prepare the designer for this phase. These may be in the form of cognitive exercises similar to puzzles and visual games.

The *communication* phase perhaps poses the bigger problem. A user interface concept is conveyed through a combination of several representations. For example: a plaster model of the product and a screen demo of the display area plus paper sketches. Making a change in one representation format is not reflected in other formats. Secondly, not all formats are inviting for even simple manipulation or annotation. A screen animation for instance can be changed or manipulated only by the author. Moreover, different team members need to interpret the conceptual representations into their own notation schemes like flow-sheets, state-diagrams and so on. Further, tools must support easy and rough sketching of ideas (and these should be demonstrably sketchy) so that one does not make an early commitment to a design. Techniques are required to facilitate making changes in several related representational formats simultaneously. Needless to say, a shared understanding of the concepts among the design team is vital to product development, and conceptual representations play an important role in the decision making process.

In the *realisation* phase, many of the computer tools that are available currently, offer at least some support. The three dimensional form of a product can be modelled fairly accurately and the files can be exported to production systems. Likewise, the functionality of a user interface can be simulated and even prototyped to some extent, though the process can be very cumbersome because of the extensive programming required. However, there are no systems to translate the simulations into concrete specifications for the user interface. The result is that these simulations (Macromedia Director files, for example) are used as illustrations and form part of the specifications. There are a few domain specific tools available for prototyping the functionality of telephones and VCRs. When the interfaces are prototyped using actual hardware connected to computers, incremental changes are made directly in the prototyping software. Therefore at the end, when a fully working product is made, there may not be any complete documentation of the user interface specification. Also, there are no industry practices or known formats for user interface specification as applicable to consumer products. Support tools could be developed for making comprehensive specifications for production purposes and translating these into user manuals at a later stage.

From the above analysis, we can conclude that support for interaction design is required at different levels:

1. at the *cognitive* level to develop skills in visualising dynamic structures,
2. at a *communication* level to share a common understanding of concepts among team members and
3. at *production* level to be able to specify the interface precisely and accurately.

It should be noted that these are mainly for support of interaction design and not related areas such as usability evaluation or software engineering which are also integral parts of user interface development. Let us look at the wider issue of integrating the user interface development process with the software engineering process.

5. Integrating the Human factors & Software Development Processes

Digital technology is transforming the look and function of many electronic products which provide a great deal of flexibility. However, flexible products are very complex to design and manufacture. Consequently, there are many problems facing the industry. The increasing complexity of products requires expertise from several specialised fields outside of the manufacturing sector. Bringing in specialists from non-engineering fields like human factors, ethnology and linguistics for example, makes team communication slow and difficult because of the different working methods, culture and vocabulary of specialists (Grudin 1982). Also, standard development methods may not always be applicable for new products. Very often, project specific tools and methods have to be custom-made and some of them must even be developed simultaneously along with the actual product.

The convergence of computers, communications devices and consumer electronics gives rise to a new generation of highly interactive products where the user interface is a critical component that enables the consumers to comprehend and use a product. A user interface is that aspect of the product involved in its operation or use. Typically, a user interface is formed of the displays, buttons, knobs and connectors. As more and more consumers face usability problems, the design of user interfaces has become extremely important in product development.

In software, a user interface is essentially screen-based and is dependent on the operating system. On the other hand, user interfaces for consumer appliances may have both screen-based (or soft) and physical (or hard) elements. Examples of products with such interfaces are: TVs, VCRs, fax machines, plain paper copiers and phones, which have "hard" knobs and buttons as well as on-screen displays.

Consider the Waterfall Model. This is a description of the software development process which most can recognise whatever process they themselves use. Essentially, the Requirements Specification phase is followed by the Design, Code, Test and Maintenance phases. It is becoming common practice to develop prototypes of a software product and increasingly to then conduct usability evaluations. Whilst this is a vital first step to improve product usability, it leads to an *evaluation centred* approach and any impact on the user interface (UI) would largely be limited to re-arranging the layout or renaming menu items, for example. Additional techniques need to be applied; interviews of users and observational studies, for example. Usability is becoming accepted as an important product release criterion; it has to be designed into a product and cannot be added on late in its development. A *design centred* approach must replace the evaluation centred approach which is presently commonplace; both are important. Alternative views of an integrated cycle are given in (Browne 1994), (Bass & Coutaz 1991), (Sutcliffe & McDermott 1991), (Catterall 1991), (Macaulay 1990), (Curtis & Hefley 1994); an early example is described in (Wasserman 1987).

The first step towards a better user interface is realising that good design begins in the requirements definition stage and not when implementation is under way. Indeed, human factors input should inform the design of the application, in addition to the interface. However, software engineering methodologies do not provide any guidance on how to integrate the knowledge gained from human factors studies, into the software. For example, typical questions a development manager might have are:

Which HF techniques are to be used?

- Should they be scheduled in the Requirements Phase or in the Design Phase?
- Do specialist HF people have to be brought in or can SE people apply the techniques?
- How is the HF knowledge gained to be documented?
- At what stage(s) should the software engineers and human factors personnel exchange and review their respective design documents?

There are two problem areas. First, how is UI design to be undertaken? Second, how are the HF and SE personnel to communicate? MUSE (Method for USability Engineering) (Lim & Long 1994) developed at the Ergonomics & HCI Unit, University College London, addresses these problems and suggests a mechanism whereby both the process and products of UI design might be integrated with an SE method. Let us first look at the design problem and the MUSE method before looking at the integration problem.

5.1 UI Design

As Graphical User Interfaces have become prevalent, so have software tools for their creation. The mere use of windows, icons and a mouse do not guarantee high quality. The interface design problem stems from the perception that one only needs an interface to enable data input and result output. This constrains one to a rather device dependent design - at the level of windows & dialogue boxes and relegates UI design to the mere creation of "pretty pictures". However, if we consider an interface as supporting users in their tasks then we will have a wider device independent understanding.

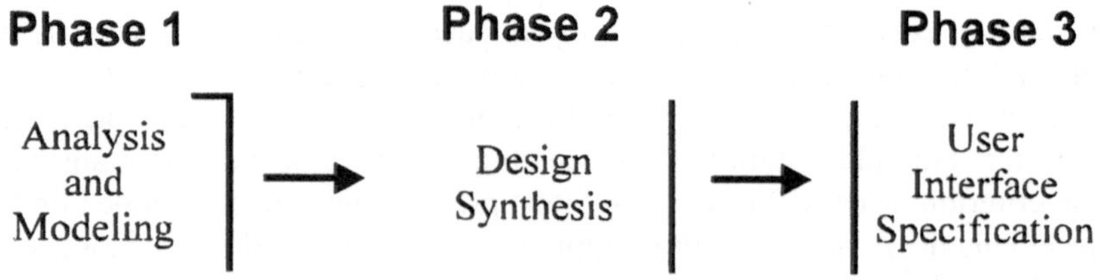

Figure 1. The three phases of MUSE

Following the MUSE method (cf Figure 1), we begin with a very general Requirements Specification and analyse the tasks people do, which may not be

computer supported. Many such task descriptions are then merged to create one Generalised Task Model (GTM) for all tasks the target system should support. Successive decompositions then identify the sub-tasks which are to be executed by the software (on-line) and those to be executed by the user (off-line) - a System & User Task Model (SUTAM). This, in simple terms, leads to a basis for designing the look (screens) and feel (interaction).
The three phases of the MUSE approach and the supporting notation enables analyses of user tasks and importantly, analyses of target systems, to be described in a form that is universally understandable - i.e. by designers, implementers and managers alike. Various intermediate products developed during the user interface design process might need to be checked - with the user or with the software engineers; and a simple structured diagrams (as easy to understand as flow charts) and supporting tables, enable the necessary information exchange.

5.2 Integration

We have defined the points where the human factors and software streams should "*handshake*", i.e. cross-check and exchange information. Four such handshakes have been defined (cf Figure 2):

- First, the User Requirements Specification (URS) must be agreed by both the streams. Omissions and inconsistencies must be resolved and a common understanding secured.
- Second, when the Task Models and initial Domain Analysis have been completed, each design team should ensure that their *understanding* of the domain's objects and activities is the same. The Task Models need to be linked to the object descriptions, attributes and relationships that are developed by the software engineers (particularly if following an Object-Oriented design method). Different disciplines sometimes develop their own subtle meanings for words, causing major communication difficulties, a problem that has been identified by (Grudin 1982). This handshake helps reduce such problems.
- Third, after the System and User Task Model has been developed, it must be reviewed by the software engineers to ensure that the proposed distinction in system and user tasks is matched by the software engineering analysis. Additionally, the software engineers will wish to ensure that only the functionality that is absolutely required will be implemented - and that no more and no less is included in the Functional Requirements Specification. A similar form of assessment is found in (Catterall 1990).
- Finally, the products that embody the look and the feel of the interface, namely the Visual and Interaction Design Specifications, are reviewed by the software engineers to ensure implementability. It may be that UI design has not adequately been informed of the capabilities of the delivery platform and certain widgets, for example, cannot be implemented. Review by the software engineers is able to put this right. This handshake is also useful for the software engineers; they will be coding the interface and will need to include aspects of the Visual and Interaction Design Specification in the Software Requirements Specification.

Additional informal handshakes may be defined, which can take place at points defined by the software engineering method in use. These handshakes can, for example, be used to ensure the two streams are using the same vocabulary to describe the *application* domain. In current best practice e.g. (Taylor 1990), human-factors engineers and software engineers may well meet to discuss the needs of the user interface, and to negotiate the requirements for functionality; with integration methods such as MUSE, early identification of the handshakes is encouraged so as to ensure timely alignment of the two activities.

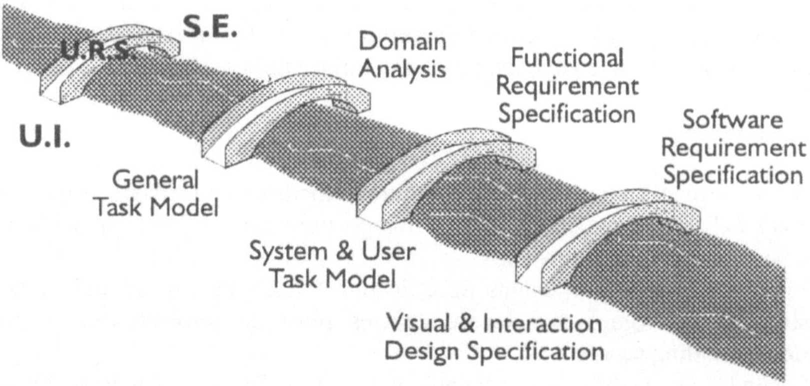

Figure 2. The integration of software engineering and user interface design processes - a document-oriented perspective

5.3 Benefits of Performing and Documenting Analyses of Current Systems

MUSE provides guidelines for identification of suitable systems for analysis (related & partial), and phase one of the method is oriented towards the documentation of these analyses and the generalisation process which informs design of the target system. The knowledge about people - their goals, preferences and working styles - gained from task analysis at the start of the design process is invaluable. The analysis phase is a rich source of innovative design ideas as well as a means of identifying procedural norms. The information gained during the analysis phase is a major contributor to the requirements elicitation and specification process, and encourages early collaboration between members of the Human Factors and Software Engineering streams. The task analysis and modelling stage is a highly iterative process with respect to requirements, i.e. initial requirements direct analysis towards specific users and/or current systems, which in turn lead to new requirements and further analyses.

5.4 Benefits of Support for Communication

The notation utilised within MUSE - the Structured Diagram Notation (SDN) taken from the Jackson Structured Design method - has proven to be easily understood by software engineers, designers and human factors experts. This is of great benefit for it means that a design team which is both multi-disciplinary and geographically distributed will be able to discuss issues related to analysis or early design with little chance for ambiguity. The notation is able to capture various features of observed tasks such as whether they may be executed in any order, or may take place in parallel or whether one of many tasks is executed depending on some condition being fulfilled.

6. Issues Outstanding for Design Methods

Whilst HF design methods offer improvements to the product development process, they cannot guarantee a good design, indeed they should not be expected to. We have identified some requirements, the following of which are particularly important:

- Supporting domain knowledge is often elicited by HF analysts, yet cannot be adequately described in documents such as Task Descriptions. It is often necessary to communicate aspects of this knowledge to the software engineers, however, the notation and accompanying tables cannot capture the breadth of information which is elicited during the task analysis phase.
- What the notation lacks is the means of linking domain information, such as object descriptions and attributes, to the task descriptions. This is a difficult problem as the levels of abstraction at which HF and SE people work are so different.
- Designers of methods assume that a generic HF person will be working on a project. They therefore do not analyse and address the communications problems within the different specialisms - experts in visual and interaction design, the use of colour, auditory interfaces, multi-media etc. to name a few.
- Contextual Inquiry encompasses organisational analysis & modelling, workflow, and user analysis & modelling. The knowledge elicited from the application of these techniques, needs to be used at various stages in the design process. This is an area where methods fail to give adequate support.
- The influence of using a tool or computer system to support a task can actually change the task, and more support to help pre-empt, document, analyse and otherwise support task redesign is needed.
- Screen layout, for example the grouping of buttons - say based on card sorting - cannot be described in design methods. The design rationale for particular layouts is not captured and nor is its derivation supported. This problem is exacerbated for multi-media interfaces and compounds the dependency upon good guidelines and good Human Factors expertise.
- Conversations with users during Task Analysis about how they use a system might reveal metaphors they use. Verbs like go and move might indicate a physical space metaphor; verbs like ask and answer might indicate a

conversation metaphor; verbs like know, make and do (attributed to the computer) might indicate an anthropomorphic or organism metaphor. Methods for metaphor design must be integrated into interface methods so as to ensure that documentation, analysis and derivation of metaphors is based on sound principles.

- Scenarios can help make concrete the abstract task models developed by the HF stream and the object oriented designs developed by the SE stream. As they embody interaction with the device from the perspective of the end user, they also help bridge the gap with the customer. By providing a set of real problems they also help usability evaluation. Design methods that support the timely construction of scenarios (Bernsen & Klausen 1993) must be better integrated with interface design and evaluation methods.

Having looked at the problems that arise when integrating the software engineering an human factors processes, we will now examine a part of the interface design process in more detail. This serves as an exemplar of the many problems that we have only mentioned; one can expect additional problems specific to other processes within interface design.

7. Issues Outstanding for Tool Support

Based on our knowledge of current research efforts in tool provision and of our experience in interdisciplinary design, the following requirements of a prototyping-centred user interface design tool are outlined. We have already identified requirements for tool support in the earlier stages of product development and for support in process integration, and this section goes on to discuss the needs for tool support for the exploration and implementation of design ideas.

7.1 Support for Integrated Methodologies

In order to support the take-up of usability engineering techniques and "good" design by the wider software development community, much more of the methodological knowledge for design needs to be supported by tools. Such tools could support usability engineering methods such as MUSE as well as providing support for UI design by integrating usability guidelines such as those of (Smith & Mosier 1986) Furthermore, support could be provided for construction and integration of design rationales (MacLean, Young, Bellotti & Moran 1991) and, later on in the life cycle support for the design and execution of usability evaluation. It may not be necessary for one tool to support all the activities required for good design, but tool support should be sought which enables the members of an interdisciplinary design team to maximise their contribution to the final product.

7.2 Use of User Interface Models

One of the major reasons for the lack of high level tools for producing user interfaces or user interface prototypes with high expressivity is the absence of suitable, high level structural models of the user interface. There already exist several structural models of the user interface but most of them are oriented towards implementation, for example the event model , object oriented concepts (Cox 1986), production systems (Olsen 1990) and constraints (Vander Zanden 1992). All of these are used as the basic concept of a programming language and are not intended for use by a designer. Also they do not explicitly support graphics. Other models, like state transition diagrams (Jacob 1986) or the dialog transaction model (Hix 1989) are not suited for modelling modern, metaphor based user interfaces.

The lack of a suitable structural model limits the work of the designers because they have to think in concepts of the model they use (incorporated into a specification language or a tool). (Hutchins, Hollan & Norman 1986) coined the term *semantic distance* which describes the ability of a user to execute a task with a given user interface. The same *semantic distance* applies to designers as users of user interface tools. The question here is: Is it possible for a designer to express a design in a certain language (a specification language or a tool) and if so, how easy is it? If a model does not provide suitable concepts for expressing a design, then the semantic distance of the tool will be high and it will be less usable.
A suitable model for modern user interfaces would support the whole life cycle. It would be easier for designers to communicate because they can express ideas in the concepts of the model. The lack of a suitable model is the reason for the lack of suitable tools and thus also for the many sub-optimal user interfaces that abound.

7.3 Designers are Users

Most paper-and-pencil specification methods are complex, hard to understand and don't include visual design. More and more human activities are computer supported. User interface design also should be computer supported to facilitate organisation of the design process and reuse. Tools should support interactive design of user interfaces.
As user interfaces of many applications improve, many of them have achieved a high usability standard by applying the knowledge that has been acquired through years of HCI research. Design tools also have a user interface. Why is so little effort spent on the user interface of a design tool? Often designers are seen as experts who have the time to specialise in the usage of a certain tool. This need not be the case. The inherent interdisciplinarity of the field implies naive users. Psychologists, Human Factors Experts etc. are not computer experts and cannot be expected to spend their time reading heavy user manuals.
Additionally, a user centred i.e. designer centred tool should support the diverse working methods of designers. They should not be forced into an inflexible process but be free to work top-down or bottom-up as they like. Many designers prefer to draw pictures first so they also need a graphic package that lets them sketch initial designs.

7.4 Prototyping Support

Rapid prototyping is touted as a suitable method for iteratively approaching the ideal design solution. ("A picture says more than a thousand words"). Specifications that are hard to understand can cause expensive communication problems. A prototype on the other hand is likely to be understood by everybody. Prototyping goes together with usability. The easier it is to use a tool, the easier it will be to create a prototype. Modifiability forms an important precondition for prototyping and also goes together with usability - the easier it is to create a prototype the easier it usually is to change it. To support prototyping it also should be possible to simulate incomplete prototypes.

7.5 Design the Optimal Interface

A designer should be encouraged to design the best possible user interface, not considering any constraints in the first run. If designers are forced to design under platform or software engineering constraints, then limited improvements will be made in user interface design itself. Compromises can be made after the first design approaches exist. This requirement implies that the design of innovative, non-standard user interfaces must be supported by a design tool.

7.6 Functionality Requirements

Modern software packages are expected to fulfil certain requirements to comply with industry standards. Products are expected to facilitate import and export of components and reuse of project parts by the use of software libraries. Portability is a major requirement and applies both to the kind of platform a tool is running on and to the kind of platform the output software is running on. Last but not least, tools as well as the output software are expected to have good performance to enable rapid development.

8. Conclusion/Research Agenda

This paper has indicated how early consideration of user interface issues is impaired by inadequate support in both methods and tools. User interface design is a multi-disciplinary task and each specialist in the team uses a different set of tools: usability specialists use special software for analysing video protocols; interaction designers use an animation tool for presenting ideas; and software engineers use a user interface toolkit for prototyping.

We have looked at the problem of integrating design methods in the wider product development process and found the methods and tools wanting; notwithstanding the additional problems introduced by the need for integration. Methods need to ensure inclusion of domain knowledge, organisation analysis & modelling, support for development of scenarios and support for exploration of alternative metaphors. Tools must support fast prototyping with high expressivity while not constraining designers to a metaphor or to a set of widgets. Concentrating on one interface design activity as an example, namely, interaction design, we find that conceptualising, visualising and specifying dynamic behaviour remains a challenge.

In general, most design professions have excellent tool support for the later stages of the design process and almost none for the conceptual phase, where group discussions, brainstorms and pen & paper, (excellent tools in their own right) are used out of necessity. Likewise, in interaction design, many key activities of the conceptual phase such as making flow-sheets, analysing information in tabular format or making story-boards, are done manually.
Perhaps, the most important problem for multi-disciplinary design teams is that of communication. The issues related to communication need to be addressed early-on and awareness of potential problems must be maintained during the development life cycle. Developers of design methods need to recognise these needs as well as tool developers.

Acknowledgements

Thanks are due to many; for the sake of brevity we only mention a few, namely Prof. J. Long, A. Stork, J. Middlemass, Prof. R. den Buurman, Prof. J. Hennessey, A. Vermeeren, K. Sittig, T. Bekker, I. McWilliam & J. Band.

Chapter 10: User Centred Complex System Design: Combining Strategy, Methods and Front End Technology

Bryan Murray, Linda Candy & Ernest Edmonds

1. Introduction

Delivering effective and appropriate software solutions to user communities within acceptable time and resource constraints is recognized to be a major challenge by the software industry. Software suppliers endeavour to deliver timely, reliable and useful applications to an increasingly competitive market. However, particularly in the field of scientific computation, it has been recognized for some time that the needs of users are not being met by most current software applications (Hague & Reid 1990). The problem with these applications is that they usually require users to grapple with general purpose programming languages and move between a range of systems even for the completion of a single task. This is a costly and frequently ineffective way of ensuring task efficiency and user satisfaction.

Our domain of interest is the development of complex systems that employ re-usability, task support, and the integration of application functionality and for whom the user population consists of professional workers. An important characteristic of the target users is that they are skilled professionals employed in critical problem solving roles and, as such, they have considerable discretion as to how they complete their tasks.

Computer technology, such as graphical user interfaces and multi-media, may enable developers to construct better users interfaces to established systems. However, we argue that this must go further than providing mere "facades" (Windsor 1990). To meet the needs of users for diverse task and organizational purposes, enhancing established systems will require different solutions ranging from improvements in the user interface presentation and dialogue to the integration of a number of applications that support complex tasks. If the system is to be tailored to the needs and tasks of professional expert users, there is a need for task specific support which is achieved by mapping the users' expertise and the functionality of existing applications. This support would depend upon a unifying, consistent, user interface that augments productivity and learning. If the systems are to meet the needs of these people fully, a user-centred strategy and a coherent enabling technology for development is required. The distinguishing features of the approach described here is that these twin elements are seen to be mutually interdependent.

User Interface System Engineering (UISE) addresses the above issues and more general problems that bring together ideas and work from various disciplines. In addressing the problems of developing complex systems we have utilised and combined several strands of UISE. The provision of suitable levels of task support requires the incorporation of task models into the system (Copas & Edmonds 1994). The Front End System (FES) technology utilises the combination of task and dialogue models as the foundation of system development. The implementation of this model based approach employs a flexible, distributed architecture and a set of rapid development tools. The technology originated in Interactive Systems development, including User Interface Management (UIM) systems. The major components and relationships within the architecture are shown in

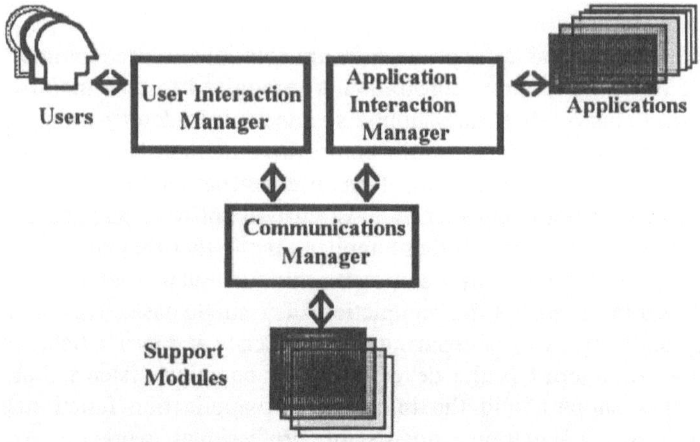

Figure 1: Front End System Technology Architecture

Our approach to the development of user centred complex systems is based upon the premise that advanced software technology is not in itself sufficient to realise high quality usable systems. To be effective it must be accompanied by appropriate development strategies and supporting methods designed to ensure the quality of the resulting system. The development strategy and associated methods are drawn from a wide spectrum of studies in Human-Computer Interaction (HCI) and practical applications in the general Software Engineering field. The FES architecture and tools were developed together with the methods to support a particular development strategy as part of an ESPRIT 2 project called FOCUS.

The chapter begins with an introduction to the FOCUS strategy and methods. This is followed by a description of the FES technology and its relation to the development strategy. Finally, an example of the use of the combined approach in a complex application domain is described.

2. Strategy and Methods

The FOCUS strategy for FES development is an iterative process within which the role of prototyping and evaluation are key elements. This development strategy and the methods that have been developed to support requirements analysis and the

evaluation of prototype systems are described in this section. These take account of a number of existing methods for user-centred design, the envisaged development context and the software technology. The methods described in section 2.2 below, are based upon a study of a range of approaches to user-centred design. Their particular content and form was driven by two main objectives: first, that they should be accessible and usable by conventionally trained system developers, and second, that they should be flexible enough to be customised for different development contexts. Each one is best applied at different points in the life cycle of the system development but this is not a rigid demarcation and not all the methods need be applied. An iterative development strategy provides a basic structure within which account can be taken of prevailing constraints of time and resources. The elements of that strategy are shown in figure 2 below.

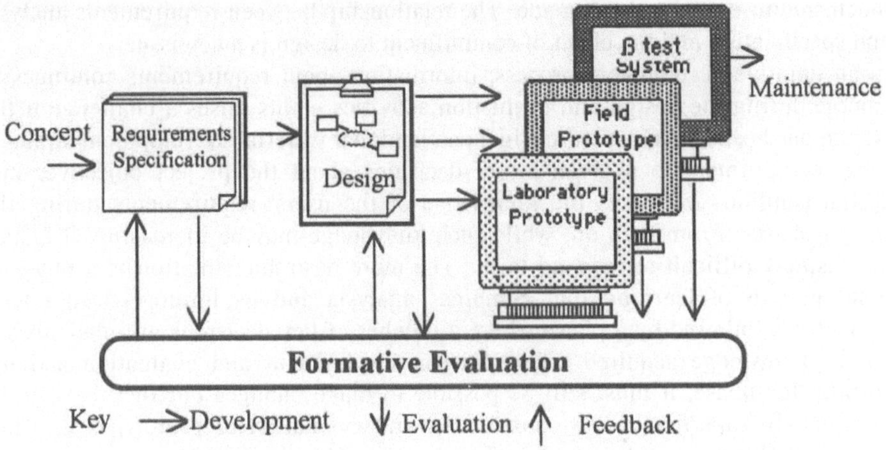

Figure 2: An Iterative Development Life Cycle

2.1 Iterative Design and Development

System development methodologies that are primarily based on a waterfall model of the life cycle assume that one can complete one information activity in full before moving on to the next. Thus, for example, Ashworth and Goodland (1990) in their guide to SSADM recommend that the outcome of the analysis is a specification that need not be substantially changed for the rest of the project, forming the basis for all design and implementation work. In contrast to this approach, an iterative development strategy assumes that even where a rigorous requirements and task analysis has taken place, changes will still be necessary during the total life cycle and, therefore, makes explicit the need for this in the process. Iterative development is increasingly acknowledged to be a viable approach in the design of interactive systems (Gould et al. 1991, Ince 1991) and is being used increasingly by software houses (eg. Philips - McClelland & Brigham 1990, Hewlett-Packard - Stevens 1991).

Early analysis prior to design assumes that users can articulate all their requirements in the absence of any design proposals. Eason presents a convincing list of reasons why users have difficulty with this (Eason 1988). Users also find it hard to verbalise their task behaviour (Berry & Broadbent 1984). For these reasons, ways of enabling the process of user articulation are critical requirements of any user centred development strategy. To that end, the interaction with a prototype system, however incomplete, may enable them to express ideas and knowledge that was either implicit or had been previously overlooked.

A basic premise of the FOCUS strategy is that interactive systems design for complex task support is best served by an iterative development life cycle. This of necessity must include the construction of prototype systems which can be evaluated by users, the results of which are fed into the design activities before too much commitment has been made. The relationship between requirements analysis and specification and the effect of commitment to design is a key issue.

In an iterative development process, information about requirements continues to emerge during the design and evaluation activities. This raises a challenge if the system has been implemented usnig a conventional waterfall development strategy. Here, commitment to a given set of decisions about the project objectives and design solutions overtakes the knowledge of the users' requirements during the design phase. From then on, while such knowledge may be increasing, it is also increasingly difficult to respond to it. The more desirable situation is a phase of rapid growth of learning that combines analysis and exploratory design with evaluations followed by a phase where a number of key decisions are made, based on the knowledge acquired before further development and evaluation activity. During this phase, it must still be possible to make changes but they have to be increasingly superficial. The construction and evaluation of prototypes is a key element of the strategy described in this chapter and is described below.

2.1.1 Prototyping

An iterative development process requires the generation of prototype system designs which act as tools for user requirements elicitation as well as furthering the design and development process. The speed with which prototypes that embody minimal commitment (whilst enabling evaluations to be performed) are generated is a critical factor.

Prototype systems take different forms according to their role and place in the life cycle. There arc three types envisaged: Laboratory, Field and Delivery (ßtest). Prior to the design and implementation of the Laboratory prototype, screen simulations (i.e. screen display and minimal dialogue simulation) may also be generated and evaluated with users immediately as part of the preliminary requirements analysis. However, for the purposes of acquiring information from users about more fundamental issues, such as degree of task support, more than a 'facade' is required.

Laboratory prototypes have a minimum of function calls but are not sufficiently robust to be installed in user sites for unsupported use. They are used by developers to evaluate technical issues and also to carry out usability tests with users in

experimental task scenarios. Field prototypes can be delivered to the user work environment where they are used to evaluate the support the system provides for real tasks and the impact this has on the general work design. They need to be more robust than the Laboratory prototypes but may not necessarily provide full functionality. They are used to to validate the requirements specification in a more realistic situation run in parallel with existing methods of performance. Thus, a prototype may be be developed to evaluate a user interface design, to establish the technical feasibility of an implementation solution, or to attempt to represent a given body of knowledge within a knowledge-based component. Alternatively, it could just be an early version of the full system with complete functionality.
In the development context envisaged, the generation of prototype systems requires quick and efficient software tools to which developers have ready access. To that end, the FOCUS technology support for prototype construction has been developed and is described in Section 3 below. Having constructed the prototypes, developers then require effective and practical methods for evaluating them, not only on a technical basis but more critically, for checking that the design meets the user requirements in full. The combined capacity for iterating rapidly through a number of design alternatives using tools that support rapid prototyping with methods that are quick, easy to perform and able to generate useful information is the central point of the approach adopted here.

2.1.2 Evaluation

Evaluation can take many forms and different methods are best suited to different evaluation objectives. It is important, therefore, to understand the differences that lie behind the performance of an evaluation. The act of performing evaluations is not sufficient in itself to ensure good system design. They must be applicable to the role of the prototype and what information is required from its use. Most important, they must be appropriate for the existing skills of the development team and be achievable within a given set of resources and timescales.

The evaluation of prototype systems with users represents a vital mechanism for achieving a full and accurate understanding of the objectives of the system design (Candy & Edmonds 1988, Fitter et al. 1991). When assessing evaluation methods, they are often valued in terms of how much they may yield about the number of usability problems. Less consideration is given to the extent to which the evaluators are able to identify significant new information about user needs as a result of the evaluations. The classification of evaluation methods into "measurement" and "diagnostic" (Wilson & Whitefield 1989) also denies this role for evaluation. The concept of the diagnostic method certainly suggests simply finding things that are at fault and obtaining information to correct them.
Formative evaluation is seen as an activity in support of design, leading to improvements in design rather than simply in its assessment. Evaluation of this kind supports design by enabling learning to take place of the different factors and issues that will determine success as well as learning about whether a given design

is in need of improvement. Scriven (Scriven 1967) in his original definition of the term, contrasted Formative Evaluation with Summative Evaluation. The latter refers to evaluations that examine the impact of a system and attempt to measure the extent to which it has met its objectives or provided an improvement over existing systems. Formative evaluation is important early on when most learning needs to be done and therefore is a significant activity. This can be done using user interface simulations without real functionality. However, as calls to the functional units are developed these can be included in the prototypes and incorporated in the evaluation activities.

The FOCUS evaluation methods for FES development are primarily directed towards the formative evaluation of different system prototypes, the results of which are fed back into the design process as early as possible in the total life cycle. They also offer support for the configuration, the execution of the evaluations and the analysis of the resulting data by the development team. In section 2.2. below, the FOCUS suite of methods for requirements analysis and evaluation of prototypes at different stages of development are described.

2.1.3 Project Management

An Iterative development strategy implies a need for mechanisms and strategies for effective management control of the process. It is important to avoid the situation where after the initial requirements analysis, a series of prototypes are generated and gradually improved until resources run out and the current prototype is hurriedly turned into the delivered system. Thus, an important issue is that there needs to be careful management of the prototyping activities (Edmonds et al. 1989, Born 1988).

Included in the FOCUS methods suite is a Project Management Guide (PMG) that provides advice about planning the FES development project. It highlights some of the key considerations that need to be taken into account in the particular area of FES development. It is assumed that a thorough feasibility analysis has been performed in the manner described in the Feasibility Analysis Method (FAM). A key point made is that the essence of good planning lies in anticipating resource requirements and building flexibility into the plan in order that additional requirements can be handled.

2.2 Requirements Analysis and Prototype Evaluation Methods

Methods for user centred system design have been devised to support different development strategies. From collaborative work in industrial and commercial environments, we have identified a need for methods that can be applied at different levels of complexity, according to the needs of the problem domain and development context. No single method is likely to be appropriate for all environments and therefore, the methods have been tailored and tested in real use and are available to developers as "toolbox" selection. Methods must also offer effective support for user centred analysis but at a lesser cost than existing methods.

In that respect , they should not be perceived as demanding extensive investment of time and effort. They should, however, increase the focus on the users' characteristics, task and requirements, by encouraging the identification of key areas of information that need to be collected and providing useful notations for representing the information.

A number of existing methods were researched and assessed in relation to the requirement for cost effective and practical resources for use by system developers. The following methods in particular were drawn upon: HUFIT PAS toolset (Taylor 1990), the USTM methodology (Macaulay et al. 1990), Contextual Inquiry (Wixon et al. 1990) Hierarchical Task Analysis (HTA) (Annett & Duncan 1967) and Task Allocation Charts (TAC) (Ip et al. 1990). They were customised and tested in the design and development process of a number of FES systems. Modifications and improvements were then carried out in the light of practical experience.

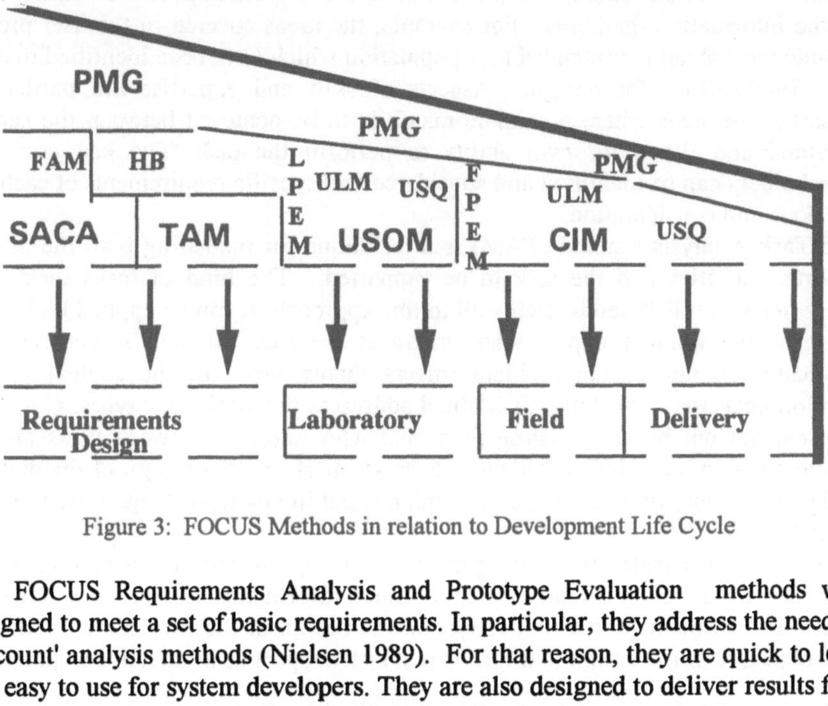

Figure 3: FOCUS Methods in relation to Development Life Cycle

The FOCUS Requirements Analysis and Prototype Evaluation methods were designed to meet a set of basic requirements. In particular, they address the need for 'discount' analysis methods (Nielsen 1989). For that reason, they are quick to learn and easy to use for system developers. They are also designed to deliver results from relatively short contact with representatives of the user population. They may form the basis for evaluation reports or simply result in changes to a prototype leading to the next version. A suite of methods was developed for FES developers to accompany the FOCUS toolkit (Candy & Rousseau 1995). The methods in relation to the development cycle are illustrated in Figure 3.

As the figure illustrates, the application of the methods at different points reduces over the life cycle. If the results achieved are valuable and are applied in the revised system design successfully then this reduction of effort should be matched by an increase in user satisfaction. It should be noted that it is not necesssary to apply all the methods in all cases but to select as the situation demands.

2.2.1 Methods for Requirements Specification

The methods for Requirements Analysis and Specification are : Project Management Guide (PMG), Feasibility Analysis Method (FAM); Stakeholders and Context Analysis (SACA), Task Analysis Method (TAM). Each comprises a set of forms for data collection and guidance about how to proceed. Two examples are described in brief in this section, the Stakeholders And Context Analysis (SACA) and Task Analysis method (TAM) see (Candy & Rousseau 1995).

The objective of SACA is to obtain a good profile of the individual users, stakeholders and their working environment that might be relevant in the design of an FES. It enables the development team to perform user and expert profile analyses, working environment analysis including physical conditions and existing equipment, stakeholders requirements analysis including costs and benefits in relation to other stakeholders and a design and life cycle implications summary of all the information gathered. For example, the areas covered in the user profiles include facts about the intended user population which have been identified that can have implications for design. Aspects of skill and expertise are particularly important in areas where a suitable match is to be achieved between the support provided and the users' own ability to perform the task. The key users and stakeholders can be identified and considered and specific requirements of each will be taken into consideration.

The Task Analysis Method (TAM) is a technique for modelling both the domain expert's activities and the task to be supported. The kind of tasks most often supported by an FES lends itself well to this approach. It can be applied both to the work of the domain expert who interfaces between problem solvers and the application(s) and to the problem solvers themselves. In the context of FES development, the Task Analysis Method addresses two basic task types. One is the task carried out by any existing personnel who interface between users and the applications to be included. This will form the basis for the design of the dialogue and problem solving strategy that is implemented in any Knowledge Based Support Modules.

Task Analysis enables the development of an appropriate understanding of task activities and problem solving strategies. Such information is necessary so that key questions can be answered that reflect on the design of the user-system dialogues. The objective of the design of a FES is that task support be as effective as possible.

2.2.2 Methods for Prototype Evaluation

The main FOCUS methods that support the evaluation of prototypes are discussed in this section. The User-Software Observation Method (USOM) and the Contextual Inquiry Method (CIM) both involve users performing tasks and developers observing and discussing task performance with the users. Other methods include, the User Satisfaction Questionnaire (USQ) which is a simple questionnaire that obtains a single global measure of user satisfaction, and the User Logging Method which offers advice about recording users' actions at any point in the development of the prototype systems: see (Candy & Rousseau 1995).

The User/Software Observation Method (USOM) is an evaluation method which uses observational and verbal protocol techniques. It is based on a technique for evaluating prototypes which is akin to the York Manual (Wright & Monk 1992). It offers a quick and easy way of obtaining feedback from users about designs and highlights usability problems. The objective of the method is to identify points where users have some difficulty carrying out their task using a Laboratory prototype, to diagnose the cause and propose some remedy. The method works best as a formative evaluation tool, that is, an activity in which feedback from users influences specification and implementation of the software. The method should be used to examine how users interact with a system in a situation where the tasks have been set up expressly for evaluation purposes rather than as normal on site activities.

The type of information derived from using the method will be qualitative rather than quantitative, and focused on major usability problems. The data can not be subjected to statistical tests of reliability so if you require predictive measures or wish to compare design alternatives, use another method. Using the method will also provide an opportunity to test out existing understanding of the users' task and skills. New information about these areas may also come to light.

The FOCUS CIM is a method for obtaining information about the difficulties users have when interacting with a Field prototype. It involves observing a subject in the performance of a task using an FES in the work context, followed by an interview. The objective of the method is to obtain a better understanding of the user's task and to identify points where the user has some difficulty in its performance, in order to be able to diagnose the cause and propose some remedy. This method is a quick and easy to use way of getting feedback about the initial system design and further information about requirements. It can be used, therefore, at the stage in the iterative development when a prototype has been constructed that is sufficiently robust and complete in its functionality that it can be introduced at the user site. In particular, this method can be used after having obtained some usage data using User Logging, in order to answer any questions that have been raised from the data collected.Two types of information are gathered: first, a deeper and more accurate picture of the tasks that users need the system to support and second, a body of qualitative data about usability problems with the Field prototype.

2.3 Methods Support for Software Development

Information from the requirements analysis and evaluations will have a profound effect on both the design of the final system and the development process. The impact of this information will be in a variety of areas, that derive in the main from the FES architecture. Consequently, they relate to different parts of the implementation. Information about the users, their skills and their task will impact directly on the design of the system. These implications can be divided into those that apply to: functionality, dialogue, presentation format, distribution of platforms, on-line help and user support in general.

The requirements and task analysis will provide the foundation information for the design of initial prototype solutions. SACA, for example, provides information about the potential system users, their environment and concerns; from this information the development team are able to build a model of the generic user of the system on which much of the system and particularly dialogue design will be based. Task analysis provides more detailed information which will provide a variety of inputs to the system, of particular importance is the development of the task and dialogue models. For example the task information to support the development of the dialogue model would be:

- An understanding of the task context
- An understanding of the task and goal structure
- A comprehensive list of the actions and related objects that are involved in the task performance
- An understanding of how the task is allocated between individuals and current tools

A fundamental assumption is that the process of requirements gathering and design is an on-going one. Consequently, the major role of the evaluation methods is to further refine the requirements, task and user information gathered during the initial design phase. The type of information gathered and the areas of impact of that information will be similar to those in the initial prototype design. Essentially the evaluation can be seen as requirements gathering employing an artefact (the prototype) to assist users in further articulating their needs.
While the methods allow the gathering, and refining of this specific information it is necessary to have a technology that can adequately support the different aspects of the iterative development strategy and the effective utilisation of the methods. Clearly, to be effective the development of the methods and the technology must be carried out in parallel, as has been the case in FOCUS. In the following sections the technology is described and its specific support to the main areas of the strategy. There is also an example presented of the use of the combined methods and technology package to address a complex support system development

3. Focus Development System

The iterative development strategy requires a technology that can support both the rapid development of a range of prototypes and evaluation. The methods described in the previous sections support the strategy and a task-based approach to system development. However, the nature of the technology will influence the emphasis placed on the types of methods selected to support system development. Rapid prototyping implies a high level specification that employs the minimum of detail with the system supplying default parameters where ever possible. Formative evaluation requires that changes to prototype design can be effected quickly and, ideally, interactively, where the user is able to select between design alternatives.

The utilisation of existing functionality speeds up the development and prototyping process by making functionality available at an early stage of system design. A technology that employed a modular architecture with each component dedicated to providing particular specialised functions is suggested to maximise efficiency and flexibility. These requirements are addressed by the Front End System technology.

A Front End System is a separable user interface system that can integrate both new and existing applications, services and knowledge-based task support in order to provide specific users with tailored solutions. This is achieved through the employment of a model based approach that utilises Task, Dialogue and Application models and provides for the integration of application functionality to address user task requirements. The details of our model based approach will be presented in the next section while a discussion of the architecture and tools developed to implement this approach will be discussed in the following section.

3.1 Model Based Approach

The overall aim of the system is to facilitate the rapid development and re-design of various types of prototypes leading to a deliverable system and thus enable the cost effective utilisation of an iterative development strategy. The model based approach provides the opportunity for rapid development through its support for high level descriptions of the system.

Model based systems aim to move interface development up a level from the definition of syntax to the specification of semantics. The semantics modelled have varied depending primarily on whether the system is user or application controlled. Application semantics have been modelled in various ways (Singh & Green 1989, Olsen 1989, Sukaviriya et al. 1993, Paterno' & Pangoli 1995). Of particular interest is the utilisation of the software engineering domain's data models (Hudson & King 1986, de Baar et al. 1992, Janssen et al. 1993). However, a problem here is that the dialogues generated are somewhat generic and, as other authors have attested, (Gullikson & Sandblad 1995) interfaces need to be tailored to the individual user task rather than being generic. Work has been reported that provides more fine-grained control of the generated dialogues (Janssen et al. 1993); however, to provide greater flexibility requires a system that is user rather than application controlled. Various work has been reported on user centred systems that employ models, usually of tasks or users, variously defined and combined (Szekely et al. 1993, Palanque & Bastide 1995, Bodart et al. 1995).

In FES technology, the domain model may contain a task model, a dialogue model or an integration of the two models, as in the SEPSOL example below. In this approach, the task model can be viewed as a high level abstraction of the dialogue model. Hence, a top level controlling dialogue model may not be explicitly represented in the system. The effective use of the two models requires that there is a separation between them (Copas & Edmonds 1994), although the separation can be either logical or physical. The reason for this separation is to enable the task

model to be clearly identifiable and therefore effectively maintained and developed. The integration of the models involves the task model exchanging state information and data with the dialogue model. Data generated from the execution of the dialogue is passed back to the task model. Where the separation is physical, the models would probably reside in separate Support Modules and communication would be facilitated by the message system. Logical separation would involve both models residing in a single Support Module and communication would be via sub-goals and argument instantiation, as in the example below.
The FES technology implements the use of these models through the Support Modules (see 3.2) component of the architecture and tools. The Support Module enables a logical model of both the Task and the Dialogue to be developed. The declarative nature of these models and the separation of the sub-tasks means that a flexible dialogue can be supported rather than the somewhat restricted dialogue/user options possible where a more procedural model is used.

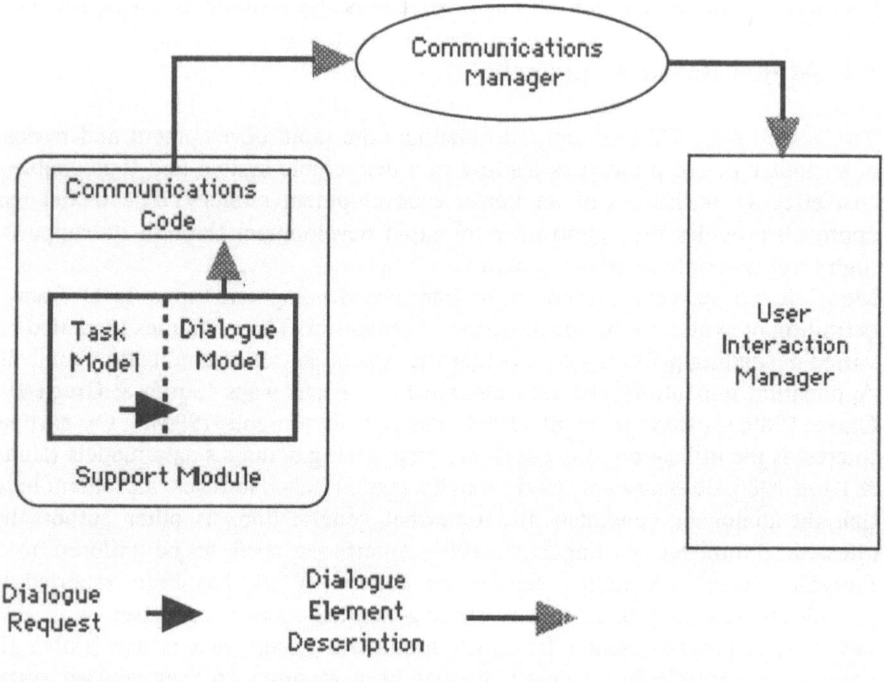

Figure 4. Dialogue Generation

The above issues are now discussed in the context of an example system. SEPSOL (Murray et al. 1992; see section 4.5) is a complex multi-application system that supports chemists using statistical design to identify suitable models for their experiments. The dialogue is generated from the integration of the task and dialogue models. Thus, for example, there is a sub-task that requires the display to the user of the results of the analysis. This 'dialogue request' is passed to the dialogue model and a suitable dialogue element is selected and instantiated with

the results data. The dialogue element is specified using the AIO specification method and passed to the User Interaction Manager (UIM) for realisation, via the message system. Figure 4 below shows this process in terms of the logically separated models, as employed in SEPSOL, and the architectural components.
The user is able to interact with the interface object displayed. The user's interaction would cause the UIM to send a return message to the Support Module and further sub-dialogues may be generated depending on the definition of the dialogue element.
The Task model enables an application function integration that is transparent to the user. This is achieved through the Application Interaction Manager (AIM) (Prat et al. 1990) module of the FOCUS architecture. The available application functionality can be aggregated into task objects that constitute the application model. The application function models are held in the AIM and are integrated with the Task model to support the user tasks. Where necessary they are integrated with the dialogue model and define particular dialogue requirements. The task objects (function aggregation) are not static and can readily be re-defined. Clearly, there is the opportunity of developing dynamically re configurable task objects to support newly defined tasks.
As an example, in SEPSOL the AIM has a set of task objects defined in terms of function models of several statistical packages. The integration of application functions is achieved as follows: at a point in the problem solving process when the task model requires the generation of a specific model (e.g. d-optimal) an application independent task object is specified along with the necessary data and communicated via the message system to the AIM. The example below shows a typical message:

```
message(sepsol115, [ aim_goal, be_generated_design(d_optimal,
                [4,2,0,0,0,0,_,_,_,16], [X,Y]) ], sepsol:aim).
```

The second parameter contains the task object identifier and the data required. The AIM then maps this task object to individual application functions, accesses these functions and returns the generated model to be integrated into the problem solving process. The process is completely transparent to the user and the applications actually used can be changed as required with no impact on the systems working.

The FES model based approach has been outlined in this section. The following section introduces the implementation of these ideas in the FES architecture and tools.

3.2 Architecture and Tools

The Front End System Technology is based on an extended Seeheim model, with a distributed modular architecture that employs a client-server level of separation between the modules. It has a specialised Application Interface Module and includes a completely new module, the Support Module to address current concerns in the areas of task support and highly interactive applications. This formed the basis for the production of a set of construction tools centred on the main modules of the architecture. The architecture is based on the premise that user task support is a basic requirement for a modern system. The fundamental concepts were described by Edmonds & McDaid (1990) and refined in (Edmonds et al. 1992). The major components and relationships within the architecture are shown in Figure 1 above.

The kind of modular architecture shown in the figure above can only work if communication between its components is simple, fast and flexible. Communication is handled by 'messages', which are routed by the Communications Manager. The same message format applies to all messages, that is: a unique identifier, routing information supplied automatically by the sending module and a *contents* argument that contains the data to be exchanged. There are two basic messages types, either control or communication. *Control* messages, such as a request to activate or terminate a particular module, are dealt with by a module within the Communications Manager. *Communication* messages are used for data exchange and communication between any of the modules, although they are generally directed to the user in which case they will contain dialogue descriptions employing the FES AIO specification notation (Edmonds et al. 1992).
The following sections briefly describe the concepts involved and the function of each component shown in the architecture.

3.2.1 User Interaction Manager (UIM)

The User Interaction Manager provides user interface presentation and dialogue services to the other modules in the architecture. In addition, it controls access to the user and mediates between modules in conflict for access to the user. Its main function is to create and realise the details of the object oriented dialogue specification it receives via the central message system.
Dialogue management and specification involves an hierarchical structure that is based on, and managed by, a task model integrated with a dialogue model (Murray & Edmonds 1993, Copas & Edmonds 1994). These models would normally be contained in one or more Support Modules. The task model initiates an abstract dialogue request, for example, to obtain information from the user. The dialogue elements may be specialised for individual requests and will necessarily be application dependent. The resulting dialogue may be single level or involve sub-dialogues and thus the resulting hierarchy can have several levels in a complex dialogue sequence. For example, the dialogue request may be for a filename, in which case the dialogue model would select a suitable filename request dialogue element. This may involve a directory request, followed by the display of the directory contents and selection of a filename by the user.

The specification of the dialogue objects used to present the dialogue element to the user are based on a specification method employing Abstract Interaction Objects (Edmonds et al. 1992). An Abstract Interaction Object (AIO) is a prototype object in which the details of presentation are not specified. The UIM maps this information to the window manager which is being used and realises the completed object on screen. The impact of the nature of the task on the dialogue model, particularly the details of the interface objects is considerable. Various work has been reported in this area (see Murray 1994 for a review) of interest is that of Casner (1990) and Sutcliffe (1995).

3.2.2 Application Interaction Manager (AIM)

If existing software is to be integrated to support a user's task, it cannot directly use standard messages to communicate. Therefore, these applications must be integrated into the Front End System technology through the Application Interaction Manager (AIM) (Prat et al. 1990). The AIM can be seen to perform a mapping function between the application's existing I/O and the standard message structures of the FOCUS system. The AIM consists of two main components. The Task Manager deals with abstract application independent tasks and models of application functionality. It passes a request to the Application Action Manager which has within it all the information necessary to realise that task in an application specific manner.

3.2.3 Support Modules

The Support Module (SM) is the component within the architecture that contains the models (i.e. task and dialogue) described in section 3.1. The SM can vary from having a general purpose dialogue model to having a task specific dialogue that involves an integration of dialogue model and task model. The SM communicates directly with the rest of the architecture using messages. It is a new piece of code that can have a variety of roles, although it may be re-usable in different systems. SMs may provide a range of functionality, such as analysis or complex knowledge base manipulation or visualisation tools. It would typically support complex tasks and would contain knowledge based task and domain support.

4. Technology Support to Strategy

The technology and strategy have been described above, however it is the combination of them that produces the significant results. It is important that this combination is rather an integration so that the two exhibit more than mere high level similarities. Therefore, the integration needs to be of a reasonable depth to produce an effective solution. The section below discusses the integration between the technology and the strategy and methods.

While the Iterative Development Strategy is a combination of ideas that have been previously suggested by other authors there has always been the lack of a suitable enabling technology for implementation. It is by the provision of this technology that the utilisation of the strategy becomes a commercial and realisable possibility. The Front End System technology directly supports the strategy in two major areas:

Prototyping and Formative Evaluation. This is shown in Figure 5. In addition it provides considerable support for the overall management of the software development process. This Project Management support is important in making the strategy a commercial and realisable possibility.

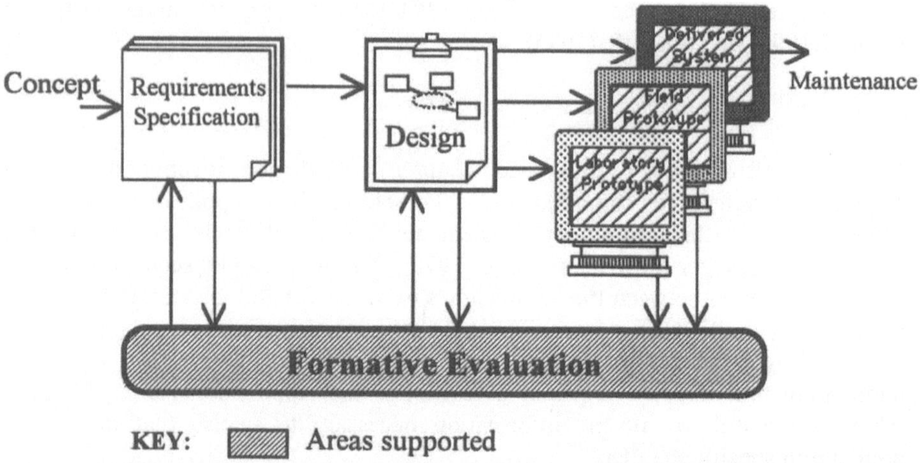

Figure 5. Front End System Technology support for the Iterative Development Strategy

The modular construction of the architecture has important implications for the control and management of the software development process. Individual modules can be developed in parallel and various teams can be created to construct the different modules. The development task is, therefore, broken down into manageable development components supported by the underlying architecture. The minimal interfaces between the architectural components eases the management of the development process by limiting the inter-dependencies that have to be managed.

4.1 Support for Prototype Construction

The speed with which prototypes that embody minimal commitment whilst enabling valid and informative evaluations to be performed, are generated is a critical factor. The Front End System toolkit enables the developer to specify user-system dialogues much more rapidly than using conventional programming languages. This rapid development is made possible by several features of the FES technology. A dialogue is defined at an abstract level, leaving details of presentation to the User Interaction Manager to determine. The definition is minimal and is described using the FES AIO specification that provides a rapid specification method with a limited learning curve and the use of defaults to further accelerate the specification process.

The quality and usefulness of the generated prototype, particularly for evaluations, depends on its fidelity to the finished, or 'target' system. As the FES technology prototyping tools are also the delivery tools, the prototypes will be faithful in 'look and feel' to the proposed system. Thus, it is incremental prototyping that is employed and therefore the costly re-engineering associated with throw-away prototyping is completely avoided. In addition, the use of the delivery tools to develop prototypes means that the Field prototypes are suitably robust for use and evaluation in the user work environments.

To enable the acquiring of more detailed information prototypes must be more than mere 'facades'. FES technology enables prototypes to be developed that simulate calls to underlying functionality that may not yet have been connected. This means that the Front End System technology can support rapid user interface prototyping ahead of full functionality development. Also, when building a Front End to existing functionality, one does not have to implement the underlying functionality one can immediately create prototypes that provide functionality. In particular, it will be much quicker and easier to alter such function calls than it would be to change the actual functional code. This means that even prototypes offering extensive functionality can still be changed with relatively little effort.

4.2 Support for Evaluation

The Front End System technology provides a range of support for evaluation, both formative and summative. The support for formative evaluation is in two main areas; the provision of specialist facilities such as user logging; and the ability to generate changes to prototypes rapidly in a structured and well managed manner. The availability of prototypes is important in the formative evaluation process. Therefore, if there are considerable time periods when the prototypes are not available because they are being developed this will impact negatively on the process. The speed with which changes can be made using the FES technology means that prototypes will be almost continually available. For example, the problems identified from a USOM evaluation can be implemented in, possibly, a few days and re-presented to users while the original problems are fresh in their minds. It is even possible to effect the necessary design changes interactively with the user thus enabling them to select between several possible solutions. This is particularly helpful with the early stages of prototyping (simulations and laboratory) where the proposed solutions are more tentative. This takes the notion of exploiting users ability to articulate their ideas in response to tangible objects to another level with users interactively involved in design changes to the actual prototype.

SEPSOL (Murray et al. 1992), for example, is a Front End system built using the technology, strategy and methods. It is interesting as the nature of the problem necessitated a parallel development programme. SEPSOL is a complex multi-application system that supports chemists using statistical design to identify suitable models for their experiments. The chemists were the initial intended users (although subsequent events have lead to the statisticians wanting to use the system as well) and as such they were the group that was studied using a combination of

techniques from the FOCUS methods. However, in addition, the statisticians were also studied as they were the ones to provide the domain knowledge and the task model that would be at the heart of the system.
The FES technology enabled the developers to be providing at an early stage screen simulations and even laboratory prototypes of user system dialogues, while at the same time other members of the team were beginning to develop the task model and gather the domain knowledge from the statisticians. As the functional adequacy was being developed it could be integrated into the prototypes. User evaluations using USOM and later CIM were employed to gather evaluation data. The functional accuracy of the system was also being monitored during development and prototype Support Modules with appropriate user interfaces were available to the statistician to evaluate the accuracy of the system. Eventually, the two parts of the system were fully integrated and final summative evaluations were conducted involving both the intended users and the statisticians. In this way the development time for the system was considerably reduced.

5. Conclusion

It is generally acknowledged that quality is a critical concern in the development of computer systems. Quality Assurance must involve the specification of certain standards and criteria against which the product of development activities can be assessed. However, it is impossible to take account of all the elements involved in FES design and arrive at a satisfactory solution that will meet a given standard first time around. In practice, the development process must be one of generating a design solution, assessing it against the standard and then revising it. This will carry on until an acceptable solution is found.

To make this a practicable approach requires a technology to enable the fast and cost effective development of prototype solutions and a set of methods that will support the design and evaluation of these prototypes. The technology, strategy and methods have been used to develop various Front End systems (DOX: Prat et al. 1992, KAFTS: Edmonds et al. 1991, SEPSOL: Murray et al. 1992) which are currently in use in commerce and industry.

This paper has presented the FES technology and FOCUS methods that were developed in tandem to provide an integrated support package for the iterative development approach. It has also shown the level of integration necessary between these components to achieve a suitable standard of finished system. Finally, an example system has been described, that was constructed using the FES technology and FOCUS methods, to demonstrate the utility of the products

Acknowledgements

The work described in this paper was partly funded by ESPRIT 2 FOCUS Project 2620. The authors would like to thank the partners of the project: NAG Limited,

Imperial College of Science & Technology, Philips, Solvay, Universitat Politecnica de Catalunya and Westfälische Wilhelms Universität. In particular, the technical contributions of Nick Rousseau, Jacqui Smith and Susan Heggie were an important part of the foundations of the chapter.

Part IV: Architectures for User Interface Software

In this part of the book, we move from the high level concerns of methodologies, tools and design models to the details of software architectures for interactive systems. Work on software architectures started about ten years ago and has made significant progress since then. The principal aim of software architectures is to propose a structural framework for the code produced during the development of interactive systems. The structuring of the code according to the architecture allows developers to improve the design of the system by enhancing the reusability, maintainability, and the overall quality of the software.

During the last ten years, much has been written about which representation of software is most appropriate for which purpose. The original idea of separating the presentation and underlying structure of both concrete, interaction objects and abstract objects is usually traced back to the Seeheim model. In Chapter 11 a lucid review of a number of the most significant architectures for interactive systems is provided. The chapter describes what the characteristics of the new kind of interactive systems are that have to be included in the future software architectures for interactive systems. Work deriving from the European Amodeus project is presented which has led to a number of useful heuristics; rules of thumb which designers can use in the development of user interface software.

The Seeheim model provides a representation in which separates the 'functional core' from the presentation of the system. However, there can, arguably, never be a complete separation of these two aspects. Chapter 12 presents an architecture which sets out to deal with these interdependencies. It begins with the recognition that software is generally long-lived and describes a flexible architecture specially designed to accommodate the modifiability of user interface software. This architecture gives a very clear example of what is an architecture for interactive systems, how it can be used and what benefits can be expected from the use of an architecture at design time.

Chapter 11: Agent-Based Architecture Modelling for Interactive Systems

Joelle Coutaz, Laurence Nigay & Daniel Salber

1. Introduction

A software architecture is an organisation of computational elements and the description of their interactions. Although specialists still argue about a precise definition of this concept, it is widely recognised that software architecture designs can no longer simply emerge from craft skills. The increasing complexity and size of software systems require sound engineering principles and frameworks to formally structure the design process into multiple but consistent perspectives. Possible perspectives on software architectures include the functional partitions of the system, the structural view in terms of components and connectors, the dynamic coordination model (Abowd & Bass 1994). All of these representations should be the result of an explicit design rationale. They should be analyzable, communicable, and maintainable.

Architectural styles such as pipes and filters, object-oriented organisations and layered structures, can be used as generic vehicles to express architectural solutions. An architectural style makes recurring organizational patterns explicit (Garlan & Shaw 1993). A style defines a vocabulary of design elements, imposes configuration constraints on these elements, determines a semantic interpretation that gives meaning to the system description, and enables analysis of the system properties. As a result, architectural styles not only lead to different design solutions but to designs with significantly different software properties (Shaw & Garlan 1995).

In the domain of user interface, a number of architectural styles have emerged. Seeheim, Arch, MVC, PAC, and others can be considered as canonical references. They primarily provide a framework for performing functional partitioning and allocation of function to structural components based on system and user-centred properties. One lingering problem in user interface software design is that off-the-shelf tools such as interaction toolkits, application skeletons, and user interface builders do not make explicit the link between the facilities they provide and the underlying architectural framework they convey. The software architecture is lost in the resulting code or difficult to extract:

- Interaction toolkits such as Motif (OSF 1989) do not embed the architectural principles that software designers need to build interactive systems effectively. For example, the "call-back procedure" paradigm made popular by X Window (Scheifler & Gettys 1986), does not enforce the distinction between task domain concepts and presentation specific issues. Thus, without an adequate software framework, the resulting interactive system may be an incredible mixture of concerns.

- In order to exploit object-oriented application frameworks like MacApp (Schmucker 1986), the programmer needs to reverse-engineer the architecture of the existing code. This task can be made easier if the underlying organisation of the environment were made explicit to programmers. A good example is the MVC model that structures the Smalltalk programming environment in a systematic way.
- User interface generators, which they alleviate the programming task, tend to provide a false sense of confidence that software architecture is no longer an issue. We call this attitude "the ABS syndrom": a false sense of security. It is true that some implicit architecture is embedded in the code generated by such tools. However, the software designer must understand the functional coverage of the generated code in order to devise what needs to be developed by hand. In addition, the developer has to discover how to integrate and coordinate the hand-coded portion with the generated code in a way that supports the design requirements. Without an architectural framework to structure the problem, it is difficult to properly achieve this task.

Software tools for the construction of user interfaces will not eliminate architectural issues as long as the construction of user interfaces requires programming. Clearly, developers and maintainers of interactive systems need to rely on canonical models for identifying software components, for organising their interconnections, for reasoning about them and for maintaining them in a productive way.

The literature shows a wide variety of architecture styles for interactive systems revealing distinct goals, usages, and scientific beliefs. The purpose of an architectural description may be to support assessment against specific properties as described in the SAAM method (Kazman et al. 1994). Another goal may be to communicate a design solution to another development team. Then the description should be unambiguous, with possibly clear reference to the implementation tools, and no opportunity for misinterpretations. In a nutshell, an architecture design expresses what is important[1]. And what is important depends on the purpose.

In this chapter, we present agent-based architectural styles for the purpose of assessing software designs. In Section 2, we discuss the concept of agent as well as the general properties that agent-based models tend to support. In Section 3 we present our own work in this area: the principles of the PAC-Amodeus model. In 4, we show how PAC-Amodeus can be used in practice to reconcile conceptual design with software properties and requirements.

2. Agent-Based Models

Agent-based models structure an interactive system as a collection of specialised

---

1Len Bass from SEI Carnegie Mellon University, should be thanked for this remark computational units called agents. An *agent* has a state, possesses an expertise, and is capable of initiating and reacting to events. Agents that communicate directly with the user are sometimes called *interactors*. An interactor provides users with a perceptual representation of its internal state. The terms interactor and agent are sometimes used indifferently even if there is no direct interaction with the user. Interactors are also coined as *interaction objects*. An object is a generic term that covers a computational element with a local state. It can either be viewed as a concept or as the technical structure that underpins the object-oriented programming paradigm. In the following discussion, we will consider an object as a generic concept.

Our view of the concept of agent is one perspective of the more general definition used in distributed Artificial Intelligence (A.I.). In A.I., agents may be cognitive or reactive depending mainly on their reasoning and knowledge representation capabilities (Demazeau & Muller 1991). A cognitive agent is enriched with inference and decision making mechanisms to satisfy goals. At the opposite, a reactive agent has a limited computational capacity to process stimuli. It has no goal per se but a competence coded (or specified) explicitly by the human designer. In current interactive systems, agents are reactive. In the following discussion, we will not make the distinction between cognitive and reactive agents although current models developed for the software design of user interfaces have considered reactive agents only.

Having presented the vocabulary of the agent-based style, we need to discuss the advantage of this modelling technique and compare several of the approaches using this style as a basis.

2.1 Benefits from the Agent-Based Style

Agent models stress a highly parallel modular organisation and distribute the state of the interaction among a collection of co-operating units. Modularity, parallelism and distribution are convenient mechanisms for supporting the iterative design of user interfaces, for implementing physically distributed applications, and for handling multi-thread dialogues:

- An agent defines the unit for functional modularity. It is thus possible to modify its internal behaviour without endangering the rest of the system.
- An agent defines the unit for processing. It is thus possible to execute it on a processor different from the processor where it was created. It is also possible to use instances of a class of agents to present a concept on distinct workstations. This property is essential for implementing groupware.
- An agent can be associated to one thread of the user's activity. Since a state is locally maintained by the agent, the interaction between the user and the agent can be suspended and resumed at the user's will. When a thread of activity is too complex or too rich to be represented by a single agent, it is then possible to use a collection of co-operating agents.

In addition to satisfying requirements for better user interfaces, agent models can easily be implemented in terms of object-oriented languages: an object class defines a category of (reactive) agents where class operators and attributes respectively model the instruction set and the state of an agent category, and where an event class denotes a method. An object and an agent are both highly specialised processing units, and both decide about their own state: a state is not manipulated by others but results from processing triggered by others. The sub-classing mechanism provided by object-oriented languages can be usefully exploited to modify a user interface without changing the existing code.

A number of agent-based models and tools have been developed along these lines. MVC (Goldberg 1984), PAC (Coutaz 1987), ALV (Hill 1992), the CNUCE (Paterno' et al. 1994) and York (Duke & Harrison 1993, Duke & Harrsion 1994) models, are typical agent-based styles. Interviews (Linton & Dunwoody 1986) and Aïda (Ilog 1989) are examples of toolkits based on such a model, whereas Serpent (Bass & Coutaz 1991) and Sassafras (Hill 1986) are run time kernels and user interface generators organised as a multi-agent structure. All of these models and tools push forward the separation of concerns advocated by seminal Seeheim (Pfaff et al. 1985). They generalise the distinction between concepts and presentation techniques by applying the separation at every level of abstraction. In order to do so, they distribute the separation of concerns among co-operating agents. They differ however in the way they perform the distribution and the co-operation. This is the topic of the next section.

We propose to compare agent-based models according to their functional structure and according to the MSM dimensions (Coutaz et al. 1993).

2.2 Comparative Analysis Based on Agent Structures

In MVC (Model, View Controller), an agent is modelled along three functional perspectives: the Model, the View, and the Controller. A Model defines the abstract competence of the agent (i.e., its functional core). The View defines the perceivable behaviour of the agent for output. The Controller denotes the perceivable behaviour of the agent for inputs. The View and the Controller cover the user interface of the agent, that is, its overall perceivable behaviour with regard to the user.

PAC (Presentation, Abstraction, Control) conveys similar ideas: the facets of an agent are used to express different but complementary and strongly coupled computational perspectives. A PAC agent has a Presentation (i.e., its perceivable input and output behaviour), an Abstraction (i.e., its functional core), and a Control to express dependencies. The Control of an agent is in charge of communicating with other agents as well as expressing dependencies between the Abstract and Presentation facets of the agent. In the PAC style, no agent Abstraction is authorized to communicate directly with its corresponding Presentation and vice versa. In PAC, dependencies of any sort are conveyed via Controls. Controls serve as the glue mechanism to express coordination, formalism transformations that sit between abstract and concrete perspectives.

ALV (Abstraction, Link, View) has a similar decomposition to PAC except that a

Link has a more restricted role than the PAC Control. An ALV Link is in charge of expressing constraints between the View and the Abstraction whereas PAC Controls may be used to express relationships with other agents. Whereas PAC does not prescribe any form of implementation (i.e., whether an agent should be built from three objects in an object-oriented development environment like MVC, or simply as a single C module), ALV implies the decoupling of the agent into three distinct pieces.
A CNUCE agent possesses four perspectives inherited from the computer graphics modelling techniques: the Collection and the Abstraction facets define the functional core aspect of the agent for input and output respectively; the Measure and the Presentation cover the user interface side of the agent for input and output respectively. In addition, two triggers express the conditions under which input and output may occur.
A York agent has two perspectives: the presentation and its internal behaviour. This decomposition is similar to the structure chosen for InterViews.

In summary, MVC and CNUCE decouple input techniques from outputs, whereas ALV, PAC, and York concentrate them in the notion of Presentation or View. Contrary to PAC and ALV, MVC has no explicit notion of arbitrator for expressing the relationships and the co-ordination between agents. In the Lisbon model (Duce et al. 1991), agents do not have perspectives but are organised as specialised categories to model the user interface portion of an interactive system.

2.3 Comparative Analysis Along the MSM Dimensions

The MSM (Multi-Sensori-Motor) framework has been devised to support reasoning about current and future interactive systems (Coutaz et al. 1993). The framework is comprised of 6 dimensions. The first two dimensions deal with the notion of physical devices: the number and the nature of these devices (i.e., input vs output). The other four dimensions are used to characterise the degree of built-in cognitive sophistication of the system: levels of abstraction, context, fusion/fission, and parallelism.

2.3.1 Input and Output

All of the models considered in our discussion stress the fact that an agent may communicate with multiple agents. Agents have multi-channel capabilities. However, not all of the agent-based models make explicit the communication channels their agents support. For example, MVC does not say how communication occurs between the agents of an interactive system. The question is left opened until implementation.

In PAC, on the other hand, the Control facet of an agent supports communication in two ways: first, it is as an explicit bridge between the two facets it serves (the Abstraction and the Presentation may use different formalisms as well as distinct time basis); second, it is used as the switchboard of the agent: it receives inputs and outputs from other agents. At the opposite of CNUCE, however, PAC does not make explicit how inputs and outputs are processed and dispatched within the agent.

In CNUCE and York, input and output channels are clearly expressed. For example, the Measure of an agent is modelled as the local process specialised in processing inputs from lower level agents. The Collection has a similar role for processing inputs from higher levels of abstraction. The Presentation and the Abstraction are the output channels for lower levels and higher levels of abstraction respectively.

2.3.2 Levels of Abstraction

The notion of level of abstraction expresses the degree of transformation that the interpretation and rendering functions perform on information. The sequence of input transformations forms the interpretation function whereas in the other direction, internal information (e.g., system state) is transformed to be made perceivable to the user by a sequence of output transformations called the rendering function. The notion of level of abstraction also covers the variety of representations that the system supports, ranging from raw data to symbolic forms.

Information acquired by agents is transformed by a population of agents before reaching the functional core of the system. In the other direction, agents concretise information from to functional core into perceivable behaviour. The successive steps of such input and output transformations define levels of abstraction. In the conceptual architectural models considered in our discussion, abstracting and concretising are performed by agents organised into levels of abstraction.

Within CNUCE, levels of abstraction are defined in two ways: within an agent and in the form of a composition mechanism.

- A CNUCE agent stresses a clear distinction between the rendering and the interpretation functions. These functions operate along a 2 step process. Each step defines a level of abstraction within the agent. For rendering, information from higher levels of abstraction is received by the Collection and delivered to lower levels by the Presentation. For interpreting, the Measure receives information from lower levels whereas the Abstraction communicates with higher levels.
- CNUCE agents can be composed into more powerful, abstract agents with composition operators such as the interleaving operator (Paterno' et al. 1994). By doing so, an agent is defined as a hierarchy of agents composed of a parent and a set of interleaved child agents.

PAC and MVC adopt a similar approach for modelling levels of abstraction. Like CNUCE, they do not make explicit the nature of these levels. The Lisbon model, on the other hand, introduces classes of agents, i.e., Conceptual objects (CO's), Interaction Objects (IO's), and Transformer Objects (TO's) as an indication of what these levels might be.

In the Lisbon model, CO's are "the user interface accessible representation of an object the functional core wishes to make visible" (Duce et al. 1991). In the user interface portion of an interactive system, CO's are the proxies of the task domain concepts manipulated by the functional core. IO's support the translation process between CO's inputs and outputs and low level input and output devices. As in CNUCE, "Composite IO's may be formed from single IO's to handle arbitrarily complex threads of dialogue" (Duce et al. 1991). TO's provide the basic mechanism for managing the relations between different objects of the user interface. Examples of such relations include constraint management to maintain consistency between IO's, context switching between dialogue threads, integrity mapping between CO's and IO's, etc. TO's are in charge of similar functions as PAC Controls.

2.3.3 Context

The capacity of a system to interpret and render information may vary dynamically with respect to "contextual variables". Contextual variables are like cognitive filters. They form a set of internal state parameters used by the representational processes to control the interpretation/rendering function. Agents, which are the processes of the user interface, are good candidates for being the owners of local contexts.

2.3.4 Fusion and Fission

Fusion refers to the combination of several chunks of information to form new chunks. Fission refers to the decomposition phenomenon. Fusion and fission are part of the abstracting and materialization phenomena.

The composition mechanism within York, MVC, PAC, and CNUCE was primarily introduced for the expression of levels of abstraction. One side effect of this mechanism is that composition provides a sound foundation for fusion and fission. Fusion and fission are part of the internal processing capabilities of an agent (which owns contexts to perform its computation). A more detailed discussion about fission and fusion can be found in (Coutaz et al. 1993)

2.3.5 Parallelism

Representation and usage of time is a complex issue. In our discussion, we are concerned with the role of time within the interpretation and rendering functions. How does time relate to levels of abstraction and contexts? How does it interfere with fusion and fission? Parallelism at the user interface may appear at multiple grains: at the physical level (multiple I/O devices may be used simultaneously), at the task level (the user or the system may execute multiple tasks in parallel), and at the task cluster levels (the user or the system may carry multiple types of activities at the same time or in an interleaved way).

An agent is a processing unit that can operate in parallel with other agents. It results from agent-based architectures that multiple interpretation and rendering activities can take place simultaneously. Therefore, agents can be defined to represent parallelism at the appropriate grain of concurrency. It is important to note however that, at the implementation level, an agent is not necessarily an actual process (in the sense of the underlying run-time platform).

Allocation in architectural design is a multiple step activity. It includes the allocation of functions to structures, the allocation of structures to system processes, and the allocation of processes to physical processors. Allocation depends on non functional requirements such as the characteristics of the run-time platform. Clearly, implementing an agent as a Unix process would be inefficient, but at the conceptual level of design, one should view an agent as an entity capable of initiating actions in parallel to other agents.

Having presented general issues about agent-based styles, we now describe our own approach: PAC-Amodeus.

3. PAC-Amodeus: the principles

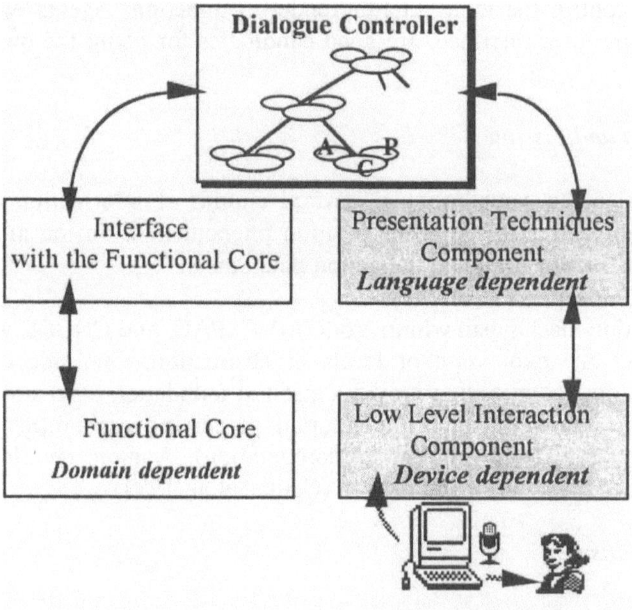

Figure 1. The PAC-Amodeus functional components.

PAC-Amodeus uses the Arch model (Arch 1992) as the foundation for the

functional partitioning of an interactive system and populates the key element of this organisation, i.e., the Dialogue Controller, with PAC agents.
Basically, Arch is a revisited Seeheim that provides hooks for reasoning about software engineering properties such as code re-usability, portability, and modifiability. PAC-Amodeus incorporates the two adaptor components of Arch, the Interface with the Functional Core and the Presentation Techniques Component, to insulate the keystone component (i.e., the Dialogue Controller) from modifications in its unavoidable neighbors: the Functional Core and the Low Level Interaction Component. A detailed discussion on the advantages of these adaptors will be presented in Section 4.

The Arch model however, does not provide any guidance about the decomposition of the Dialogue Controller nor does it indicate how the MSM features (such as parallelism) can be supported within the architecture. PAC, on the other hand, stresses the recursive decomposition of an interactive system, in terms of agents, but does not pay attention to engineering issues such as the existence of implementation tools. PAC-Amodeus gathers the best of the two worlds. Figure 1 shows the resulting structure.
As shown in Figure 1, PAC-Amodeus adopts the same overall structure than Arch but goes one step further in two ways:

(1) PAC-Amodeus makes explicit the boundaries of the Presentation Techniques and the Low Level Interaction components using the notions of physical device and interaction language. A *physical device* is an artefact of the system that acquires (input device) or delivers (output device) information. Examples of devices include the keyboard, mouse, microphone and screen.
An *interaction language* defines a set of well-formed expressions (i.e., a conventional assembly of symbols) that convey meaning. The generation of a symbol, or a set of symbols, results from actions on physical devices. Examples of interaction languages include pseudo-natural language and direct manipulation.
In PAC-Amodeus, the overall functional partitioning of an interactive system should be defined according to the following rule: the Low Level Interaction Component should be device dependent and language dependent; the Presentation Techniques Component is device independent but still language dependent; the other components of the interactive system, including the Dialogue Controller, should be both device and language independent.

(2) PAC-Amodeus decomposes the Dialogue Controller into a set of cooperative PAC agents. The set is derived for a particular system using the heuristic rules presented in Section 4. These rules, which consider the external specifications of the system as the driving rationale, offer a bottom-up approach to the process of functional decomposition. Other rules, based on a task description, support a top-down partitioning process (Paterno' et al. 1994). Both approaches are valid. If the external specifications are consistent with the task model, bottom-up and top-down reasoning should lead to the same set of cooperative agents.

Although agents provide a sound approach to the refinement of an Arch Dialogue Controller, we need to clarify how they are connected to the functional neighbours of the Dialogue Controller. As shown in Figure 2 an agent is related to the Interface with the Functional Core (IFC) and to the Presentation Techniques Component via its Abstraction and Presentation facets. The Abstraction is connected to one or multiple entities of the IFC. Depending on the case at hand, the connector is implemented as a procedure call, as a pointer, or as any other protocol suitable for the system requirements. Similarly, the Presentation facet of an agent is connected to one or multiple entities of the Presentation Techniques Component.

In summary, the hierarchical organisation of the Dialogue Controller in terms of PAC agents is motivated by the necessity of modelling computation at various levels of abstraction, the necessity of expressing the fusion and fission phenomena as well as parallelism at various levels of granularity. In addition to the hierarchical information flow, (and in contrast with the original PAC model (Coutaz 1987)), communication can also occur horizontally at various levels of abstraction through the Abstraction and Presentation facets of the PAC agents.

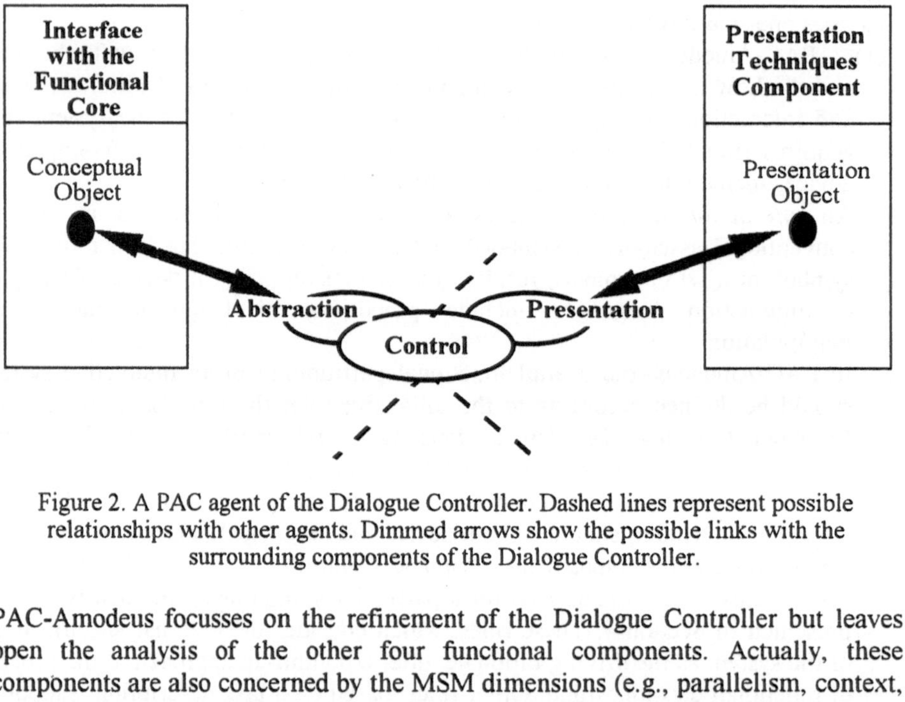

Figure 2. A PAC agent of the Dialogue Controller. Dashed lines represent possible relationships with other agents. Dimmed arrows show the possible links with the surrounding components of the Dialogue Controller.

PAC-Amodeus focusses on the refinement of the Dialogue Controller but leaves open the analysis of the other four functional components. Actually, these components are also concerned by the MSM dimensions (e.g., parallelism, context, levels of abstraction, fusion and fission). As a result, the agent-style applies equally well to all of the components of the Arch. We have chosen not to do so for several reasons: either these components are fully covered by dedicated implementation tools (therefore, the architecture is already there) or they are partially covered by the development environment (then, it is difficult to provide systematic rules at the conceptual level that fit every situation). It is however possible to model an interactive system in a systematic way using an agent style to prove user-centered properties as in the interactor theory (Duke & Harrison 1993, Duke & Harrison 1994). If, on the other hand, the goal is to formulate an architecture with the perspective of an implementation using off-the-shelf tools, then the hybrid PAC-Amodeus model, which combines agents and gross functional components, is a good candidate to start with.

4. PAC-Amodeus in Practice

Conceptual models like PAC-Amodeus are ideal views of a complex world. They are very attractive as style guides in a book but are difficult to relate to the practical activity of design. This section shows how PAC-Amodeus can be used to reason about a particular design when confronted with practical software requirements. First, we present possible usages of the PAC-Amodeus adaptors, then we comment on the lingering problem of allocating functions to structural components. In 4.3, we close the discussion with our set of heuristic rules for refining the Dialogue Controller in terms of PAC agents.

4.1 Interpreting the PAC-Amodeus Adaptors

PAC-Amodeus reuses the two adaptors of the Arch model: the Interface with the Functional Core and the Presentation Techniques Component.

4.1.1 The Interface with the Functional Core: Temporal Strategies and Data Exchanged

The Interface with the Functional Core (IFC) serves as a mediator between the Dialogue Controller and the domain-specific concepts implemented in the Functional Core. It is designed to absorb the effects of changes in its direct neighbors. As any boundary, it implements a protocol. A protocol is characterized by temporal strategies and by the nature of data exchanged (Coutaz & Balbo 1991). A *temporal strategy* defines the coordinating rules for transfering information between two communicating entities such as the Functional Core and the Dialogue Controller. The coordination may be fully synchronous or fully asynchronous or may alternate between the two extremes. Synchronous coordination implies that the sender waits for the receiver before its own processing can resume. In the context considered here, synchronous coordination models the mutual control of the Functional Core and the Dialogue Controller: either one has the initiative, but the initiator is directly controlled by its partner. Asynchronous coordination allows communicating entities to exchange information without waiting for each other. With such a communication scheme, the Functional Core and the Dialogue Controller are two equal partners sharing a common enterprise: that of accomplishing a task with the user.
Using a synchronous scheme, either the Functional Core controls the interaction in

a query-answer style, or the Functional Core is controlled by the user interface. Most legacy functional cores, which perform the well-known Pascal "writeln's" and "readln's", comply to the query-answer style. On the other hand, implementing a user interface on top of X Window forces to model the Functional Core as a passive server of the user interface. Possible conflicting requirements may emerge from this situation, for example, upgrading the user interface of a legacy system using X Window. If so, the Functional Core and the user interface should be run by distinct processes and the Interface with the Functional Core should be used to synchronise these processes.
From the user's point of view, synchronous coordination results in single threads of dialogue or, at best, in interleaved threads. If mono-threading is not consistent with the user's requirements, then asynchronous coordination should be adopted. Asynchronous coordination supports multiple concurrent threads of dialogue: the user may issue multiple commands simultaneously or in an interleaved way while the Functional Core may have its own processing going on. Functional Cores that implement dynamic systems such as a robot or a nuclear plant, and provision for end-user's control over the on-going process, call for asynchronous coordination. In turn, asynchronous coordination leads to allocate the Functional Core to a dedicated process.
Exchange of data between the Functional Core and the user interface is performed through the IFC in terms of domain objects. A domain object is an entity that the designer of the Functional Core wishes to make perceivable to, and manipulable by the user (cf. the CO's of the Lisbon Model). Ideally, it is supposed to match the user's mental representation of a particular domain concept. It may be the case however that the Functional Core, driven by software or hardware considerations, implements a domain concept in a way that is not adequate for the user.

Semantic enhancement (Bass & Coutaz 1991) may be performed in the IFC by defining domain objects that reorganize the information modeled by the Functional Core. Reorganizing may take the form of aggregating data structures of the Functional Core into a single domain object or, conversely, segmenting a concept into multiple domain objects. It may also take the form of an extension by adding attributes and operators, which can then be exploited by the other components of the user interface. Note that the CO's of the Lisbon Model fit in the Interface with the Functional Core.

4.1.2 The Presentation Techniques Component

The Presentation Techniques Component (PTC) acts as a mediator between the Dialogue Controller and the Low Level Interaction Component (LLIC). Because it is device independent, it is generally viewed as a logical LLIC. As shown in Figure 3, we propose to refine the PTC into two layers of abstraction: the Extension Layer and the Interaction Toolkit Adaptor. The Interaction Toolkit Adaptor defines a virtual toolkit used for the expression of presentation objects. This expression is then mapped into the formalism of the actual interaction toolkit used for a particular implementation. Switching to a different toolkit requires rewriting the mapping rules, but the expression of the presentation objects remains unchanged.

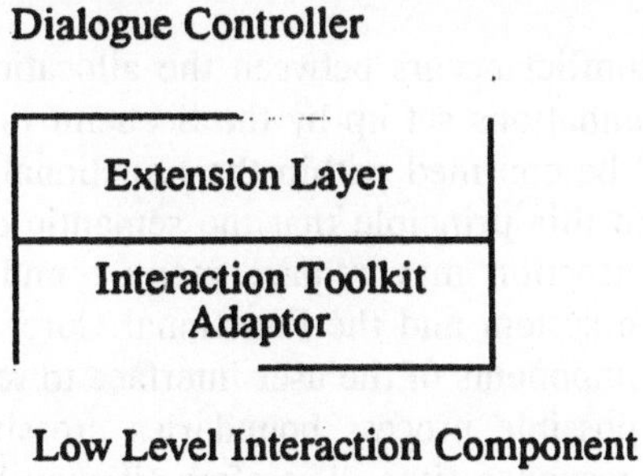

Figure 3. Refinement of the Presentation Techniques Component.

Interaction objects are generally constructed from entities made available in interaction toolkits. In general, interaction toolkits such as the X Intrinsics (OSF 1989), provide an abstraction mechanism for defining new interaction objects. However, it is not always possible to build new interaction objects from the predefined building blocks of the toolkit. For example, in an earlier version of the X Intrinsics, widgets (i.e., interaction objects) would occupy rectangular areas only. Under such conditions, the notion of a wall in a floor plan drawing editor could not be implemented as a diagonal line widget. Instead, a presentation object "wall" would have to be defined as a new presentation object outside the toolkit.

The wall example shows that the Presentation Techniques Component should, conceptually, be structured into two layers. Specific-interaction objects, which can be built from the building blocks of the toolkit, should belong to the toolkit. Those which cannot be built with the toolkit should be part of the Extension Layer. The Interaction Toolkit Adaptor, such as XVT (Valdez 1989) defines the boundary between these two layers.

Sometimes, the location for implementing a presentation object is not as straightforward as the wall example. If located in the toolkit, then the presentation object becomes a general purpose interaction object and thus, should be implemented according to the programming rules imposed by the toolkit to guarantee reusibility. If located in the extension layer, the private status of the presentation object relaxes the reusability constraints of the underlying platform.

This example is merely a simple illustration of a more general problem: that of identifying the appropriate location for software functionalities.

4.1.3 Allocating functions to structural components

Experience shows that no single architectural model can satisfy all of the software design factors and criteria such as those reported by McCall (McCall 1977). Factors and criteria may be conflicting. For example, portability and modifiability may impede efficiency. In PAC-Amodeus, the two adaptor components have been reused from the Arch model to minimize dependencies from the modifications of the Functional Core as well as from user interface toolkits. Conversely, these abstract machines may have an adverse effect on the speed of the run-time end product.

Another example of conflict occurs between the allocation of functionalities and response time. The foundations set up by the Seeheim model stress that domain-specific objects should be confined within the Functional Core and its extension, the IFC. It results from this principle that the semantic quality of feedback for a single user-system transaction may require many round trips between the user interface portion of the system and the Functional Core. This long chain of data transfer between the components of the user interface to reach the Functional Core and vice versa, plus possible process boundaries crossing, may be costly with respect to the system response time. Therefore, it may be inconsistent with the expectation of the end-user.

Domain-knowledge delegation[2], which consists of down-loading Functional Core knowledge into the user interface, is a way to reduce transmission load at critical points (Coutaz & Balbo 1991), therefore to improve response time when this criteria has been identified as an important requirement. For example, rubber-banding in direct manipulation interfaces, requires high performance at the user interface. In particular, if the Functional Core is implemented as a distinct process running on a distinct processor, it may be judicious to delegate domain knowledge into the user interface portion of the interactive system. By doing so, semantic knowledge is readily available in the user interface and can be rendered to the user within the response time constraint. Communication with the Functional Core can be postponed when response time is not critical.

The Slinky metamodel acknowledges the fact that software architectures for interactive systems must be tailored to the requirements and criteria selected for the particular case at hand (Arch 1992). "The term "Slinky" was selected to emphasize that functionalities can shift from component to component in an architecture depending on: - the goals of the developers, - the weighting of development criteria, -the type of system to be implemented. This concept is loosely represented by the flexible Slinky™ toy." (Arch 1992, pp. 35).

Thus, the Slinky metamodel is a generic framework from which particular instances of arches can be derived. For example, if efficiency prevails against toolkit portability, then the Interaction Toolkit Adaptor may not be needed. If the Functional Core provides the "appropriate interface" in accordance with the user's requirements, and if the Functional Core will not evolve in the future, then the Interface with the Functional Core can be scaled down to a simple connector (e.g., a set of procedure calls). If high quality semantic feedback and efficiency are important requirements as in semantically rich rubber-banding tasks, then domain-knowlege delegation may be performed. Such decision may result in reducing the relative importance, thus the code size, of the Functional Core.

PAC agents of the Dialogue Controller provide a way to perform domain-

[2] The term "semantic delegation" was previously used by Coutaz to denote "domain-specific delegation".

knowledge delegation without jeopardizing the basic "separation of concerns" principle. The Abstraction facet of agents can be used to locate domain-dependent information. This information may be a copy of the original information maintained in the Functional Core or a copy from an adapted version maintained in the Interface with the Functional Core, or even the domain-knowledge per se (with no equivalent copy in the Functional Core). Duplicating information is one way of improving local efficiency. However, it introduces an additional complexity for maintaining consistency between the copies in the Dialogue Controller and the Functional Core (or the IFC). If consistency is not guaranteed then honesty (Abowd et al. 1992) is not satisfied. If consistency is difficult to maintain, then the designer may decide to not implement the domain concept in the Functional Core and use a PAC agent instead. Pushing the rationale further, the Functional Core may be empty by allocating and distributing its functional capabilities across a set of PAC agents.

4.2 Heuristic Rules for Devising PAC Agents

The following rules have been devised for PAC-Amodeus and have been implemented in the form of an expert system, PAC-Expert (Nigay 1994). As mentioned above, they imply a bottom-up analysis starting from the external specifications of the system. They are organised along four issues: window existence, window content, window links, and hierarchy revision.

4.2.1 Window Existence

Generally speaking, a window is a rendering surface for displaying information on the physical screen. A distinction should be made between main-dialogue-thread windows, which display domain concepts exported from the Functional Core, and convenience windows, such as dialogue boxes and forms used in sub-dialogues to inform users that an abnormal condition has occurred or to offer them the opportunity to enter the parameters of a command.

Rule 1: Model a "main-dialogue-thread window" as an agent.
The Presentation facet of an agent of type "main-dialogue-thread window" manages the window itself (that is the interaction technique "window" offered by the toolkit component), including the title and the windowing commands such as the resize and move functions. In addition, if the agent is a leaf in the PAC hierarchy, its presentation facet also manages the presentation of the concepts it renders to the user.
If a "main-dialogue-thread window" agent is a leaf in the PAC hierarchy, its Abstraction facet maintains an abstract representation of the concepts (i.e., the domain objects) it renders or at least the links between these concepts.
We observe that, in general, the presentation of a hierarchy of concepts is displayed within the window technique associated with the "main-dialogue-thread window" agent. Although general, this property is not always true. It may be the case that

the selection of the representation of a sub-concept in the "main-dialogue-thread window" agent opens a new window. In turn, this window, which displays domain objects, is modelled as a child "main-dialogue-thread window" agent.

Rule 2: Use an agent to maintain visual consistency between multiple views.
If multiple views about the same concept are allowed and if each view is modelled as an agent, then a Multiple View parent agent is introduced to express the logical link between the children view agents. Any user action with semantic and visual side effect on a view agent is reported by the view agent to its parent, the Multiple View agent, which in turn broadcasts the update to the other siblings.

4.2.2 Window Content

It is often the case that the user interface presents a list of the classes of concepts from which the user can create instances. For example, a drawing editor includes the classes circle, line, rectangle, and so forth. In general, these classes are gathered into palettes or tear-off menus. Let's call such presentation techniques "tool palettes". Tool palette agents provide a good basis for extensibility, reusability and modifiability. Note that we must make a distinction between tool palette agents, which render classes of concepts, and main-dialogue-thread-window agents, which represent instances of concepts.

Rule 3: Model a tool palette as an agent.
The Abstraction facet of a tool palette agent contains the list of the classes of instantiable concepts. In general, the Presentation facet of a tool palette agent is built from interaction objects offered by the Low Level Interaction Component. It is in charge of the local lexical feedback when user actions occur on the physical representation of the concept classes (e.g., reverse video of the selected icon). These actions are then passed to the Control facet.
The Control facet of a tool palette agent maps user actions to the list maintained in the abstraction facet. It transforms these actions into a message whose level of abstraction is enriched (e.g., a mouse click on the “circle” icon is translated into the message "current editing mode is circle").

Rule 4: Model the editable workspace of a window as an agent.
A window may contain an area where the user can edit concepts. In this case, this area should be modelled as a "workspace" agent. A workspace agent is responsible for interpreting (1) the user actions on the background of the window, (2) the user actions on the physical representations of the editable concepts when these concepts are not managed by any special purpose agent, (3) messages from the child agents when those agents represent editable concepts. In addition, a workspace agent may be in charge of maintaining graphical links to express logical relationships between the editable concepts. In summary, a workspace agent has the competence of a manager of a set of concepts.
At the opposite, a non-editable area of a set of concepts is not modelled as an

agent. It is embedded in the "main-dialogue-thread window" agent which displays these concepts.

Rule 5: Model a complex concept as an agent.
A complex concept may be either a compound concept, or it may have a structured perceivable representation, or it may have multiple renditions.

1. A compound concept is built from sub-concepts, and this construction must be made perceivable to the user. In general, a hierarchy of agents in the user interface maps the composition of the compound concept.
2. When involving a set of rendering items, a simple concept may be modelled as an agent. For example, the concept of wall, whose presentation is built up from a line, a hot-spot (to select it), and a pop up menu (to invoke an operation on the wall), can be modelled as an agent.
3. An elementary concept may be presented in multiple locations. In addition, each presentation may be different. One agent is introduced to maintain the consistency between the multiple presentations.

4.2.3 Window Links

Window links fall into three categories: open links, syntactic links, and semantic links.

Rule 6: If the access to a "main-dialogue-thread window" is allowed from another "main-dialogue-thread window", a parent-child relation is modelled by an agent.
We use the term "open link" to refer to the relation that describes the possibility for the user to open a "main-dialogue-thread window" from another one. This relationship is controlled by a dedicated agent.

Rule 7: An agent is introduced to synthesised actions distributed over multiple agents.
Windows agents are related by a "syntactic link" when a set of user actions distributed over these windows can be synthesised into a higher abstraction (i.e., the fusion phenomenon). For example, to draw a circle, the user selects the "circle" icon in the tool palette agent, then draws the shape in the workspace agent. These distributed actions are synthesised by a cement agent into a higher abstraction (i.e., the command "create circle"). This agent, which maintains a syntactic link between its sub-agents, is called a "cement agent".

Rule 8: An agent is introduced to maintain a semantic relation between concepts included in distinct windows.
This rule is identical to the previous one except that the competence of the Semantic agent is to maintain a semantic relation and not to synthesise the user's actions.

4.2.4 *Hierarchy Revision*

Once the hierarchy of agents have been devised according to the rules above, we recommend to analyse the hierarchy using the following rules.
We have observed that users of PAC-Amodeus have difficulty in bounding the recursive decomposition of the agent hierarchy. As a pedagogic material, we recommend the following approach: refine the decomposition down to the elementary interaction objects as specified in the external specifications (e.g., a push button, a menu), then prune the hierarchy using the following rule.

Rule 9: If the development tools used at the LLIC or PTC levels can implement an agent in a straightforward way, then turn the agent into an interaction (or presentation) object and make it part of the Presentation facet of the parent agent (i.e., the facet gets connected to the interaction/presentation object).

Rule 10: If a parent agent has one single sibling, if future evolution of the system does not lead to additional siblings, and if information transfer between agents is not for free, then it may be useful to combine the two agents into a single one.

4.2.5 *About Agent Facets*

Our heuristic rules imply that not all agents have a Presentation nor an Abstraction facet. Typically, multiple view agents, which maintain some consistency between their siblings, have no Presentation and no Abstraction. They are pure controllers.
Other agents, like cement agents, which combine information from multiple sources into higher abstractions, have no Presentation but may have an Abstraction in case domain-knowledge is needed to perform data fusion. In addition, the Abstraction facet may be a simple connector to the IFC or, if there is no IFC, to the Functional Core.
Agents that are pure controllers may not be explicit components of the architectural design. As mentioned in the introduction, a design solution expresses what is important. If by chance, the designer can draw upon a dedicated language or tool to express dependencies such as FLO (Ducasse & Fornarino 1993) and Link (Hill 1992), then the design solution may simply show a connection between the dependent agents. Because the controller is automatically generated by a tool (as opposed to program it explicitly in C code), it is no longer an issue, and it disappears from the architectural design solution. Similarly, the fusion algorithm that we have developed to support multimodal interaction (Nigay & Couatz 1995), is not part of a PAC-Amodeus architecture. It sits behind the scene as a reusable mechanism.

5. Conclusion

Architectural modelling is becoming a central problem for large, complex systems. With the advent of new technologies and user-centred concerns, the user interface portion of interactive systems is becoming increasingly large and complex. Although interface builders tend to alleviate the problem, they are limited in scope and apply to mundane cases for which the user interface is often a second class component. Architecture design of user interfaces needs better support.

In this chapter, we have focussed on agent-based architectural styles and showed how sound tradeoffs between conflicting requirements and properties can be done using the PAC-Amodeus conceptual model. Although we have provided some practical guidelines for the software design of user interfaces, we do not claim exhaustiveness. In particular, we have not discussed how PAC-Amodeus can be extended to groupware (Salber 1995), and we still do not have operational generic heuristics to bridge the gap between architectural design and implementation tasks.

Acknowledgements

This work has been supported by project ESPRIT BR 7040 Amodeus

Chapter 12: Towards A Flexible Software Architecture of Interactive Systems

Michael Goedicke & Bettina Sucrow

1. Introduction

It is a generally accepted fact that with the possible exception of throw away prototypes software systems have a long life time. This implies that software systems have to survive many change requests. Thus the design process from very early on has to consider likely changes. The design for potential change is the key to the success of a software system. This means that the investment in a software product is justified only if at least potential changes are considered and reflected in the design i.e. the software architecture of a software system (Ghezzi, Jazayeri & Mandrioli 1992).

Modern interactive software systems allow the direct manipulation of the system's state via multi dimensional and multi modal input/output devices. Thus such software systems face at least two important design problems. One is the design of the user interface, the other is the design of the overall software architecture of the interactive software system. The latter is especially in charge of representing all relevant objects of the system internally thus providing the required functionality and data. Thus we distinguish internal and external representation of the system's information. Many models for this interaction have been proposed which clearly separate the two aforementioned properties of software systems (see, for example the Seeheim Model (Pfaff 1985) or the MVC (Goldberg 1984, Krasner & Pope 1988) model as the first attempts in this area and also (Coutaz & Bass 1991) and (Götze 1994) for a good overview and classification).

The implication of these two design problems is that interactive systems have to face at least two streams of change requests. The user interface design is dominated by questions resulting from a human factors oriented analysis of the system's actual tasks. The internal object model of the application is dictated by other considerations. For example, the evolvability of the software system and / or the connection to other software systems may prescribe certain object structures. The most important aspect of the internal object model is, however, the desired degree of object (data) consistency the system has to achieve. This notion of consistency is similar to traditional database consistency. However, in contrast to traditional database applications advanced applications require often a new and often less rigid notion of consistency. This notion is often application specific which is mostly due to the distributed nature of the application domain.

In this contribution we discuss the relation of user interface models to the software architecture and the implications to the software architecture of the entire interactive software system. These models emphasize the user interface and address the interaction with the rest of the software system only in a limited way. This discussion leads to a software architecture scheme which employs a specific notion of consistency. This notion applies to the internal and external objects as well and forms a semantic frame for both the internal and external presentation and manipulation possibilities.

Starting from a brief analysis of related work below we develop an architectural scheme which emphasizes the relation between user interface elements and the internal architecture of the software. This is achieved by describing explicitly the connections between the related 'internal' and 'external' software components (Goedicke & Sucrow 1994).

A set of different architecture models for the construction of user interfaces has been developed in order to achieve flexible software systems. User interfaces are the medium for the user to communicate with the underlying application. It is therefore very important that the user interface allows the user to interact with the underlying application in a correct and convenient manner.

The notion of flexibility means here evolvable software systems. In particular, a software system in this context has to integrate the user interface and the underlying data and operations up to a certain granularity on the one side and at the same time dialog independence up to a certain degree on the other side. Starting with such considerations as a first approach in this area a linguistic model of interaction has been outlined in the so-called *Seeheim model*, developed at the Seeheim Workshop on User Interface Management Systems (Pfaff 1985).

Starting from the Seeheim model another important idea has been developed, the *multiagent model* of a user interface architecture. A number of architecture models for interactive systems has been developed on the basis of the multiagent model. We mention the Model-View-Controller (MVC) (Goldberg 1984), the PAC (Bass & Coutaz 1991) and the DIWA (Voss 1990), for example (see s n 11.2 for a comprehensive discussion of various architectural issues related e multiagent model).

According to the two main architecture models MVC and PAC interactive systems are organized as communicating agents or interaction objects. However, in neither model a clear structure of the integration between the underlying application and its man-machine interface is shown. A well structured architecture of the software components integrating presentation *and* application offers powerful possibilities for supporting semantic feedback and also other features which are very important for highly graphical manipulation interfaces.

Therefore, we will discuss in the next section the idea of our architecture model of interactive systems which is based on the idea of maintaining various kinds of consistency relations. It will become obvious, for example, how suitable semantic feedback, an essential feature of modern graphical user interfaces, will be supported through our approach. After that we will show the flexibility of our approach by analysing some important categories of change requests to an interactive software system.

2. The Architectural Model

In this section we discuss two important consistency relations which exist between the application and the presentation of the application. These are

- relations between the (graphical) presentation of internal information on the one side and the application and its internal state information on the other side
- relations between various presentations of the internal state information which may be alternative and or complementary presentation (of the internal state).

We start with analysing these kinds of consistency relations. The focus lies here on relations of the first kind where the consistency relations of the second kind are discussed in (Goedicke & Sucrow 1995). From this analysis we show how architectural software components and their interconnection can be derived. This will describe our approach to structure the software architecture of interactive software systems.

The Seeheim model proposed to realize separation of concerns for interactive systems by having three components at the top level of the software architecture. The question is: How to keep this desirable separation between the various properties of an interactive software system and achieve at the same time modularity at a finer level.

We argue that at the level of software architecture a notion of component and interconnections of components is important. In the discussion below we assume only a general notion of object where an object is encapsulating certain resources by allowing only object-specific operations to manipulate the object's resources. Since objects represent state and state manipulation during the runtime of a system we also use the notion of an object type which allows to speak about the properties of an object defined prior to any execution and which are valid during the system's or object's lifetime respectively. A component is described in terms of various object types.

2.1 Conceptual Structure of Internal and External Representation of Interactive Software Systems

In order to explain our structuring approach integrating both views we have to compare the roles of the various "objects" within the system. The objects we consider here are the user interface (graphic-) objects (UI-objects for short) and the objects maintained internally by the application (AP-objects for short). UI-objects are the focus of the UI-Design process while the AP-objects are the centre of the "normal" software engineering process. We argue that both types of objects reflect different aspects of the entire system (part) under consideration. In order to show this we discuss a number of propositions.

Proposition 1 For every type of AP-object there is a corresponding external representation by a number of UI-objects and vice versa.

This follows from the observation that any AP-object exists and is maintained within a software system since it represents directly or indirectly some property to be managed by the system. This implies that information about the systems application domain has led to the inclusion of such AP-objects within the system design. The same information needs to be presented to the user of the system. Thus the same aspect of the system's application domain is reflected both in its internal and external representation as well. Of course, there are possibly auxiliary objects needed to allow speedier access to or manipulation of the system's state. However, this does not invalidate the statement above: the mapping between the internal and external need not be a one to one. We believe that in general the mapping can be quite complex in order to keep the various displays and interaction elements for the user at an acceptable level of complexity. However, the inherent structure of the information of the system's application domain suggests a certain structure which will also be a structured mapping between internal and external representations. This leads to our next

Proposition 2 The construction of AP-objects is reflected in the (graphic) construction of its external representation and vice versa.

This means that the construction of the UI-objects follows to some extent the construction of the AP-objects. This is not to say that e.g. an E/R-modelling of the system's data should dictate the system's user interface. A more detailed look and systematic development is necessary. Thus a systematic analysis of the structure and operations demanded by the information to be manipulated by the envisaged system leads to design decisions i.e. software architecture relevant for internal and external representation of information in question.

This approach also includes the poss ity that findings in the design process of the UI-objects influence the structure and construction of the AP-objects. For example, if it turns out that a particular piece of information can only be shown in a useful way in the context of other information pieces, this additional information must be provided by the AP-objects. Such a design decision might sometimes necessitate the addition of additional auxiliary AP-objects or additional object links.

Consider an editor capable of designing modular software systems. The editor supports textual and graphic editing of system structure concurrently. Also different degrees of detail can be displayed. In Figure. 1 a sketch is given how the external appearance of such an editor could look like. Of course, all three views may be open at any given time for a configuration of modules and may also be manipulated. The various operation offered by the editor vary from view to view due to the different degree of detail shown in the views. E.g. in View 2 only boxes i.e. modules may be created, given an name and can be connected. While in View 3 the most detailed description of each module may be entered textually. The manipulation of a graphic module representation through a view will normally affect one or more modules. The internal representation is a database of modules (a module library) which has to be updated accordingly. Analysis actions performed on the module database may reveal inconsistencies between modules which in turn are represented by special graphic elements in the various views.

Returning to our discussion about correspondences between internal and external representations of objects in the editor two kinds of boxes or a text fragment are possible external representations of a module description. The module description of each module is represented internally by a respective object containing all relevant information about a module. If a module is inserted and connected to other modules corresponding objects representing modules and module connections are

placed in the module database. This is only to sketch the ideas of a module editor and to highlight the idea about internal and external representations.
From this discussion follows also the next

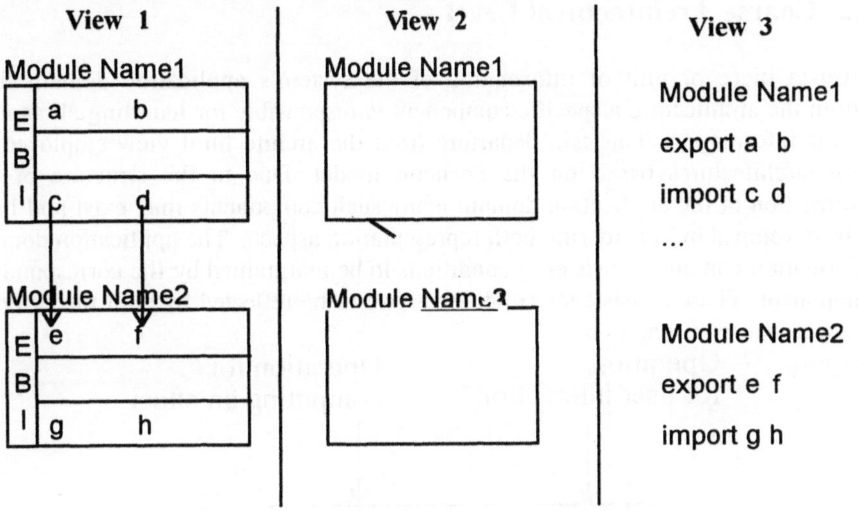

Figure 1 Three different views of a module editor

Proposition 3 Execution of operations on the AP-objects may cause changes in the external representation (UI-objects) and vice versa.

This means that the system as well as the user may initiate operations which may change the internal and external structure and contents of the system's state.
In the example this may be seen if one considers moving boxes around in order to achieve a particular graphic layout. This means that the existing module connections have to be changed as well. This is an example of an operation which changes the external appearance of a module configuration only. This implies that the graphic information associated with each module has to be changed while the corresponding AP-object storing the modules export and import interface, for example, is left unchanged.
Another example is an operation which adds a new connection between modules in one of the views. This implies not only adding an arrow to all the graphic views of the module system (view 1 and 2) but also the creation of an AP-object representing the information about the module connection. Studying the module connections more thoroughly a specific architectural aspect of the module editor system is revealed. E.g. by deleting a module from a module configuration all connections from and to this module have to be erased as well. In a traditional textual syntax oriented editor this causes only minor problems since the context analysis of the specification text fragments updates the module connection information. However, in order to provide instantaneous response to the graphic operation "box-removal" it is necessary to associate which each AP-object representing a module also the information about AP-objects representing module connections involving the module to be removed.

In the following we would like to summarize the findings from above and develop an architectural scheme. We describe this at two levels.

2.2 Coarse Architectural Level

Given a piece or unit of information of the system's application domain then within the architecture a specific component is responsible for handling all aspects of this information. This is a departure from the architectural view employed by those architectures based on the Seeheim model. Due to the structure of the information of the application domain many such components may exist and have to be developed by considering both representation aspects. The application domain information contains consistency conditions to be maintained by the corresponding component. These consistency conditions have to be reflected by both the external and internal representation.

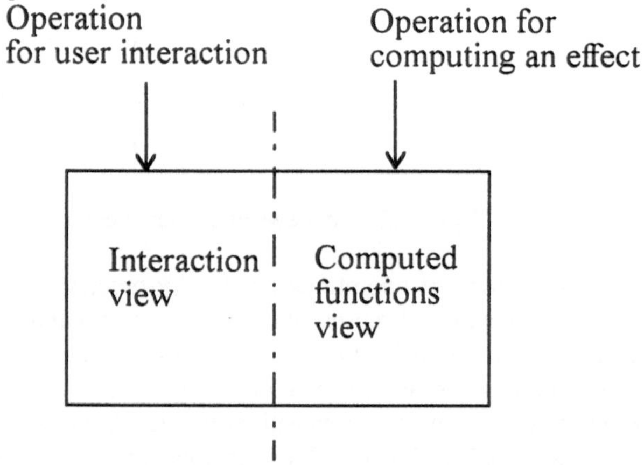

Figure 2 Views of a component

From the structural analysis of the application domain information also the structure and the connections of the architectural components follow. Such an approach integrates the internal and external representation of the system's state. Since the interaction between user and system on one side and UI-Objects and software component on the other side is established on a finer grain the semantic feed back can be realized faster and structurally more adequate than in the case of separating the entire system into three (monolithic) building blocks implied by the Seeheim model. The combination of the external and internal representation in selfcontained software components at a level of finer granularity results in a design employing smaller components compared to the Seeheim model. Since smaller components are easier to analyse the amount of checking and duplication of design work is also less than in the case of the big building blocks implied by the Seeheim approach. Of course, the inherent complexity of the problem is not reduced by any clever technique. In our approach the connections between the various components incorporating the UI-objects and AP-objects have to be considered carefully. This approach advocates for a component concept capable of expressing user-interaction and computational properties in one modular description. One could regard this as different (complementary) views of a component. However, the design of such software structures is in many cases not trivial and needs systematic development. In order to guide the developer the design space has to be limited in a certain way. This is not to restrict the designer but to offer a structural model serving as a blueprint for searching an adequate software architecture. Such a concept is also called canonical software component and using this notion we present below the modular structure of a system part sketched in Figure 2.

2.3 A More Detailed Architectural Level

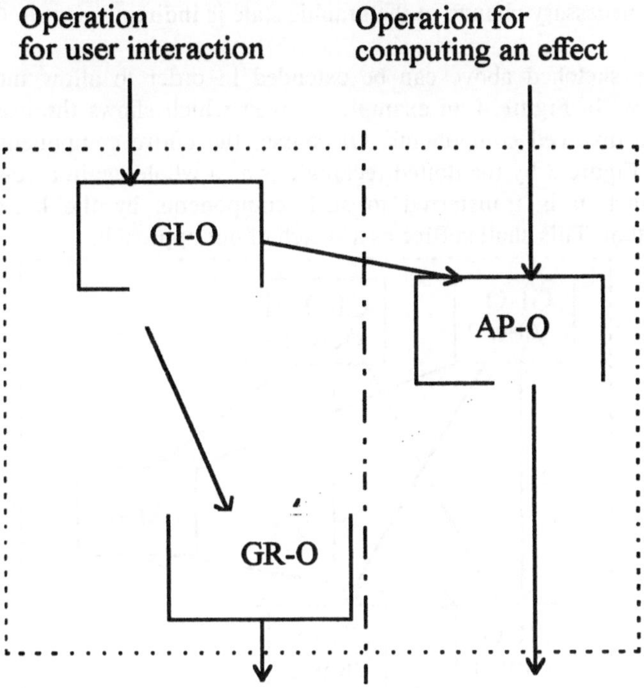

Figure 3. Use-Relationship between modules realizing the "interactive" component sketched in Figure 2

The structure for Figure 2 at a more detailed level is again a configuration of components which realize the desired interaction and computation. The constituent “boxes” are labelled GI-O, GR-O and AP-O. The box/module GI-O represents the interface to windowing systems i.e. to widgets etc. In particular it is responsible for detecting and managing the user's interaction e.g. entering a command, clicking a mouse button. The crucial task within the GI-O-component is to decide on the knowledge of the graphic state whether only syntactic or semantic operations need to be invoked. In the first case only the external representation has to be changed,

but no change to the internal representation is necessary. In the second case e.g. moving a box over the trash icon for erasing the box changes to the internal representation are necessary, hence an appropriate operation has to be invoked.
In such a case the AP-O component comes into play. It is responsible to realize the internal representation of the involved objects. Thus it implements and maintains the various consistency rules derived from the analysis of the system's application domain.
When graphic properties of the external representation need to be changed the GR-O-component of Figure 3 has to perform its task. The GR-O-component maintains the graphic state of the objects maintained in the AP-O component. A change can be caused by a simple "box"-move, for example. In such a case the direct use-relation between GI-O and GR-O is important. If there are semantic interactions of the user the necessary change in the graphic state is indirectly sent to GR-O by AP-O.
The scheme sketched above can be extended in order to allow more than one external view. In Figure 4 an example is given which shows the use-relationship between the involved components. Of course, the entire component sketched in Figure 4 or Figure 3 by the dotted rectangle is as a whole again a component. The user's interaction is transferred to such components by the basic underlying window system. This shall suffice as a sketch of our approach.

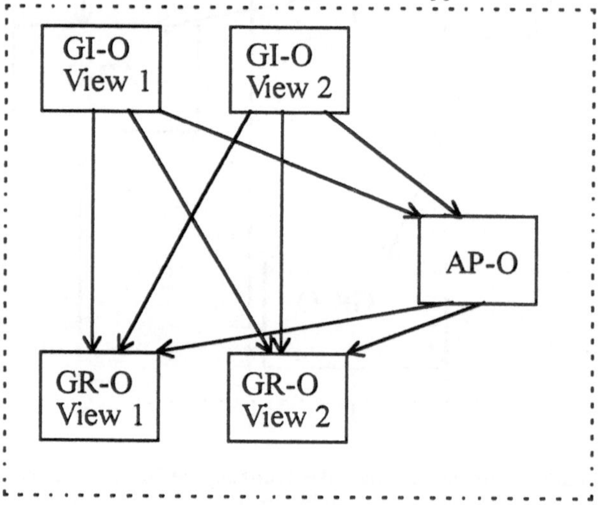

Figure 4 Component implementing two external Views

So far we have presented the scheme for constructing the software architecture of interactive systems. Below we now present another example of our approach and evaluate it with regard to architectural flexibility.

3. Analysis of the Architecture Model wrt. Flexibility

In this section the focus of attention is on the desire to change a particular software

system with respect to some concern. The desired change has consequences regarding the software architecture of the entire system. The interesting questions are, which changes or development actions have to be performed as a result of a particular change request and how the architecture is modified.
For example, a change request in an interactive system may concern the underlying application. However, not only the specific part of the application has to be changed, but such a change request may also affect the interaction between the system and the user. Thus, the goal is that the software architecture of the system allows this change request in an easy and comprehensible way.
This problem will be discussed using an example of an interactive software system which has been designed and partly implemented (Goedicke & Sucrow 1994) at the University of Essen. This system is designed using the component oriented module architecture (Goedicke 1993) specified through the description language _ (Cramer et al. 1991) and realizes the known (IFIP) Conference Planing System.
Below we first will describe the architecture of the software system for the Conference Planing System example before the change request with respect to a specific concern takes place and its consequences are discussed.

3.1 Architecture Before the Desired Change Request

We discuss here the part of the IFIP Conference Planing System where assignment between papers and referees takes place. In particular, we look at the components responsible for handling papers and referees and assigning individual papers to referees or vice versa. To understand the change request later on we describe this relevant part of the system more precisely.
Consider the following state of the system: After starting the system a window appears representing a listbox which in turn presents the submitted papers. A menu enables the user to assign a referee to a selected paper in the list. In Figure 5 and Figure 6 it is sketched how the system presents itself in these situations.

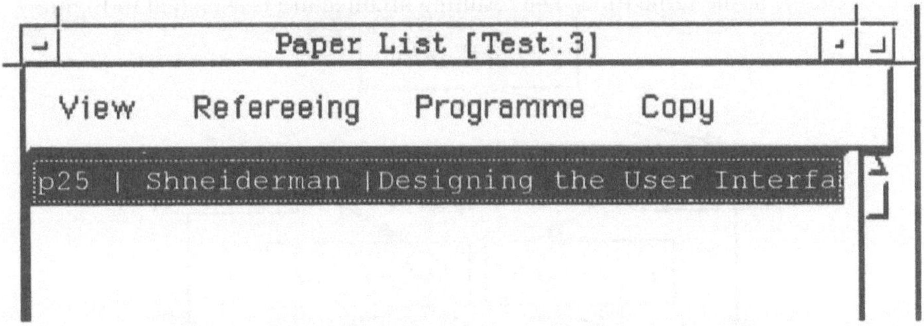

Figure 5 Part of the Paper - Referee assignment dialogue

Having shown the graphical representation of the system we now consider its software architecture. The entire architecture is divided into three main parts at a coarse level: These parts shall be *PaperWindow*, *Papers* and *Referees*. The user may interact with the system via the component *PaperWindow*. She can select a certain paper presented by *PaperWindow* in the listbox. *PaperWindow* in turn needs informations about the papers to be handled and the referees involved. Therefore there exists a connection between *PaperWindow* and *Referees* for providing more detailed informations about the referee entries to the component *PaperWindow*.

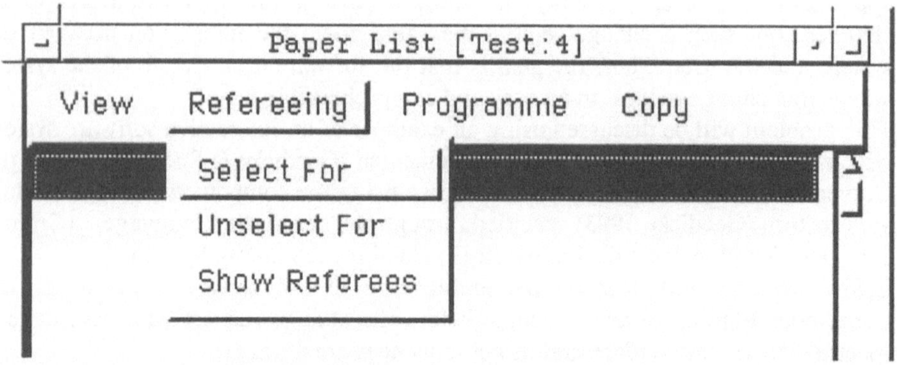

Figure 6 The Selection of a Referee for a chosen Paper

It is most important for the assignment of referees to papers to maintain consistency between all papers and referees during the whole runtime of the interactive system. The focus lies here on the datatype model. Internally the datatype schema for a paper and a referee is specified as follows. The papers are organized as a table where each paper entry consists a paper_id and a paper_information part. Analogously, the referees are represented through entries in a table, each entry consisting of a referee_id and a referee_information part. Consistency maintenance between papers and referees is achieved through storing the assigned referee(s) for a paper in the information part of this paper and vice versa, i.e. storing all papers to which a referee is assigned in the information part of the referee, at the same time. The resulting architecture is sketched in Figure 7.

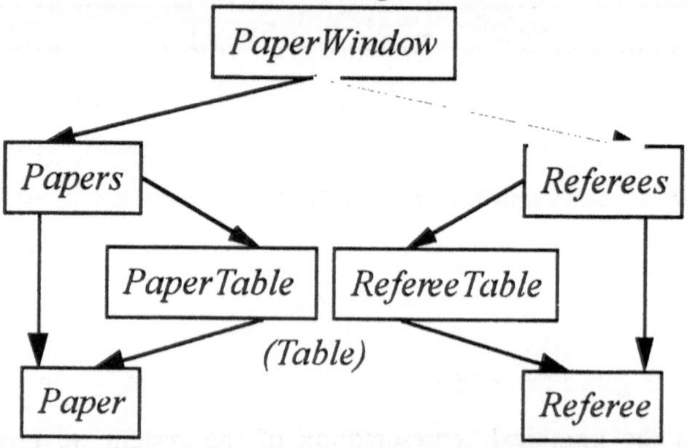

Figure 7 Software Architecture of a part of the IFIP Conference Planning System before the change request

In order to explain the interplay between the various modules more in detail we consider the component *PaperWindow*. This component itself has a structure as suggested in Figure 3. The top level component *PaperWindow* realizes the GI-O - component as can be seen in Figure 8 by the attached boxes close_box_click and select_for_referee. These boxes represent sample operations in charge of handling related graphical user interactions. The GR-O-component contains three modules Paper_window, Frame and Paper_Window_Item, which together are responsible for correctly constructing the graphical components of the *PaperWindow* appearing on the screen. The component Frame realizes the entire window layout while Paper_Window_Item realizes the display of the various entries shown within such a window. The AP-O-component of *PaperWindow* contains the two modules PaperHandling and 2Tupel which together are responsible for handling papers entered in the database. PaperHandling handles the papers by using 2Tupel for structuring papers and referees, respectively. Finally, the GR-O-component uses primitive graphical operations and features realized by the basic window operations of the windowing system.
The above detailed described architecture of the part *PaperWindow* of the software system is sketched in Figure 8.

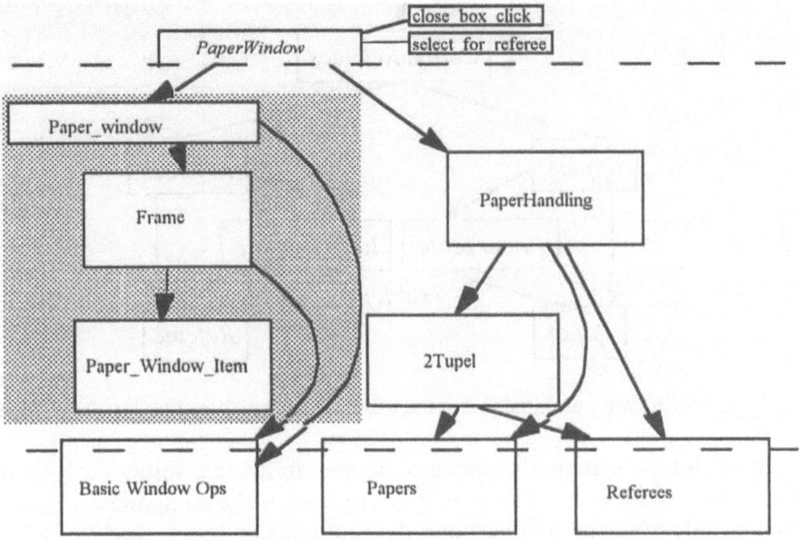

Figure 8 The fine grain architecture of component Paper-window

In the same way, that is with components GR-O, AP-O and GI-O respectively, are structured more concretely the other components *Papers* and *Referees*.

3.2 Change Request and Proposed Architectural Change

Suppose now, the interactive system should be changed in the following way: immediately, after the receipt of papers (just after passing of the deadline of submission) and before reviewing the papers there will be introduced a so called *coarse* reviewing phase. During this phase only a few referees (probably a subset of all referees) look at the papers and choose a subset of all of these papers (perhaps the highest number of papers which can be accepted for the conference) for reviewing in the usual manner. For this case there has to be considered, how the relevant part of the entire software system has to be changed in an effective and suited way.

Of course, the first thought is to add a further component to the system, which is responsible for all things concerning the referees of this coarse phase of reviewing (the corresponding component will be called *CoarseReferees*). The main differences to the original system will be sketched below.

The new component *CoarseReferees* handles for all submitted papers which of the papers will be reviewed by whom of the coarse referees. For example, it should be possible, now, to list all papers with their informations about referees and coarse referees who reviewed these specific papers. Moreover, it should also be possible to list only those papers with their respective informations, which have been accepted for the conference.

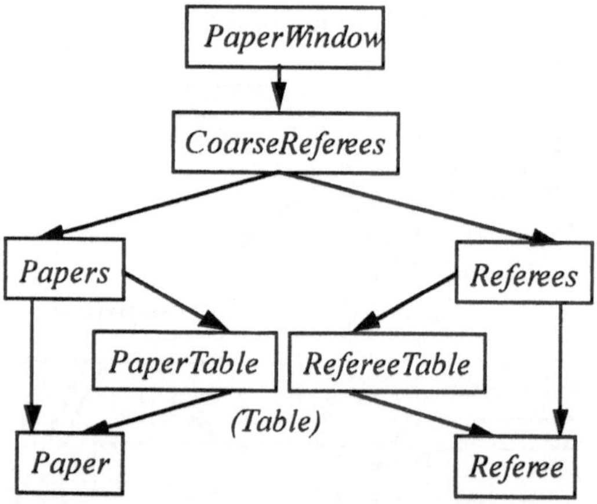

Figure 9 Software architecture of the example system after the desired change

This new situation requires changes of the following kinds: the component *CoarseReferees* can now be seen as a filter between the component *PaperWindow* on the one side of the system part and the components *Papers* and *Referees* on the other side. For the goal of *CoarseReferees* to act as a filter the connections between the related components have to be changed as well. The connections from *PaperWindow* to *Papers* and *Referees* will be removed and replaced by an equivalent connection from the component *PaperWindow* to component *CoarseReferees*, which in turn will get connections to the components *Papers* and *Referees*, respectively. To obtain the additional informations about reviewing of papers through coarse referees the internal datatype schema has to be extended. More in detail, the paper entries, consisting of a paper_id and a paper_information part in each case, will receive an additional information entry about coarse reviewing in their respective paper_information part.

Thus, one result for the new evolving software architecture of the relevant part of the entire system will be, to connect the components or modules *PaperWindow*, *Papers*, *CoarseReferees*, *Referees* and *Table* according to their uses-relationships as described above, and as shown in the figure below.
Of course, also this new architecture reflects our proposed model of modules realizing the interactive component in its components (see also Figure 3). Here lies a big flexibility in organizing the three components GR-O, AP-O and GI-O in the component *CoarseReferees* in an desired and effective way. This means according to the new desired graphical user interface and according to an effective software architecture of the whole new system again.

4. Evaluation and Conclusion

In this contribution we have discussed the critical issue of designing the software architecture of an interactive software system. Many approaches focus on either side of the problem. We have argued to include both properties in the design considerations in order to achieve a high semantic feedback in the resulting software system thus increasing its usability. We used a part of the IFIP - Conference planning system to show how a change request can modify the architecture of the system. Introducing the requirement to include a refereeing process at a "coarse" - level results in an additional component. The process of adding the new component shows the following properties of our architectural scheme.

- Due to the chosen components the new component fits well into the existing architecture. This feature can be described by "locality of change". This means that changes to the architecture affect only the relevant components. Such a property follows from a careful analysis of the various objects and object-types involved. This is also partly due to the chosen component concept not explained here in full length. See (Goedicke 1993) for a full discussion of software component concepts.
- The separation a software system's task into external presentation and internal management of state is applied to every constituent component of the software system. This applies also to the new component as a result of the change request. In particular this means that the presentation part of the new component and the internal management part can be dealt with separately to a great extent on the one side and the interaction between both can be dealt with together in order to achieve the high degree of semantic feedback from the system to the user on the other side.

Our work presented here has shown the feasibility of the approach. It also showed that the entire software system can be structured in such a way that man machine issues and traditional software engineering issues can be dealt with either separately or in common depending on the development situation. Currently we apply our concepts to the design of a number of non trivial example systems. These are mostly mixed textual and graphic editors, information systems like the IFIP Conference planning system and distributed systems in the area of CSCW.

Part V: Critical Issues for the Future of User Interface Systems Engineering

This last part of the book presents two different new trends for the future of user interface system engineering. Both chapters in this part deal with a need rather than existing technologies. They point to areas where there is inadequate support at present.

The first chapter focuses on the incorporation of the context for improving the usability and the efficiency of the interactive system. It explores many different relationships which can exist between contextual information and design. Five principle types of notation are identified which are required to support the whole system development life cycle: notations for envisonment of designs, for context, design rationale, system behaviour and system construction. These are required because of the different needs for information at different stages of design. This chapter proposes an approach known as 'Literate Development' to deal with these issues and with the problems of gaps between notations. The gap is much larger between context and design than it is in the traditional areas of study, which focus on design and construction

Chapter 14 discusses an important issue which, up until now, has been only superficially addressed: the design of metaphors. The use of metaphor in user interfaces allows users to develop their model of the system more quickly as they can use their existing knowledge to infer characteristics of the system. The problem is, of course, that if the metaphor is poorly chosen then the users will make incorrect inferences. This chapter presents a thorough analysis of how designers should go about the task of designing metaphors and on the software tools which are needed if designers are to be given adequate support.

Chapter 13: Literate Development: Weaving Human Context into Design Specifications

Gilbert Cockton, Steven Clarke, Phil Gray & Chris Johnson

1. Towards Systematic Extensive and Full Use of Human Context

HCI approaches have distinguished themselves by their user focus, considering users' needs, analysing their tasks, investigating their preferences and differences, and understanding physical, social, organisational and even technological facets of their environment. When much HCI writing was polemic, it was enough to stress the need for understanding the context of human usage and to describe some system failures brought about by incompatibilities with context. Almost everyone accepts the polemic now and it has been overlain by commercial lip service to participative, stakeholder-consulting, user-driven, activity-based validated system development. Much of HCI is seen as common sense, and it would appear that this sense is (at long last) becoming more common.

The limits of common sense are, however, quickly reached. For many, the first problem is deciding what is meant by 'Context', as borne out in a special issue of *Human-Computer Interaction* by 24 commentaries on one paper (Seely-Brown & Duguid 1994). These positions are unsettling the existing *status quo*, which distinguished users, their tasks and their environment (Maissel et al., 1993). A similar classification in an early HCI text book adopted a long standing HCI trinity and organised user needs analysis into three checklists: user (Booth 1989, p.114), task (p.115) and situational characteristics (p.116). Current concerns about the nature and use of context signal the end of innocence: mere knowledge of the trinity of users, their tasks and their work environments cannot ensure that useful information about human context is gathered and systematically put to effective use.

This chapter introduces one response to the problem of really using contextual information. The problems are not artefacts of introspection on the essence of systems' contexts. The problems are real, as the literature on problem analysis and requirements engineering bears out.

In the remainder of this introduction, the experiences of a typical requirements capture project are summarised to provide a concrete example of the problem that this chapter addresses. This problem is then defined. Lastly, we present our position on valid solutions to the problem of really using contextual information when making design decisions. This position defines a research programme on *Literate Development*.

Section 2 introduces the concept of Literate Development, relates it to a V-model of software development, and argues that the use of contextual and design notations is key to effective Literate Development.

Section 3 reports on the use of contextual and design notations in a development

case study. An information system is under participative development in a real work context, and we are using the contextual information and design documents for this application to develop our understanding of the requirements for Literate Development.
Section 4 summarises our current understanding of the requirements for Literate Development. These requirements extend beyond the use of notations to higher level issues such as how different methodologies differ in their relation of contextual information to design decisions.
Lastly, Section 5 summarises the potential for Literate Development as a strategy for full and effective use of contextual information. The status of our current work is assessed and ongoing work is described.

1.1 A Typical Experience

There are many published reports of the difficulties of using contextual information in design that can provide concrete examples of the problem that this chapter addresses. We very briefly consider one example, an interim report from the CAR project (Powrie & Siemieniuch 1990), which investigated applications for integrated broadband communications in the European automobile industry. The reported experiences are typical of attempts to make a systematic use of human context.

The CAR project focused on co-operative design using multimedia communications. Interviews with staff identified tasks performed within their organisation and, in particular, how introduction of integrated broadband communications may affect it. The CAR project was systematic in its capture of human context (further studies were to include tracer studies of documents). There are clearly no problems in collecting volumes of contextual data. What is interesting is what the volume was and what was done with it. Approximately seven hundred user requirements were derived. These were broken down into a smaller set of "minimal requirements". Two were:

- interaction with each graphical application should be as consistent as possible;
- users should have access to facilities that let them express and explore their ideas formally and informally using graphics.

Such requirements could apply to *any* design environment, so the question arises as to where the specific contexts of automobile CAD come in. Some appear to have been left out, as they were "extraneous data." Some appear to have been unusable, as senior management had not been well enough briefed to get a coherent, representative view of their companies. However, even if these problems of data collection are overcome, the issue of how to use contextual data remains.

1.2 The Problem

Contextual information can be easily gathered, but there is a problem in using it fully and effectively. The problem can be reduced simply to understanding the relationships between human contexts and systems designs. To understand these relationships, we require descriptions of human contexts and systems designs, and ways of linking between these descriptions. We need to prepare these descriptions without prior commitment to any prescribed methodology for moving from context to design (or vice-versa). The problem thus changes from that addressed in the CAR and similar projects (ie, transforming context data into requirements), to one of finding a more systematic way of underpinning design decisions with contextual knowledge.

The problem is thus not to determine how contextual information can be used to form requirements. The problem is to use it fully and effectively throughout the whole development life cycle. In long-lived systems, contextual information remains relevant until decomissioning, i.e., decisions on maintenance and modifications should refer back to the original context of design, if only to decide with confidence that this context either no longer holds or is irrelevant to the proposed changes. The use of context should not be restricted to the early stages of development.

Furthermore, a deep understanding of the relations between context and design will provide firm foundations for reliably and effectively transforming contextual information into formal requirements specifications. As it is currently not clear how contextual information can be reliably and effectively used in design decisions, all current attempts to deduce formal requirements from it will remain speculative.

A root and branch approach to the problem is necessary. The problem must be studied in its purest form, taking descriptions of human context and descriptions of system designs and to thoroughly explore the interconnections that can be profitably made.

1.3 Full And Effective Use of Contextual Information

With a clean slate, we can examine the role of notations in recording, structuring and guiding the use of contextual information over the whole development life cycle from problem analysis to maintenance and operation. Our goal here is to extend development documentation so that full and effective use can be made of information about the human context for planned systems:

- *full* use requires a systematic approach to data collection that would result in fewer “extraneous” context data (i.e., they would have a clear delayed use if not, they would not be recorded and structured)
- *effective* use would result in clearer design hypotheses (ie, the rationale for design decisions would be some contextual criteria), and also support the assessment and preservation of a design's internal consistency.

Our position is that contextual information can only be used fully and effectively if:

- collected contextual information is recorded, processed and made accessible (in raw and processed forms) to software staff;
- the complete design is recorded;
- design decisions are identified as 'positions' in the complete design description;
- unadopted design options can be 'overlaid' on the complete design description;
- design decisions are linked to the contextual information that raised the design

question and/or provided criteria for the choice of the adopted option.

There is clearly a role for contextual and design notations in the above ("collected contextual information is recorded", "the complete design is recorded", "design decisions are identified", "unadopted design options can be overlaid"). The challenge lies in the last requirement. This chapter addresses this by examining the scope for weaving links between HCI notations. Such linking must be systematic and effective in order to meet our goals of extending notational support to new aspects of communication, modelling and planning during software development.

With systematic and effective use of contextual information, moving *between* context and decisions will be less of a creative leap. Each explicit link contributes a strand to a bridge between context and design, facilitating simple shifts of focus as developers shift around Carroll's task-artefact cycle (Carroll & Rosson 1992).

2. Literate Development

Weaving links between HCI notations is the key feature of *Literate Development*. Literate Development is inspired by, but is more extensive than, Knuth's (Knuth 1984) Literate Programming. Literate Programming tools link design (in the form of stepwise refinements) to itself (refinement steps) and to implementation (PASCAL code).

Literate Development tools will require far more extensive links, as they must link contextual data, surrogates for that data (e.g., scenarios), complementary design representations (design rationales, behavioural specifications, constructional specifications), and internal software specifications (software architectures). Knuth's web thus spreads from the narrow centre of programming in the small to the full span of developing in the large.

The idea of Literate Development is due to the convergence of two streams of work within the GIST group at Glasgow. One author has been using representations of context (Johnson 1994) to extend the webs of Literate Programming to specification. In such *Literate Specifications*, formal requirements statements are linked to Design Rationales (Johnson 1995). The other authors are addressing the broader problem of relating context to design (Cockton et al. 1995). A Literate Development approach absorbs the explicit representations and links of Literate Specification into a broader framework that covers more representations and more links. More representations are covered because all phases of the development life cycle can be potentially addressed. More links follow from this cornucopia of representations. The high level structure of these links can be related to the development life cycle.

2.1 The Potential for Literate Development

Webs of Literate Development extend beyond the refinement-code links of Literate Programming, and the specification-rationale links of Literate Specification, to links between anything produced during the phases of software development. Thus links are possible between specifications, context analyses and software design

documents. Such links are not entirely novel, since long links between early and late development already exist in the 'V model' of software development.
The 'V model' (Figure 1) relates development phases to immediate successors (as in the waterfall model), and also to ones on the 'same level'. *Levels* are due to phase outputs that are not used by the next logical phase. System Installation (where acceptance tests may still be conducted) is on the same level as Requirements Specification (where acceptance tests are created). System Integration (where modules are combined) is on the same level as System Design (where systems are decomposed into modules). Similarly, tests devised during Module Design are used during Module Construction.

Links in the 'V model' are examples of *delayed use*, where documents prepared in one phase (e.g., acceptance tests, integration plans, test plans) are not used in immediately subsequent ones. Generally, delayed use arises when tests/integration are planned before the artefacts to be tested/integrated have been constructed. Given this, the delayed use of contextual information is not alien to software development. Contextual information can have other uses than immediate transformation into requirements.

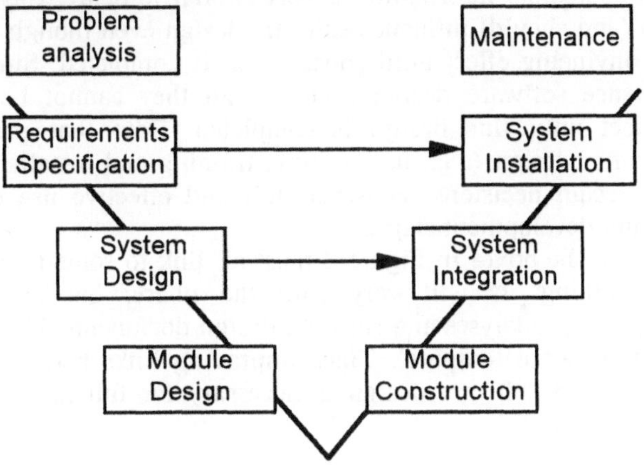

Figure 1: A V model for software development

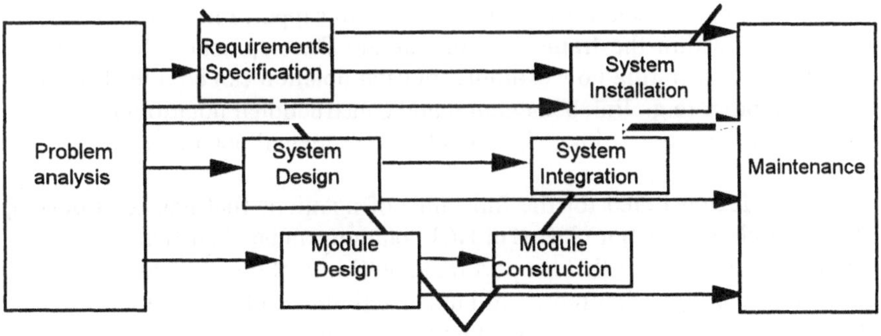

Figure 2: A V model for contextualised software development

2.2 Realising the Potential for Literate Development

In the V-model, only development phases are with the V. Problem Analysis (where contextual information is gathered) and Maintenance phases (where context remains relevant) are placed above it. Literate Development aims to fully integrate the use of contextual information during software development. The V-model must thus be extended to link in these phases.

Contextual information cannot become linked to design decisions until the *System Design* and *Module Design* phases. This is a form of 'delayed use' as already encountered in the V model of the software life cycle. Once linking of contextual information to design is considered to be a form of delayed use, the V model can be easily extended to link in previously excluded phases (Figure 2).
The model in Figure 2 treats outputs of contextual (problem) analysis as both design and test inputs (so long delays across a whole level are possible). Contextual information thus includes constraints (tests) that cannot be considered extensively and systematically until a design is completed (point 2 of our position, Section 1.3). Delayed use of contextual information is very similar to delayed use of test plans. Test plans can (and should) influence software design even though they cannot be fully used to convincing effect until construction is completed. Similarly, context data can influence software design even though they cannot be fully used to convincing effect until this design is completed. Data that primarily guides activities long after design (e.g., user testing, training and installation plans) can still influence design decisions. However, full and effective use of this data is delayed until later development stages.
The links between the boxes in Figure 2 must all link to something in the boxes. What the 'something' is will vary with the phase, but examples include specifications, context analyses and software design documents. Notations are used for many of these phase 'outputs'. Thus, improving links between notations for problem analysis and software design is necessary for full and effective use of contextual information.

2.3 The Place of HCI Notations in Literate Development

We believe that design notations can be extended to support full and effective use of contextual data within the framework of Literate Development. These extensions will involve demonstrating how examples of each notation can be inter-linked:

- with each other (e.g., link behavioural and constructional notations)
- with context data (e.g., link behavioural and contextual notations

This must be demonstrated for the full range of notations that has been developed by HCI research. Five major classes of HCI notation can be identified:

- *envisionment notations* that support rapid outlining of possible designs;
- *contextual notations* that represent human activities and environments;
- *design rationale notations* that capture the reasons behind design decisions;
- *behavioural notations* that represent systems from users' viewpoints;
- *constructional notations* that represent systems from developers' viewpoints.

We have used a range of notations in the design of an information system. Section 3 presents an example for all but one class (we have only recently used envisionment notations) and shows how it has been used in our design experiment. The notations are:

- Flow Model Diagram (contextual notation)
- QOC (design rationale notation)
- UAN (behavioural notation)
- NUF (constructional notation)

The notations are now briefly introduced in the following subsections. Readers who require more detail should follow up the appropriate references. However, NUF is a novel notation under development at Glasgow (Cockton 1992) and up to date details of this notation are not widely available. A brief appendix is thus provided at the end of this chapter that outlines the main features of the current version of NUF.

2.3.1 Contextual Enquiry Notations

Several notations have been developed for representing aspects of human context. For example, the Contextual Enquiry approach uses several diagrammatic representations (Holtzblatt & Beyer 1993). Diagrams represent work flows, responsibilities and relationships and physical layout (an example flow diagram is presented in Section 3.1). Such diagrams can be regarded as 'contextual surrogates', which provide specific views onto raw contextual information. Scenarios are another form of contextual surrogate that use a narrative structure to organise diverse aspects of context.

2.3.2 Design Rationale Notations

> "Design can be viewed as an exploration of a space of alternatives. That is, there are a host of alternative designs that fulfil the system's specification and the process of design involves identifying the one, or ones, that satisfy the system's constraints and goals as closely as possible." (Preece et al. 1994)

Designers often compare different design decisions, but rarely systematically, which often leads to designers not really reviewing all possibilities. They do not cover the whole design space and unconsciously reject what could be better solutions.

MacLean and colleagues devised the QOC notation (Questions, Options and Criteria, (MacLean et al. 1991)) for comprehensive exploration of the design space. Questions focus on a design issue. Options are possible design decisions. Criteria are (generally contextual) factors that (dis)favour the adoption of an option. QOC is a graphical representation of the design space for an interactive artefact. Questions, Options and Criteria are presented as columns of boxes, with linking lines to indicate positive or negative interactions between options and criteria (see Figure 4

in section 3.2).
QOC lets stakeholders gain a better understanding of a design and forces designers to explicitly discuss the pros and cons of various options in a QOC diagram.

2.3.3 Behavioural Notations

Behavioural notations specify the behaviour of the interface, as users will experience it, as opposed to the construction of the interface as software developers will suffer it. UAN describes user interaction with an interactive system (Hartson et al. 1990).

UAN describes the behaviour of the system in terms of feedback and visible actions which the system can perform. User actions, corresponding feedback and system actions are represented at the lowest level. For example, mouse clicks, mouse movements and icon highlighting are examples of the low level constructs in UAN. As an example , consider the following UAN description of the task "move a file icon".

TASK: Move a file icon

USER ACTIONS	**INTERFACE FEEDBACK**
~[file_icon] Mù	file_icon!
~[x,y]* ~[x',y']	outline of file_icon follows cursor
M^	display file_icon at x',y'

Mù means "depress mouse button"
M^ means "release mouse button"
~[x,y] means "move the cursor to position (x,y)"
(*) means one or more repetitions of the associated action
! means highlight

The two columns in the above example are the basic form of UAN. More columns can be added. Some can act as a bridge to more constructional notations. For example, "interface state" and "connection to computation" columns describe both state information such as the object which is the currently selected objects (e.g., file, window) and any relevant information for computation such as underlying command procedures (see Section 3.3).

Task sequences can be encapsulated and named to arbitrary levels of abstraction. A complete UAN description of an interface is a hierarchy of individual UAN descriptions. The hierarchy emerges from use of the task name (e.g., "Move a file icon") in other User Actions columns (just like a procedure call in programs).

2.3.4 Constructional Notations

Constructional notations can be mapped directly onto the structure of a software implementation. Thus dialogue notations such as transition networks can be mapped directly onto case statements (Denert 1977). Constructional notations can address different levels of abstraction for interactive systems (Cockton et al. 1995). NUF addresses the functional level. It was originally called DICM, as it described the designer's intended conceptual model. It is now called NUF (Notation for User Functionality) to reflect its constructional nature. NUF represents the objects and attributes of an interactive application as designers would like users to think about them. Therefore, NUF does not describe the interface as it appears on the screen nor any implementation details but simply concentrates on the objects and attributes which the designer believes are vital for a correct understanding of the application.

NUF combines the syntactic and semantic levels of Moran's Command Language Grammar (CLG — Moran 1981) with features of object-modelling language (Cockton 1992). Following Moran's CLG, a frame-based syntax is used. A *frame* is a set of slots. A *slot* is a name-value pair. Three key aspects of an application domain can be modelled in NUF slots:

- *relationships between domain objects* can be modelled (CLASS for generalisations, ISA for inheritance, ATTRIBUTES for part-of relationships);
- *features of domain objects* can be modelled (ROUTE slots for regularly accessed 'landmark' objects, COUNT s   or instance restrictions);
- *properties of domain objects* can be modelled (CONSTRAINT slots for the domain aspects of the fixed context).

ach abstract operation in NUF is an *abstract command.* Command slots have a rich subslots structure that distinguishes:

- *the assumed user intention* (ENACTS subslot for key action);
- *error detection, recovery* and *prevention* (AVOID ... BY subslots for detection and recovery; AVAILABILITY for prevention; BLOCK ... WHEN subslots for complete breakdowns);
- *task steps* that can be (partially) *automated* by the system (automatic AVOID ... BY and FOLLOW_UP subslots).

A brief appendix to this chapter summarises the current version of NUF.

3. The Use of HCI Notations in a Development Project

Literate Development involves linking across the complete development life cycle. Such links must be anchored in outputs from each phase (e.g., reports, analyses, specifications, software designs, training plans). We are using a development case study to explore how such *anchor points* can be located and exploited.

We have recently completed a study of the admissions process for our Master of Science course in Information Technology. This is a key postgraduate course in our university, with strands in humanities, computational physics, medical informatics and management, as well as mainstream computing. It thus involves many (potentially conflicting) stakeholders and is ‘business-critical’, bringing significant income to the department and the university.

We are now prototyping a new applications processing system, based on a design that is strongly influenced by the results of an extensive contextual analysis. We have used a range of notations to capture context and to express elements of the design. Exploratory links have been formed between these context and design documents

3.1 A Contextual Enquiry Flow Diagram

We have prepared versions of all Contextual Enquiry diagrams for the case study. Figure 3 shows a flow diagram for our MSc applications process. Such diagrams model "the important roles people take on". Roles are defined as "a set of responsibilities and associated tasks for the purpose of accomplishing a part of the work". Therefore, we can see that the *Applications Secretary's* main responsibility is to transfer information from applicants to the *Applications Officer* or the Faculty Office and vice versa. For example, the Application Secretary passes all the application details to the Applications Officer to make a decision. The Application Secretary then relays this decision to the applicant or Faculty Office. The Application Secretary's tasks generally involve filing, photocopying, sending mail, or updating information in files. The Applications Officer's responsibility is to decide what to do with each application (whether to accept it or not). These tasks involve communicating with the other involved strand co-ordinator (if appropriate) and the application secretary.

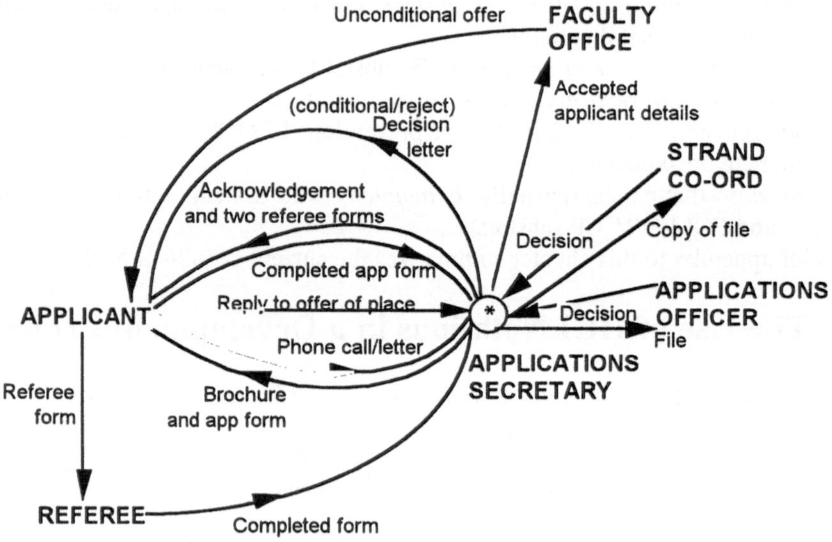

Figure 3: Flow Model for IT Applications Process

3.2 QOC

The Applications Secretary is frequently interrupted by phone calls about the progress of an application. Two design questions that arise are "when should phone queries be handled?" and "how can application details be accessed?". QOC diagrams for both questions are now presented. Both are illustrative in that the full range of options and criteria are not explored.

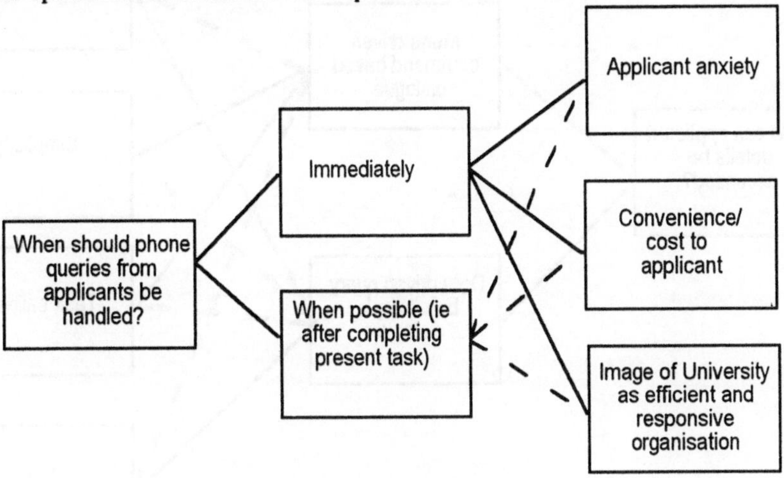

Figure 4: QOC for responding to phone queries

Figure 4 addresses when the applications secretary should be able to answer a phone query from an application. The two options are (i) immediately or (ii) when possible. The criteria to evaluate these options are aspects of the system's human context. These may appear to vary in generality from the almost universal (anxiety, cost, convenience) to the specific (image of university). However, all are specific to the relevant context, which gives rise to anxiety, costs and inconvenience. Applicants are understandably anxious about their educational future, and would like immediate answers to queries (otherwise they would not phone). Cost is important, particularly if applicants are overseas. Lastly, universities should give applicants the best possible service.
In QOC diagrams, solid lines represent positive interactions between design options and (contextual) criteria. Dashed lines represent negative interactions. Hence, for Figure 4, the first option is chosen since it always interacts more positively than the second with the criteria (as long as queries can be dealt with quickly).

The QOC diagram in Figure 5 shows a less clear cut choice about the choice of dialogue style, but we need not resolve this near universal HCI dilemma here. Suffice to say that decisions are not based on comparisons of simple counts of solid and dashed lines. Note here however that the context is largely general. These criteria apply to almost all human-computer interaction. However, the extent of a 'long time' is clearly determined within this system's context by the cost of an international phone call. Similarly, the need for flexibility arises from phone-based queries where applicants may not have 'key' field values to hand (e.g., application reference number). Thus again, specific contextual information will help us to resolve the question.

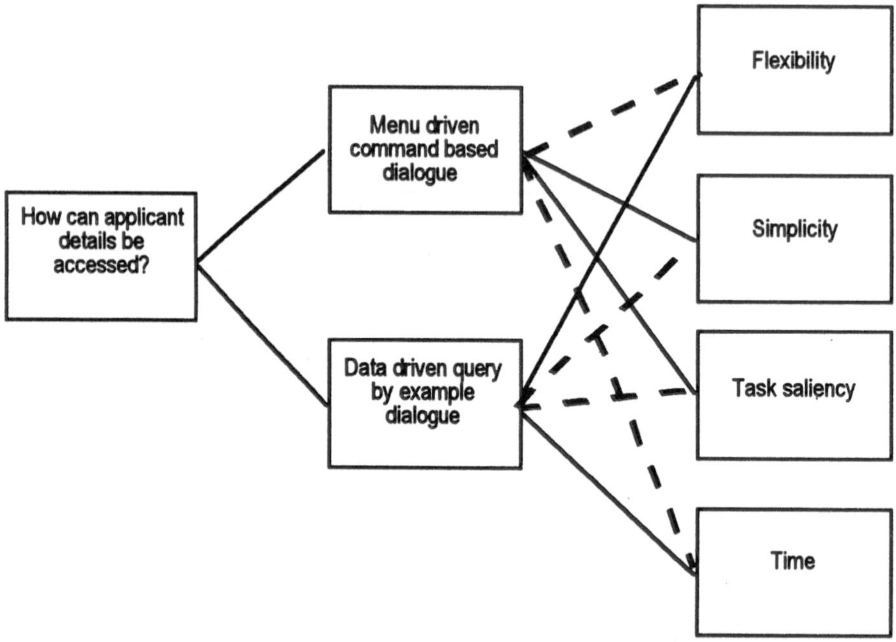

Figure 5: QOC for accessing application details

3.3 A UAN Example

The second option for Figure 5 has been chosen for the admissions system prototype. A UAN specification for the query specification task is given below. It uses the two extra columns mentioned in section 2.3.3 (@ means "in the display area").

The above example outlines a Query-by-Example interface for retrieving applicant details. It is a first cut (it ignores existing values in fields and what to do with them, and it omits selection of the CreateNewQuery command). The specification clearly addresses a choice made for Figure 5. It also prepares for the use of constructional notations, as it contains dialogue fragments (first two columns), as well as references to abstract commands (last column) and objects (CurrentResults: of AdmissionsSession).

TASK: SpecifyQuery

USER ACTIONS	INTERFACE FEEDBACK	INTERFACE STATE	CONNECTION TO COMPUTATION
~[aField@ ApplicantView]			
MV/\	display[I-beam@aField]		
Specify(aField, aValue)	display[aValue@aField]	aField.val := aValue	SetNewValue(aField)
	display[results@ CurrentQueryView]	results := CurrentResults: of AdmissionsSession	

3.4 An NUF Fragment for the Admissions System

Abstract objects and commands that are relevant to the above task fragment are described in NUF below:

CLASS FOR: AdmissionsSession
    COUNT: 1
    ATTRIBUTES
        TheMScApplications : list of MScApplications
        CurrentViews : list of list of MScApplications
        CurrentApplicant : a MScApplication
        CurrentQuery : a Query
        CurrentResults : aQueryResult [handler=Add(CurrentResults :, CurrentViews:)]
        .
        .
        .

CLASS FOR : a MScApplication
    ATTRIBUTES
        UniqueID: *format to be decided*
        TheApplicant : an ApplicantDetails
        Education: an EducationDetails
        TheStatus : a Status
        Notes : *free text format to be decided*

CLASS FOR: a QueryResult
    ATTRIBUTES
        TheseApplications : list of MScApplications

CLASS FOR : a Query
ATTRIBUTES
    Fields : List of ApplicationFields
    COMMANDS
        SetNewValue(AField)
        ENACTS: QueryReplace(Fields:, AField)
            FOLLOWUP FindAllApplicationsFor(Fields:) into CurrentResults: of AdmissionsSession

The objects behind the UAN task are a Query object comprising a list of field values (including undefined values) and the CurrentResults object comprising a list of application values, which is updated whenever the SetNewValue command is called, as its key action is followed by a recomputation of the query. Applications matching the query are assigned to the CurrentResults object. This object is active, as it has a handler property that automatically adds the new results to the CurrentViews.

3.5 Summary

While all four notations may be useful for existing design approaches, they do not provide enough support for linking to context. This is not surprising, since they have been designed for 'immediate use', that is in a waterfall relationship between adjacent development phases. Still, this does admit short links between the notations. Thus links from analysis/requirements to design are possible for QOC and UAN. Similarly, NUF allows links from design to construction.

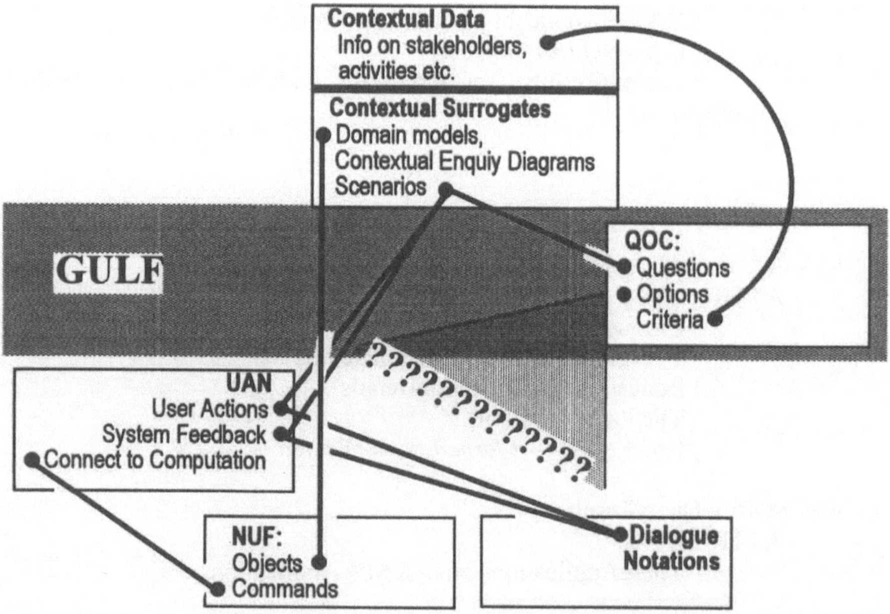

Figure 6: The first strands of literate development

Despite these limitations, we have made more rapid progress than we had expected on linking notations into a web of development decisions. Work on the IT MSc admissions system has let us construct several classes of links between context and design which are illustrated in Figure 6.

In Figure 6, contextual notations are placed above the 'gulf' between context and design, and design notations are placed below it (with behavioural ones above constructional ones). Dialogue notations appear in Figure 6 even though none were discussed in Sections 2 or 3, since there are clear transformations between UAN and such notations (Palanque, Bastide & Sengès 1995) Design rationale notations are placed in the gulf, for reasons which will be explained below.

Behavioural notations such as UAN have a key role in providing the initial links between the human context of a system (as envisionment scenarios) and its software implementation (as required task sequences). There are clear anchor points for linking between behavioural and constructional specifications. Links to context are more straightforward when surrogates rather than unstructured contextual

information is used. Thus UAN task descriptions can be written for scenarios that represent human context as a set of narratives. In contrast, criteria in design rationales can be linked to basic contextual information.
Design rationales are placed 'in the gulf', because they currently produce vague options that have no obvious link to design decisions in either behavioural or constructional notations. This is illustrated by the shaded fan out from options, bounded by question marks. Systematic refinement of design rationales may move this vague boundary towards firm anchor points in behavioural and constructional notation, but this has not yet been achieved for the current development exercise.

4. Requirements for Literate Development Environments

The case study has let us stretch some life lines across the gap between context and design. Bridges may follow. However, our experience to date indicates that reliable bridges will depend on several requirements being met.

4.1 Literate Development will Involve Different Types of Links

The understanding communicated in Figure 6 largely uses contextual information as a constraint on design. This is only one of the possible relationships between context and design. For example, within Figure 6 there are also some transformational relationships, such as the archetypical transformation of a scenario into UAN and then into a dialogue structure.
Transformation is the preferred relationship in engineering approaches. Structured development methods attempt to transform context information into requirements and/or designs (just as the transform designs into software architectures that in turn provide inputs to module design).
Constraint and transformation are only two of several possible relationships between context and design. Each form of relationship will give rise to different types of links within a Literate Development environment. Contextual information may be used as criteria during formative analytical evaluation. It can also be used during empirical evaluation (formative or summative) as a source of scenarios for user tests. There is a further reversed relationship that needs to be considered, where design analyses act as prompts for iterative contextual enquiries (Carroll's task-artefact cycle captures this inverse relationship as well as the favoured top-down transformational one). Where rapid design sketching is employed, designs may precede any context analysis and thus wholly drive the piecemeal elicitation of contextual information.
Another special form of link is arises as a result of using multiple notations, especially contextual surrogates, which can introduce overlaps and redundancy. However, this is a not a consequence of Literate Development (which involves more than multiple notations), but is actually addressed by it (e.g., by "these are the same thing" links).

In summary, several relationships between contextual information and designs are possible. Research is needed into the advantages and disadvantages of each relationship, the circumstances which determine the appropriate choice of relationship, and the implications for the development life cycle of each form of relationship. Literate Development Environments (Section 4.6 below) are required to let these issues be explored systematically.

4.2 Support for Different Context Maps

Developers must be able to gather different groups of contextual information and structure it in different ways. Development teams will want to develop their own context map, locating information as user-, task-, role-, organisation- or whatever related *as they see fit.* Tools for using context in design must thus let development teams build their own contextual structures, although they can provide standard ones (e.g., Maissel et al. 1993) as starting points, as well as ideas drawn from specific projects (e.g., Will (1992) has identified *dogmatism* as a key user characteristic!)

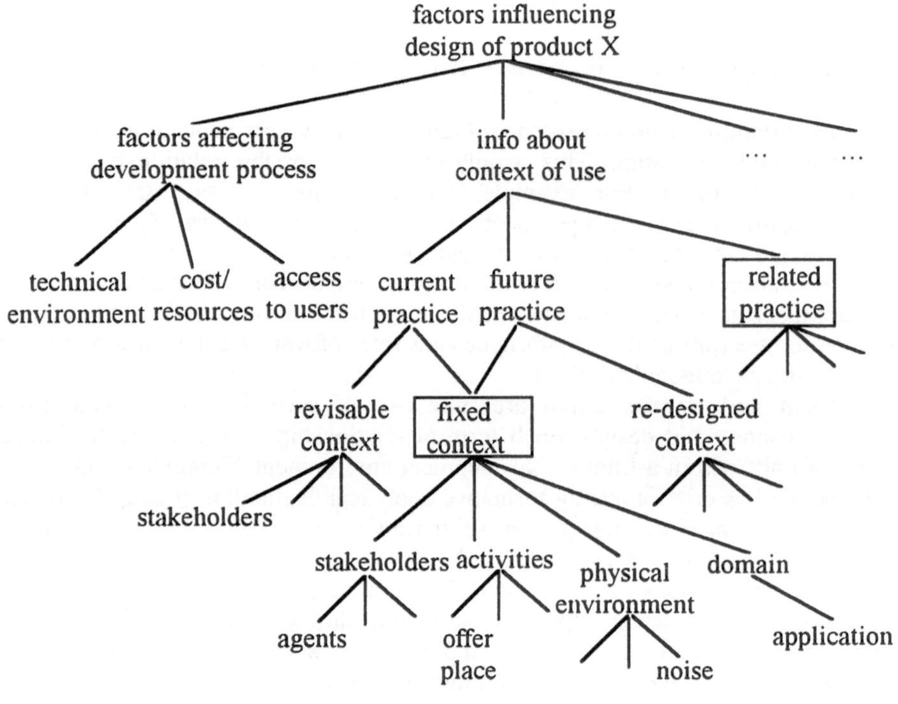

Figure 7: A possible structure for a system's context

Developers must actively and reflectively structure context. They have to organise information about the context of development and the context of use. They have to further distinguish fixed and revisable context. The *fixed context* is anything that *cannot be changed* or, if *changed or ignored by a design, will reduce the quality of achieved work or incur unacceptable costs.* The revisable context is everything else. One of the main problems for a development team is to make these distinctions. Tool support is required for separating the two forms of context, and to record the supporting rationales for probable quality degradation or unacceptable cost. An example of fixed context is our university regulations, which require a Faculty Office to make all offers of a place (Figure 3). Our new system *cannot* change this.

We can thus see developers building a structure like the one in Figure 7 using a context information management tool:

In Figure 7, boxed nodes represent context that can or should not be changed. The development team have decided to consider *related practice* separately from all aspects of the fixed context of the new system. This provides a sharper focus on the fixed context, and gathers secondary information in one place.

4.3 Support for Different Development Contexts

Contextual structures go beyond the context of usage. We need to map out the context of *development* as well as the context of use. Factors affecting the development process such as cost, resources and access to users will all affect the subsequent design in some way. Context maps need to include these factors, but should keep them separate from information about context of use (as in Figure 7).

4.4 Support for Iterating Context

Things change. Things get missed. The context will change. Understandings of it will change. Literate Development must embrace the origins of changing requirements rather than pretend (as some would prefer) that they do not exist.

The iteration in iterative development is generally seen as an iteration of the designed artefact. However, the case study has driven home the fact that if we record descriptions of context and process descriptions to produce contextual surrogates, then these documents and artefacts must also be iterated no less than the system design.

For example, interpretations of fixed and revisable context do change during development, although the purpose of a system is to revise some context, and thus some revisable context is likely to remain so, unless development is abandoned.

4.5 Literate Linking Requires Anchor Points in Notations

Our vision of literate development has many links woven between documentation for all development phases. Notations have to provide *anchor points* for these links. These anchor points provide support for delayed use, encapsulating interpretations and decisions that cannot be fully exploited until much later development phases.

Use of the notations reported in Section 3 revealed variations in provision of good anchor points. Diagrams from Contextual Enquiry have no obvious anchors for the Questions of a design rationale, and few anchors for its Criteria. Options in most design rationales are a long way removed from the detail of interaction in UAN. Options can be refined by further QOCs that could eventually reach UAN details.

However, we expect developers to make the same sort of jumps that experienced programmers make in stepwise refinement, moving immediately to coding when they reach manageable code fragments.
UAN in contrast offers clear anchors for constructional notations such as dialogue specifications (from user action and system feedback columns), as well as to display models (feedback columns) and application models (connection to computation).
Although UAN addresses the issue of task, it is not at a high enough level to allow short and straightforward links to many contextual surrogates. UAN specified tasks generally address work system rather than work goals (i.e., goals that users will have because they are using a specific system rather than goals they will have because they are doing some specific work). Although an arbitrary amount of abstraction can be employed using UAN, a task goal is highly unlikely to match work goals as UAN has no constructs that address goals at this level. We therefore need *envisionment scenarios* that portray key tasks with a broad brush. These would mostly describe work situations, but would include proposed design features for a new system (e.g., automatic warnings on problem applications in our case study). Such descriptions would provide the necessary anchor points for liking high level work goals to lower level UAN goals. We have recently completed envisionment scenarios for the case study, but have not had time to reflect on our experiences.

NUF is used to express the concepts which the designer wants the user to be aware of and could therefore use important aspects of context (command names, attributes and objects from the context of use). Close links between contextual surrogates such as domain models (Dowell & Long 1994) are thus possible. NUF's slots allow almost direct correspondences between system object descriptions and domain objects, providing a specification basis for the proposal for models of the application domain within interactive systems (Fischer 1993). However, the only links between objects are inheritance links, and these may not be sufficient for representing all inter-object relations in a system's context.

Experiences to date thus suggest the need for extra types of description (e.g., envisionment scenarios) and more types of link. The lack of both is apparent from the nature of the remaining gaps between context and design that we are aware of:

- the gap between models of work activities and design questions in QOC;
- the gap between contextual information and criteria in QOC;
- the gap between models of work activities and low level UAN task structures;
- the gap between vague design options in QOC and low level UAN/NUF details.

The gaps are this largely between context and design, rather than between design and construction, whereas UAN has clear anchor points linking to constructional notations.

4.6 Literate Development Needs Tool Support

The relationship between human context and design is an open research issue, and thus tools must support exploration of this relationship. The key requirement is flexibility with respect to different structures for context and different forms of link between context and design. We are aware of radically different approaches to both structuring contextual information and to the way that it is used. A tool that imposed a single approach would be doomed to failure given our current understanding.

More technical requirements are:
- to allow selection of anchor points;
- to create links between anchor points;
- to create and revise context maps;
- to find and report on design and context features that could be affected by changes to content and links elsewhere in a Literate Web.

We are developing a Literate Development Environment (LDE) that lets developers collect and structure contextual information, devise contextual surrogates, create design descriptions and rationales, and then link all these development documents together.

When changes are made, other context and design features that are linked to them are found and reported to the developer. Without software support for linking, it is simply too hard to move between UAN and, for example, NUF (try it with the Section 3 examples).

5. Conclusions and Further Work

We have a vision of Literate Development as a solution to the incomplete, ineffective, unguided and unsystematic use of information about human context in software development. We see links between development documents a basis for a web of relationships between all phases of software development. Although existing notations were developed for immediate use within a waterfall model of development, some already have good anchor points. Software based links between these anchor points would greatly speed up the reading of related development documents and improve consistency across this documentation. However, many critical gaps remain, and we have only established the potential of our approach. Much more work is needed, especially in structuring and labelling contextual information in order to provide anchor points for delayed use of this information.

We are advancing our understanding of literate development by implementing and evaluating the admissions system for our MSc in IT. The results of this evaluation will be used to assess the structures created in a literate development tool that will be implemented over the next year. Further case studies are planned.

Acknowledgements

The idea of Literate Development is a very simple extension of Chris Johnson's recent analogy between *Literate Specification* and literate programming. We have found this analogy very useful for communicating our vision of inter-linked notations in an interactive systems development environment. Steven Clarke is supported by a EPSRC PhD research studentship. Our tool ideas are inspired by work by Hermann Kaindl and colleagues at Siemens AG, Vienna (Kaindl 1993). Some of our general ideas about the relationship between context and design arose during the IFIP WG13.2 and WG2.7 Joint Workshop in Loughborough (September 1994, Sutcliffe et al. 1995). Many ideas have been influenced by the editing of a monograph by IFIP WG2.7 members on design principles (Gram & Cockton 1995).

Appendix: The NUF Notation

This appendix provides an easy to access summary of the current state of the NUF notation. The appendix is based on a paper presented by the first author at the Model-Based User Interface Specification Workshop, held at GVU, Atlanta, November 1993. This version is the March 1995 update that was prepared for the utest list (email first author for details).

A1. OVERVIEW

NUF Object classes are represented by frames with these slots:

CLASS FOR	a class name
COUNT	— unlimited/a number
ROUTES	— path through instance hierarchy to an object
ISA	— a list of class names
ATTRIBUTES	— attribute specifications (A1)
PROJECTIONS	— projection specifications (A2)
CONSTRAINTS	— constraint specifications (A3)
COMMANDS	— command specifications (A4)
LINKAGE	— linkage specifications (A5)

The notation encourages designers to think about unreasonable and/or nuisance restrictions on the object population by providing an INSTANCES slot to make such restrictions clear. The notation admits multiple inheritance via multiple class names in ISA slots (you manage the resulting problems!) There is thus no class hierarchy in NUF. The main structure is the instance hierarchy, which arises from the attribute slot of a NUF slot. Attributes slot values are a list of attribute subslots. Each has the form:

attribute name : class name or constructor or expression

Structured attributes can be formed by a constructor (generally for enumerations) or a separate class description. This implicitly specifies an instance hierarchy, but there should be a separate explicit graphical representation. Expressions allow the specification of virtual attributes that users can think of as being real and separate, although they are computed from other attributes (this can be used to created a dependency network).

Optional qualifiers are postfixed after the above, eg

: *property list*

A default value can be postfixed after the property list, prefixed by a slash, eg:

/default value

An example property is read-only. Other properties include queue-all, part of ENUF, the extended notation that is used to manually link the application interface model to the concrete user interface and the underlying functionalities (see A5). These extensions are only needed for detailed software design, they are not part of the application model. For example, handler indicates an active attribute.

A2. PROJECTION SPECIFICATIONS

Projections slot values are a list of projection subslots. Each projection has the form:

projection name is *list of attribute names*

projections can be used to guide concrete user interface design (e.g., for display groups), but they can also be used to highlight consistency in the application model.

A3. CONSTRAINT CONFIGURATIONS

Constraint configurations combine assertions with constraint restoration actions. Constraints slot values are a list of constraints, each with the form:

Constraint identification phrase
ENFORCE *logical expression => logical expression*
BY *action or procedure reference*

Constraints centralise follow ups (post-conditions) that would otherwise be distributed (creating consistency and maintenance risks) across several commands (A4 below).

Logical expressions may reference relations, which are specified along with actions and procedures in the linkage specification (A5 below). Action and relation references may also include function references.
Parameters may appear in the constraint identification phrase and in subslot values. Parameters are enclosed in angle brackets. Attribute values are postfixed with ':'.

A4. COMMAND CONFIGURATIONS

Commands slots are lists of command values. Each command has the following form
(note that multiple BLOCK WHEN and AVOID subslots are allowed):

Command identification phrase
ENACTS: *action or procedure reference*
AVAILABLE: *logical expression*
BLOCK WHEN: *logical expression*
DOING: *action or procedure reference*
AVOID: *logical expression*
BY: *query, action or procedure reference*
FOLLOW UP: *action or procedure reference*

Parameters may appear in any command identification phrase and in subslot values. Parameters are enclosed in angle brackets. Attribute values are marked by : postfix.

There is some command engine with a specific algorithm that visits each slot in a particular order. Specifying its behaviour is not a problem in a paper notation, but it needs to be sorted out for a computer-based tool.

A5. LINKAGE CONFIGURATIONS

This slot constitutes the bulk of the ENUF extension (the remainder provides subsubslots for attributes to link them to streams of underlying values). It can be just a list of action, relation, query and function identifiers in initial eNUF (sic!) configurations (as a design notation, NUF allows comments to be used in place of any (sub)slot value). The linkage specification describes the computational universe that is used by commands and constraints.

Linkage slots have up to six subslots:

ACTIONS	SIGNALS
FUNCTIONS	QUERIES
RELATIONS	PROCEDURES

Each subslot has a list value, with each element being an individual action, function, relation, query or procedure description that begins with an identification phrase. These elements have their own frame structures that generally link them into the underlying functionalities via an IMPLEMENTATION subsubslot (signals raise model events for communication with the concrete user interface). Further details of these subslots and their use are available by email from the first author

Chapter 14: Metaphors in User Interface Development: Methods and Requirements for Effective Support

Manfred Tscheligi, Kaisa Väänänen-Vainio-Mattila

1. Introduction

Metaphors can provide paths through the jungle of functionality. Let us take the metaphor included in the previous sentence to outline the general components of a metaphor. A metaphor is a rhetorical device (rhetoric: techniques for communicating messages) to describe an object or event, real or imagined, using concepts that cannot be applied to the object or event in an conventional way (Indurkhya 1992). The object being described is called the target (other terms sometimes used are topic, object and tenor), and the concepts that cannot be applied conventionally are called the source (vehicle). There exists a metaphorical mapping between these two domains which is a cognitive process of combining the target and source. In our initial sentence the target is the complexity of software systems, the source is the jungle where it is usually not easy for the untrained to find the right way. The essence of a metaphor is understanding and experiencing one kind of thing in terms of another (Lakoff & Johnson 1980). In visual user interfaces the concepts of the source are presented in a visual form. So given an appropriate mapping the user may not be aware of the existence of an explicit metaphor. It is the challenge for the designer to select the right metaphor source with appropriate mappings to the target visualized with appropriate visual elements.

There are some other terms often mentioned in relation to metaphors like similarity or analogy or some other forms of rhetorical devices (Marcus 1993). We do not make this differentiation here and use these terms as synonymous. User interface engineers using a metaphor-based design procedure need not know about all the different (more or less) theoretical interpretations of these terms. They need some guidelines, procedural advice and "computational" (Carroll & Rosson 1994) support in using metaphorical concepts for their design problems.

Evidence for the usage of metaphors comes from several different viewpoints. Metaphors are studied in linguistics and cognitive science, and are used as a design source and as a design method. Metaphors as a linguistic concept is a constant part of our everyday speech (Lakoff & Johnson 1980). Johnson gives revealing examples of metaphor usage in computer discourse (Johnson 1994). Metaphors are embedded in the terms we use everyday to talk about computers. Metaphors as a cognitive concept comes from the understanding of our world through metaphors. Thought is metaphoric and proceeds by comparison and the metaphors of language derive therefrom (Carroll & Mack 1985). Learning by analogy may be the only way humans actually learn. Whether or not explicit metaphors are designed for a user interface it is likely that people will generate metaphoric comparisons on their own. There is empirical evidence which supports these claims (Carroll et al. 1988)

Metaphors support the formation of a mental model. The mental model can be seen as the result of metaphor-supported learning and problem solving processes. Metaphors as a design source provide the underlying images, terms and concepts that make communication possible at all (Marcus 1993). At least they are good at suggesting general orientations even if they not encode all application semantics precisely. The explicit representation of the analogy in the design helps the user to understand the system. Metaphors as design technique are effective creativity aids for the designers (Mountford 1990), generating design ideas (MacLean et al. 1991) and disciplining the designer (Hammond & Allinson 1993) New ideas for the electronic world can come from careful examination of the traditional way of performing tasks (Mountford 1990). In Erickson's "design by symmetry" technique (Erickson 1990), extended, precise analogies are applied to design problems. Analogy has an important role in inspiring the designer even if the analogy is not represented in the visual realization of the user interface itself. MacLean reports the experience of a bagel store, where queues are handled by having employees work along the queue and helping in the preparation of the customer choices before they reach the counter. They explain the choices available and give support to fill in the orders on a form. This experience was used an a metaphor for the idea of having bank cards the customers could preprogram while waiting in an ATM line.

In this paper we will address the problem of metaphor usage from an engineering viewpoint. Developers need support in carrying out the activities in course of an metaphor-oriented and metaphor-based design approach. We will first present a procedural model of the necessary activities during the design (section 2). Then we give requirements of metaphors regarding some quality aspects from the user's and designer's viewpoint (section 3). In section 4 an outline of support modules is developed which can be used as a requirements framework for future metaphor-oriented design environments.

2. Metaphor-Oriented Development

The first support user interface engineers need to be able to use in a metaphor-oriented methodology is a conceptual map of activities needed during such a design process. We will provide such a conceptual map by introducing a general model of metaphor-based design showing the participating domains and the main activities. Each of these activities are described later on in more detail. Suggestions for the design of user interface metaphors have already been made by some researchers in the field (Carroll et al. 1988), (Erickson 1990), (Lee 1993), (Madsen 1994), (Lovgren 1994). We will combine and extend these approaches to achieve a common methodological basis for our proposed support environment.

2.1 Domains and Activities

Figure 1 shows the main components and the main activities necessary in designing user interface metaphors. The analysis activity leads to the modeling and description of the application domain which covers the features of the system being described with the metaphor. The mapping activity results in conceptual metaphor concepts forming the metaphor domain. The metaphor domain contains the metaphor concepts selected as candidates for the presentation in the user interface. The visual domain results from the visualization activity where the metaphor concepts are mapped onto a specific visual representation. The visual realization has to be evaluated with the user.

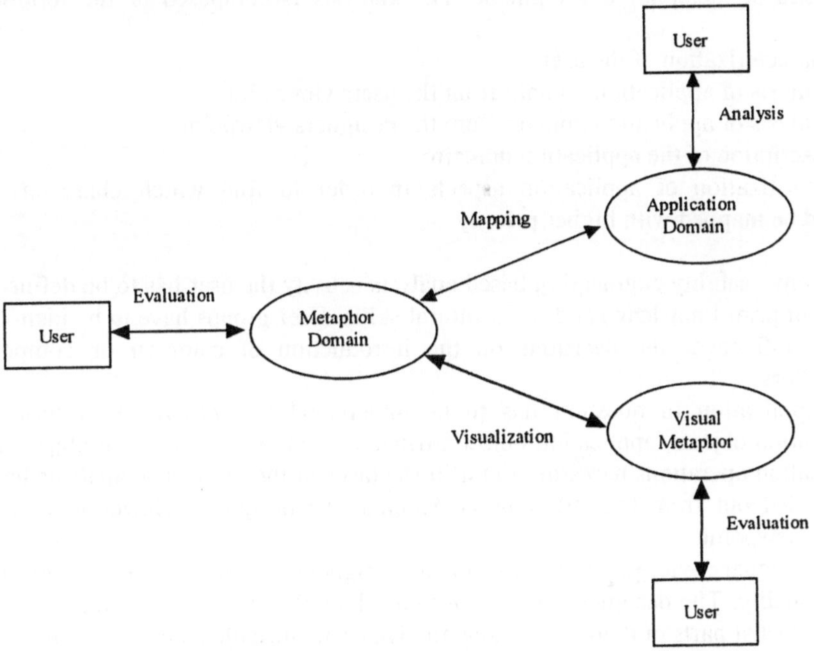

Figure 1: Main activities during metaphor development

The activities have to be carried out in highly iterative manner influencing the domains at both end of an activity links. The work on the mapping may have influence on the application domain (e.g. the metaphor selected results in new application functionalities) and the work on the visualization may have some influence on the metaphor domain (e.g. the presentation of a particular component of the metaphor cannot be done and so the metaphor chosen has to be changed accordingly). Furthermore the decisions in the visual domain have some influence on the application domain via the metaphor domain (e.g. if no satisfying representation can be found for a particular function and therefore this function will not be included in the system).

The user is involved in all three domains. At the application domain at the metaphor concept level to find good metaphor domains which should be transformed to the visual domain. The visual presentations have to be tested in detailed usability studies to get additional feedback regarding the quality of the visual presentation, the quality of the transformation between metaphorical concepts and visual presentation and the appropriateness of the visual metaphor to represent the application domain.

2.2 Analysis Activity

The general goal for this activity is to provide all the information for the following activities of metaphor development. The analysis is composed of the following steps:

- characterization of the user
- analysis of application domain from the users viewpoint
- analysis of application domain from the designers viewpoint
- description of the application domain
- prioritization of application aspects in order to find which characteristics should be mapped with higher priority

As in any usability engineering based analysis activity the user has to be defined in terms of prior knowledge and sociocultural skills. User groups have to be identified which influences the decisions on the introduction of common or composite metaphors.

The application in question has to be understood and described in terms of application objects, application object attributes, relationships between objects and application operations necessary to fulfill the tasks of the users. The analysis has to be carried out from two different viewpoints: the designer's viewpoint and the user's viewpoint.

The designers viewpoint results in a designer's model of the application functionality. The designer has to understand how the system really works and to identify what parts of it are most likely to give users difficulty. The user's viewpoint covers the fact that the metaphor must be in the user's sphere of knowledge and identifies the user's model of the application functionality. To listen how users understand their application domain can be used as a useful source for finding metaphors later in the design process. Analyzing representative, goal-directed user scenarios that exhaust the set of things people will really do with the system can be of great value for understanding and identifying potential user problems.

Together this results in a description of the application domain. The application domain should then be prioritized to identify the salient features of the application domain. This focusing based on the prioritization of application domain concepts reduces complexity as not every characteristic of the application domain can be mapped onto the metaphor domain and therefore can be of great value. It also helps during the finding and rating of candidate metaphors.

All these activities with special orientation to metaphor should be integrated into the analysis efforts done within common user interface engineering approaches. However if "normal" analysis activities are carried out special emphasis has to be put on the needs of metaphor-oriented development and developed with special emphasis on elaborating metaphorical knowledge.

2.3 Mapping Activity

The general goal of this activity is to find metaphors with appropriate mappings to the application domain which should be developed further into visual prototypes. The mapping is composed of the following steps:

- identification and generation of candidate metaphors
- description of the candidate metaphors
- matching of metaphor domain and application domain
- evaluation and rating candidate metaphors
- choosing metaphors

The first step in the mapping activity is the generation of ideas for metaphors which are able to cover the features of the system in an appropriate form. Sources for ideas are already existing user interface metaphors, metaphors implicit in the problem description either from the user's or designer's viewpoint, real world events exhibiting key aspects, metaphors coming from the application domain, predecessor systems that are going to be replaced, prior experiences of users, human properties, other realms like movies or art or the designer simply invents something new. The larger the set of potential metaphors the better.

The candidate metaphors have to be described in more or less the same form as the application domain. The description should be usable during the whole design activity and also can be combined with metaphor oriented design rationality (MacLean et al. 1991). The description of metaphor domain and application domain are the basis of the matching step. In the matching step the metaphor concepts are matched to the corresponding concepts of the application domain. The matching of each candidate metaphor build the basis for further evaluation steps.

Evaluation within this activity can be carried out without or with involvement of the user. In the next section criteria for metaphors are mentioned which can be used for assessing the goodness of metaphors. A more detailed discussion can be found in (Hammond & Allinson 1993), (Erickson 1990), (Lee 1993), (Carroll et al. 1988), (Madsen 1994), (Lovgren 1994), (Anderson et al. 1993). One can also use a more theoretically oriented framework developed by Sternberg (Sternberg et al. 1979) based on the superimposed within subspace distance and the superimposed between subspace distance. The first measures the distance between the target and the vehicle within their shared main features, the latter measures the relative distance between the two domains.

However the most important quality feature is the mismatches between the application domain and the metaphor domain. Metaphors provide only imperfect mappings to their application domain. The designer has to deal with several types of mismatches in order to further develop the metaphor domain or the application domain. We will use a notation based on Anderson (Anderson 1993) to describe the situations which will result from these partial mappings.

The activity of metaphor can be described in terms of the intersection of two sets. The first set A represents the concepts of the application domain, the second set M represents the concepts of the metaphor domain. A+M+ concepts lie in the

intersection between the two sets. A+M+ are those concepts of the application domain that map completely on to concepts of the metaphor domain. A+M- concepts are the first type of mismatch. These lie within the set of the application domain but not intersect with the set of metaphor concepts. A-M+ are the concepts that lie within the set of metaphor concepts but do not intersect with the set of application domain concepts (Anderson characterizes these set as the conceptual baggage that the metaphor brings with it). The last set are the concepts that are neither part of the application domain nor the metaphor domain.
All different types of mismatches have to be attacked by the designer in this evaluation step. Either the usage of particular metaphor leads to enhancement of the application domain, or due to important missing application concepts the candidate metaphor has to be changed or even rejected. Another possibility is the usage of composite metaphors. The third type of mismatch is covered by explicitly considering the extensions done by the user where new concepts are discovered although not presented in the metaphor domain. These new concepts were not planned for the application but such extensions have to be considered. With the selection of a particular mismatch strategy the designer has a considerable amount of influence to the application domain. New functionality can be invented and planned functionality can be discarded if it cannot be included in a satisfying way.

Not all mismatches can be resolved. According to Carroll et al. (Carroll et al. 1988) the disparity between source and target can be a potent factor contributing to the force of the metaphor. Salient dissimilarities in the context of salient similarities can stimulate thought. The key condition is that the discrepancy in the software domain must be interpretable, the mismatch should be isolable and a salient alternative course of action in the target domain should be available. It is the task of the visualization step to make clear what the metaphor hides and what it highlights.
The evaluation activity can also be enhanced by integrating the user. Metaphor concepts should be discussed with the user. By presenting verbal metaphor prototypes user feedback can be collected and ideas from the user can be used for the refinement of the concepts. The development of any visual form of prototype refers to the visualization step but has to be done in a highly iterative and integrated manner.
According to the matching and evaluation results the different candidate metaphor have to be rated according to the quality principles used. Lee (Lee 1993) proposes a pragmatic form of rating where the priority and a score based on the quality of the match is used to develop a weighting factor for each object and relationship. Based on the overall total score the metaphors can selected for further development. Other techniques have to be developed to help the designer in carrying out this step.

2.4 Visualization Activity

The concepts developed in the mapping activity have to be transformed into a visual presentation to be accessible for the user. It has to be decided which of the

concepts are explicitly presented via visual elements and behaviors and which of the concepts are implicit in the presentation (e.g. usually the conceptual relationship between houses and rooms are not conveyed through explicit visual presentations).
Different presentation possibilities for one metaphor concept have to be tried out to realize an effective communication of the metaphor concepts to the user. The metaphor can also be used only during the idea creation phase and does not necessarily have to be incorporated in the final visual design. If no good presentation can be found the designer has think about discarding the functionality at all depending on the overall importance of this function. So the visualization activity may have a considerable influence on either the metaphor domain used or even the application domain.

2.5 Evaluation Activity

With the availability of visual metaphors there is the possibility of running detailed usability studies to test the user and problem oriented quality of the metaphor concepts and their visual appearance and behavior. Existing usability testing techniques have to be used and enhanced to test specific metaphor features as addressed in (Anderson et al. 1993) and (Hammond & Allinson 1993). We are currently experimenting with techniques like priming and associating, sentence building and inductive and deductive conclusions (Musil et al. 1994) for doing empirical based evaluation. The results give additional feedback which influences all other design domains.

3. Users' and Designers' Requirements of Metaphors

When metaphors are applied in the user interfaces of interactive computer applications, two sets of requirements need to be observed in terms of metaphor quality and applicability: The user's and designer's requirements. In principle it is more important that the user who in the end uses the system is completely comfortable with the metaphor and the underlying system. However, it should be taken into account that the designer's understanding of the chosen metaphor (and the conceptual design model of the system) should be in line with the user's mental model of that metaphor. In fact, the metaphor can act as a domain for a common language for the application-dependent objects and functionality. Such common grounds can provide a valuable basis for task analysis and participatory design and this way improve the chances that the resulting application be intuitive and usable.
Nevertheless, some of the requirements that the users and authors pose on user interface metaphors differ. These requirements and the qualitative questions that arise from them are discussed below.
The user's main interest concerning user interface metaphors is that they should provide the user with an intuitive access to all functionality needed to perform the task at hand. This implies on one hand that the user should be familiar with the metaphor domain and on the other hand that the user should be able to perform the mapping between the metaphor domain and the application domain. This includes

mapping of all metaphor concepts to the respective entities in the application domain. It should be noted that this mapping need not be conscious; in fact the metaphor often remains "unnoticed" and helps the user form the mental model of the system without explicit cognitive effort.

In order to make the user interested in the system and to motivate him to use (and reuse) the system, the "visual metaphor" should be attractive and wake curiosity. The metaphor characteristics of incompleteness and open-endedness (Carroll et al. 1988) encourage active thought processes by the user and can result in high motivation levels for the user. However, it remains dependent on the application domain how "serious" and implicit or "playful" and explicit the metaphor should be (Väänänen & Schmidt 1994). Some studies show that the metaphor needs to be closely related to the application domain (Anderson et al. 1993), (Martin 1990) but this may not be true for certain application types. For example, where a medical information system in a hospital would most probably better use a metaphor that actually models the real-world objects in the task domain itself, a publicly accessible exploration or presentation system (e.g. an information kiosk) may successfully use a game-like user interface metaphor.
Furthermore, frequent users of a system may become "bored" with the metaphor if it distracts them too much from performing the task quickly and effectively. For this end, the user should have at least some amount of control over the user interface -- the system should offer methods for personalization and customization of the metaphor-based user interface. In an ideal situation, users would have a possibility to choose the user interface metaphor based on their personal preferences.

Further characteristics of metaphors are visuality, spatiality and concreteness of the "metaphor visualizations". In current interactive (often multimedia) applications the trend is more and more towards exploitation of human senses and in this context especially the visual imagery can be supported by visual presentations of objects of interest. Furthermore, metaphors should not only be composed of individual symbols or icons set together on some two-dimensional, empty electronic space (such as a window) but they should form a coherent and richly inhabited information "place". In such a place the metaphor-based objects, their relationships and behavior form an overall conceptual model that ideally matches with the user's mental model of the application.
Naturally, many of the designer's requirements match with the users' requirements of metaphors. The designer's task is to provide the best possible user interface for the user, and the requirements that user has are thus automatically transferred to the designer's consideration.
The main problem the designer has with metaphors is to find a suitable one for the application under construction. The "matching" problem becomes the first issue the designer has to consider after first ideas of possible metaphors have been created. Mismatches of all sorts of the metaphor may lead to inadequate presentation of the application domain. The greatest pitfalls of metaphor usage lie in wrong cues about

the metaphor-based functionality of the application objects, and in worst case leads to wrong expectations by the user and resulting frustrations about the trustworthiness of the system.

Another major requirement of metaphors from the designer's point of view is flexibility and extensibility of the user interface metaphor (see section 2 and (Erickson 1990)). Since the application requirements often change or the application is extended with new functionality, it is essential that the metaphor is not totally rigid and static. It has to have extra components that can be used if the system evolves. Another alternative to extending a metaphor is to use composite metaphors; to bind a new metaphor together with the old one in a way that seems logical and natural from the user's point of view.

One further requirement from the designer's side of the metaphor application is the relatively easy implementation of the metaphor-based user interface. Metaphor can be presented by using only text, but visual imagery and further multimedia presentations -- even Virtual Reality -- can make the user interface more attractive and comfortable to use. However, very realistic and high-dimensional presentations are more expensive to produce and may be more difficult to modify because of the increased editing effort.

Different types of metaphors are needed for the modeling of complex application domains. For example, for multimedia information systems three major categories of user interface metaphors are organizational, navigational and functional metaphors. Organizational metaphors are needed to provide the user with an orientation and structural information about the application. Navigational metaphors are used for moving around in the information space formed by the organizational metaphor. Functional metaphors provide the user with the means for controlling and interacting with the individual application and user interface objects.
Further metaphor types are for example task metaphors, tool metaphors, meeting place metaphors and agent metaphors. Different metaphor types can be combined for the application under construction to achieve an overall metaphor-based model of the system.

4. Metaphor-Based User Interface Development Environment

4.1 Existing Approaches

Some work on computational support has already been done within the domain of linguistic metaphors for the analysis and comparison of metaphorical concepts (Martin 1990), (Indurkhya 1992). Blumenthal (Blumenthal 1990) provides some support for user interface metaphors, in particular for database applications. His system reasons about a description of an application, a description of a real-world metaphor source and a set of relations mappings. The support for metaphors is also the main theme of the FRIEND21 project (Nonogaki & Ueda 1991). They focus on providing multiple metaphors and maintaining the relationships between the constituent metaphors.

Informal and pragmatic techniques usable within metaphor design are proposed by (Lee 1993), (Carroll et al. 1988), (Anderson et al. 1993) and (Hammond & Allinson 1993). Carroll shows an informal scenario-based technique to compare source and target at the levels of tasks, methods and appearance. Anderson uses a visual set diagrams technique to show the amount of overlapping entities between the source and target. Hammond also uses visual cues to indicate shared mappings across the two domains. Lee uses a so-called object model notation to model objects and structural relationships between the object for the modeling of the target and source. He uses simple tables for the mappings and the rating of the candidate metaphors. All of these techniques have to be refined to be of better use for an user interface engineer in development situations.

This section examines the support tools necessary for the metaphor-based user interface development process as it was discussed in section 2. First an existing approach is described based on the ShareME multimedia authoring tool. Then, an "ideal" environment for more complete support of the development of metaphor-based user interfaces is sketched.

4.2 ShareME: A Metaphor-Based Authoring Tool for Multimedia Environments

ShareME (Shared Multimedia Environments) is an authoring tool for construction of multimedia information environments (Väänänen 1993a), (Väänänen 1993b). ShareME embodies several organizational and navigational metaphors that can be used as generic components in the construction of multimedia information systems with hypermedia capabilities.

The author first chooses the organizational metaphor that best suits the structure and characteristics of the information base under construction. Then, the author instantiates the metaphor-based components through graphical object inspectors and creates an environment with a needed amount of metaphor-based components or "containers" in which the multimedia information is then inserted. Each organizational metaphor is associated with several navigational metaphors that can optionally be used by the user during the navigation. Figure 2 shows the main components of ShareME.

The ShareME organizational metaphors include the House, the Library and the Television metaphors that are further structured according to their real-world models (e.g. rooms, books and channels). Furthermore, the House metaphor offers the Guides, Search Desk and History List, and the Library metaphor includes the Table of Contents, Index and Bookmarks as additional navigational metaphors. In addition, there is a "Dummy" metaphor that offers the same structure and functionality as the House but does not employ the metaphor-based visualizations but a rather standard WIMP-based presentations based on the standard components of the NeXT Interface Builder. (The "Dummy" has only been used for comparative. tests of the metaphor-based approach of ShareME.)

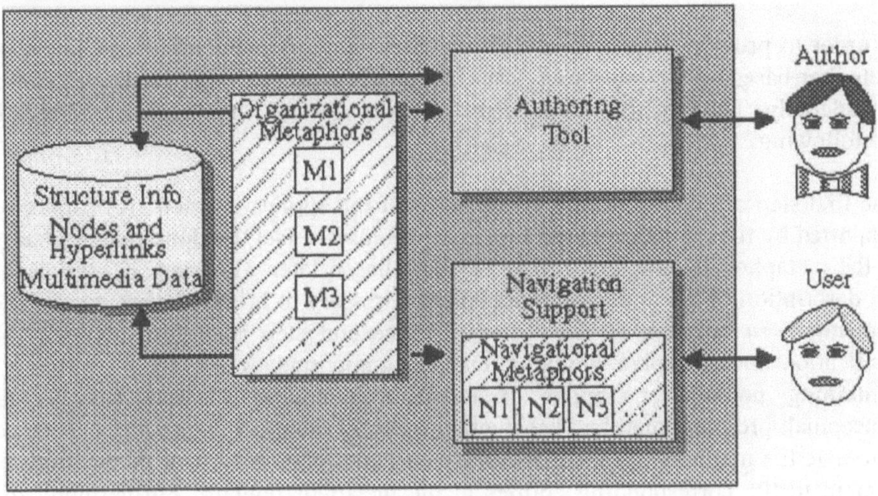

Figure 2: The ShareME metaphor-based authoring and navigation tool

The empirical tests performed with ShareME authoring tool have shown that the metaphor-based authoring templates are both quantitatively and qualitatively better for the authors than authoring templates based on the WIMP-paradigm alone. The metaphor-based approach is more valuable to novice computer users; computer experts more often prefer to construct information environments without explicit and concrete metaphors. However, the usage of a metaphor in the final application should always remain an option dependent on the end-user characteristics and application type.

One major problem with the ShareME approach is that the metaphors offered are too inflexible (in particular, they are not editable to a large extend). This problem is due to the trade-off between the amount of design/implementation work the author has to do and the inflexibility that follows from such pre-designed and pre-implemented user interface and structuring components. The experiences with ShareME imply that more flexibility and customization of the metaphor-based components is required. There are also far too few metaphors in ShareME for any realistic authoring situation; this should be overcome by providing the tool with a large set of various types of metaphors.

4.3 Towards an Ideal Design Environment for Metaphor-Based User Interfaces

The main steps in the metaphor-based design process, as decribed in section 2, are:

- analysis of the application domain
- mapping of the application domain to the metaphor domain

- visualization of the metaphor domain with user interface presentations
- evaluation

In order to provide the designer with an "ideal" environment for development of metaphor-based user interfaces, the ShareME approach has to be extended considerably. The essential components of such an environment are described in the following.

The first step of the design process (analysis of the application domain) cannot be supported by the metaphor-based tool since it must, in fact, be done independently of the metaphor domain that might only be chosen later. However a notation for the description of the application domain is necessary to bring the concepts of the application in question in the system. The second step (mapping between the application and metaphor domains) could be supported by a "metaphor library" containing potential metaphor or metaphor templates (descriptions of the conceptual, presentational and behavioral aspects of them). A "mapping tool" could automate the mapping of the objects, attributes and relationships of the application domain to the corresponding entities in the metaphor domain. Furthermore, the system can offer "built-in guidelines" or some other form of assistance within an "advice tool" and that the designer choose a suitable metaphor for the application under construction. for the application under construction. The third step (visualization of the metaphor) could also be supported by the metaphor library containing alternative visual designs of the metaphor-based objects and moreover, by a "metaphor design tool" that would allow the designers to extend and edit the existing metaphors and also create their own metaphors (both presentational and behavioral aspects of them). In all these parts advanced information visualization techniques play a very important role.
These modules are described below in more detail.

4.3.1 A Metaphor Library with Predesigned Metaphor Templates

The metaphor library contains specifications and implementation templates for a wide variety of metaphor types. Using the metaphor library the designer can scan through the existing metaphors, and choose one or more of them for further development or customization. This library can function both as an original idea source for the designer or as an implementation support once the metaphor has been chosen. Newly designed metaphors are stored in the library for future use. The available metaphors need to have a wide variability in terms of the structure, presentation and behavior characteristics.
To support the distinction between the metaphor concepts, visual aspects and behavior the library has three parts: one for the concepts, one for the visual presentations of metaphor elements and one for the behavior of the metaphor-based objects. Each metaphor concept may have one or several presentations and behavioral characteristics associated with it. The designer may first select the metaphor concept independently of the presentation, and then either choose one of

the existing visualizations or design a new one. Here the behavior means the operations that can be performed on the visual representations of the metaphor-based objects.

4.3.2 A Metaphor Mapping Tool

The metaphor mapping tool will calculate the correspondencies between the application domain and the different metaphors in the metaphor library in terms of their overall structure (objects, attributes and relationships). The mapping tool is able to read the generic metaphor concepts stored in the metaphor library and instantiate an appropriate structure for the given application. The designer can furthermore edit the structures with the structure editor of the structure tool if they are not matched completely. This is enabled by the structure editor that can read the notation used by the mapping tool and allows the designer to add and eliminate objects and their attributes in the metaphor description. With the mapping tool the designer may experiment with different metaphors that are appropriate for the current application domain.
The tool is a visual graph mapper that first shows the structures of the application domain (as generated from a description notation used for modeling the application domain) and then finds the most appropriate metaphor (or metaphors) for it in the metaphor library. The corresponding structures are shown by overlaying the graphs and highlighting the components that match and the ones that do not match (different types of mismatches). An additional rating scheme could be used to help the designer decide which of the possible metaphors is the best for the application.

4.3.3 Advice Tool

The designer could be offered guidance by an advice tool regarding what might be a suitable metaphor for the application under construction. The system could ask general questions about the application, such as

- what is the user like?
- what is the application type?
- where and how often will the system be used?

(see also the criteria presented in Section 3).
The system would then use built-in guidelines to give suggestions about the possible metaphor in terms of metaphor characteristics and presentation attributes described in Section 3. (The previously done mapping process would have already eliminated those that do not match based on the metaphor concepts.)

4.3.4 A Metaphor Design Tool

The metaphor design tool needs to have separate editors for visual presentation and behavior of the metaphor. These editors have access to the metaphor library and the metaphor mapping tool. The presentation tool has access to various graphical and multimedia editors and allows the designer to create and edit the visual

presentation layer on top of the metaphor concept. The behavior tool lets the designer define the operations that can be performed on the metaphor-based visual user interface elements. The design tool could be based on an underlying user interface management system.
The metaphor design tool will -- together with the mapping tool -- serve also for metaphor composition and customization. The design can be based on existing designs in the metaphor library or the designer can start the design "from scratch". This tool could be extended to support creative processes that the designer performs during the early design phases by providing the designer with an intelligent assistant or an "idea generator" for new metaphors.

4.3.5 A Short Scenario

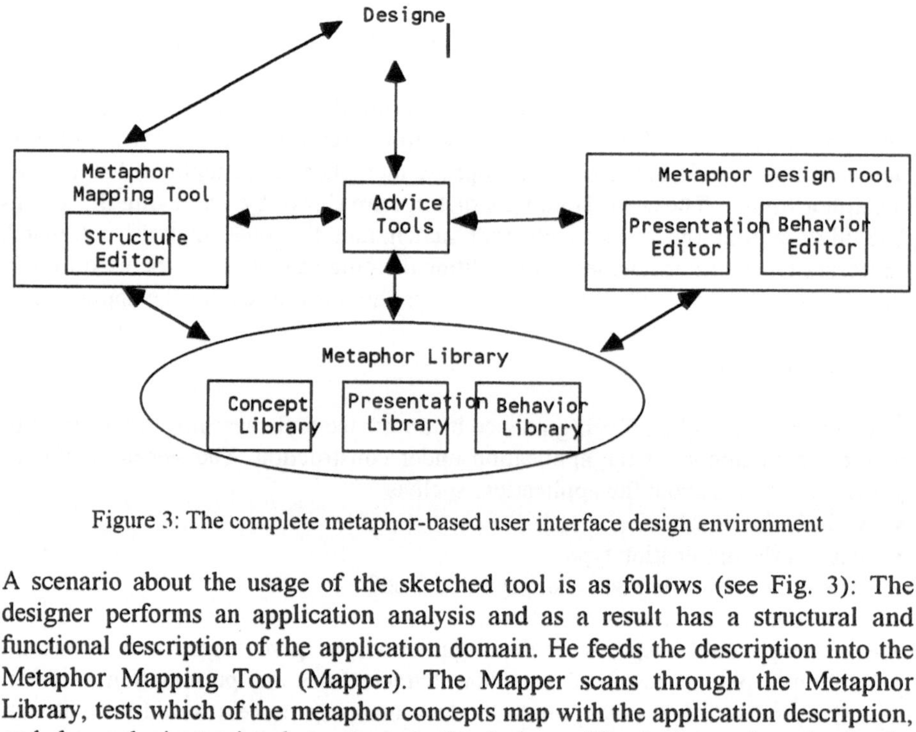

Figure 3: The complete metaphor-based user interface design environment

A scenario about the usage of the sketched tool is as follows (see Fig. 3): The designer performs an application analysis and as a result has a structural and functional description of the application domain. He feeds the description into the Metaphor Mapping Tool (Mapper). The Mapper scans through the Metaphor Library, tests which of the metaphor concepts map with the application description, and shows the instantiated structures to the designer. The designer then checks the found metaphors for their appropriateness (possibly supported by ratings given by the system). The structures of the metaphor can be edited with the Structure Editor offered within the Mapping Tool. The Advice Tool with its built-in guidelines are used when there are several mapped metaphors and the decision about their applicability must be made. When the metaphor concept is chosen, the Library presents the designer with the alternative visualizations for the metaphor. The designer can select one of these, edit it with the Design/Presentation Tool, or if none of the existing presentations is satisfactory, a new presentation is designed with the Design Tool. Finally, the behavior of the metaphor -- the operations that can be performed with the visual elements making the visual metaphor -- can be edited by the Behavior editor of the Design Tool.

The total metaphor development environment could be integrated in an existing user interface management/development environment. It would therefore use standard user interface widgets (windows, buttons, scroll bars etc.) as a basis for the metaphor-based components. However, it is of a central importance that the resulting metaphor-based user interfaces be distanced from the WIMP-style user interfaces. It is therefore essential that the standard widgets be "disguised" behind the metaphor behavior and presentation to allow the user to fully benefit from the power of the metaphor.

5. Conclusions

Based on the experiences in metaphor-based design we proposed an environment for supporting the user interface engineer in the production of modern interaction environments which are based on the usage of metaphors. The environment is based on a methodological model of user interface design which identifies the main activities of metaphor based design: analysis, mapping and visualization. This activities lead from the application problem to conceptual metaphorical concepts and end in a visual metaphor composed by visual and manipulable elements the user gets to solve the tasks in question.

The whole development process can be supported by notations and tools to reduce the complexity of generating novel user interface ideas and their implementation. The designer needs some possibility for describing the application domain in a metaphor oriented representational form, help for finding potential metaphors, problem and user oriented quality control support, documentation of mismatches and support for solving these mismatches and finally the user has to be supported in the transformation to visual metaphor instances.

A lot of work has to be done to realize all parts of such a "user interface metaphor management system". In this paper we tried to establish a common understanding of the value for the designer. In discussing the requirements and sketching such an environment we want to initiate further efforts to achieve a considerable amount of support for alternative user interface design activities.

References

Abowd G., Coutaz J. & Nigay L. (1992) Structuring the Space of Interactive System Properties, Proceedings of the IFIP TC2/WG2.7 on Engineering for Human-Computer Interaction, Ellivuori, Finlande, pp. 113-128.

Abowd G. & Bass L. (1994) Software Architecture: A Tutorial Introduction, Software Engineering Institute, Carnegie Mellon University, Pittsburgh, USA.

Aldersey-Williams H. (1994) Use Scientists, Design, May, 1994, pp 32-377.

Amodeus (1994) Glossary of terms. At http://www-lgi.imag.fr/Les.Groups/IHM/AMODEUSGlossary/GlossaryEntries/task.html

Anderson J.R. (1983) The Architecture of Cognition. Harvard Press, Cambridge

Anderson B., Smyth M., Knott R.P., Bergan M., Bergan, J. & Alty, J.L. (1994) Minimising Conceptual Baggage: Making Choices about Metaphor. Proceedings of BCS HCI'94 Conference, People and Computers IX, Cambridge University Press, pp. 179-194.

Annett J. & Duncan K.D. (1967) Task analysis and training design. Occupational Psychology, 41, 211-221.

Annett J.K. et al. (1971) Task analysis. HMSO, London.

Arch (1992) A Metamodel for the Runtime Architecture of an Interactive System, The UIMS Tool Developers Workshop, SIGCHI Bulletin, ACM, 24, 1, pp. 32-37.

Ashworth C. & Goodland M. (1990) SSADM: A Practical Approach. London: McGraw-Hill.

Baecker R.M. & Buxton W.A.S. (1987) Design Principles and Methodologies, Chapter 11, in R.M. Baecker, W.A.S. Buxton, Readings in Human-Computer Interaction - A Multidisciplinary Approach, Morgan Kaufmann Publishers, Los Altos (Californie), pp. 483-491.

Barlow J., Rada R. & Diaper D. (1989) Interacting WITH computers. Interacting with Computers 1 (1) 39-42

Barnard P., Wilson M. & Maclean A. (1988) Approximate modelling of cognitive activity with an expert system: a theory-based strategy for developing an interactive design tool. The Computer Journal, 31(5), pp. 445-456.

Barnard P. (1991) Bridging between Basic Theories and the Artifacts of Human-Computer Interaction, in J.M. Carroll (Ed.), Designing Interaction: Psychology at the Human-Computer Interface. Cambridge Univ. Press, Cambridge, pp. 103-127.

Bass L., & Coutaz J. (1991) Developing Software for the User Interface, Addison-Wesley.

Bekker M.M. and Vermeeren A.P.O.S. (1992) Human-Computer Interface Design in Practice: Variability, Constraints and Information Sources, Contemporary Ergonomics, Proceedings of Ergonomics Society, Taylor & Francis, pp 352-357.

Belkin N., Canter L., & Rivers R. (1985) 'Characterising user navigation through complex data structures', Behaviour and Information Technology, 4(2): 93-102.

Bench-Capon T.J.M. & McEnery A.M. (1989a) People interact through computers not with them. Interacting with Computers 1(1) 31-38

Bench-Capon T.J.M. & McEnery A.M. (1989b) Modelling devices and modelling speakers. Interacting with Computers 1(2) 221-224

Benyon D.R. & Skidmore S.R. (1987) A Tool-kit approach to information systems development. The Computer Journal 31(1)

Benyon D.R. (1990) Information and Data Modelling, Blackwell Scientific Publications, Oxford

Benyon D.R. (1991) The role of task analysis in systems design. Interacting With Computers, 4(1): 102-123

Benyon D.R. (1992a) The Role of Task Analysis in Systems design in Interacting with

Computers 4(1),

Benyon D.R. (1992b) Task Analysis and Systems Design: The Discipline of Data. In Interacting with Computers, 4(2) 246-259

Benyon D.R. (1993) A Functional Model of Interacting Systems; A Semiotic approach in Connolly J. H. & Edmonds E.A (eds.) CSCW and AI Lawrence Erlbaum, London,

Bernsen N.O. & Klausen T. (1993) COSITUE: Towards a Methodology for Constructing Scenarios, The Amodeus Project, ESPRIT Basic Research Action 7040, UM/WP13.

Berry D.C. & Broadbent D. (1984) On the relationship between task performance and associated verbalizable knowledge. Quarterly Journal of Experimental Psychology, 36A, 209-231.

Bibby P.A. & Payne (1993) S.J.. Internalization and Use Specificity of Device Knowledge. Human-Computer Interaction 8(1), pp. 25-36.

Blumenthal B. (1990) Incorporating Metaphor in Automated Interface Design, in Diaper, D. et al. (Eds.) Proc. of Human-Computer Interaction INTERACT'90, Elsevier Science Publishers B.V. (North-Holland), pp. 659-664.

Bodart F. & Pigneur Y. (1989) Conception assistée des systèmes d'information - méthodes, modèls, outils, 2nd ed., Masson, Paris.

Bodart F. & Provot I. (1989) Eléments de modélisation et d'architecture des IHM dans les SI - Une approche pragmatique, Rencontres Lausannoises sur les Interfaces Homme-Machine, Troisième Cycle Romand d'Informatique, Lausanne.

Bodart F., Hennebert A.-M., Leheureux J.-M., Sacré I. & Vanderdonckt J. (1993) Architecture Elements for Highly-Interactive Business-Oriented Applications, in Lecture Notes in Computer Science, Vol. 753, L. Bass, J. Gornostaev and C. Unger (Eds.), Springer-Verlag, Berlin, pp. 83-104.

Bodart F. & Vanderdonckt J. (1994), On the Problem of Selecting Interaction Objects, in Proceedings of HCI'94 (Glasgow, 23-26 August 1994), G. Cockton, S.W. Draper, G.R.S. Weir (Eds.), Cambridge University Press, Cambridge, pp. 125-143.

Bodart F., Hennebert A.-M., Leheureux J.-M. & Vanderdonckt J. (1994a) Towards a Dynamic Strategy for Computer-Aided Visual Placement, in Proceedings of 2nd Workshop on Advanced Visual Interfaces AVI'94, Bari, T. Catarci, M.F. Costabile, S. Levialdi, G. Santucci (Eds.), ACM Press, pp. 78-87.

Bodart F., Hennebert A.-M., Leheureux J.-M., Provot I. & Vanderdonckt J. (1994b) A Model-based Approach to Presentation: A Continuum from Task Analysis to Prototype, in Proceedings of Eurographics Workshop on Design, Specification, Verification of Interactive Systems, Carrara, Eurographics Series, pp. 25-39.

Bodart F., Hennebert A.-M., Leheureux J.-M. & Vanderdonckt J. (1995) Computer-Aided Window Identification in TRIDENT, in Proceedings of Fifth IFIP TC13 Conference on Human-Computer Interaction INTERACT'95, Lillehammer, Chapman & Hall Publishers.

Bodart F., Hennebert A-M., Leheureux J-M. Provot I., Vanderdonckt J. & Zucchinetti (1995) G. Key dimensions for a development methodology of interactive applications. Critical Issues in User Interface Systems Engineering. Benyon, D. & Palanque, P. (Eds.), this volume.

Booch G. (1992) Object-oriented design with applications Benjamin/Cummings

Booth P. (1989) An Introduction to Human-Computer Interaction, Lawrence Erlbaum Associates, Hove.

Borälv E., Göransson B., Olsson E. & Sandblad B. (1994) Usability and efficiency. The HELIOS approach to development of user interfaces. CMPBEK 45 (Suppl.) S47-S64. In U. Engelmann, F. C. Jean, P. Degoulet (Eds.) The HELIOS Software Engineering

Environment, Supplement to Computer Methods and Programs in Biomedicine, Vol. 45, pp. 47-64.
Born G. (1988) Guidelines for Quality Assurance of Expert Systems. 1.1. Computer Services Association, CSA Working Group on QA & Expert Systems Working Paper.
Braudes B. (1990) Report of the Design Methodologies Subgroup, SIGCHI Bulletin, Vol. 22, No. 2, pp. 42-44.
Brown M.D. et al.(1978) Preparing Dance Notation Scores with a Computer, Computers and Graphics;3:1-7.
Brown C.M. (1988) Human computer interface design guidelines. Ablex, Norwood, NJ.
Browne D. (1993) STUDIO Prentice Hall
Browne D. (1994) STUDIO Structured User-Interface Design for Interaction Optimisation, Prentice Hall.
CACM (1990) Communications of the ACM 33(9)
Candy L. & Edmonds E.A. (1988) Expert Systems Development for an Office Environment: Users, Evaluation & the Design Process. IFIP Conference on Man-Machine Systems, Finland.
Candy L. & Rousseau N. (1995) FOCUS Evaluation Methods. Report 95/K/LUTCHI/0176.
Card S. Moran T. P. & Newell A. (1980) The Psychology of Human-Computer Interaction. Lawrence Erlbaum Associates, Hillsdale, NJ
Card S.K., Moran T.P. & Newell A. (1983) The Psychology of Human-Computer Interaction. Lawrence Erlbaum Ass., Hillsdale, New Jersey.
Card S.K., Robertson G.G. & Mackinlay J.D. (1991) The information visualiser, Proceedings of CHI 91, Eds
Cardelli L., Pike R. (1985) Squeak: a language for communicating with mice, ACM SIGGRAPH'85 Conference Proceedings, Computer Graphics, 19, 3, pp.215-224.
Carlsen N., Bass L., Cokton G., ten Hagen P. (1991) On Defining the Application Interface to the UIMS: A Conceptual Framework for Interactive Software Systems, in User Interface Management and Design, D.Duce (ed.).
Carr D.A. (1994) Specification of Interface Interaction Objects, in Proceedings of the Conference on Human Factors in Computing Systems CHI'94, Boston, B. Adelson, S. Dumais, J. Olson (Eds.), ACM Press, New York, pp. 372-378.
Carroll J.M. & Mack, R.L. (1985) Metaphor, computing systems, and interactive learning. International Journal of Man-Machine Studies, 22, pp. 39-57.
Carroll J.M. & Olson J.R.. (1988) Mental Models in Human Computer Interaction, in M. Helander (Ed.), Handbook of Human-Computer Interaction, . Elsevier Science Publishers B. V., North-Holland, pp. 45-65.
Carroll J. & Rosson M.B. (1992) "Getting Around the Task-Artifact Cycle: How to make Claims and Design by Scenario", ACM Transactions on Information Systems, 10(2), 181-212.
Carroll J.M. & Rosson M.B. (1994) Putting Metaphors to Work. Proceedings of Graphics Interface'94, Banff, Alberta, Canada, pp. 112-119.
Carroll J.M., Mack R.L. & Kellogg W.A. (1988) Interface Metaphors and User nterface Design. In Helander,M. (Ed.), Handbook of HCI, Elsevier, North-Holland, pp. 67-85.
Carroll J.M. (1990) Infinite detail and emulation in an ontologically minimised HCI in J.C. Chew and J. Whiteside (eds.) Empowering People; CHI '90 Proceedings ACM press
Casner S.M. (1990) A Task-Analytic Approach to the Automated Design of Information Graphics. Ph.D Thesis, University of Pittsburgh, Pittsburgh, USA.
Catterall B. J. (1990) The HUFIT Functionality Matrix. In Proceedings. of INTERACT'90, Diaper D. (ed) et al., pp 377-381.

Catterall B. J. (1991) Three approaches to the input of human factors in IT systems design: DIADEM, The HUFIT Toolset and the MOD/DTI Human Factors Guidelines, Behaviour & Information Technology, Vol 10, No 5, pp 359-371.

Checkland P. B. (1981) Systems Theory, Systems Practice. Wiley

Chen P. P-s (1976) Towards a unified theory of data ACM Transactions on database systems vol 1 (1) pp. 9-36

Cherry C. (1966) On Human Communication (2nd edition) MIT press

Coad P. and Yourdon E. (1992) Object-Oriented Analysis. and edition Prentice-Hall

Cockton G. (1987) A New Model for Separable Interactive Systems, in Proceedings of the Second IFIP TC13 Conference on Human-Computer Interaction INTERACT'87, Stuttgart, H.-J. Bullinger, B. Shackel (Eds.), Elsevier Science Publishers, Amsterdam, pp. 1033-1038.

Cockton G. (1991) The Architectural Bases of Design Re-use, in User Interface Management and Design, D.A. Duce, M.R. Gomes, F.R.A. Hopgood and J.R. Lee (Eds.), Springer-Verlag, Berlin, pp. 15-34.

Cockton G. (1992) Architecture and Abstraction in Interactive Systems, PhD Thesis, Heriot-Watt University, Edinburgh, 1992.

Cockton G., Clarke S. & Gray P. (1995) Theories of Context Influence the System Abstractions Used to Design Interactive Systems. People and Computers X, eds. M.A.R. Kirby, A.J. Dix and J.E. Finlay, Cambridge University Press: Cambridge.

Conklin J. (1987) Hypertext: an introduction and survey, IEEE Computer, 20(9): 17-41.

Copas C.V. & Edmonds E.A. (1994) Executable Task Analysis: Integration Issues. People and Computers IX, Cockton, Draper & Weir (Eds.), Cambridge:Cambridge University Press, 339 -352.

Coutaz J. (1987) PAC, an Object Oriented Model for Dialog Design, in Proc. Interact'87, North Holland, pp. 431-436.

Coutaz J. & Balbo S. (1991) Applications: A Dimension Space for User Interface Management Systems, in Proc. CHI'91 Human Factors in Computing Systems, ACM Press, pp. 27-32.

Coutaz J., Nigay .L. & Salber D. (1993) The MSM framework: A Design Space for Multi-Sensori-Motor Systems, in Proc. East/West Human Computer Interaction, EWHCI'93 Moscow, Springer Verlag Publ., LNCS Vol. 753, pp. 231-241.

Coutaz J., Nigay L. & Salber D. (1995) Agent-based agent modelling for interactive systems. This volume

Cox B. J. (1986) Object Oriented Programming - An Evolutionary Approach, Addison Wesley.

Coy W. (1989) Brauchen wir eine Theorie der Informatik? Informatik-Spektrum, Vol. 12, pp. 256-266. (in German)

Cramer J., Fey W., Goedicke M. & Große-Rhode M. (1991) Towards a formally based component description language - a foundation for reuse, in Structured Programming, Springer, 12, 91-110

Cross N. et al. (1992) Research in Design Thinking, Delft University Press, Delft.

Curtis B., & Hefley B. (1994) A WIMP No More - The Maturing of User Interface Engineering, ACM Interactions, pp 22-34.

Date C.J. (1986)An introduction to Database Systems 4th edition Addison-Wesley

Davis A. M. (1993) Software Requirements; Objects, Functions and States. Prentice Hall

de Baar D.J.M.J., Foley J. & Mullet K.E. (1992) Coupling application design and user interface design. In Proceedings of CHI'92, (3-7 May, Monterey, California), Reading: Addison Wesley, 256-266.

de Bruin H., Bouwman P. & van den Bos J. A. (1994) Task-oriented Methodology for the Development of Interactive Systems as Used in DIGIS. In: Tauber, M.J., Traunmüller, R. and Kaplan, S. (eds.) Proceedings Interdisciplinary approaches to system analysis and design. Schaerding, Austria.

de Haan G., van der Veer, G.C., & van Vliet, J.C. (1991) Formal Modelling Techniques in Human-Computer Interaction. Acta Psychologica; 78: 26-76.

de Haan G. & van der Veer G.C. (1992) Analyzing User Interfaces: ETAG validation studies. Proceedings Task-Analysis in Human-Computer Interaction, Schärding, Austria, 9-11 June, 1992.

de Haan G. & van der Veer G.C. (1992) Etag as the Basis for Intelligent Help Systems. In: van der Veer, G.C., Tauber, M.J. and Bagnara, S. (eds.). Proceedings ECCE-6: Tasks and Organisation. CUD, Rome, Italy, pp 271-283.

de Haan G. (1994) An ETAG-based Approach to the Design of User-interfaces. In: Tauber, M.J., Traunmüller, R. and Kaplan, S. (eds.) Proceedings Interdisciplinary Approaches to System Analysis and Design. Schärding, Austria.

de Haan G. (1994) How to Cook ETAG and Related Dishes: Uses of a Notational Language for User Knowledge Representation for User Interface Design. In: Stary, C. (ed.) Proceedings Cognitive Modeling and User Interface. Vienna, Austria.

de Haan G. (1995) ETAG-based design: User Interface design as User Mental Model design. This volume

de Haan G. (1995) The Psychological Basis of a Formal Model for User Interface Design. Submitted to the International Journal of Human-Computer Studies 1995.

De Marco T., (1978) Structured analysis and system specification. Yourdon press, N.Y.

DeMarco T. Structured Analysis, Systems Specification. 1979 Prentice Hall

Demazeau Y. & Müller J.P. (1991) "From Reactive to Intentional Agents", Decentralized Artificial Intelligence, vol. 2, Demazeau & Muller eds., North Holland, Amsterdam.

Denert E. (1977) "Specification and design of dialogue systems with state diagrams," in ACM European Chapters Computing Symposium (Liege), E. Mortlet and D. Rubbens (eds.),ACM Press, 417–424.

Diaper D. (1989) (ed.) Task Analysis for Human-Computer Interaction. Ellis-Horwood,

Diaper D. & Addison M. (1992) Task Analysis and Systems Analysis for Software Development. In: Interacting with Computers vol 3(3) pp 124-139,

Dowell J. & Long J. (1994) A Domain Analysis of Air Traffic Management can be Used to Rationalise Interface Design Issues, in People and Computers IX, G. Cockton, S.W. Draper and G.R.S. Weir, Cambridge University Press: Cambridge, pp. 53–65.

Downs E., Clare P. & Coe I. (1991) Structured Systems Analysis and Design Method: application and context. Prentice Hall, New York.

Draper S. (1993) The notion of task in HCI. In Ashlund, S., Mullet, K., Hendersen, A., Hollnagel E. & White T. (eds)Proc of Interchi '93 Adjunct proceedings ACM press

Ducasse S. & Fornarino M. (1993) Protocol for managing dependencies between objects by controlling generic function invocation, in OOPSLA'93 workshop on Object-Oriented Reflection and Metalevel Architectures, Washington, ACM.

Duce D., Gomes M.R., Hopgood F.R.A. & Lee J.L. (eds) (1991) "User Interface Management and Design", Eurographics Seminars, Berlin: Springer-Verlag, pp. 36-49.

Duke D. & Harrison M. (1992) Abstract Models for Interaction Objects, Computer Graphics Forum, 12 (3), pp.25-36.

Duke D. & Harrison M. (1993) Towards a Theory of Interactors, The Amodeus Project, Esprit Basic Research 7040, Amodeus Project Document, System Modelling/WP6.

Duke D.& Harrison M. (1994) Folding Human Factors into Rigourous Development, in the

Proc. of Eurographics Workshop Design, Specification, Verification of Interactive Systems, F. Paterno' Ed., pp. 335-352.

Dzida W. (1987) On Tools and Interfaces. In Frese, M., Ulich, E., Dzida, W. (Eds.): Psychological Issues of Human-Computer Interaction in the Work Place. North-Holland, Amsterdam, pp. 339-355.

Eason K.D. (1988) Information Technology & Organisational Change. London: Taylor & Francis.

Eco U. (1976) A Theory of Semiotics Indiana University Press, Bloomington.

Edmonds E.A., Candy L., Slatter P.S. & Lunn S. (1989) Issues in the design of expert systems for business. Expert Systems for Information Management, 2, 1.

Edmonds E.A. & McDaid E. (1990) An Architecture for Knowledge-Based Front Ends. Knowledge-Based Systems. 3, 4, 221-224.

Edmonds E.A., Southwick R., Prat A., Catot J.M., Lores J. & Fletcher P. '1991) Using the FOCUS Architecture for Developing Knowledge-Based Front Ends: KAFTS - a KBFE for Forecasting. In Human Aspects in Computing, H.-J. Bullinger (Ed.), Elsevier, Amsterdam, 825-829.

Edmonds E.A., Murray B.S., Ghazikhanian J. & Heggie S.P. (1992) The re-use and integration of existing software: a central role for the intelligent user interface. People and Computers VIII. Monk, Diaper and Harrison (Eds.), Cambridge:Cambridge University Press, 414-427.

Erickson T.D. (1990) Working with Interface Metaphors. In Laurel, B. (Ed.), The Art of Human-Computer Interface Design, Addison-Wesley, pp. 65-73.

Faraday P.F. and Sutcliffe A.G (1993) A method for multi media design. In People and Computers VIII, Proceedings of the BCS HCI-SIG Conference. Eds Alty J.L, Diaper D. and Guest S., pp 173-190, Cambridge University Press, Cambridge

Figarol S. & Javaux D. (1993) From Flying Task Description to Safety Assessment, Le Transpondeur.

Fischer G. (1989) Human-Computer Interaction Software: Lessons Learned, Challenges Ahead IEEE Software, (January) pp 44-52

Fischer G. (1993) Beyond Human Computer Interaction: Designing Useful and Usable Computational Environments, in People and Computers VIII, (eds) J.L. Alty, D. Diaper and S. Guest, Cambridge University Press: Cambridge.

Fitter M., Robinson D., Rector A., Horan B., Nowlan A., Wilson A. & Newton P. (1991) Supportive evaluation handbook: a methodology to facilitate system development in the health care domain. HRC/ESRC Social and Applied Psychology Unit, Univ. of Sheffield.

Foley J.D. & Sukavirya P. (1993) A Second generation User Interface Design Environment: The Model and The Runtime Architecture. Proc. INTERCHI'93 (Amsterdam, April 1993), pp. 375-382.

Frese M. & Zapf D. (1994) Action as the Core of Work Psychology: A German Approach, in Handbook of Industrial and Organizational Psychology, H.C. Triandis, M.D. Dunnette, L.M. Hough (Eds.), Vol. 4, Consulting Psychologists Press, Palo Alto, pp. 271-340.

Galitz W. O. (1987) Handbook of screen format design. 2nd ed. QED Publications, Wellesley, MA.

Garlan D. & Shaw M. (1993) An Introduction to Software Architecture, Advances in Software Engineering and Knowledge Engineering, V. Ambriola and G. Tortora Eds., Vol. 1, World Scientific Publ., pp. 1-39.

Gellersen H.-W. (1993) Graphical Design Support for DCE Applications. In Schill, A. (Ed.): OSF - Distributed Computing Environment, First Interantional DCE Workshop,

Karlsruhe, Germany, Lecture Notes in Computer Science 731, Springer Verlag, pp. 231-241.

Gellersen H.-W., Mühlhäuser, M. & Frick, O. (1994) Multi-user and Multimodal Aspects of Multimedia. In Herzner, W., Kappe, F. (Eds.) Multimedia and Hypermedia in Open Distributed Environments, First EuroGraphics Symposium, Graz, Austria, EurographicSeminars, Springer Verlag, pp. 278-297.

Gellersen H.-W. (1995) Toward Engineering for Multimodal Interactive Systems. First International Workshop on Intelligence and Mulimodality in Multimedia Interfaces (IMMI-1), Edinburgh, Scotland.

Ghezzi C., Jazayeri M. & Mandrioli D. (1992) Fundamentals of Software Engineering, Prentice Hall

Goedicke M. (1993) On the Structure of Software Description Languages: A Component Oriented View, University of Dortmund, Dept. of Computer Science, Dortmund, Research Report, No. 473, Habilitation

Goedicke M. & Sucrow B. (1994) On the Software Architecture of Interactive Systems, Position Paper in Proceeding of the Joint Workshop on Software Engineering and User Interface of the IFIP Working groups 13.2 and 2.7 in Loughborough.

Goedicke M. & Sucrow B. (1995) Using Graph Grammars For Specifying Graphical User Interfaces, Software Engineering Memo, Univ- Essen, Fb Math & Computer Science.

Goedicke M. & Sucrow B. (1995) Towards a flexible software architecture of Interactive Systems. This volume

Götze R. (1994) Dialogue Modelling for Multimedia User Interfaces, Dissertation (in german) Research Report 1/94, Dept. of Computer Science, University of Oldenburg

Goldberg A. (1984)Smalltalk-80: The Interactive Programming Environment, Addison-Wesley, Readings, Mass.

Goldberg M. & Robson D. (1983), Smalltalk-80: The Language and Its Implementation. Addison Wesley Publishing Company, Reading MA.

Gould J.D., (1987) How to design usable systems. In proceedings Interact 87; Eds Bullinger H-J and Shackel B., North Holland, Amsterdam.

Gould J.D., Boies S.J. & Lewis C. (1991) Making usable, useful, productivity-enhancing computer applications. Communications of the ACM, 34, 1, 74-85.

Gram C. & Cockton G. (eds), (1995), Design Principles for Interactive Software, monograph by members of IFIP WG2.7(13.4) to be published by Chapman-Hall.

Grudin J. (1982) Utility and Usability: research issues and development contexts. Interacting with Computers, vol. 4, no 2, pp 209-217.

Guest A.H. (1990) Dance Notation, Perspecta - the Yale Architectural Journal, 26, 203-214.

Gulliksen J. & Sandblad B. (1995) Domain specific design of user interfaces. Critical Issues in User Interface Systems Engineering. Benyon, D. & Palanque, P. (Eds.), this volume.

Gulliksen J. & Sandblad B. (in press) Domain specific design of user interfaces. International Journal of Human-Computer Interaction, Ablex Publishing Corporation, Norwood, New Jersey.

Gulliksen J., Johnson M., Lind M., Nygren E. & Sandblad B. (1993). The need for new application specific interface elements. In G. Salvendy and M.J. Smith eds. Proceedings of HCI International'93, pp.15-20, Elsevier.

Gulliksen J., Lind M., Lif M. & Sandblad B. (1995) Efficient Development of Organisations and Information Technology – A Design Approach. In Y. Anzai and K. Ogawa (eds.) Proceedings of the 6th International Conference on Human-Computer Interaction, Pacificio Yokohama, Yokohama, Japan.

Hague S. & Reid I. (1991) The changing face of scientific computing. Human Aspects in

Computing: Design and Use of Interactive Systems and Information Management. H.-J. Bullinger (Ed.), Amsterdam: Elsevier, 791-795.

Hakiel D.R. (1991) User Interaction Reference Model: Introducing a Framework for HCI Design Support, Contemporary Ergonomics, Taylor & Francis, pp 163-168.

Halasz F.G.; (1989) Reflections on notecards: Several issues for the next generation of Hypermedia systems.; Comms of the ACM, Vol 31(7), pp 836-852.

Hall W. et al (1992) Towards an integrated information environment with open hypermedia, in Proceedings of ECHT'92, 4th ACM Hypertext Conference.

Hammond N. & Allinson, L. (1993) The Travel Metaphor as Design Principle and Training Aid for Navigating around Complex Systems Proceedings of BCS HCI'93 Conference, People and Computers VIII, Cambridge University Press, pp. 75-90.

Hammond N.V. & Allinson L.J. (1988) Travels around a learning support environment: Rambling, orienteering or touring? In Soloway, E., Frye,D. & Sheppard,S.B. (eds), CHI'88 Conference Proceedings: Human Factors in Computing Systems, ACM: Washington DC, 15-19 May, pp 269-273.

Harada A. (1992) The Interface Design Edge, Industrial Design (Japanese), 157, 1992.

Harrison M. & Barnard P. (1992) "On Defining Requirements of Interactions", Proceedings IEEE Requirements Engineering, pp.50-54.

Hartson H.R.A., Siochi C. & Hix D. (1990) "The UAN: A User–Oriented Representation for Direct Manipulation Interface Designs," in ACM Transactions on Information Systems, 8(3), pp.181–203.

Hartson R. & Gray P. (1992), "Temporal Aspects of Tasks in the User Action Notation", Human Computer Interaction, Vol.7, pp.1-45.

Hennebert A.-M. (1994), La hiérarchie des Objets de Contrôle: Règles de construction, Internal TRIDENT report, Institut d'Informatique, Namur.

Hill R.D. (1986) Supporting Concurrency, Communication, and Synchronization in Human-Computer Interaction-The Sassafras UIMS, ACM Transactions on Graphics, Vol.5, No.3, pp.179-210.

Hill R.D. (1992) The Abstraction-Link-View Paradigm: Using Constraints to Connect User Interfaces to Applications. In proceedings CHI'92, ACM:New York, pp. 335-342.

Hitch G. J. (1987) Working memory, in B. Christie and M. M. Gardiner (eds.), Applying cognitive psychology to user interface design. Wiley, London.

Hix D. & Hartson H. R. (1993) Developing User Interfaces Wiley

Hix D. & Hartson H.R. (1993) Developing User Interfaces: Ensuring Usability Through Product & Process. Wiley Professional Computing.

Hix D. (1989) Developing and evaluating an interactive system for producing human-computer interfaces, Behaviour and Information Technology, Vol 8, 4:285-299.

Hoare C.A.R. (1985) Communicating Sequential Processes, Prentice Hall International, London.

Hobday J.S., Rhoden D., Bright C.K. & Earthy J.V. (1994) Aiding the control of emergencies on ships. IN Proceedings of IMAS-94, Fire Safety on Ships: Development into the 21st century, pp 23-27

Holtzblatt K. & Beyer H. (1993) Making Customer-Centred Design Work For Teams, Communications of the ACM, 36(10), pp 93-103

Howard M. (1993) Work Flow Applications: Top-down Perspective, Bottom-up Implementation. In The Work Group and Beyond: Exploiting the Transformation of Office Information Systems. Gartner Group, Inc. Stamford, Conn., U.S.A.

Hudson S.E. & King R. (1986) A generator of direct manipulation user interfaces. ACM Transactions on Graphics, 5, 4, 283-317.

Hutchins E.L., Hollan J.D. & Norman D.A. (1986) Direct Manipulation Interfaces. In: Norman D. A., Draper S.: User-centered system design: New perspectives in human-computer interaction, Hillsdale, NJ, Lawrence Erlbaum Associates, pp 87-12.4

Ilog (1989) "Aïda, Environnement de développement d'applications", Reference manual Aïda, Version 1.32, Copyright Ilog.

Ince D. (1991) Methods of evolving order out of chaos. Computing, 30, 20-21.

Indurkhya B. (1992) Metaphor and Cognition: an Interactionist Approach. Studies in Cognitive Systems, Volume 13, Kluwer Academic Publishers.

Ip W.K., Damodaran L., Olphert C.W. & Maguire M.C. (1990) The Use of Task Allocation Charts in System Design: A Critical Appraisal. In Proceedings of INTERACT'90, IFIP TC 13 Third International Conference on HCI, Diaper, D.,Gilmore, D., Cockton, G. and Shackel, B.(Eds), 289-294.

ISO (1989) ISO/IEC-JTC1/SC21/FDT/C, IPS - OSI - LOTOS, a Formal Description Technique Based on the Temporal Ordering of Observational Behaviour, IS 8807.

ISO 9241 (1994) International Standards Organisation, Ergonomic requirements for office work with visual display terminals, Part 12, Presentation of Information, Draft International Standard.

Jackendoff R. (1983) Semantics and cognition. MIT Press, Cambridge, Massachusetts.

Jacob R.J.K. (1986) A Specification Language for Direct-Manipulation User Interfaces. ACM Transactions on Graphics 5(4), pp. 283-317.

Jacob R.J.K. (1986) A Specification Language for Direct-Manipulation User Interfaces, ACM Transactions on Graphics, 5, 283-317.

Jacobson J., Chistensen M., Johnson P. & Overgaard G. (1993) Object-Oriented Software Engineering. Addison-Wesley

Janssen C., Weisbecker A. & Ziegler J. (1993) Generating user interfaces from data models and dialogue net specifications. In proceedings of INTERCHI'93, Amsterdam, 418-423.

Johnson C. (1994) The Formal Analysis of Human Computer Interaction During Accident Investigations, in People and Computers IX, (eds) G. Cockton, S.W. Draper and G.R.S. Weir, Cambridge University Press: Cambridge. HCI 94

Johnson C. (1995) Literate Specifiaction: Using Design Rationale To Support Formal Methods In The Development Of Human Machine Interfaces, submitted to Human Computer Interaction

Johnson G.J. (1994) Of Metaphor and the Difficulty of Computer Discourse. CACM, 37(12), pp. 97-102.

Johnson P. (1985) 'Towards a task model of messaging: An example of the application of TAKD to user interface design', In People and Computers: Designing the interface. Eds Johnson P. and Cook S., pp 46-62; Cambridge University Press.

Johnson P. (1989) Supporting System Design by Analyzing Current Task Knowledge. In D. Diaper Eds Task Analysis for Human-Computer Interaction. Ellis Horwood Ltd, UK. . p. 160-185

Johnson P. (1991) Human-Computer Interaction, Psychology, Task analysis and Software Engineering, McGraw-Hill Book Company, London.

Johnson P. (1992) Human Computer Interaction, McGraw Hill, London.

Johnson P. (1992) Human-Computer interaction; Psychology, Task Analysis and Software Engineering. McGraw-Hill, Maidenhead, UK

Johnson P., Johnson H., Waddington R. & Shouls A. (1988) Task Related Knowledge Structures: Analysis, Modelling, and Application. In D. M. Jones and R. Winder Eds, People and Computers: From Research to Implementation Cambridge: Cambridge University Press. , pp. 35-62

Johnson P., Markopoulos P. & Johnson H. (1992) Task Knowledge Structures: A Specification of User Task Models and Interaction Dialogues, Proceedings in the 11th Interdisciplinary Workshop on Informatics and Psychology, Austria '92.

Kaindl H. (1993) The Missing Link in Requirements Engineering, in Software Engineering Notes, ACM, pp. 30–39.

Kangassalo H. (1983) Structuring Principles of Conceptual Schemas and Conceptual Models. In Bubenko, J. (ed.) Information Modelling Chartwell-Bratt

Katz S.D. (1991) Film Directing Shot by Shot - Visualizing from Concept to Screen, Michael Wiese Productions.

Kazman R., Bass L., Abowd G. & Webb M. (1994) SAAM: A Method for Analyzing the Properties of Software Architectures, In Proc. of the 16th International Conference on Software Engineering, ICSE'94.

Keeler M. A. & Denning S. M. (1991) The challenge of interface design for communication theory: from interaction metaphor to contexts of discovery Interacting with Computers 3(3) 283-301

Kieras D. & Polson P.G. (1985) An Approach to the Formal Analysis of User Complexity. Int. Journal of Man-Machine Studies; 22: 365-394.

Kieras D. (1988) Towards a practical GOMS model methodology for user interface design. In The Handbook of Human-Computer Interaction Helander, M. (ed.) pp 135-158 North-Holland

Knuth D.E. (1984) "Literate Programming," Computer Journal, 27(2), 97111

Kuutti K. & Bannone L. (1993) Searching for Unity Among Diversity: Exploring the Interface Concept. Proc. INTERCHI'93, ACM Press, pp. 263-267.

Krasner G.E. & Pope T.S. (1988) A Cookbook for Using the Model-View - Controller User Interface Paradigm in Smalltalk 80, Journal of Object oriented Programming, Vol. 1, No 3. pp 26–49.

Lakoff G. & Johnson M. (1980) Metaphors We Live By. The Unversity of Chicago Press.

Landay J.A. & Myers B.A. (1994) Interactive Sketching for the Early Stages of User Interface Design, Report CMU-CS-94-176, School of Computer Science, Carnegie Mellon University, Pittsburgh.

Larson J.A. & Wallick J.B., (1984) An interface for novice and infrequent database management system users. In proceedings of NCC 84, pp 524-529.

Laszlo P. (1969) System, Structure and Experience Gordon and Breach Science Publishers, London

Laurel B. (1990) Interface Agents: Metaphors with Character in B. Laurel (ed.) The Art of Human-Computer Interface Design Addison-Wesley

Lee G. (1993) Object Oriented GUI Application Development. Prentice-Hall.

Leidig T. (1994) Entwicklung kooperativer graphisch-interaktiver Anwendungen. Dissertation, University of Kaiserslautern, Germany, Verlag Shaker,. (in German)

Lewis C. & Rieman J. (1995) Task-Centered User Interface Design, shareware, available via anonymous ftp from ftp.cs.colorado.edu.

Lim K.Y. & Long J.B. (1994) The MUSE Method for Usability Engineering, Cambridge University Press.

Lim K.Y. & Long J.L. (1992) A method for (recruiting) methods: Facilitating human factors input to system design. In Human Factors in Computing Systems, Proceedings of CHI92, Eds Bauersfield p., Bennett J. and Lynch G., pp 549-555, ACM Press.

Linton M. & Dunwoody C. (1986) "Partitioning User Interfaces with Interactive Views", Computer Systems Laboratory, Stanford University, Stanford, CA 94305-2192.

Long J. (1989) Cognitive Ergonomics and Human-Computer Interaction. In P. Warr (ed.)

Psychology at Work, Penguin, Harmondsworth.
Lovgren J. (1994) How to Choose Good Metaphors. IEEE Software, pp. 86- 88.
Lyons J. (1977) Semantics Cambridge University Press,
Lyytinen K. (1983) Reality modelling considered harmful - the need for a linguistic framework. In Bubenko (ed.) Information Modelling. Chartwell-Brat
Macaulay L., Fowler C., Kirby M. & Hutt A. (1990) USTM: A New Approach to Requirements Specification. Interacting with Computers, 2, 1, 92-118.
MacLean A., Bellotti V., Young R. & Moran, T. (1991) Reaching through Analogy: A Design Rationale Perspective on Roles of Analogy. Proceedings of CHI'91, ACM, New Orleans, USA, pp. 167-172.
MacLean A., Young R.M., Bellotti V.M.E. & Moran T.P. (1991) Questions, Options and Criteria: Elements of Design Space Analysis. In Human-Computer Interaction, Special Issue on design Rationale: Carroll, J. & Moran, T. (eds.), Vol 6 (3&4), pp. 201-250.
MacLeod M. & Bevan N. (1993) MUSiC Video Analysis and Context Tools for Usability Measurement, in Proceedings of the Conference on Human Factors in Computing Systems INTERCHI'93 Amsterdam, S. Ashlund, K. Mullet, A. Henderson, E. Hollnagel and T. White (Eds.), ACM Press, New York, pp. 55.
Madsen K.H. (1994) A Guide to Metaphorical Design, CACM, 37(12), pp. 57-62.
Maes P. & Kozierok R. (1993) Learning Interface Agents AAAI '93 Conference on Artificial Intelligence, Washington,
Maes P. (1994) Interface Agents. In Communications of the ACM)
Maissel J., Macleod M., Thomas C., Renger R., Corcoran R., Dillon A., Maguire M. & Sweeney M. (1993) Usability Context Analysis: A Practical Guide,Version 3.0, National Physical Laboratory and HUSAT Research Institute, DITC, NPL, Teddington, TW11 0LW, UK.
Manhartsberger M. & Tscheligi M. (1994) Wizard: Non-wimp Oriented Prototyping of Direct Manipulative Behaviour, Conference Companion, CHI'94, pp 111-112.
Mann, W. & Thompson, S. (1988) 'Rhetorical structure theory: toward a functional theory of text organisation', Text, 6(3): 243-281.
Marcus A. (1993) Human Communication Issues in Advanced UIs. CACM, 36(4), pp. 101-109.
Marmolin H. (1992) Multimedia from the perspectives of Psychology. In: Multimedia, Systems, Interactions and Applications, Kjelldahl L (ed), Springer-Verlag, pp 39-52.
Marshall C., Nelson C. & Gardiner M.M. (1987) Design Guidelines, in Applying Cognitive Psychology to User-Interface Design, M.M. Gardiner, B. Christie (Eds.), John Wiley & Sons, New York, pp. 221-278.
Martin J.H. (1990) A Computational Model of Metaphor Interpretation. Perspectives in Artificial Intelligence, Volume 8, Academic Press.
Maybury M.T., (1993) Planning multimedia explanations using communicative acts. In Intelligent multimedia interfaces, Ed Maybury M.T., pp 60-74, MIT Press, Cambridge, MA.
McBride N. (1994) Bridging the gap between structured analysis methods and object-oriented analysis. In Object Technology Transfer Alfred Waller,
McCall J. (1977) Factors in Software Quality, General Electric Eds.
McClelland I.L. & Brigham F.R. (1991) Marketing ergonomics - how should ergonomics be packaged?. Ergonomics, 33, 5, 519-526.
Miyashita K., Matsuoka S. & Takahashi S. (1992) Declarative Programming of Graphical User Interfaces by Visual Examples. In Third Annual Symposium on User Interface Software and Technology, UIST '92, pp 107-116.

Miyata Y. & Norman D.A. (1986) Psychological Issues in Support of Multiple Activities, chapter 13, in User Centered Design - New Persepectives on Human-Computer Interaction, D.A. Norman, S.W. Draper (Eds.), Lawrence Erlbaum Associates Publishers, Hillsdale, pp. 266-284.

Moher T., Dirda V., Bastide R. & Palanque Ph. (1994) A Bridging Framework for the Modeling of Devices, Users, and Interfaces, Technical Report UIC-EECS-ICE-94-13, University of Illinois.

Monarchi D.E. & Puhr G.I. (1992) A Research Typology for Object-Oriented Analysis and Design. Communications of the ACM, 35(9): 35-47.

Moran T. (1981) Command language grammar: a representation for the user interface of interactive computer systems International Journal of Man Machine Studies 15 3

Moran T.P. (1981) The Command Language Grammar: A Representation for the User-Interface of Interactive Systems. International Journal of Man-Machine Studies; 15(1): 3-50.

Moriyon R., Szekely P. & Neches R. (1994) Automatic Generation of Help from Interface Design Models, in Proceedings of CHI'94, Boston, B. Adelson, S. Dumais, J. Olson (Eds.), ACM Press, pp. 225-231.

Mountford S.J. (1990) Tools and Techniques for Creative Design. In Laurel, B. (Ed.), The Art of Human-Computer Interface Design, Addison-Wesley, pp. 17-30.

Murray B.S. & Edmonds E.A. (1994) Flexibility in Interface Design. IEE Proceedings-E, Computers and Digital Techniques, 141, 2, 93-98.

Murray B.S. (1994) Intelligent Information Presentation Systems. Knowledge Engineering Review, 9, 3, 269-286.

Murray B.S., Edmonds E.A. & Govaert B. (1992) SEPSOL: an experimental knowledge-based front end developed using the FOCUS architecture. In the Proceeding of PRICAI'92, Soeul, Sth. Korea, 447-455.

Musil S., Giller V. & Tscheligi M. (1994) Inhouse: Designing a Metaphor Based Interaction Environment. Vienna User Interface Group Technical Report Series, TR 94/15, 1994.

Myers B. A. & Rosson M. B. (1992) Survey on user interface programming. In Human Factors in Computing Systems, CHI '92 Proceedings, ACM Press, pp. 195-202.

Myers B.A. (1990) "A New Model for Handling Input", ACM Transactions on Information Systems, pp.289-320, Vol.8, N,3.

Myers B.A. (1994) User Interface Software Tools. Scool of Computer Science, Carnegie Mellon University Technical Report CMU-HCII-94-107.

Myers B.A., McDaniel R. G. & Kosbie D. S. (1993) Marquise. Creating Complete Interfaces by Demonstration, in Proceedings INTERCHI'93, pp 293-300.

Neerincx M. & de Greef P. (1993) How to Aid Non-Experts. In: Ashlund, S., Mullet, K., Henderson, A, Hollnagel, E. and White, T. (eds.) Proceedings InterCHI'93. ACM, New York, pp 165-171.

Neilsen J. (1993) Hypertext and Hypermedia, Academic Press

Newman W. A. (1993) Preliminary Analysis of the Products of HCI Research, using Pro Forma Abstracts. In: Ashlund, S., Mullet, K., Henderson, A, Hollnagel, E. and White, T. (eds.) Proceedings InterCHI '93. ACM, New York, pp 278-284.

Nielsen J. (1989) Usability engineering at a discount. Designing and Using Human-Computer Interfaces and Knowledge Based Systems. Vol. II, G. Salvendy and M.J. Smith (Eds). Amsterdam: Elsevier. 394-401.

Nielsen J.(1993) Usability Engineering, Academic Press, London.

Nigay L. & Coutaz J. (1993), A Design Space For Multimodal Systems: Concurrent Processing and Data Fusion, in Proceedings of the Conference on Human Factors in

Computing Systems INTERCHI'93, Amsterdam, S. Ashlund, K. Mullet, A. Henderson, E. Hollnagel and T. White (Eds.), ACM Press, New York, pp. 172-178.

Nigay L. & Coutaz J. (1995) A Generic Platform for Addressing the Multimodal Challenge, in Proc. CHI'95 Human Factors in Computing Systems, ACM New York, Denver, pp.98-105.

Nigay L. (1994) Conception et modélisation logicielles des systèmes interactifs : application aux interfaces multimodales. Thèse de doctorat de l'Université Joseph Fourier.

Nonogaki H. & Ueda H. (1991) FRIEND21 Project: A construction of 21st century human interface. Proceedings of CHI'91, ACM, New Orleans, USA, pp. 404-414.

Norman D. A. & Draper S. (1986) User-centered system design: New perspectives in human-computer interaction, Hillsdale, NJ, Lawrence Erlbaum Associates.

Norman D.A. (1983) Some Observations on Mental Models. In: Gentner, D. & Stevens, A.L. (eds.) Mental Models. Lawrence Erlbaum, Hillsdale, New Jersey, pp 7-14.

Nygren E. and Henriksson P. (1992) Reading the Medical Record I. Analysis of physicians ways of reading the medical record. Computer Methods and Programs in Biomedicine (39) pp. 1-12.

Nygren E., Johnson M. & Henriksson P. (1992) Reading the Medical record II. Design of a human-computer interface for basic reading of computerised medical records. Computer Methods and Programs in Biomedicine (39) pp. 13-25.

Nygren E., Johnson M., Lind M. & Sandblad B. (1992). The art of the obvious. Proceedings of CHI'92, Monterey, California.

Oberquelle H. (1984) On Models and Modelling in Human-Computer Co-operation. In: Van der Veer, G.C., Tauber, M.J., Green, T.R.G. and Gorny, P. (eds.) Readings on Cognitive Ergonomics - Mind and Computers. Springer Verlag, Berlin, pp 26-43.

Olsen D.R. (1989) A programming language basis for user interface management. In Proceeding of CHI'89, ACM, New York, 171-176.

Olsen D.R. (1990) Propositional Production Systems for Dialog Description, Human Factors in Computing Systems, CHI '90 Conference, ACM Press, pp 57-63

Olsson E., Göransson B., Borälv E. & Sandblad B. (1993) Domain Specific Style Guide – Design and Implementation. Proceedings of the MOTIF'93 & COSE International User Conference, Washington, D. C.

Open Software Foundation, OSF/Motif Style Guide, Revision 1.1 and draft Revision 2.0

OSF (1989) "OSF/Motif, Programmer's Reference Manual", Revision 1.0; Open Software Foundation, Eleven Cambridge Center, Cambridge, MA 02142.

Palanque Ph. & Bastide R. (1995) Interactive cooperative objects: a formalism for the specification and the design of user driven interfaces. Critical Issues in User Interface Systems Engineering. Benyon, D. & Palanque, P. (Eds.), this volume.

Palanque Ph., Bastide R. & Sengès (1995) Validating interactive system design through the verification of formal task and system models. 6th IFIP Working Conference on Engineering for Human-Computer Interaction (EHCI'95) Grand Targhee Resort, Wyoming, U.S.A.

Palanque Ph., Bastide R. (1995) Verification of an Interactive Software by Analysis of its Formal Specification. Interact'95 IFIP TC 13 conference, Lillehammer (Norway), 27-29 june.

Palanque Ph., Bastide R., Dourte L. (1993b)Contextual Help for Free with Formal Dialogue Design ; Proceedings of (HCI International 93), 5th International Conference on Human-Computer Interaction joint with 9th Symposium on Human Interface (Japan), published by North Holland. Orlando, Florida (USA), August 8-15.

Palanque Ph., Bastide R., Sibertin C., Dourte L. (1993a) Design of User-Driven Interfaces using Petri nets and Objects ; In proceedings of 5th Conference on Advanced Information Systems Engineering (CAISE'93). LNCS n° 685, Springer-Verlag.

Paterno' F. & Faconti G. (1992), On the LOTOS Use to Describe Graphical Interaction, Proceedings HCI'92 Conference, pp.155-173, Cambridge University Press.

Paterno' F. & Mezzanotte M. (1994) "Analyzing Matis with ACTL and Interactors", Amodeus BRA Esprit Report, System Modelling, wp36.

Paterno' F. & Mezzanotte M. (1995) "Verification of Undesired Behaviours in the CERD case study", Proceedings EHCI'95, Chapmann & Hall, Wyoming.

Paterno' F. (1994) "A Theory of User-Interaction Objects", Journal of Visual Languages and Computing, Vol.5, N.3, pp.227-249, Academic Press.

Paterno' F. & Pangoli S. (1995) ISW: a tool for designing and prototyping interactive systems. Critical Issues in User Interface Systems Engineering. Benyon, D. & Palanque, P. (Eds.), this volume.

Paterno' F., Leonardi A. & Pangoli S. (1994) A Tool Supported Approach to the Refinement of Interactive Systems, in the Proc. of Eurographics Workshop Design, Specification, Verification of Interactive Systems, F. Paterno' Ed., pp. 85-96.

Patton P. (1992) User Interface Design: Making Metaphors, I.D., pp 62-66.

Payne S. (1989) Using models of users knowledge to analyse learnability. In Long J.B. and Whitefield A..D.; Cognitive ergonomics and Human Computer Interaction. J. Wiley.

Payne S.J. & Green T.R.G. (1986) Task Action Grammars: a model of mental representation of task languages. Human Computer Interaction, 2 (2), Lawrence Erlbaum, Hillsdale, N.J. pp. 93-133.

Payne S.J., Squibb H.R. & Howes A. (1990) The Nature of Device Models: The Yoked State Space Hypothesis and Some Experiments With Text Editors. Human-Computer Interaction; 5: 415-444.

Petoud I. & Pigneur Y. (1989a) Des specifications fonctionnelles à l'interface-utilisateur sans programmation, in Actes du Colloque sur l'ingénierie des interfaces homme-machine, Sophia-Antipolis.

Petoud I. & Pigneur Y. (1989b) An automatic and Visual Approach for User Interface Design, in Proc. of 4th IFIP Working Conference on User Interfaces, Nappa Valley.

Petoud I. (1990) Génération automatique de l'interface homme-machine d'une application de gestion hautement interactive, PhD, Ecole des Hautes Etudes Commerciales, Université de Lausanne, Chabloz, Tolochenaz.

Pfaff G.E. et al. (1985) User Interface Management Systems, G.E. Pfaff ed., Eurographics Seminars, Springer Verlag.

Pierret-Golbreich C.; Delouis, I. & Scapin D.L. (1989) An object- oriented tool for extracting and representing tasks. INRIA research report no 1063. (In French.)

Powrie S.E. & Siemieniuch C.E. (1990) "An Investigation of User Requirements for Broadband Communications in the Automotive Industry," in Human Computer Interaction – INTERACT '90, D Diaper, D. Gilmore, G. Cockton and B. Shackel (eds), Elsevier Science Publishers BV, 233–238.

Prat A., Catot J.M., Lores J., Galmes J., Riba A. & Sanjeevan K. (1992) Construction of a Statistical KBFE for Experimental Design using the Tools and Techniques Developed in the FOCUS Project, in Proc. COMSTAT 10th Symposium on Computational Statistics (Neuchatel, Switzerland.

Prat A., Lores J., Fletcher P. & Catot J.M. (1990) Back-end Manager: an Interface between a Knowledge-Based Front End and its Application Sub-systems. Knowledge-Based Systems. 3, 4, 225-229.

Preece J, Rogers Y., Sharp H., Benyon D., Holland S. & Carey T. (1994) Human Computer

Interaction, Addison Wesley, p 528.
Preece J.J., Rogers Y R., Sharp H., Benyon D R., Holland S. & Carey T. (1994) Human-Computer Interaction Addison-Wesley
Preston-Dunlop V. (1969) A Notation System for Recording Observable Motion, International Journal of Man Machine Studies, 1, 363-386.
Provot I. (1993) L'enregistrement d'une commande téléphonée, Internal TRIDENT report, Institut d'Informatique, Namur.
Rösch P., Gerteis, W., Mühlhäuser, M. & Leidig, T. (1992) Tool Support for Design Methods - The DOCASE Object-Oriented Approach. CASE for Object-Oriented Methods, ECOOP Workshop, Utrecht, The Netherlands.
Rosengren P. (1994) Applying conceptual modelling to Multimedia Information retrieval. In Proceedings of RIAO-94, Intelligent Multimedia Information retrieval systems and management. USA, October 1994, ISBN 2-905450-05-3.
Rosenquist C.J. (1982) Entity-Life Cycle Models and their applicability to information systems development life cycles The Computer Journal 25 (3) 307-315
Rosson M.B. & Alpert S.R. (1990) The Cognitive Consequences of Object-Oriented design in Human Computer Interaction vol 5 345-379
Rosson M.B., Maas S. and Kellogg W.A. (1987) Designing for Designers: An Analysis of Design Practice in the Real World, Proceedings of CHI'87, pp 137-142.
Rumbaugh J., Blaha M., Premerlani W., Eddy F. & Lorensen W. (1991) Object-Oriented Modeling and Design, Prentice-Hall, Englewood Cliffs.
Russel D.M., Stefik M, Pirolli P., & Card SK. (1993) The cost structure of sense making. In proceedings of INTERCHI'93, Eds Ashlund S., Mullet K., Henderson A., Hollnagel E. and White T., pp 269-275, ACM press.
Salber D. (1995) De l'interaction individuelle aux systèmes multi-utilisateurs. L'exemple de la Communication Homme-Homme-Médiatisée. Thèse de doctorat de l'Université Joseph Fourier.
Sarantinos E.& Johnson P. (1991) Explanation dialogues: question disambiguation and test generation, in Proceedings 11th International Conference on Expert Systems and their Applications. Avignon.
Sato K. (1992) User Interface Design Theory, Discussion on User Interface Design Methods, Industrial Design (Japanese), 157, 39-40.
Scapin D. & Pierret-Golbreich C. (1989) Towards a Method for Task Description: MAD. In: Berlinguet, L. and Berthelette, D. (eds.) Work with Display Units '89. Elsevier, North-Holland, pp 371-380.
Scheifler R.W. & Gettys J. (1986) "The X Window System", ACM Transactions on Graphics, 5(2), pp. 79-109.
Schmucker K. (1986) "MacApp: An Application Framework", Byte, 11(8), pp. 189-193.
Scriven M. (1967) The methodology of evaluation. In Tyler, R.W., Gagné, R.M. & Scriven, M., Perspective of Curriculum Evaluation, Chicago:Rand McNally and Co. 39-83.
Sebillotte S. (1988) Hierarchical Planning as a Method for Task-Analysis: the example of office task analysis. Behaviour and Information Technology; 7(3): 275-293.
Seely-Brown J. & Duguid P. (1994) Borderline Issues: Social & Material Aspects of Design, in Human-Computer Interaction, 9(1).
Shannon C.E. & Weaver W. (1949) The Mathematical theory of Communication, University of Illinois press
Sharratt B.D. (1987) Top-Down Interactive Systems Design: some lessons learnt from using command language grammar. In: Bullinger, H.J. & Shackel, B. (eds.), Proc. Interact'87. Elsevier, North Holland, Amsterdam, pp 395-399.

Shaw & Garlan D. (1995) Software Architecture. Perspectives on an Emerging Discipline, Prentice Hall.

Shepherd A. (1989) Analysis and Training in Information technology Tasks, in Task Analysis for Human-Computer Interaction, D. Diaper (Ed.), Ellis Horwood, Chichester, pp. 15-55.

Shlaer S. & Mellor S. J. (1992) Object Life cycles. Prentice-Hall.

Shneiderman B. (1992) Designing the User Interface, Strategies for Effective Human-Computer Interaction, 2nd ed., Addison-Wesley, Reading.

Singh G. & Green M. (1989) A High Level User Interface Management System. In Proceedings of CHI'89 (Austin, Texas). ACM, New York, 133-138.

Singh G., Kok C. H. & Ngan T. Y. (1990) Druid: A System for Demonstrational Rapid User Interface Development, Proceedings of the ACM Symposium on User Interface Software, pp 167-177.

Singley M.K. & Anderson (1987), J.R. A Keystroke Analysis of Learning and Transfer in Text Editing. Human-Computer Interaction 3(3), pp. 223-274.

Siochi A.C. & Hartson H.R. (1989) Task Oriented Representation of Asynchronous User Interfaces, in Proceedings of the Conference on Human Aspects in Computing Systems CHI'89, Austin, pp. 183-188.

Smith S. & Mosier J. (1986) Guidelines for Designing User Interface Software, ESD-TR-86-278 MTR 10090, The MITRE Corporation, Bedford, MA 01730-0208, USA.

Sowa J.F. (1984) Conceptual Structures: Information Processing in Mind and Machine. Addison-Wesley, Reading, Massachusetts.

Stamper R. (1977) Information B. T. Batsford Publishers, London

Sternberg R.J., Tourangeau R., & Nigro G. (1979) Metaphor and Social Policy: The Convergence of Macroscopic and Microscopic Views. In Ortony, A. (Ed.), Metaphor and Thought, Cambridge University Press, pp. 325-353.

Stevens R. (1991) Creating software the right way. BYTE, August.

Storrs G. (1989)Towards a Theory of HCI In Behaviour and Information Technology, 8(5) pp 323-334

Suchman L. (1987) Plans and situated actions: The problem of Human-Machine Communication Cambridge University Press

Sukaviriya P., Foley J.D. & Griffith T. (1993) A second generation user interface design environment: the model and the runtime architecture. In proceedings of INTERCHI' 93, Amsterdam, 375-382.

Sully P. (1994) Modelling the World with Objects Prentice-Hall

Summersgill A.R. & Browne A.D.P. (1989) Human Factors: Its Place in System Development Methods. Sigsoft Bulletin, 14(3): 227-234.

Sutcliffe A. & McDermott J. (1991) Integrating methods of human-computer interface design with structured systems development International Journal of man Machine Studies 34 631-655

Sutcliffe A. (1994) Defining the Requirement for HCI Design Methods, SIGCHI Bulletin, Vol. 26, No. 2, pp. 21-23.

Sutcliffe A. (1995) A method for task related information analysis. This volume

Sutcliffe A. (1995) Task related information analysis. Critical Issues in User Interface Systems Engineering. Benyon, D. & Palanque, P. (Eds.), this volume.

Sutcliffe A., Bass L., Cockton G., Monk A. & Newman I.(1995) Joint Workshop on Methods, Models and Architectures for Graphical User Interface Design, to appear in SIGCHI Bulletin.

Sutcliffe A.G & Faraday P.F. (1994) Systematic design for task related multi media

interfaces. Information and Software Technology. 36(4):225-234
Sutcliffe A.G. & Springett M.V. (1992) From User's Problems to design Errors: Linking Evaluation to Improving Design Practice, Proceedings HCI'92 Conference, pp.117-134, Cambridge University Press.
Sutcliffe A.G., & McDermot M. (1991) Integrating methods of Human Computer Interface Design with Structured System Development. International Journal of Man Machine Studies. Vol 34: 631-655
Sutcliffe A.G., & Wang I. (1991) Integrating human-computer interaction with Jackson System development, Computer Journal. 34(2), p. 132-142
Swenson K. D. (1993) A Visual Language to Describe Collaborative Work. Proceedings of 1993 IEEE Symposium on Visual Languages, Bergen, Norway, August 24-27, 1993, IEEE Computer Society Press.
Szekely P., Luo P. & Neches R. (1993) Beyond interface builders: Model-based interface tools, Human Factors in Computing Systems, INTERCHI'93 Conference, ACM Press, pp 383-390.
Tauber M.J. (1988) On Mental Models and the User Interface. In: van der Veer, G.C., Green, T.R.G., Hoc, J.M. and Murray, D.M. (eds.) Working with Computers: theory versus outcome. Academic Press, London, pp 89-119.
Tauber M.J. (1990), ETAG: Extended Task Action Grammar - A Language for the Description of the user's task Language, Proceedings INTERACT'90, pp.163-168.
Taylor B. (1990) The HUFIT Planning Analysis & Specification Toolset. In Proceedings of INTERACT'90, IFIP TC 13 Third International Conference on HCI, Diaper, D., Gilmore, D., Cockton, G. and Shackel, B. (Eds.), Cambridge, UK, Amsterdam:North-Holland, 371-382.
Tullis T.S. (1986) Optimising the usability of computer generated displays. In People and Computers: Designing for usability. Eds Harrison M.D. and Monk A.F.; Cambridge Univ Press.
Väänänen K. (1993a) Multimedia Environments: Supporting Authors and Users with Real-world Metaphors, Adjunct Proceedings of INTERCHI'93, Amsterdam, pp. 99-100.
Väänänen K. (1993b) ShareME: A Metaphor-based Authoring Tool for Multimedia Environments, Proceedings of Vienna HCI'93, Vienna, Grechenig, T., Tscheligi, M. (Eds.), Human-Computer Interaction, LNCS No. 733, Springer-Verlag, pp. 39-50.
Väänänen K., & Schmidt J. (1994) User Interfaces for Hypermedia: How to Find Good Metaphors?. Adjunct Proceedings of CHI'94, ACM, Boston, USA, pp. 263-264.
Valdez J. (1989) "XVT, a Virtual Toolkit," Byte ,14(3).
van Hoff J. (1982) Categories and Sequences of Behaviour: Methods of Description and Analysis. In Handbook of Methods in Non-verbal Behaviour Research, Cambridge University Press, pp 362-430.
Vander Zanden B. (1992) An Active-Value-Spreadsheet Model for Interactive Languages. In: Myers B. A., Languages for Developing User Interfaces, Jones & Bartlett Publ., pp. 147-157.
Vanderdonckt J. & Bodart F. (1993) Encapsulating Knowledge for Intelligent Automatic Interaction Objects Selection, in Proceedings of the Conference on Human Factors in Computing Systems INTERCHI'93, Amsterdam, S. Ashlund, K. Mullet, A. Henderson, E. Hollnagel and T. White (Eds.), ACM Press, New York, pp. 424-429.
Vanderdonckt J. (1994), Guide Ergonomique des interfaces homme-machine, Presses Universitaires de Namur, ISBN 2-87037-189-6.
Viereck A., Schlungbaum E. & Gorny, P. (1991) Structured Design of User Interfaces and Knowledge-based Design. In Bullinger, H.-J. (Ed.): Human Aspects in Computing,

Proceedings of the Fourth International Conference on Human-Computer-Interaction, Stuttgart, Germany, Elsevier Science Publishers, pp. 577-581.

Vissers C.A., Scollo G., van Sinderen M. & Brinskma E. (1991) Specification Styles in Distributed Systems Design and Verification, Theoretical Computer Science 89, pp.179-206.

Voss J. (1990) Design and Implementation of Graphic User Interfaces: An integrated and Object Orientated Approach, (in german) FernUniversität-Gesamthochschule-Hagen, Hagen, Dissertation.

Wasserman A. et al. (1987) Developing Interactive Information Systems with the User Software Engineering Methodology, in Readings in HCI, Baecker & Buxton (eds), pp 508-527, Morgan Kaufman.

Wasserman A.I. (1985) Extending State Transition Diagrams for the Specification of Human-Computer Interaction, IEEE Transactions on Software Engineering, vol. SE-11(8), pp. 699-713.

Wilenga B., Van de Velde W., Schreiber G. & Akkermans H., (1993). Expertise Model Definition Document. KADS project document KADS-II/M2/UvA, University of Amsterdam.

Will R.P. (1992) Individual Difference in the perfomance and use of an expert system, in International Journal of Man-Machine Studies, 37, pp 173–190.

Wilson F. & Whitefield A. (1989) Interactive systems evaluation: mapping methods to contexts. In Contemporary Ergonomics, Megan, E. (Ed.),Taylor and Francis, 62-67.

Wilson M.D., Barnard P.J., Green T.R.G. & Maclean A. (1988) Knowledge-Based Task Analysis for Human-Computer Systems. In van der Veer G.C., Green T.R.G., Hoc J-M & Murray D.M. (eds.) Working With Computers: Theory versus Outcome. Academic Press

Wilson S., Johnson P., Kelly C., Cunningham J. & Markopoulos P. (1993) Beyond Hacking: A Model Based Approach to User Interface Design. In: Alty, J.L., Diaper, D. and Guest, S. (eds.) Proceedings People and Computers VIII. Cambridge University Press, Cambridge UK., pp 217-232.

Windsor P. (1990) An object-oriented framework for prototyping user interfaces. In Proceedings of INTERACT'90, IFIP TC 13 Third International Conference on HCI, Diaper, D., Gilmore, D., Cockton, G. and Shackel, B.(Eds.),Cambridge, UK, North-Holland, 309-314.

Windsor P. & Storrs G. (1993) Practical User Interface Design Notation, Interacting with Computers, 5:423-438.

Wirfs-Brock R., Wilkerson B. & Weiner L. (1990) Designing Object Oriented Software. Prentice-Hall

Wixon D., Holtzblatt K. & Knox S. (1990) Contextual design: an emergent view of system design. In Chew, J.C. & Whiteside, J. Empowering People. In Proceedings of CHI'90, Seattle, ACM Press, 329-336.

Wright P. & Monk A.F. (1992) A cost-effective evaluation method for use by designers. International Journal of Man-Machine Studies, 35, 6, 891-912.

Wright P., Field B. & Harrison M. (1994) Deriving Human-Error Tolerance Requirements from Tasks, Proceedings ICRE'94, pp.135-142, IEEE Computer Society Press.

Zucchinetti G. (1990) Réalisation d'un éditeur d'interface homme-machine, Mémoire de diplôme postgrade en informatique et organisation, Ecole des Hautes Etudes Commerciales, University of Lausanne, Lausanne.

Index